A REFERENCE PUBLICATION IN LITERATURE
Jack Salzman, *Editor*

Three Virginia Writers;
Mary Johnston, Thomas Nelson Page
and Amélie Rives Troubetzkoy:
A Reference Guide

George C. Longest

PS
266
·V5
L64

G. K. HALL & CO., 70 LINCOLN STREET, BOSTON, MASS.

Library of Congress Cataloging in Publication Data

Longest, George.
   Three Virginia writers : Mary Johnston, Thomas Nelson
Page, Amelie Rives Troubetzkoy.

   (Reference guides in literature)
   Includes indexes.
   1. American literature—Virginia—Bibliography.
2. Johnston, Mary, 1870–1936—Bibliography. 3. Page,
Thomas Nelson, 1853–1922. Bibliography. 4. Troubetzkoy,
Amélie Rives, 1863–1945—Bibliography. I. Title.
Z1345.L64   016.81'08'09755   77–9566
ISBN 0–8161–7841–0

This publication is printed on permanent/durable acid-free paper
MANUFACTURED IN THE UNITED STATES OF AMERICA

Contents

Three Virginia Writers/Introduction

Mary Johnston, Thomas Nelson Page, and Amélie Rives were three of the best known popular writers Virginia ever produced. With the exception of Clayton L. Eichelberger's <u>A Guide to Critical Reviews of United States Fiction</u> (1971.B3; 1974.B1), however, no extensive bibliographical research has been conducted on any of the three writers. The most widely accessible and most recent bibliographies of the three Virginia writers remain those in Louis D. Rubin's <u>A Bibliographical Guide to the Study of Southern Literature</u> (1969.B3).

Mary Johnston

Mary Johnston was born on November 21, 1870 in Buchanan, Botetourt County, Virginia. The daughter of Major John William Johnston, C.S.A. and Elizabeth Alexander Johnston, she was reared in the genteel tradition of nineteenth century Southern life.

Miss Johnston's early interest in reading, particularly in history, is attributed by most early biographical accounts to her frail health. Her lively imagination is said to have been encouraged by her paternal grandmother. Her favorite readings, somewhat typical ones for late nineteenth century Southerners, included Spenser, the Scottish ballads, Shelley, Keats, and Browning.

With the exception of a period of residency in Birmingham, Alabama from 1885 to 1893 and a brief stay in New York and trips abroad, Miss Johnston spent her life in Virginia. For some time she lived in Richmond; and after 1913, when "Three Hills" was built, she took up permanent residency in Warm Springs, Virginia, where she died on May 9, 1936.

Romantic closeness to nature and mystical response were innate to Mary Johnston's disposition as woman and as writer. As novelist-romancer she was nourished, according to Lawrence G. Nelson (1961.B1), by four things: her readings, her "piety," her family tradition, and the history of Virginia. For a writer of such a disposition, considering the climate of her publication, the moment of her entrance into professional writing was indeed propitious.

INTRODUCTION

Her first major work was The Prisoners of Hope (1898), which
Walter Hines Page at Houghton Mifflin accepted for publication. The
novel achieved two things for the young novelist. First, it intro-
duced her in a major way to the American reading audience and, second,
it typed her in the minds of her readers and in the minds of some of
her reviewers as historical novelist-romancer. Such typing would
have its disadvantages when she sought in a problem novel like Hagar
to further the cause of feminism (See Edwin Francis Edgett, 1913.B15).

To Have and to Hold (1900) achieved a success that few American
romances have attained. Alice Payne Hackett (1945.B1), for example,
places it as number one on the fiction sales list for 1900. The
Dilettante (1900.B6) cited advance demand at 45,000, whereas circulation of The Atlantic was rumored, according to The Book Buyer
(1900.B10), to have been boosted by 50,000 through serial publication
of the work. The 1900 publication definitely placed Mary Johnston at
the forefront of the romancers so popular at the turn of the century.
The romance remains the one work most frequently identified with her
name.

From her very entrance into professional writing it has been
standard practice to categorize Miss Johnston's works as Virginia
romances, European romances, mystical novels, Civil War novels, etc.
Starting in the 1940's, a number of masters' theses have taken such
an approach, and Gayle Melton Hartley (1972.A2), who has produced in
her dissertation the lengthiest Johnston study, has followed a similar approach.

What is the basis for Miss Johnston's critical reputation? For
one thing, throughout the body of Johnston materials, one recurrent
judgment emerges, almost without qualification. Mary Johnston was
gifted in the creation of setting--in the vivid presentation of landscape. In this regard, she was, for example, compared by William
Morton Payne (1900.B17) with Mary Noailles Murfree. As a social historian she was able to make a "romantic rainbow of colonial civilization in Virginia" (1902.B5). Thus, Virginia works like The Prisoners
of Hope, To Have and to Hold, Audrey, and Lewis Rand enjoyed considerable success with the critics.

Reviewers and critics, moreover, have been favorably disposed to
Mary Johnston's fictional use of history. One must clarify that
assessment, however, by noting that hers was a highly romantic ver-
sion of history that appealed to the anti-realists. As one reviewer
put it, it was to be hoped that she would never emphasize "historic
truth to the point of realism" (1900.B12).

Miss Johnston's selectivity, her use of detail, her command of
historical fact have frequently been praised. Edwin Mims, for example, believed Lewis Rand to be "one of the best novels published
during the last decade" (1909.B5). By the time she came to write
The Long Roll, The Saturday Review could speak of her use of detail

in constructing a view of war as the most vivid since Zola's La Débâcle (1911.B10).

Although Miss Johnston has been praised for her picturesque settings, her use of history, her mood and atmosphere, and her romantic depictions of colonial and antebellum life, she has frequently been charged with the creation of wooden characters. Charges of artificiality and excessiveness seem more often aimed at her non-Virginia works than at her Virginia ones. In a review of Sir Mortimer, for example, William Morton Payne noted that the author seemed to be degenerating in talent (1904.B10).

Works published after 1918 seem to have been particularly vulnerable to negative criticism. Grant Martin Overton asserted that her works prior to 1918 were accessible to all readers (1928.B2). Miss Johnston's mysticism seems to have been particularly distasteful to her critics, especially in novels like Sweet Rocket, Silver Cross, and Drury Randall. Her experiments in stylistic innovation, moreover, were frequently assailed, and her early venture into feminism in Hagar viewed as propaganda, Trudy Hanmer (1972.A1) terming it a "polemic par excellence."

Since her death in 1936, Miss Johnston has been virtually ignored. There is no Johnston biography, and the amount of critical commentary available on her work is highly limited at best. Jay B. Hubbell in The South in American Literature (1954.B1), for example, briefly alludes to her work as melodrama typical of the South. The best work produced in the past forty years remains Lawrence G. Nelson's "Mary Johnston and the Historic Imagination" (1960.B1).

Thomas Nelson Page

Thomas Nelson Page was born at "Oakland," Hanover County, Virginia on April 23, 1853. With direct ties to some of the oldest and most aristocratic Virginia families, he spent his formative years in war-torn Virginia, witnessing the demise of the old order that had produced him and the Reconstruction that was to beset him.

A student at Washington and Lee, to which Robert E. Lee had retired as president, Page took his degree in law at the University of Virginia. He practiced law for a number of years in Richmond, Virginia.

In 1886 he married Anne Seddon Bruce of Staunton Hill, Charlotte County, Virginia. After her death in 1888, he continued his Richmond practice until 1893 when he married Florence Lathrop Field and moved to Washington, D. C., where he remained until 1913, when Woodrow Wilson appointed him ambassador to Italy. He died on November 1, 1922.

Introduction

Owing to his time and place in history, Page was ideally suited to writing of antebellum and Reconstruction Southern life. Achieving the highest fulfillment of the plantation tradition in writing, Page left us in his work what Francis Pendleton Gaines has termed the "supreme glorification of the old regime" (1924.B10).

Beginning in 1886 reviewers were charmed by Page's use of dialect in stories like "Marse Chan" and "Meh Lady." The two stories, which were later collected into In Ole Virginia, have consistently been cited as Page's best work (indeed, Theodore Gross has referred to "Marse Chan" as a "Virginia classic" [1961.B3]). Readers of the 1880's and 1890's, then, were attracted to the dialect, the pathos, the humor, and the Negro characterization in Page's stories, traits later cited by Louise Manly in her Southern Literature from 1879 to 1895 (1895.B7).

When, on the other hand, Page tried his hand at a novel like On Newfound River or Gordon Keith, his reception was not nearly so warm. Red Rock, one of his best received novels, was judged by William Morton Payne "one of the most satisfactory works of fiction that the South has ever produced" (1898.B15). The Independent, however, asserted that Page lacked "constructive ability and style-energy" as a novelist (1899.B8). Edward Wagenknecht (1952.B1) sees Red Rock as Page's most important novel, Arthur Hobson Quinn (1909.B11) as his best, and Harriet R. Holman (1947.A1) as his most artistic.

Page's real forté as writer, then, was in stories within the plantation tradition, dialect stories with romantic coloring and idealistic point of view, stories employing a Black raconteur. The nostalgia of a collection like In Ole Virginia or Elsket has been particularly appealing to American readers, and the author's claim to fame rests somewhat solidly on such fictional exponents of social history.

However, when Page tried his hand at more relevant materials, as in Under the Crust and The Land of the Spirit, he was thought by his publishers, as Miss Holman has so succinctly explained, to have been abandoning his true métier (1973.B1). Edwin Francis Edgett noted in his review of The Land of the Spirit (1913.B16) that the work was not in Page's best vein. John Marvel, Assistant shared a similar fate.

Page's non-fiction has attracted little critical attention. Some readers, however, recognized the charm of nostalgia in Page's essays. The New York Times, for example, noted that reading Social Life in Old Virginia Before the War was "like opening a rose jar."

Page, one recognizes, has often been viewed as the defender of the Old Order, a problem Miss Holman noted in her dissertation (1947.A1). To many, he remains the idealist who best conveys a picture of a romantic, aristocratic old South. Fred Lewis Pattee, for example, observed of Page that he was "the first writer really to

picture the South from the heart outward, to show it not as a picturesque spectacle but as a quivering section of human life"
(1916.B5). To James Kimball King, Page's work constitutes a "eulogy
of the Old South" (1964.A1).

Although there is no truly definitive Page biography or critical
study available, three book-length studies are of considerable help:
Harriet R. Holman's The Literary Career of Thomas Nelson Page, 1884-
1910 (1947.A1), James Kimball King's George Washington Cable and
Thomas Nelson Page: Two Literary Approaches to the New South
(1964.A1), and Theodore Gross's Thomas Nelson Page (1967.A1).

Amélie Rives Troubetzkoy

Amélie Louise Rives was born on August 23, 1863 in the old rec-
tory of Saint Paul's Church, Richmond, Virginia. The daughter of
Alfred Landon Rives and Sarah (Sudie) Macmurdo Rives, she was reared
in the tradition of the affluent nineteenth century Virginia aristocracy.

The years 1863-1870 were spent at the Rives family estate "Castle
Hill." There, amidst the rolling countryside of Albemarle County,
Virginia, not far from Jefferson's "Monticello," she developed a
strongly romantic disposition and a keen imagination. Although her
father's business necessitated residency in Mobile, Alabama, from
1871 through 1883, her summers were spent at the Virginia estate she
always considered home. After 1884, "Castle Hill" became her permanent home.

By the time she had reached her sixteenth birthday, she had read
not only a great deal of Shakespeare but of Elizabethan drama in
general, thus preparing the way for her earliest publications. In
1886 Thomas Bailey Aldrich accepted for publication her manuscript
of "A Brother to Dragons," a romantic tale set in Elizabethan England. Two more Elizabethan tales, "The Farrier Lass o' Piping Pebworth" and "Nurse Crumpet Tells the Story," were published in 1887.

In 1888 Miss Rives married John Armstrong Chanler, wealthy,
fashionable, prominent New Yorker. The courtship and marriage of
the two coming so close upon publication of The Quick or the Dead?
caused a number of readers to identify the young couple with the hero
and heroine of the novel, thus provoking moral censure.

The marriage was a troubled one. After extensive travels abroad,
from which came her novel According to St. John (1891), Miss Rives
divorced John Armstrong Chanler in 1895.

In 1896 Miss Rives married Prince Pierre Troubetzkoy, Russian
portrait painter, whom she had met at a London garden party. Handsome, charming, cultured, Prince Troubetzkoy was the ideal husband
for a woman of her disposition. The marriage was, therefore, an
idyllic one.

Introduction

On 24 August 1936 Prince Troubetzkoy died at "Castle Hill."   On 16 June 1945 Miss Rives died at a Charlottesville nursing home.

Although Miss Rives enjoyed considerable popular success, her critical reception has been poor and studies of her work, with the exception of George Calvin Longest's "Amélie Rives Troubetzkoy: A Biography" (1969.A1) and Welford Dunaway Taylor's Amélie Rives (Princess Troubetzkoy) (1973.A1), have been unavailable.

Early reviewers were charmed by Miss Rives' Elizabethan tales "A Brother to Dragons," "The Farrier Lass o' Piping Pebworth" and "Nurse Crumpet Tells the Story." Most appealing to her readers was her rendition of Elizabethan idiom and manners. R. T. W. Duke (1909.B1) believed her to be at her best in dealing with the Elizabethan world.

1888 is, however, the most significant year in the literary history of Amélie Rives, for it is the year of publication of The Quick or the Dead?, which most historians, perhaps wrongly, still judge her by. The work was parodied, the work was censured for its indelicacy. As late as 1947 Frank Luther Mott noted that the novel had a "morbid theme and some scenes of hysterical passion" (1947.B1).

Although her works frequently transgressed the moral values of her many readers, Miss Rives was praised for her ability to create a certain type of character, a type offensive to many. As early as 1893 Godey's Magazine observed that she was excellent at depicting women who were "proud, selfish, handsome, alluring, lacking in womanly delicacy, and, above all things, desperately self-absorbed and inconceivably mean" (1893.B2).

With such a thought in mind, it is no wonder, then, that Louise Manly (1895.B1) cited poetry and drama as Miss Rives' real forté, or that Mildred Lewis Rutherford believed that The Quick or the Dead? reflected "no credit upon the author" (1907.B2). Miss Rives had advanced in her views of women far beyond the genteel conventions of her early critics. Welford Taylor has a cogent and perceptive discussion of the author's feminism in his Rives biography (1973.A1).

Charges of artificiality, excessiveness, and false morality were frequently lodged against Rives works like Virginia of Virginia, The Witness of the Sun, According to St. John, and Barbara Dering. Later Rives works like Seléné, The Golden Rose, Trix and Over the Moon, Hidden House, and World's End received comparatively little attention.

Shadows of Flame, on the other hand, was praised for its excellent characterization. Edwin Francis Edgett of the Boston Evening Transcript spoke of its "virile force," noting that the novel had "exceptional knowledge of life and a distinctive skill in its vital presentation" (1915.B4). Welford Dunaway Taylor has an enlightening discussion of the novel in his article "A 'Soul' Remembers Oscar Wilde" (1971.B2).

INTRODUCTION

Amélie Rives' critical reputation is largely based upon her early Elizabethan tales; her romantic novels like The Quick or the Dead?, Virginia of Virginia, Barbara Dering, and According to St. John, all of which shocked Victorian America; and the more sophisticated Shadows of Flame. In such works she is largely remembered, as George Calvin Longest has observed in his biography (1969.A1), for her local color fiction, her marked use of sensuality, and, hence, for her widening of the latitude of the artist.

The present study contains entries represented in the archives of Richmond Newspapers, Incorporated; Articles on American Literature, 1900-1950, edited by Lewis Leary; Articles on American Literature, 1950-1967, edited by Lewis Leary; A Bibliographical Guide to the Study of Southern Literature, edited by Louis D. Rubin; Bibliography of American Literature (Jacob Nathaniel Blanck); Book Review Digest; Biography Index (1946-1973); Dissertation Abstracts International; Essay and General Literature Index; A Guide to Critical Reviews of United States Fiction, vols. I & II, edited by Clayton L. Eichelberger; New York Times Index; Nineteenth Century Reader's Guide; Official Index to the Times; Poole's Index to Periodical Literature, 1802-1907; annual bibliographies of The Publications of the Modern Language Association; Reader's Guide to Periodical Literature (1900-1937); Richmond Public Library Virginia Authors Files; and Theses in American Literature (Patsy L. Howard).

Whole runs of The Atlantic Monthly, The Bookman, The Dial, Harper's Magazine, The Independent, The Literary Digest, McClure's, The Nation, North American Review, Sewanee Review, and South Atlantic Quarterly were examined. Manuscript collections at the University of Virginia were helpful in the case of Mary Johnston and Amélie Rives Troubetzkoy. Because of the inaccessibility of some of the items in the manuscript collections, I have had to rely on bibliographical data supplied by the clipping services. Such items are easily identified, owing, as a rule, to the absence of page numbers and, hence, the use of the designation n.p. For further information about the three authors, the reader is referred to manuscript collections at the University of Virginia and at Duke University.

The materials excluded from this bibliography were "brief mentions," i.e., materials which attributed a work to an author or which merely typed a work generically, or which alluded to or made passing reference to an author. Works of a wholly genealogical nature and death notices were also excluded.

Because of the general scarcity and inaccessibility of materials on the three Virginia authors, I have made somewhat full annotations of items, carefully noting in each annotation the nature and extent of the item and, wherever possible, any works referred to.

INTRODUCTION

The index to the bibliography includes the titles of the author's works, the titles of writings about the author or his work (excluding newspaper titles), the authors of secondary sources, and subject headings as dictated by the nature of the materials entered in the bibliography.

Acknowledgments

I wish to express my appreciation to Doris Mitchell, reference librarian, and Jane W. Westenberger, Eileen Pearson, and Janet R. Howell, Interlibrary Loan staff, James Branch Cabell Library, Virginia Commonwealth University, Richmond, Virginia for their many efforts in my behalf.

Mary Johnston:
A Reference Guide

Writings about Mary Johnston, 1898-1976

1898 A BOOKS - NONE

1898 B SHORTER WRITINGS

1   ANON. "Current Fiction." The Literary World, 29
        (29 October), 353-55.
            The narrative in Prisoners of Hope is so interesting
        that the reader is disappointed at its "melancholy and in-
        conclusive finale."

2   ANON. "Novel Notes." The Bookman, 8 (December), 253-57.
            Prisoners of Hope is an almost perfect work, even though
        contemporary "disciples of the morbid novel" will probably
        attack it as "idealisation."

3   ANON. "Prisoners of Hope." The Critic, NS 30 (December),
        532.
            The romance suffers from "characteristic feminine super-
        lative" (i.e., excess and exaggeration). Although the
        setting is vivid, the characterization is lifeless. None-
        theless, the novel has real moments of excitement, and the
        conclusion reveals the "full scope of the author's talent."

4   ANON. "Prisoners of Hope." New York Times, Saturday Review
        of Books (1 October), p. 644.
            Those who wish to escape the realities of contemporary
        life can do so by reading Prisoners of Hope, the style and
        thought of which are "untouched by any influence later than
        'Greyslaer.'" Dialogue in the romance is excellent.

5   ANON. "Recent Fiction: Prisoners of Hope." The Independent,
        50 (29 December), 1942.
            Miss Johnston's new romance is pleasant to read but must
        be taken without a "critical wince." Although much of the
        work is less than credible, the narration and characteriza-
        tion are appealing. With considerable sentimentality, she
        focuses on the "kind of tragedy imagined by women." The

3

reviewer concludes that "if it is a first novel, the author is to be congratulated and encouraged."

6   ANON. "Recent Publications." New Orleans Daily Picayune
        (9 October), p. 6.
          Prisoners of Hope has "merit" and "bespeaks for its
        author great literary achievements." Characterization and
        style in the romance are good, and the history of the peri-
        od is vividly re-created. Because of a slight "lack of
        perspective," the latter part of the work borders on the
        "commonplace."

7   PAYNE, WILLIAM MORTON. "Recent Fiction." The Dial, 25
        (1 November), 301-06.
          Prisoners of Hope is the only Virginia romance to date
        to approach the merits of Thackeray's The Virginians. In
        her use of adventure, Miss Johnston rivals James Fenimore
        Cooper. Her representation of Governor Berkeley is the
        best to date in fiction.

1899 A BOOKS - NONE

1899 B SHORTER WRITINGS

1   ANON. "Historical Romances." The Athenaeum, 3717
        (21 January), 79-80.
          Prisoners of Hope reveals some knowledge of history but
        very little knowledge of human nature. The representation
        of Sir William Berkeley is quite poor.

2   ANON. "Novel Notes." The Bookman (London), 16 (June), 81-3.
          The Old Dominion presents very "real" scenes of the
        colonial Virginia plantation system. Many of the scenes
        are "dark and tumultuous." The "unusual power and dignity"
        of the work is quite striking, as is its style.

3   ANON. "The Old Dominion." The Saturday Review (London), 87
        (20 May), 632.
          The description of the slave quarters and the plantation
        in The Old Dominion is quite good. The only artistic weak-
        ness in the romance is Patricia's desertion of her lover,
        an action inconsistent with the behavior of an "honourable
        woman."

4   ANON. "Some Novels of the Year." The Atlantic Monthly, 83
        (January), 127-37.

Miss Johnston demonstrated in <u>Prisoners of Hope</u> that she had both "originality" and an "active imagination." Although well constructed, the romance suffers from the author's "exuberance," her excess. Miss Johnston's ability at describing the Virginia landscape is truly excellent.

<u>1900 A   BOOKS - NONE</u>

<u>1900 B   SHORTER WRITINGS</u>

1   ANON. "American Fiction." <u>The Athenaeum</u>, 3776 (10 March), 302-03.
    By Order of the Company, like <u>The Prisoners of Hope</u>, contains much "picturesque writing." Miss Johnston's villains, on the other hand, are overdone. Diction is often not historically true to the period.

2   ANON. "Books and Authors: Miss Johnston's <u>To Have and to Hold</u>." <u>Dixie, A Monthly Magazine</u>, 3 (April), 264-67.
    Miss Johnston's latest romance comes closer to equalling Thackeray's <u>The Virginians</u> than the works of John Esten Cooke, Thomas Nelson Page, or Maud Wilder Goodwin. Her romance has a "fine, ringing, masculine quality." Although the major characters in the romance are traditional to the genre, each retains considerable individuality. The work is truly a "brilliant imaginative tale."

3   ANON. "<u>By Order of the Company</u>." <u>The Saturday Review</u> (London), 89 (10 March), 306.
    Miss Johnston's "keen instinct for picturesqueness" is apparent in her latest romance. The work, moreover, has an admirably robust quality to it. Both characterization and incident are excellent.

4   ANON. "Fiction." <u>The Independent</u>, 52 (22 November), 2803-04.
    Critical weaknesses are of little import to the reader of <u>To Have and To Hold</u>.

5   ANON. "General Gossip of Authors and Writers." <u>Current Literature</u>, 28 (May), 139-43.
    Miss Johnston is a "high-bred, aristocratic girl of the South."

6   ANON. "Mary Johnston." <u>The Dilettante: A Monthly Literary Magazine</u>, 3 (July), 3-4.
    Although <u>To Have and To Hold</u> lacked the sympathy of a Hawthorne, it championed "right and virtue over scheming and treacherous villainy."

1900

7   ANON. "Mary Johnston's Triumph." Book Buyer, 20 (March),
    117-18.
        To Have and To Hold is the "work of a born story-teller,
    a straightforward, robust romance in which, praise God,
    many things come to pass in simple language." The exact-
    ness in description lends real credence to the historical
    narrative. The only negative quality of the romance is
    that the "rapid succession" of exciting events borders on
    melodrama.

8   ANON. "Miss Johnston's New Romance." The Independent, 52
    (15 March), 667-68.
        To Have and To Hold equals Prisoners of Hope. The Eliza-
    bethan diction of the former is quite good, and the romance
    is decorous enough for family reading. The history in the
    work is, unfortunately, superficial, and the conclusion of
    the romance lacks vigor.

9   ANON. "Miss Johnston's To Have and to Hold." New York Times,
    Saturday Review of Books (10 February), p. 91.
        The new romance is marked by the "author's immense im-
    provement in style and in method, and by her repeated choice
    of the better part in fiction, that of describing real men
    and women, not puppets."

10 ANON. "Miss Mary Johnston." The Book Buyer, 25 (March),
    94-96.
        To Have and to Hold is reputed to have increased the
    circulation of The Atlantic by 50,000. Miss Johnston's
    early childhood spent in Buchanan, Virginia, no doubt
    formed the foundations of her new romances as well as her
    love for landscape description.

11 ANON. "Notes." The Sewanee Review, 8 (April), 248-56.
        The Atlantic Monthly is doing very well under the edi-
    torship of Bliss Perry and especially owing to its serial
    publication of To Have and to Hold.

12 ANON. "Novel Notes." The Bookman, 11 (March), 91-95.
        Both To Have and to Hold and Prisoners of Hope are ex-
    cellent novels for the presentation of setting, atmosphere,
    and knowledge of human nature. The conclusion of the for-
    mer is "pre-eminently unconventional and original." One
    hopes that Miss Johnston will never succumb to the pitfall
    of emphasizing "historic truth to the point of realism."

13   ANON. "Novel Notes." The Bookman (London), 18 (April), 27-29.
         By Order of the Company is a truly good historical ro-
      mance. The plot is tightly constructed, the character
      finely delineated, and the author's touch strong.

14   ANON. "Recent Publications." New Orleans Daily Picayune
         (25 February), part 3, p. 3.
         To Have and to Hold more than fulfills the promise of
      Prisoners of Hope. Miss Johnston is able to convey the
      "spirit of the times." Although the romance may not be a
      "great book," it is definitely a "fascinating" one.

15   ANON. "To Have and to Hold." The Literary World, 35
         (3 March), 69-70.
         Miss Johnston's second romance has "all the power, pa-
      thos, and picturesque quality of the first." Added to
      those merits are a "ripeness of touch and a happier ending."
      A "beautifully written" romance, the only notable flaws are
      excessive use of incidents and poor illustrations.

16   DIXON, THOMAS, JR. "Miss Johnston's Virginia." The Bookman,
         12 (November), 237-38.
         Cobb's Island, Virginia was not the scene for the pirate
      duel in To Have and to Hold but Smith's Island, Virginia,
      site of the Cape Charles Lighthouse. Tidewater Virginia
      remains much as Miss Johnston described it in her work.

17   PAYNE, WILLIAM MORTON. "Recent Fiction." The Dial, 29
         (1 July), 21-25.
         The success of To Have and to Hold is truly deserved.
      The protagonists of the romance are genuinely interesting.
      Unfortunately, a bit of melodrama is obvious in the ro-
      mance. Description of the landscape is the strongest
      feature of the work and merits placing Miss Johnston along-
      side Mary Noalles Murfree.

18   PRATT, CORNELIA ATWOOD. "Miss Johnston's 'Velvet Gown.'" The
         Critic, 36 (April), 351-52.
         To Have and to Hold is a "prince among churls, clad in
      the very purple and fine linen of romance." The romance
      has everything which the recent sensational successes in
      historical romance have had, and it has style, charm and
      "lift" besides.

19   SIMONDS, WILLIAM E. "Three American Historical Romances."
         The Atlantic Monthly, 85 (March), 408-14.
         To Have and to Hold fulfills the promise of Prisoners of
      Hope. With a "style of dignity and grace," Miss Johnston

1900

has unusual powers of description. Plot construction is
excellent since the author pays particular attention to the
laws of probability. Characterization is strong.

1902 A BOOKS - NONE

1902 B SHORTER WRITINGS

1 ADCOCK, A. ST. JOHN. "Miss Johnston's New Novel." The
Bookman (London), 22 (April), 26-27.
Audrey is worthy of Miss Johnston's earlier Virginia
romances. The new romance is marked by strong characterization, "imaginative insight," and deft description. Audrey
herself is the real center of this "beautiful and poetic
conception."

2 ANON. "Audrey." The Independent, 54 (20 March), 696-97.
Audrey does not rely upon "the forest tragedy" that has
become so identifiable with American historical romances.
The town scenes are, therefore, refreshingly original to
the genre. Miss Johnston's portrayal of Evelyn Byrd is
admirable. Although the style of the romance is an improvement over the author's earlier style, the narrative is
not nearly as interesting.

3 ANON. "Audrey: Miss Johnston's 'Atlantic' Novel Just Ready
in Book Form." New York Times, Saturday Review of Books
and Art (22 February), p. 123.
Miss Johnston has improved considerably since To Have
and to Hold. For Miss Johnston "the setting of her stories,
notably of Audrey, is illustrative of character." The
greatest strength of the romance is its portrayal of Evelyn
Byrd. Despite its occasional stylistic weaknesses, Audrey
is her best work to date.

4 ANON. "Books of the Week." The Outlook, 70 (15 March),
687-90.
Audrey may be the best Johnston work to date, for the
heroine is "sympathetically and clearly drawn." With a
"somber tone" throughout, the romance avoids the pitfall
of sentimentality.

5 ANON. "Books of the Year." The Independent, 54 (20 November),
2769-80.
In works like Audrey, Miss Johnston was able to make a
"romantic rainbow of colonial civilization in Virginia."

6 ANON. "Current Books." Overland Monthly, 39 (May), 917.
    Audrey is a "marvelous romance" filled with "picturesque
    diction and episode, fire and dramatic feeling." The weak-
    ness of the romance is its abrupt, nearly "melodramatic end-
    ing." Since the reader tends to see Audrey as a "dryad,"
    her sudden appearance as an actress detracts from the credi-
    bility of the work.

7 ANON. "New Novels." The Athenaeum, 3885 (12 April), 463-64.
    Audrey is fairly accurate in its rendition of life in
    colonial Virginia. The major characters typify those of
    romance; the minor characters are more individually drawn.
    Although the plot is refreshing, the ending succumbs to
    melodrama.

8 ANON. "Recent Novels." The Nation, 74 (13 March), 213-18.
    The love story in Audrey commands the readers' attention,
    and the heroine is altogether fascinating. The historic
    verisimilitude of the romance is quite good.

9 ANON. "Sable Threads in Cloth of Gold." The Literary Digest,
    24 (5 April), 476.
    Audrey is superior to To Have and to Hold. The great
    strength of the new romance is its portrayal of Audrey, a
    "child of nature." On the other hand, Miss Johnston's
    beautiful descriptions tend to impede narrative progress,
    and the main characters are not too well done.

10 ANON. "Six Months of American Literature." The Saturday
    Review (London), 93 (29 March), 405.
    Audrey is a "study of manners." With more substance
    than earlier Johnston works, the new romance is written in
    an admirable style.

11 ANON. "Talk About New Books." The Catholic World, 75 (June),
    410-11.
    Audrey, Miss Johnston's love story concerning a frontier
    girl and a polished Virginian, has a unity never attained
    by To Have and to Hold. The romance, moreover, is marked
    by a highly descriptive power. On the other hand, there is
    a tendency in the romance to bring in "crowded passages on
    colonial times."

12 BOYNTON, H. W. "Books New and Old." The Atlantic Monthly, 89
    (May), 706-11.
    Audrey is replete with accurate local color, and his-
    toric verisimilitude. The work, however, must be considered
    a romance and not a historic novel.

1902

13 HARKIN, E. F. and C. H. L. JOHNSTON. <u>Little Pilgrimages</u>
    <u>Among the Women Who Have Written Famous Books</u>. Boston:
    L. C. Page & Company, pp. 299-313.
        Miss Johnston was instantly recognized as a writer of
    considerable talent when her publishers accepted the manu-
    script for <u>Prisoners of Hope</u>. Her ancestry is a dis-
    tinguished one--both in its British and American branches.
    She became interested in books for two reasons: her frail
    health pushed her towards reading as a pastime, and her
    paternal grandmother cultivated her imagination. <u>To Have</u>
    <u>and to Hold</u> was one of the most popular books by a female
    author at the turn of the century. The romance has "vividly
    portrayed" characters, unity of scenes, and historic veri-
    similitude. Miss Johnston's home in Birmingham is "well
    regulated" and "typical of the old homes of the South,
    without, however, suggesting the colonial."

14 H. T. P. "Books of Some Importance." <u>The Bookman</u>, 15 (March),
    59-73.
        <u>Audrey</u> is superior to <u>To Have and to Hold</u> in every pos-
    sible way. The new romance may be viewed as a "study in
    temperamental psychology." The author's style is excellent.
    Audrey's transformation into actress, however, is a strain
    on credibility. The romance should end with the twenty-
    fourth chapter.

15 M. H. V. "Miss Johnston's 'Audrey.'" <u>The Critic</u>, 40 (March),
    260.
        When Scott was alive, there was a "<u>raison d'être</u> for the
    historical romance." Current romancers, however, live in
    "no dream of the Middle Ages." Mary Johnston's <u>Audrey</u> is
    an example of the best of the current vogue, for, despite
    its shortcomings, it is a "pretty, touching story." Any
    significant weaknesses in the romance are owed to the "class
    of books to which it belongs."

16 PAYNE, WILLIAM MORTON. "Recent Fiction." <u>The Dial</u>, 32
    (1 April), 245-48.
        <u>Audrey</u> is guilty of "straining for effects and a more
    liberal allowance of 'manners and customs.'" Adventure is
    strong in the romance.

1903 A BOOKS - NONE

1903 B SHORTER WRITINGS

   1 BODDINGTON, E. S. "Mary Johnston in Birmingham, Alabama," in
Women Authors of Our Day in Their Homes. Edited by Francis
Whiting Halsey. New York: James Pott and Company,
pp. 91-99.
      Because of her frail health, Miss Johnston received much
of her education at home in Botetourt County, Virginia,
under the supervision of her aunt and, later, under govern-
esses. After a stay at boarding school in Atlanta, she was
sent, because of poor health, back to her Birmingham home.
The Birmingham home was built primarily for comfort. The
library in the home contained few modern works, emphasis
falling instead upon Shakespeare, Marlowe, Spenser, eight-
eenth century essayists, Scottish ballads, Shelley, Keats,
and Browning.
      Miss Johnston had no particular hour or place for her
composition. Prisoners of Hope was begun, for example, at
San Remo but largely written in Central Park. A good deal
of To Have and to Hold was composed at a small resort in the
mountains of Virginia. Although her readings obviously prepared her for the "spirit and speech" of the times with
which she dealt, the tremendous popularity of her work is
attributable to her rich imagination.
      Mary Johnston's knowledge of "voyage and shipwreck" in
To Have and to Hold is owed to her stays on an island off
Virginia's Eastern Shore. The real key to understanding
Audrey is to be found in Wordsworth. Miss Johnston's talent
for description of military scenes is owed in large part to
her father, who served in the Civil War.

   2 HENNEMAN, JOHN BELL. "The National Element in Southern
Literature." The Sewanee Review, 11 (July), 345-66.
      In 1900 To Have and to Hold experienced "phenomenal ad-
vertising and sale."

1904 A BOOKS - NONE

1904 B SHORTER WRITINGS

   1 ADCOCK, A. ST. JOHN. "An Elizabethan Romance." The Bookman
(London), 26 (June), 101-102.
      It would be difficult to find a nobler love in romance
than that in Sir Mortimer, "altogether a brilliant piece of
work." The characters are indeed lively, the plot plausible
and soundly constructed.

1904

2   ANON. "Johnston--Sir Mortimer." The Critic, 45 (July), 94-95.
        Although the illustrations in Sir Mortimer are good,
    they do not redeem the wooden characters. The "dull" ro-
    mance of Elizabethan life reads like a work of history.

3   ANON. "Miss Johnston's Latest Story." New York Times,
    Saturday Review of Books and Art (2 April), p. 224.
        Emphasis on honor and on dueling are apparent in Sir
    Mortimer, the movement of which is often "clogged" by an
    ornate dialogue. The romance will appeal to those who con-
    tinue to hold "medieval ideals" of manhood.

4   ANON. "Recent Fiction." The Literary World, 35 (May), 144-48.
        Sir Mortimer lives up to Miss Johnston's high standards
    of writing. The romance is marked by a musical quality and
    a plot of considerable interest.

5   ANON. Review of Sir Mortimer. The Saturday Review, 98
    (27 August), 276.
        Miss Johnston's new romance contains "interesting and
    even brilliant passages, but its artificiality is never
    successfully concealed."

6   ANON. "Sir Mortimer." The Independent, 56 (19 May), 1143-44.
        Miss Johnston is the "lady minstrel of historical fic-
    tion in this country." Sir Mortimer lives up to her repu-
    tation and is one of the "most beautifully written books"
    of the day.

7   HALSEY, FRANCIS W. "Novels of Importance." Book Buyer, 24
    (November), 128-29.
        Audrey demonstrates that Miss Johnston's "grasp is more
    firm, and her imagination is held in better restraint" than
    in To Have and to Hold. One feels, moreover, the historic
    verisimilitude of this new romance. Her craftsmanship here
    compares very favorably with that of William Dean Howells,
    Mary E. Wilkins Freeman, or Jane Austen.

8   LEONARD, PRISCILLA. "Sir Mortimer; or, A Romance of the
    English Court and the Spanish Main." Current Literature,
    37 (August), 184-85.
        Miss Johnston's new romance is as "dull as Walter Scott
    ever chose to be." With a brilliant unity and true vivid-
    ness, however, the later portion of the romance is quite
    entertaining. The psychological improbability of the ro-
    mance and its sudden reversal of things at its conclusion
    will not affect those who prefer a "thrill" in reading.

9   MOSS, MARY. "Five Books of the Day." The Bookman, 19 (June),
    388-95.
        Sir Mortimer suffers from excessiveness and an improper
    mixture of styles.

10 PAYNE, WILLIAM MORTON. "Recent Fiction." The Dial, 36
    (1 June), 366-68.
        Sir Mortimer is a "disappointment" in that Miss Johnston
    seems to have forgotten "how to tell a straightforward
    story in fitting language." Her attempts at rendering
    Elizabethan ways tend to impede the narrative progress.
    She seems to be degenerating in her writing.

1907 A BOOKS - NONE

1907 B SHORTER WRITINGS

1   ANON. "Books." The Spectator, 99 (2 November), 635.
        Miss Johnston's The Goddess of Reason is a "poetical
    drama as her romances would lead us to expect." With his-
    toric verisimilitude, the play achieves admirable "dramatic
    moments." The only weakness in the play is that her talent
    is "a little too delicate to reproduce the rude horrors of
    the Revolution."

2   ANON. "A Guide to the New Books." The Literary Digest, 35
    (13 July), 61-62.
        The Goddess of Reason is an "extraordinary literary per-
    formance, very uneven in character." Despite its consider-
    able historic interest, the play is marred by mediocre verse
    and broken unity.

3   RUTHERFORD, MILDRED LEWIS. The South in History and Litera-
    ture: A Handbook of Southern Authors. Atlanta, Georgia:
    The Franklin-Turner Company, pp. 612-14.
        Prisoners of Hope had a "freshness and vigor about it"
    that made it popular. To Have and to Hold was an improve-
    ment on the former, both of which were set in Cobb's Island,
    Virginia.

1908 A BOOKS - NONE

1908 B SHORTER WRITINGS

1   ANON. "Autumn Fiction." The Independent, 65 (19 November),
    1181-83.

1908

> Lewis Rand is Miss Johnston's best work to date, for she attains in it real depth in characterization.

2 ANON. "Books: Lewis Rand." Outlook (24 October), n.p.
The new novel lacks the "poetry of the past" of earlier works by Miss Johnston. The background of the novel is too large for the characters in the narrative. Miss Johnston, moreover, has failed to develop the dramatic possibilities inherent in her narrative.

3 ANON. "Current Fiction." The Nation, 87 (1 October), 317-19.
Lewis Rand contains admirable analysis. Landscape description is also quite good. The theme of the novel is the "triumph of character over temperament."

4 ANON. "Fiction." Times Literary Supplement (5 November), p. 390.
Lewis Rand suffers from "padding" and is often slow moving and marred by "empty" dialogue. The novel does, however, attain a "genuine eloquence and pathos."

5 ANON. "The Great Novel of the Year: Lewis Rand by Mary Johnston." Charlottesville Daily Progress (7 November), p. 5.
This advertisement praises Lewis Rand for its vivid presentation of American life of the nineteenth century and commends Mary Johnston for her use of "personal complications and dramatic situations resulting from political warfare."

6 ANON. "Johnston, Mary. Lewis Rand." American Library Association Booklist, 4 (November), 269-70.
Lewis Rand is a "self-made man whose ambition overreaches his moral sense." Characterization in the novel is strong, and the pleasant life of wealthy Virginians contrasts effectively with the "somberness of the main plot." The novel is an improvement over earlier works by Miss Johnston.

7 ANON. "Julia Marlowe Charms in Goddess of Reason." The Boston Journal (22 December), n.p.
There are "fine lines in the play, lines glowing with true poetic charm and vibrant with true dramatic energy." Miss Johnston's characterization, particularly that of the heroine, is quite strong.

8 ANON. "Lewis Rand by Mary Johnston." Catholic World, 88 (November), 259-60.

Miss Johnston gives the reader "some picturesque scenes of public and private Virginian life" in her new novel and exposes the "caste" system of early Virginia. Rand, however, is occasionally represented with a sentimentality inconsistent with his strength of character.

9   ANON. "Lewis Rand." The Spectator, 101 (28 November), 387.
    Miss Johnston is able to recapture the beauty of a by-gone era in her new novel, the focus of which is Virginia political life and its human ramifications. Both plot and characterization are a real credit to the author.

10 ANON. "Lewis Rand." Times Literary Supplement (5 November), p. 390.
    Much of the material in Miss Johnston's new novel strikes one as padding. Rand is "part genius and part adventurer." The new novel may be marred by "emptiness and redundancy" but its style approaches "eloquence and pathos and sometimes very near to beauty."

11 ANON. "Mary Johnston's New Novel." San Francisco Chronicle (11 October), p. 10.
    The Revolutionary War romance Lewis Rand is superior to all Johnston works to date except To Have and to Hold. The characterization of Lewis Rand, however, is conflicting and the historical background weak.

12 ANON. "Miss Johnston's Best Novel." The Independent, 65 (24 December), 1563-64.
    Lewis Rand has for its historical setting the most romantic period in American life. Miss Johnston's knowledge of history, however, outdistances her knowledge of the dramatic.

13 ANON. "New Novels." The Athenaeum, 4227 (31 October), 536-38.
    Miss Johnston is at her best in Lewis Rand when she writes of "love and jealousy" intertwined with the narrative concerning Jefferson and Burr.

14 BOWDOIN, W. G. "A Selection from the Year's Holiday Books." The Independent, 65 (17 December), 1457-68.
    Miss Johnston's Lewis Rand is an excellent historical novel because it has "real people instead of lay figures in antiquated costumes."

15 COOPER, FREDERIC TABER. "The Historical Background and Some Recent Novels." The Bookman, 28 (October), 140-46.

1908

Miss Johnston is excellent at the painting of landscape, especially Virginia landscape, yet her novels suffer from an "over-emphasis of the historic background."

Lewis Rand displays Miss Johnston's increased "understanding of the subtleties of life."

16 PAYNE, WILLIAM MORTON. "Recent Fiction." The Dial, 45 (1 November), 294-97.

Lewis Rand has a strong narrative replete with all the "accessories of historical fact and of the manners of Virginians a century ago." The novel is superior to earlier Johnston works.

1909 A BOOKS - NONE

1909 B SHORTER WRITINGS

1 ANON. "In the Realm of Bookland." Overland, NS 53 (January), 52-58.

The characterization of Jefferson is quite good in Lewis Rand. Miss Johnston has great talent for the use of historical setting.

2 ANON. "Mary Johnston A Suffragette: Gives Out Statement Telling Why She Is One." Baltimore American (15 November), n.p.

Mary Johnston, the "well-known Virginia authoress," has issued a signed statement explaining that since she is subject to all the duties of citizenship, surely she is entitled to the vote.

3 ANON. "Novel Notes." The Bookman (London), 35 (January), 198-200.

The protagonist of Lewis Rand is a "man of supreme abilities and of a certain innate nobleness." Rand's downfall was his intrigues in treason. The romance presents "a great theme greatly handled."

4 ANON. "Why She Is A Suffragist: Mary Johnston, The Author Thinks Suffrage A Right." New York Sun (15 November), n.p.

Mary Johnston, author of Lewis Rand, has explained that since she is subject to all other duties of citizenship, surely she is entitled to the vote.

5 M[IMS], E[DWIN]. "Lewis Rand." The South Atlantic Quarterly, 8 (January), 98-99.

Lewis Rand is "one of the best novels published during the last decade." The novel has both a good style and a strong insight into life.

6   PLEASANTS, WILLIAM H.   "Mary Johnston" in Library of Southern Literature. Edited by Edwin Anderson Alderman, et al. 17 volumes. Atlanta: Martin & Hoyt Company, 1909, vol. 10, pp. 2757-79.
    Discusses three influences on Mary Johnston's development--heredity, environment, and education. Miss Johnston's works are often historical in fact as well as in "spirit." Three favorite eras in the Johnston canon include the period just after the restoration of Sir William Berkeley to the governorship of Virginia in 1660 (Prisoners of Hope), Jamestown under Governor Yeardley (To Have and to Hold), and the administration of Alexander Spottswood (Audrey). Sir Mortimer, on the other hand, reverts to Elizabethan England yet retains Miss Johnston's historical authenticity. Her drama The Goddess of Reason reverts to the turbulent days of the French Revolution. Miss Johnston should be ranked alongside Scott, Thackeray, and Kingsley.

7   SIMONDS, WILLIAM EDWARD.   A Student's History of American Literature. Boston: Houghton Mifflin Company, p. 347.
    Mary Johnston is the author of three "successful romances" set in colonial Virginia: Prisoners of Hope, To Have and to Hold, and Sir Mortimer.

1910 A   BOOKS - NONE

1910 B   SHORTER WRITINGS

1   LLOYD, WILLIAM.   "Book of the Week." London Sunday Sun (8 November), n.p.
    Lewis Rand is the "tragedy of a man's soul." The English reviewer notes that one might divide novels into three types--the "Puzzle," the "Parable," and the "Picture." The third type, the best of the three types, provides a "true picture of men, women, and events." Lewis Rand is a highly successful "Picture" novel.

THREE VIRGINIA WRITERS

1911

<u>1911 A BOOKS - NONE</u>

<u>1911 B SHORTER WRITINGS</u>

1   ANON. "Civil War Epic." Los Angeles, California <u>Time</u>
        (19 June), n.p.
        <u>The Long Roll</u> is Mary Johnston's best novel to date and
    possibly the best work to treat the Civil War from a
    Southern point of view. The novel is a "long and vivid"
    portrait of Jackson. In her extensive use of details,
    Miss Johnston rivals Hugo, Zola, Balzac, and Tolstoi. The
    novel is "fact tinged with art."

2   ANON. "Concerning New Novels." London <u>Sketch</u> (9 August),
        n.p.
        <u>The Long Roll</u> contains a "stirring" narrative. The
    themes of the novel are "love, love of woman and country,
    finely tempered by war, and War, whose wounds are dressed
    by Love."

3   ANON. "Current Fiction." <u>The Nation</u>, 92 (25 May), 530-32.
        <u>The Long Roll</u> suffers from excessive details. Mary
    Johnston gives the reader an "ingenious collocation of
    facts rather than . . . a piece of life." Her style, more-
    over, is "pretentious and labored."

4   ANON. "Johnston, Mary. <u>The Long Roll</u>." <u>American Library
    Association Booklist</u>, 7 (June), 445.
        Mary Johnston presents a detailed study of Jackson, in-
    teresting for its revelation of Southern attitudes towards
    the general. As fiction, it is inferior to her other works.

5   ANON. "<u>The Long Roll</u> by Mary Johnston." Des Moines <u>Capital</u>
        (12 July), n.p.
        The panoramic nature of the new novel is oftentimes
    marked by a heaviness of detail. The portrait of Jackson
    is the focal point. History consequently becomes a major
    interest in the work.

6   ANON. "<u>The Long Roll</u>. By Mary Johnston." <u>The North American
    Review</u>, 194 (August), 303-304.
        <u>The Long Roll</u> is the best novel to date to treat the
    Civil War, for its details make history come alive.

7   ANON. "<u>The Long Roll</u>." <u>The Catholic World</u>, 94 (November),
        247.
        Miss Johnston emphasizes history at the expense of ro-
    mance. The work is characterized by its "historical

accuracy" and "vivid realism." The novel, on the other
hand, suffers from an extreme "Virginianism" and "too
flaring a color."

8   ANON. "The Long Roll: Miss Johnston's Story of Stonewall
      Jackson and His Battles." Charleston, South Carolina News
      (28 May), n.p.
          The new novel is replete with vivid description and pre-
      sents its protagonist as a somewhat mad military officer.
      Because Miss Johnston does not render a completely coherent
      narrative of the war--realistically, an impossibility--her
      novel attains an admirable "verisimilitude."

9   ANON. "The Long Roll." The Saturday Review, 112 (12 August),
      211.
          The true value of Mary Johnston's new novel lies in its
      "truthful and dramatic description of the great war and the
      men it produced." Her picture of war is the most vivid
      since Zola's La Débâcle.

10   ANON. "The Long Roll." The Spectator, 107 (16 September),
      424.
          Miss Johnston presents an "admirable picture" of Jackson
      in her new novel. Although she obviously takes the Southern
      point of view, her characterization is excellent.

11   ANON. "The Long Roll: Striking Portrait of Stonewall Jackson
      in a Novel by Mary Johnston." Newark, New Jersey Evening
      News (3 June), n.p.
          Stonewall Jackson is a "veritable triumph in military
      portraiture." Since the focus of the novel is often broad,
      the plot tends to be crowded. Conversation in the novel
      is often flat.

12   ANON. "Mary Johnston Has Splendid New Book." Dallas, Texas
      News (26 June), n.p.
          The Long Roll is a "remarkable work" for a woman writer.
      Although romance pervades the novel, history is its major
      focus. The scope of the novel is panoramic and its realism
      powerful.

13   ANON. "Mary Johnston On Progress." Boston Woman's Journal
      (11 March), n.p.
          In her speech at a Baltimore suffragette dinner, Mary
      Johnston notes the important role of women in the evolution
      of humanity.

1911

14   ANON. "Miss Mary Johnston: A Suffrage Worker." New York Times (11 June), p. 8.
        Having finished writing The Long Roll, Miss Johnston is about to sail for Europe. Miss Johnston states that as a eugenist she must support the enfranchisement of women. She adds that someday she may very well write a novel concerned with the suffrage movement.

15   ANON. "New Novels." The Athenaeum, 4370 (29 July), 124-25.
        Miss Johnston's use of the Civil War in The Long Roll lends new interest to an old subject. Although somewhat lengthy, the new novel seems thoroughly researched.

16   ANON. "Recent Fiction and the Critics." Current Literature, 51 (July), 107-110.
        The Long Roll places romance in the background and history in the foreground. Although the Southern "side" of the Civil War is convincingly presented, the romance "suffers in consequence."

17   ANON. "Some of the Season's Best Fiction." The American Review of Reviews, 43 (June), 757-62.
        Mary Johnston's presentation of Civil War conflicts in The Long Roll is without parallel in American literature. The work, a truly admirable one, appears more a "chronology" than a novel owing to its "tremendous array of verifiable information."

18   ANON. "Talk About Books." The Chautauquan, 65 (December), 140-44.
        The Long Roll is enriched by materials drawn from both public and private sources. Jackson is "awkward, prayerful, masterful." The fiction in the novel is, however, "negligible."

19   ANON. "Three American Backgrounds." The Outlook, 98 (27 May), 145-47.
        Miss Johnston recalls the gallantry of old Virginia in The Long Roll. With epic sweep, the novel focuses upon Stonewall Jackson and the Civil War years in Virginia. She handles the mass of details with considerable skill.

20   ANON. "Votes for Women: Some Newsy Bits of Interest to Suffragists." Philadelphia Record (26 February), n.p.
        Notes that Mary Johnston is to address the suffrage dinner at the Stafford Hotel, the week of 26 February 1911.

21 ANON. "War Time Heroes in The Long Roll." Philadelphia Record
    (9 September), n.p.
        Mary Johnston's use of details in The Long Roll is effec-
    tive, suggesting considerable historical investigation on
    her part. The novel, moreover, displays a "vigor in Miss
    Johnston's method, and charm in her matter."

22 ANON. "The Women Coming To the Front." Clinch Valley News
    (24 February), p. 1.
        The unexpected happened when the Baptist ministers con-
    ference invited Mary Johnston to address them. Since her
    address stirred no public criticism, it is difficult to
    assess her influence on the audience.

23 HARRIS, MRS. L. H. "The Long Roll." The Independent, 71
    (6 July), 39-40.
        The Long Roll ranks alongside Hugo's Les Misérables, for
    the Johnston masterpiece dramatizes "the private life of a
    great army with the heart of it in one man's bosom and the
    head of it on one man's shoulders." Her main purpose in
    the novel is to "interpret the real mind and character" of
    Stonewall Jackson.

24 PAYNE, WILLIAM MORTON. "Recent Fiction." The Dial, 51
    (16 July), 48-51.
        The Long Roll is too serious in nature to be a novel.
    Because the novel was so extensively researched, it is more
    properly speaking a "military history."

25 ROGERS, JOSEPH M. "For the Reader of New Fiction: Miss
    Johnston's 'The Long Roll.'" Book News Monthly, 29 (July),
    733-34.
        The Long Roll, heavy on local color but slightly short
    on romance, presents a "fine portrait of Stonewall Jackson,"
    for the work presents a "good setting of Jackson in his own
    environment."

26 TORRENCE, WILLIAM CLAYTON. "General Stonewall Jackson and
    The Long Roll." Richmond Times-Dispatch (19 November),
    p. 9.
        In defending The Long Roll from its critics, Torrence
    cites the humaneness of Miss Johnston's protagonist and
    the fact that the protagonist is viewed through the eyes
    of those who knew him. In order to defend the novel's his-
    toric authenticity, Torrence quotes from Colonel Henderson's
    Stonewall Jackson and the American Civil War.

1911

27   W. H. W. "The Long Roll." South Atlantic Quarterly, 10
         (October), 397.
            Mary Johnston's new novel is a "rhapsodic prose epic,"
         somewhat overly detailed yet highly imaginative in nature.

1912 A   BOOKS - NONE

1912 B   SHORTER WRITINGS

    1   ANON. "Cease Firing." The Independent, 73 (19 December),
         1430-31.
            Cease Firing, an extension of The Long Roll, lacks
         "proportion" and is marred by an "artificial style."

    2   ANON. "Cease Firing." Times Literary Supplement (12 December),
         p. 578a.
            The "grimness and power" of Cease Firing are owed to its
         "many vignettes of death." Mary Johnston's search for
         realism in the novel leads her, however, into a betrayal of
         her readers.

    3   ANON. "Current Fiction." The Nation, 95 (21 November),
         482-84.
            Mary Johnston relies too heavily on coincidence in
         Cease Firing. Her style is "inflated" and her dialogue
         characteristically stilted.

    4   ANON. "Miss Johnston's Second War Story." New York Sun
         (23 November), p. 8.
            The opening descriptions in Cease Firing are truly
         "eloquent." Dialogue, on the other hand, is particularly
         weak. The descriptions of battle are comparable to those
         in Stephen Crane's The Red Badge of Courage.

    5   ANON. "The New Books." The Outlook, 102 (30 November),
         776-79.
            Cease Firing is a sequel to The Long Roll and is evi-
         dently a carefully researched novel. The novel is somewhat
         similar to Tolstoi's War and Peace. Miss Johnston tells
         her story without "rancor."

   *6   ANON. Review of Cease Firing. Springfield Republican
         (21 November), p. 5.
            Unlocatable. Listed in Book Review Digest for 1912,
         p. 248.

7 ANON. "A War as War." New York Times, Saturday Review of
   Books and Art (17 November), p. 677.
      Cease Firing is not a novel but a "series of pictures--
   thrilling, piteous pictures."

8 COOPER, FREDERIC TABER. "The Theory of Endings and Some
   Recent Novels." The Bookman, 36 (December), 433-39.
      Cease Firing contains "a certain epic sweep of action, a
   sense of the havoc of war." The novel represents some of
   Miss Johnston's best work to date.

9 TYLER, ALICE. "Cease Firing!: Mary Johnston's Second Civil
   War Novel." Book News Monthly, 29 (November/December),
   239-43.
      Miss Johnston has achieved a "War Epic" in her new
   novel. The backdrop of nature adds much to this new work.

1913 A BOOKS - NONE

1913 B SHORTER WRITINGS

1 ANON. "Cease Firing." South Atlantic Quarterly, 12
   (January), 92.
      Miss Johnston's excellent descriptions in Cease Firing
   suggest exhaustive research on her part.

2 ANON. "Critical Reviews of the Season's Latest Books."
   New York Sun (1 November), p. 8.
      Hagar is not a plea for justice for women but an "asser-
   tion" of women's rights. Although the early portion of the
   novel is well written, the latter section lacks unity.

3 ANON. "Current Fiction." The Nation, 97 (30 October), 409-11.
      Mary Johnston's Hagar may be to females as Uncle Tom's
   Cabin was to blacks. She has mastered "artistic exaggera-
   tion" by discovering in her new novel that logic must always underlie hyperbole.

4 ANON. "Five New Novels By Women." The Outlook, 105
   (15 November), 570-72.
      Hagar may strike some readers as too much like a tract
   and too little like a novel. The novel is nonetheless
   "revolutionary" feminist propaganda. The earnestness of
   the protagonist leads to the overloading of the novel.

5 ANON. "Hagar." Times Literary Supplement (20 November),
   p. 555a.

1913

Mary Johnston's Hagar suffers from her purpose in writing the novel, for the heroine is too often an exponent of feminism and her father too obviously an extreme chauvinist.

6 ANON. "Johnston, Mary: Hagar." American Library Association Booklist, 10 (December), 157.
Hagar's development into feminist is seen amidst a "well-drawn conservative southern background." The work is too obviously propaganda.

7 ANON. "Johnston (Mary), Hagar." Supplement to the Athenaeum, 4492 (29 November), 643.
Hagar is an unduly long novel about "women's development in social service." The contrast between New Yorkers and Virginians, however, is very well done.

8 ANON. "The New Books." The Independent, 76 (30 October), 218–220.
The opening chapters of Hagar create a number of "sympathetic portraits" which are all but abandoned by Miss Johnston's absorption in social movements in the latter half of the novel.

9 ANON. "New Novels: Cease Firing." London Christian World (16 January), n.p.
Cease Firing and The Long Roll constitute an "epic of war, unparalleled in the history of fiction." The moving narrative of Civil War conflicts is enhanced by the "splendid imagination of an author who sees beyond the sordid misery and the wrong, the finest qualities of men and women being tested, purified and strengthened."

10 ANON. "Novels." The Saturday Review, 116 (15 November), 623.
Mary Johnston always writes "pleasantly and easily, never forcing the note or attempting modern tricks of cleverness." Hagar is an excellent portrait of the modern female. Although the novel lacks humor, the heroine is truly genuine.

11 ANON. "Recent Novels." The Literary Digest, 47 (15 November), 953–57.
Hagar is a "careful and sympathetic study" of the feminist movement. The feminine movement, moreover, has never had a more "human exposition."

12 ANON. "Recent Novels." The Literary Digest, 46 (1 February), 238–41.

Mary Johnston's descriptions of Civil War battle scenes in Cease Firing are excellent. Although her views are essentially Southern, she deals impartially with both sides involved in the war.

13 ANON. "The South Paid Bitterly." Minneapolis, Minnesota Journal (5 January), n.p.
Cease Firing emphasizes the fundamental brotherhood of North and South. The novel will do much toward achieving reconciliation of North and South.

14 BULLIS, HELEN. "A Feminist Novel: Miss Johnston's Hagar a Tale and a Theory." New York Times Review of Books (2 November), part 6, p. 277.
Hagar is a "plea for greater freedom for women, and a very pleasant story." Although Hagar's childhood is convincingly drawn, her womanhood in the novel leaves something to be desired.

15 EDGETT, EDWIN FRANCIS. "Mary Johnston's Feminist Novel." Boston Evening Transcript (25 October), part 3, p. 8.
Mary Johnston's fatal mistake in Hagar is that she admires her protagonist too much and is too determined to advance the feminist cause. Her new novel is unfortunately a "polemic." The novel blunders, moreover, in bordering upon the comic when it strives for the serious. Miss Johnston's true talent is obviously not with the problem novel but with the romance.

16 HOOKER, BRIAN. "Mary Johnston's Hagar." The Bookman, 38 (December), 426-28.
Hagar contains a "'glowing argument for feminism.'" The novel, however, is plotless since Miss Johnston's purpose is to present a thesis concerned with feminism and since she allows propaganda to overshadow narrative. The novel must consequently be judged as a tract and not as a tale. It does not equal To Have and to Hold.

17 LUBLIN, CURTIS. "Some Recent Books." Town and Country, 22 (November), 35.
The characters in Hagar are fully developed. Hagar herself did not "turn into a suffragist; she was compressed into one." The novel is "thought-awakening, thought-inspiring and thought-convincing in its mission as a plea for certain ideals.

1914

1914 A   BOOKS - NONE

1914 B   SHORTER WRITINGS

1   ANON. "Brief Notes Concerning Books and Writers." Richmond
         Times-Dispatch (18 October), part 4, p. 10.
            Publishers have reported a heavy advance demand for Mary
         Johnston's The Witch.

2   ANON. "Deeds Done and Dreams Dreamed." Boston Advertiser
         (11 November), n.p.
            The Witch disproves the notion that the reading audience
         demands a happy ending.

3   ANON. "Mary Johnston's Story of the Brave Man Who Feared a
         Bully." Greensboro, North Carolina News (8 November), n.p.
            The Witch violates the pattern of conventional romance
         in its choice of setting, character, and event. The work
         is in part an attack on religious orthodoxy and bigotry and
         is nearly allegorical in its presentation of a man who
         "sought Truth in an age of blindness and found only Death."

4   ANON. "Mary Johnston's Suffrage Speech." Current Opinion, 56
         (January), 49.
            Hagar has been hailed "'the Uncle Tom's Cabin of the
         woman movement.'" The reviewer believes, however, that
         Hagar "flys [sic] too high, particularly after she reaches
         maturity."

5   ANON. "Miss Mary Johnston's New Novel, The Witch." Houston,
         Texas Post (29 November), n.p.
            The Witch is a "well told and effective story, the most
         artistic that Miss Johnston has written, even if she allows
         ill fortune to keep up too heavily on her unlucky victims."

6   ANON. "The New Books." The Outlook, 108 (11 November),
         603-05.
            The Witch is a return to Mary Johnston's "more attrac-
         tive manner." With excellent landscape painting and ex-
         citing events, the novel never loses its momentum.

7   ANON. "Novels of Significance." The American Review of
         Reviews, 50 (December), 764-65.
            The Witch returns to the romantic vein of Miss Johnston's
         To Have and to Hold. The novel is "intense, highly drama-
         tic, full of spirit and pictorial phraseology, but so over-
         done and flamboyant in spots as to be unconvincing."

8   ANON. "Pseudo Historical." The New Republic, 1 (28 November),
      28.
          The Witch has "all the trappings of romance and none of
      its glamor, all the seriousness of fact with none of the
      vitality that immortalized fact into truth." The work is
      truly "pseudo-historical."

9   ANON. "Recent Reflections of a Novel-Reader." Atlantic
      Monthly (April), 491.
          Hagar is "lacking in vitality, spirit, fresh air, faith
      and charity." The novel is weakened by an unpleasant at-
      mosphere and a heroine with whom one cannot sympathize.

10   ANON. "Reflections By W. J. C.: English and American Novels
      Compared." Detroit News Tribune (13 March), n.p.
          A casual comparison of the English and American novelist
      suggests that the former has the "greater sense of society,"
      and the latter the "greater sense of the individual." Miss
      Johnston did excellent portrayal in The Long Roll and Cease
      Firing. Although we observe the progress of war, we become
      acquainted with but a few men.

*11 ANON. Review of The Witch. Springfield Republican
      (3 December), p. 5.
          Unlocatable. Listed in Book Review Digest for 1914,
      p. 291.

12   ANON. "The Witch." The Athenaeum, 4542 (14 November), 502.
          The Witch is a "drama which frees imagination, and
      chains sympathy to its appointed end." The novel is quite
      "realistic," its events quite plausible.

13   ANON. "The Witch." Christian Work (5 December), n.p.
          Mary Johnston has achieved a "full play of her dramatic
      gift, and has harmoniously associated her rich imagination
      with facts."

14   ANON. "The Witch." New York Times Book Review (1 November),
      part 6, p. 474.
          The theme of The Witch is that "real and permanent hap-
      piness can be found only in freedom of the spirit." The
      motivation of the hero and heroine is primarily love of
      truth.

15   ANON. "The Witch." The Saturday Review, 118 (14 November), 6.
          The "stirring events" of Elizabethan England form the
      basis for The Witch. Reading the "admirable" novel is a
      pleasant diversion from the weariness of the present war.

1914

16 ANON. "The Witch." South Bend, Indiana Tribune (10 October), n.p.
Joan Heron and Dr. Aderhold are strongly drawn charac- ters. As a picture of Elizabethan life, the novel is with- out equal.

17 ANON. "The Witch." Times Literary Supplement (29 October), p. 481.
Mary Johnston is an "able American novelist" who, in The Witch, can transport us to the Elizabethan era and conjure up its vividness and color.

18 ANON. "Witchcraft Novel By Mary Johnston." The North American (10 October), n.p.
Mary Johnston writes in The Witch in a "glowing, sympa- thetic vein of imaginative portrayal, presenting strong and highly-vitalized characters, instinct with the spirit of the time." The new work is a tragedy, not a romance.

19 BOYNTON, H. W. "Recent Novels." The Nation, 99 (3 December), 652-54.
Miss Johnston's The Witch is fortunately more akin to her early work Audrey than to her later Civil War novels.

20 EDGETT, EDWIN FRANCIS. "Mary Johnston and the Witch." Boston Evening Transcript (24 October), part 3, p. 8.
The Witch is marked by the "elements of a vigorous old- fashioned romantic novel." The history of Renaissance England furnishes the substance of this new romance. Despite the credibility of the novel and the appeal of its narrative, Miss Johnston is guilty, at times, of a lack of restraint.

21 O'CONNOR, MRS. T. P. My Beloved South. New York: G. P. Putnam's Sons, p. 371.
In speaking to Rosewell Page of the Knights of the Golden Horseshoe, Mrs. O'Connor observes, "How charmingly Mary Johnstone [sic] uses that incident in Audrey."

22 REELY, MARY KATHARINE. "The Witch." The Publishers' Weekly, 86 (12 December), 2010.
The Witch takes a well deserved shot at the myth of the good old days. Miss Johnston, moreover, provides excite- ment in the new novel without catering to the reading pub- lic's love of sentimentality and happy endings.

1915 A BOOKS - NONE

1915 B SHORTER WRITINGS

1   ANON. "Current Fiction." The Nation, 101 (2 December),
        657-59.
            The narrative of The Fortunes of Garin is filled with
        "movement and color." The heavy seriousness of Miss
        Johnston's purpose, however, detracts from the novel.
        Garin's pursuit of his love becomes the pursuit of an ideal.

2   ANON. "Double Toil and Trouble." The Independent, 81
        (1 February), 176.
            The Witch, like other recent Johnston fiction, is
        "rather too gruesome to be quite healthy."

3   ANON. "Fiction." Times Literary Supplement (16 December),
        p. 478c.
            Miss Johnston is able to paint the days of Richard the
        Lionheart with a "picturesque touch." With a well construc-
        ted narrative, The Fortunes of Garin suffers only from a
        "conscious literariness in its style."

4   ANON. "Fiction." Wisconsin Library Bulletin, 11 (December),
        371-72.
            Mary Johnston's hero and heroine in The Fortunes of
        Garin are extremely well done.

5   ANON. "The Fortunes of Garin." Lafayette, Indiana Journal
        (24 October), n.p.
            The reviewer finds it odd that Miss Johnston should
        write a romance like The Fortunes of Garin when her own era
        is such a troubled one. The reviewer finds grammatical
        constructions in the novel a major flaw.

6   ANON. "Johnston, Mary. The Witch." American Library
        Association Booklist, 11 (January), 221.
            The Witch is a "somber and tragic story" exposing the
        inhumanity of Puritan England.

7   ANON. "Mary Johnston's Historical Romance." New York Times
        Book Review (24 October), part 5, p. 402.
            The Fortunes of Garin is a fascinating, dramatic romance
        with life-like characters set in a period "full of con-
        trasts." Although Garin supplies the title for the book,
        it is the Princess Audiart who "dominates it all."

1915

8   ANON. "Notes on Current Fiction." The American Review of
     Reviews, 52 (December), 765.
          The Fortunes of Garin has a richly colored background
     drawn from an age of chivalry and the crusades.

9   ANON. "Review of New Books." Springfield Republican
     (24 October), p. 15.
          With painstaking research and considerable talent for
     the romance, Mary Johnston is quite successful in The For-
     tunes of Garin. Although the narrative is a bit slow at
     times, the climax of the romance is very satisfying.

10   ANON. "Some Costume Novels: Representative of Current
     Fiction." The Nation, 100 (14 January), 52-53.
          The Witch is a "labored" romance, the style "tricky
     rather than original," the suspense unrelieved.

11   ANON. "Tournament and Troubadour." The Independent, 84
     (22 November), 318.
          Mary Johnston's Fortunes of Garin, a medieval romance,
     stands in pleasant contrast to the unpleasant events oc-
     curring throughout the year of its publication.

12   ANON. "The Witch." South Atlantic Quarterly, 14 (January),
     90-91.
          The Witch contains "strong and vital characters" and is
     based upon an interesting love affair. The historical novel
     is marked by Miss Johnston's "imaginative comprehension of
     times past."

13   COOPER, FREDERIC TABER. "Some Novels of the Month." The
     Bookman, 40 (January), 552-57.
          The Witch is an exciting tale that degenerates into
     "sheer melodrama." The latter half of the novel is a "re-
     version to the picaresco type."

14   _____. "Some Novels of the Month." The Bookman, 42
     (December), 467-71.
          The Fortunes of Garin does not equal Miss Johnston's
     earlier fiction. The conclusion to the novel is quite
     obvious.

15   EDGETT, EDWIN FRANCIS. "Mary Johnston in Medieval France."
     Boston Evening Transcript (20 October), p. 21.
          Mary Johnston makes the past "one vast poetic dream" in
     The Fortunes of Garin. The romance is marked by an illusion
     that is "perfect" and is hence a much better novel than The
     Long Roll or Cease Firing.

16   KELLOGG, ELENORE. "A Plea for Freedom." Chicago Post
         (26 February), n.p.
             The Witch is an "intellectual protest" that grows from
         the setting of the romance. One is tempted to read this
         romance as allegory and to see Aderhold as "understanding--
         clear and unobstructed vision."

17   LYND, ROBERT. "The Fortunes of Garin." The Publishers'
         Weekly, 88 (11 December), 1964-65.
             Those who like romances set in the days of knighthood
         will appreciate The Fortunes of Garin, a romance which cap-
         tures the atmosphere of medieval France.

18   WILLCOCKS, M. P. "Books of the Day." London Chronicle
         (2 January), n.p.
             The Witch is an "interesting spiritual study, in which
         the woman is far less important than the wizard, . . . a
         man who refuses, in days when such a refusal was very dan-
         gerous, to express his philosophy in any of the usual creeds
         or shibboleths." Aderhold is a more absorbing character
         than Joan.

1916 A   BOOKS - NONE

1916 B   SHORTER WRITINGS

1   ANON. "Johnston, Mary. The Fortunes of Garin." American
         Library Association Booklist, 12 (January), 194.
             Mary Johnston's new romance set in southern France during
         the crusades is "fresh and spirited and the characters stand
         out vividly."

2   ANON. "Reviews of New Books." The Literary Digest, 52
         (22 January), 185-86.
             The Fortunes of Garin is a charming romance, a pleasant
         departure from Miss Johnston's Civil War novels. The plot
         of the romance provides her with the opportunity for con-
         siderable landscape painting.

3   HALE, EDWARD E. "Recent Fiction." The Dial, 60 (20 January),
         78-79.
             The Fortunes of Garin is marked by its "vitality." Al-
         though Miss Johnston may lack "the intensity of imagination
         necessary to fuse everything in one great impression," the
         new romance is still a "fine" work.

1916

4   PAINTER, FRANKLIN VERZELIUS NEWTON. An Introduction to
        American Literature. Boston: Sibley & Company, p. 316.
            Mary Johnston is a "well-known novelist and lecturer on
        woman's suffrage."

5   PATTEE, FRED LEWIS. A History of American Literature Since
        1870. New York: The Century Company, p. 403.
            Mary Johnston's To Have and To Hold, which had sold
        285,000 copies as of the summer of 1901, is an example of
        the fashion in that era for historical romance.

1917 A BOOKS - NONE

1917 B SHORTER WRITINGS

1   ANON. "Johnston, Mary. The Wanderers." American Library
        Association Booklist, 14 (December), p. 96.
            The Wanderers is, properly speaking, not a novel but "a
        series of tales" concerned with women's progress towards
        equality through the ages.

2   ANON. "The Light That Never Was." The Nation, 105
        (1 November), 486-87.
            The Wanderers has the usual Johnston weakness: exces-
        sive seriousness. The novel is all dark and no light and
        is "a history of Woman as feminism sees her."

3   ANON. "Male and Female." New York Evening Post (27 October),
        n.p.
            The material of The Wanderers is based upon the "rela-
        tionship between the sexes in all its changing aspects,
        the political and economic not least." Freedom is the
        major note of the novel, the dominant theme sexual equality.
        The theme of the novel, however, is far too large for Miss
        Johnston's treatment of it.

4   ANON. "New Fiction by American Writers." New York Times
        Review of Books (30 September), part 4, p. 566.
            The Wanderers is a series of nineteen short stories,
        each of which reveals some aspect of "the changing rela-
        tions of men and women through the ages." The work demon-
        strates "thought and a good deal of study."

5   ANON. "Novels and Short Stories." <u>The American Review of</u>
     <u>Reviews</u>, 56 (November), 555-57.
          <u>The Wanderers</u> is a collection of short stories which
     view love between men and women throughout history. The
     stories bear a realistic atmosphere and perspective of each
     age examined.

6   ANON. "<u>The Wanderers</u>." <u>The Catholic World</u>, 106 (December),
     400.
          Mary Johnston's new work is comprised of a number of
     sketches involving the "'love relation.'" The scope of the
     work, however, is far too wide to manage, for the novelist
     has been overshadowed by the feminist.

7   ANON. "<u>The Wanderers</u>." Newark, New Jersey <u>Evening News</u>
     (3 November), n.p.
          <u>The Wanderers</u> is a series of unconnected short stories,
     each story containing a woman as the major character.

8   ANON. "Woman and Civilization." <u>Springfield Republican</u>
     (7 October), p. 17.
          The two themes of <u>The Wanderers</u> are love and the origins
     of man's dominance over woman. Miss Johnston demonstrates
     in the novel that "the higher the civilization, the greater
     become the limitations of woman's freedom and independence
     in the interest of a broadly social ideal." The novel is
     a "landmark in the season's fiction."

9   BOYNTON, H. W. "A Stroll Through the Fair of Fiction." <u>The</u>
     <u>Bookman</u>, 46 (November), 337-42.
          Mary Johnston's <u>The Wanderers</u> is a refreshing departure
     from her former works. The new novel is a "series of tales"
     dealing with love between men and women and the effect of
     such love on history.

10   D. L. M. "<u>The Wanderers</u>." <u>Boston Evening Transcript</u>
     (3 October), part 2, p. 6.
          Mary Johnston's works have often been marked by a didac-
     ticism that imparts her vision of the past. <u>The Wanderers</u>
     is an intensification of that didactic impulse. Miss
     Johnston's artistry forces us to see each of the nineteen
     sets of characters in the new work, which traces out the
     history of womankind and the love relationship. The work
     is marked by "deep insight" and "dramatic intensity."

1918

1918 B SHORTER WRITINGS

  1   ANON. "Latest Works of Fiction." New York Times Review of
      Books (3 November), part 3, p. 3.
        Foes is like a "beautifully formed crystal." With ef-
      fective characterization, attractive setting, and sound
      character motivation, the novel is truly moving.

*2   ANON. Review of Mary Johnston's Foes. New York Evening Post
      (30 November), p. 2.
        Unlocatable. Item is listed in Book Review Digest for
      1918, p. 240.

  3   BRADSHER, EARL L. "Book Publishers and Publishing," in The
      Cambridge History of American Literature. Edited by
      William Peterfield Trent, Stuart P. Sherman, and Carl Van
      Doren. New York: G. P. Putnam's Sons, pp. 91, 287, 550.
        Mary Johnston "must have made from $60,000 to $70,000
      on To Have and to Hold, which statement may be taken as
      some fair gauge of the returns of a modern best seller."

  4   EDGETT, EDWIN FRANCIS. "Mary Johnston's Romance of Scotland."
      Boston Evening Transcript (27 November), part 2, p. 8.
        Despite the variety in her choice of time and place,
      Mary Johnston is always, in everything she has written, a
      romanticist. The theme of her new romance Foes is "a boy-
      ish friendship and love turned into implacable hate." The
      unity of the work is marred, however, by "omissions" and
      "gaps."

  5   J. L. "The Factor of Sex." New Republic, 13 (5 January),
      289-91.
        The Wanderers views life with a "feministic universal
      eye." Its major concern is male-female relationships from
      earliest times to the French Revolution. The work unfor-
      tunately becomes a "grindstone for the feminist axe."

1919 A BOOKS - NONE

1919 B SHORTER WRITINGS

  1   ANON. "In the Name of the Past." The Nation, 108
      (1 February), 173-74.
        Mary Johnston tries much too hard for historic verisimi-
      litude in Foes. Although her characters speak "by the
      calendar," Miss Johnston's "accent" is always present.

1919

2   ANON. "Johnston, Mary. <u>Foes</u>." <u>American Library Association</u>
      <u>Booklist</u>, 15 (January), 145.
         Mary Johnston's new romance is a "dramatic picturesque
      story of the time of the Stewart uprising in Scotland."
      The work has a number of colorful scenes of foreign lands
      and equally strong characterization.

3   ANON. "<u>The Laird of Glenfernie</u>." <u>Times Literary Supplement</u>
      (4 September), p. 472c.
         Although <u>The Laird of Glenfernie</u> is based upon "old ro-
      mantic incidents," the treatment of material is refreshing
      and the dénouement quite subtle. Characterization in the
      new work is excellent.

4   ANON. "Mary Johnston's Mystical Novel and Other Recent Works
      of Fiction." <u>New York Times Review of Books</u> (14 December),
      part 7, p. 741.
         <u>Michael Forth</u> both pleases and puzzles a reader. The
      latter half of the work seems a departure from the opening.

5   ANON. "New Books." <u>The Catholic World</u>, 109 (June), 397-412.
         Mary Johnston's <u>Pioneers of the Old South</u> is written
      like a novel. Miss Johnston views both pleasant and un-
      pleasant moments of history.

6   ANON. "<u>The Pioneers of the Old South</u>." <u>The Dial</u>, 67
      (6 September), 216.
         As historical writing, <u>Pioneers</u> suffers from serious
      weaknesses, for Johnston often focuses on personalities at
      the expense of "political and social conditions in England."
      The work, moreover, dwells more on Virginia under the
      Stuart kings than it does on the South.

7   ANON. "Readable History." <u>The Independent</u>, 99 (13 September),
      368.
         Mary Johnston's <u>Pioneers of the Old South</u> is written as
      fluently as <u>To Have and to Hold</u>.

8   EDGETT, EDWIN FRANCIS. "Mary Johnston's World-Wanderings."
      <u>Boston Evening Transcript</u> (24 December), p. 6.
         Mary Johnston's early works about colonial Virginia were
      marked by an "abundance of color" and a sensitivity to
      history. <u>Michael Forth</u> is not "a tale of the New South
      and its reconstruction on the ruins of the old," for the
      novel "degenerates into a series of rhapsodic chapters."
      As usual, Miss Johnston is guilty of "fine writing" and
      "flamboyant style." The new novel is obviously no equal
      to <u>To Have and to Hold</u> or· <u>Lewis Rand</u>.

1920

1920 A BOOKS - NONE

1920 B SHORTER WRITINGS

1   ANON. "Fiction." Times Literary Supplement (22 July),
p. 474b.
     Michael Forth reflects the current metaphysical vogue
for "'The New Thought.'" The work is comprised of a
"pseudo-spiritual quest," inflated language, and "stylistic
affectations." The new work suggests the continued decay
of the English language in America.

2   ANON. "Johnston, Mary. Michael Forth." American Library
Association Booklist, 16 (January), 134.
     Mary Johnston's latest work minimizes both "plot and in-
cident" in order to focus on the change of the old South
into the new. The novel has limited appeal.

3   ANON. "Mary Johnston's Philosophy." Springfield Republican
(10 December), p. 8.
     "Wordsworthian in intensity" and love of nature, Sweet
Rocket lacks Wordsworth's "simplicity and poetic sense,"
for Miss Johnston lacks a sense of "proportion."

4   ANON. "Michael Forth: A Splendid Picture of the Old South
in Reconstruction Days--By Mary Johnston." Philadelphia
Public Ledger (3 January), n.p.
     The first part of Michael Forth is commendable reading.
The latter part, however, is highly "psychic" and consequently quite confusing.

5   ANON. "Reviews of Books: Books of American History."
American Historical Review, 25 (January), 290-311.
     The Pioneers of the Old South uses traditional inter-
pretations of history without taking into account newer
studies.

6   ANON. "Sweet Rocket." New York Evening Post Literary Review
(20 November), p. 10.
     Most Mary Johnston fans will be disappointed to discover
that Sweet Rocket contains the "spiritual quest" apparent
in Foes and Michael Forth. The new novel, properly speaking, is not a novel, for it contains "neither action nor
character analysis."

7   ANON. "Sweet Rocket." New York Times Review of Books
(21 November), part 3, pp. 21-22.
     Those who delight in description at the expense of nar-
rative will enjoy Sweet Rocket.

8   ANON. "We're All Part of the Is-ness." Chicago Herald
     Examiner (25 January), n.p.
          Michael Forth is a "graceful, winning tale of a fine old
     Virginia family." A major theme of the novel is immortal-
     ity, Johnston's thesis being "'We are all a part of one
     great whole.'"

9   EUBANK, J. A. "Sweet Rocket." Richmond Times-Dispatch
     (14 November), pp. 8-10.
          Mary Johnston's new novel is a "mystical novel full of
     subtle beauties." The work gives the author "a rare dis-
     tinction in the field of spiritual quest."

10   F. M. W. "Sweet Rocket." Boston Evening Transcript
     (4 December), part 6, p. 5.
          The characters in Mary Johnston's new book reside in a
     place of "surpassing beauty," each character having had a
     "'vision of Oneness.'" She has "revealed with keen percep-
     tion the idea of individual growth and expansion toward
     Godhood, and the setting of her book is of idyllic beauty."

11   S. W. C. "Mary Johnston's Latest Novel 'Michael Forth,' And
     Other Recent Tales." Brooklyn, New York Eagle (17 January),
     n.p.
          Mary Johnston's new work is primarily autobiographical.
     A romantic narrative with heavy emphasis on spiritualism,
     the novel creates a "delightful character."

1921 A BOOKS - NONE

1921 B SHORTER WRITINGS

1   ANON. "Sweet Rocket." Times Literary Supplement (5 May),
     p. 290d.
          William Dean Howells often joked that in his own novels
     nothing really happened. In Mary Johnston's Sweet Rocket
     (English edition) even less happens. On the other hand,
     much of a philosophical or occult nature does happen to the
     inhabitants of the old house.

2   BOYNTON, H. W. "More of Less Novels." The Bookman, 52
     (January), 341-45.
          Sweet Rocket is "monotonously in the vein of all of Miss
     Johnston's recent books." The new novel is marked by a
     "painful sense of strain, of feverish insistence, about
     this exposition of a theory of perfect peace and rest."

1921

   3   VAN DOREN, CARL. The American Novel. New York: The MacMillan
Company, pp. 248-49.
     Mary Johnston's Prisoners of Hope was one of the success-
ful historical romances which deluged the market from 1896
to 1902.

1922 A BOOKS - NONE

1922 B SHORTER WRITINGS

   1   ANON. "Age of Miracles." Springfield Republican (23 April),
p. 15a.
     Only the very perceptive reader will be able to grasp
Silver Cross with its blending of "superstition and mysticism." The romance transports one from this contemporary
world of materialism and science.

   2   ANON. "Books in Brief." The Nation, 115 (2 August), 131.
     Silver Cross demonstrates Miss Johnston's continued con-
cern with the supernatural but is marked by a "new, vivid
style which has now the pungency of imagism and now the
stiffness of a manner not quite at ease with itself."

   3   ANON. "Fiction." Wisconsin Library Bulletin, 18 (June),
156-57.
     Silver Cross deals with the "worldly envy" of one monas-
tic order for another.

   4   ANON. "Johnston, Mary. Silver Cross." American Library
Association Booklist, 18 (June), 331.
     Silver Cross attains a feeling of "time and place." Its
"rhythmic prose" will attract some and repel others.

   5   ANON. "The Literary Spotlight." The Bookman, 55 (July),
491-95.
     Focuses on Mary Johnston's warmth of personality, her
mystical experiences, and her fondness for seclusion.
References are made to Foes, To Have and to Hold, Sweet
Rocket, Prisoners of Hope, Audrey, and The Long Roll. This
article was later incorporated into John Chipman Farrar's
The Literary Spotlight (See 1924.B5).

   6   ANON. "New Novels: Faith and Fraud." The Times (25 May),
p. 16c.
     Silver Cross employs an old theme. The novel, however,
weakens as it nears its conclusion, for Miss Johnston
leaves too many questions unanswered. The romance contains

remarkably good scene-painting, a talent the reviewer notes as having been apparent in The Long Roll and Cease Firing.

7   ANON. "Shadow and Substance." The Independent and the Weekly Review, 108 (8 April), 354.
      The substance of Silver Cross is "highly artificial." Most Johnston fiction takes on a "deadly seriousness."

8   ANON. "Silver Cross." Boston Evening Transcript (8 April), part 4, p. 8.
      Silver Cross presents a "colorful pageant of life as it was lived in old England." Despite the romance of the narrative, Miss Johnston lapses into a "highly spasmodic prose, intensely modern, intensely futuristic." Plain English would be far preferable in this work, for the novel is very difficult to read.

9   BENET, WILLIAM ROSE. "Telegraphic Romance." Literary Review of New York Evening Post (18 March), p. 503.
      Silver Cross is a romance with a "purposely mannered style," thus a "pointilliste painting." With great strength of narration and description and a staccato style, the new romance attains an almost "telegraphic" style.

10 BOYNTON, H. W. "Shadow and Substance." The Independent, 108 (8 April), 354.
      Although Mary Johnston is a major historical romancer, her major weakness is her "deadly seriousness." Silver Cross is a "romantic fable of medieval chicanery and superstitition."

11 FIELD, LOUISE MAUNSELL. "Mary Johnston in a New Field." New York Times Review of Books (19 March), part 3, p. 24.
      Silver Cross, filled with "variety" and "drama," is a "fascinating compound of history and romance and mysticism."

12 OVERTON, GRANT S. "Mary Johnston's 1492: A Novel of Curious Charm." Philadelphia North American (16 December), n.p.
      1492 is better history than fiction. Style in the novel is particularly weak, the point of view being a hindrance to dramatic development.

13 PANGBORN, GEORGIA WOOD. "New Fiction in Varied Forms." New York Herald (12 November), section 8, p. 15.
      1492 suggests that Mary Johnston is a "poet gone somehow wrong." Her weakness in clarity and style may be owed to the "'school' of Amy Lowell."

1922

14   S. L. C. "In Days of Columbus." Boston Evening Transcript
         (15 November), part 4, p. 7.
              The point-of-view character in 1492 is Don Jayme De
         Marchena. The new work is more of a "careful sketch" than
         a novel. Miss Johnston's weakness here is her attempt to
         "make history into a romance instead of allowing history
         to spin its own gorgeous web." In 1492 she has a "style
         without a conviction. Her early enthusiasms had both."

15   ŠMERTENKO, JOHAN J. "Mary Johnston's Art." New York Evening
         Post (30 December), n.p.
              Mary Johnston throughout her career has been implying
         one major goal: "the interpretation of the South of to-day
         in terms of its historic backgrounds and origins." Hagar
         is consequently her great work, a novel with "dramatic in-
         terest," excellent characterization, and sound motivation.

16   TOWNSEND, R. D. "The Book Table: A Group of Some Novelists."
         The Outlook, 131 (10 May), 74-76.
              Silver Cross is a "delicately wrought tale." Mary
         Johnston's eighteenth century English diction may be quite
         authentic. The narrative of the novel is "purposely ab-
         rupt" and is complemented by a "rapid movement."

1923 A BOOKS - NONE

1923 B SHORTER WRITINGS

1   ANON. "Croatan." The Literary Digest International Book
         Review, 2 (December), 72-73.
              Highly imaginative and quite vivid, Mary Johnston's
         Croatan is "an old-fashioned romance."

2   ANON. "Croatan." New York Times Review of Books (28 October),
         part 3, p. 8.
              Mary Johnston's primary concern in Croatan is "the
         spirit that lured those early settlers to the New World;
         the thing that happened to them here, and their relations
         with the Indians." The concluding love story in the novel
         is a "serious fault."

3   ANON. "Fiction." Wisconsin Library Bulletin, 19 (December),
         508-10.
              Those who relish historical romance will be interested
         in Mary Johnston's Croatan, which has "touches of her early
         manner" as well as something of her "later influences."

4   ANON.   "Fiction." Wisconsin Library Bulletin, 19 (January),
         24-26.
            1492 is "romantic history" which provides a "vivid pic-
         ture of the period." The work is recommended for high
         school use.

5   ANON.   "1492." Springfield Republican (14 January), p. 72.
            History and romance are "deftly interwoven" in 1492.
         Miss Johnston has succeeded in presenting an accurate pic-
         ture of Columbus and in capturing the spirit of Spain in
         an era of colonization.

6   ANON.   "The New Books." The Outlook, 135 (26 December),
         729-30.
            Virginia Dare is the "charming" heroine of Croatan, a
         romance with "just the right tinge of historical flavor."
         Despite the weakness in diction towards the end of the
         novel, the earlier half is "admirable in its plain but
         picturesque narrative."

7   ANON.   "Virginia Dare, Captive." New York World (23 October),
         p. 7e.
            Croatan returns to the literary tradition of Mary
         Johnston's To Have and to Hold. The new romance contains
         a "steadily running interest."

8   HANEY, JOHN LOUIS. The Story of Our Literature. New York:
         Charles Scribner's Sons, pp. 250, 357.
            Mary Johnston is the author of a number of "good his-
         torical novels" set in her native Virginia. References are
         made to Prisoners of Hope and To Have and to Hold.

9   LOVEMAN, AMY. "A Tale of Virginia." The Literary Review of
         The New York Evening Post (27 October), p. 183.
            Although Croatan, like To Have and to Hold, is set in
         colonial Virginia, it is more realistic than Miss Johnston's
         early romantic works. The new work is confusing because of
         its "kaleidoscopic shifting of episode." Her true vein is
         obviously romantic, not realistic. Croatan, unfortunately
         marred by realism, "remains disjointed and artificial."

10   S. L. C. "Croatan and Its Settlers." Boston Evening
         Transcript (31 October), part 3, p. 4.
            Although Croatan returns to the Johnston milieu of To
         Have and to Hold, it fails to equal the "spiritual entirety"
         of that romance. The new work, however, contains a re-
         straint that is not only "good policy but good art."

Three Virginia Writers

1924

1924 A BOOKS - NONE

1924 B SHORTER WRITINGS

1   ANON. "Bringing in the Slaves." Greensboro, North Carolina
     Daily News (30 November), p. 12b.
        Continuing the vein of the historical novel, Miss Johns-
     ton has presented the pros and cons of slavery in The Slave
     Ship. Although the climax of the novel is an "unwelcome"
     one, the new work presents a "vivid picture of the time
     with which it deals."

2   ANON. "Mary Johnston's Novel Out of Africa." New York Times
     Book Review (16 November), part 3, p. 8.
        With a bit of "romance and mystery" Miss Johnston's The
     Slave Ship is a "vivid" novel. The general nature of her
     novel, however, suggests the qualities of "naive medieval
     morality plays." The novel, moreover, is marred by false-
     ness in diction.

3   ANON. "The Slave Ship." The Independent, 113 (22 November),
     429.
        The Slave Ship presents "more gravity and power" than
     any earlier Johnston work. The theme of the work is a
     "stark, somber one."

4   CLARK, EMILY. "Africa in Exile." New York Herald Tribune
     (7 December), part 4, p. 9e.
        With a tinge of mysticism, The Slave Ship is in the best
     tradition of Mary Johnston's writing. The new novel focuses
     more upon the spiritual progression of the protagonist than
     upon his physical struggles. Johnston, moreover, presents
     a sympathetic view of Negroes and leaves us with a real
     feeling for Virginia life and landscape.

5   FARRAR, JOHN CHIPMAN. The Literary Spotlight. New York:
     George H. Doran, pp. 43-50.
        Focuses on Miss Johnston's warmth of personality, her
     mystical experiences, and her fondness for seclusion. Re-
     ferences are made to Foes, To Have and to Hold, Sweet
     Rocket, Prisoners of Hope, Audrey, and The Long Roll.

6   J. W. C. "History in Fiction." New York World (9 November),
     p. 9e.
        In The Slave Ship Mary Johnston "not only delivers her
     subject of all its implications of drama and color, but
     transmutes it into a profound comment on a universally fet-
     tered existence." David Scott, the hero, is a highly

42

effective character, and his "spiritual conflicts" are quite engrossing.

7   MANN, DOROTHEA LAWRENCE. "A Jacobite Aboard A Slave Ship." Boston Evening Transcript (15 November), part 6, p. 4.
    The Slave Ship is a novel of "spiritual progress," for the novel concentrates on the soul and its relationship to this world. David Scott consequently becomes the central figure of the novel and a kind of symbol for man's struggle against slavery as he grows in conscience.

8   OVERTON, GRANT MARTIN. Cargoes for Crusoes. New York: D. Appleton & Company, pp. 208, 376-89.
    Michael Forth is a "chrysalis." Mary Johnston, who ranks with Dickinson, Emerson, Thoreau, Whitman, and Melville, was a strong mystic. An account of her birth, residency, reading habits, and travel is included. She was an avowed idealist. An account of her mystical moments is included. Strong mystical elements pervade The Witch, Foes, Michael Forth, and Sweet Rocket.

9   PANGBORN, H. L. "Fiction With a Feminine View-Point." The Literary Digest International Book Review, 3 (December), 18-19.
    Female writers have made considerable progress in their work since 1900. Mary Johnston's The Slave Ship is, for example, marked by a "girl's vision which refuses really to grow up." With a smooth narrative, the work may be her best historical novel yet.

1925 A   BOOKS - NONE

1925 B   SHORTER WRITINGS

1   ANON. "Johnston, Mary. The Slave Ship." American Library Association Booklist, 21 (January), 153.
    Mary Johnston's new work presents the "spiritual struggle of a hard-headed but mystical young Scotchman" sold into slavery. The historical background is quite good.

1926 A   BOOKS - NONE

1926 B   SHORTER WRITINGS

1   ANON. "Johnston, Mary. The Great Valley." American Library Association Booklist, 23 (October), 40.

1926

Mary Johnston's latest work, although slow moving, contains a vividly drawn background.

2   ANON. "Novels in Brief." The Nation and Athenaeum, 39
(17 July), 450-52.
The "pathos and passionate emotions" which characterized Mary Johnston's earlier works are absent from The Great Valley. The focus of the new novel is on the effect of the wilderness on "natures marked out by a poetic mysticism of Celtic birth."

3   BENÉT, STEPHEN VINCENT. "Out of Focus." The Saturday Review,
2 (15 May), 786-87.
Despite the fact that The Great Valley is a "well-written, painstaking historical novel," it is, as a whole, a failure, for its unity is violated.

4   BORG, DOROTHY. "Mary Johnston's The Great Valley." New York
World (2 May), p. 7.
The Great Valley is a "mellow and earnest book." Although there is something of the old fashioned romance in the new novel, The Great Valley avoids the excessive "strut and a bright costuming" of Mary Johnston's early works.

5   COBLRNTZ, STANTON A. "The Great Valley." The Literary Digest
International Book Review, 4 (August), 588.
Mary Johnston's The Great Valley emphasizes history at the expense of plot and characterization. The novel is "too disconnected and kaleidoscopic to be impressive."

6   EDGETT, EDWIN FRANCIS. "In the Great Valley of Virginia."
Boston Evening Transcript (24 April), part 6, p. 4.
Mary Johnston is best known to readers for her "panoramic pictures of Virginian history during its earlier epochs." The Great Valley is in this tradition of her writing and holds that "mercy is an attribute too seldom recognized and too infrequently remembered." The reviewer finds it an "excellent example of historical fiction at its best."

7   FIELD, LOUISE MAUNSELL. "Mary Johnston Recites an Epic of
Colonial Days." New York Times Book Review (2 May),
part 3, p. 11.
The Great Valley is the chronicle of the Selkirk family, an unforgettable "chronicle of the winning of America."

8   MIMS, EDWIN. The Advancing South: Stories of Progress and
Reaction. Garden City, New York: Doubleday, Page &
Company, pp. 203, 206-07.

Hagar is a "realistic story of the reaction of a Southern girl against current standards and taboos." In The
Long Roll and Cease Firing, Miss Johnston pictures the
Civil War without "romance" or "glory." Her portrait of
Stonewall Jackson, although offensive to the United Daughters of the Confederacy, is quite a tribute to Jackson's
leadership.

9   PARSONS, ALICE BEAL. "The People of Youth." The Nation, 122
     (30 June), 727-728.
         The characters of The Great Valley strike one as similar
     to people he has known in his youth. The novel does not
     supply "sophisticated thrills" but "understanding."

10   PATERSON, ISABEL. "Our Fathers That Begat Us." New York
     Herald Tribune Books (2 May), p. 4.
         There is a "natural piety," like patriotism, in Mary
     Johnston which prompts her view of American history and
     keeps her apart from the realism that marks Ellen Glasgow's
     Barren Ground. The Great Valley is "epic in outline, the
     people heroic in moral stature."

1927 A   BOOKS - NONE

1927 B   SHORTER WRITINGS

1   ANON. "Books in Brief." The Nation, 125 (7 December), 663.
         Despite its delicacy of style, The Exile is written with
     a dull "thinness and unreality."

2   ANON. "Bridge Into the Future." New York World
     (18 September), p. 6m.
         The theme of The Exile is the "nature of existence."
     The new novel represents something of a departure from the
     historical romances of Miss Johnston's early career and is
     marked by "charm, beauty, and a serious subtlety."

3   ANON. "The Exile." The Spectator, 139 (19 November), 894.
         The major attraction of The Exile is not the excitement
     of its wars but the psychology underlying its characters.
     Miss Johnston's notion of reincarnation is "interestingly
     though not convincingly set out." The landscape of the
     novel is "charmingly drawn and full of poetic feeling."

4   ANON. "The Exile." Springfield Republican (20 November),
     p. 7f.

1927

The Exile contains more thought than action and is somewhat "intangible." The atmosphere of the novel is particularly effective, Miss Johnston's descriptions excellent.

5   ANON. "Johnston, Mary. The Exile." American Library
    Association Booklist, 24 (December), 120.
        The Exile is a "romance of mysticism." The work is a
    disappointing one in comparison with her earlier works.

6   CARTER, JOHN. "Mary Johnston and the Millenium." New York
    Times Book Review (11 September), part 3, p. 4 ff.
        "Much effort and no little literary skill" have gone
    into the creation of a Utopian setting for The Exile.
    "Vague and transcendental" the novel is often difficult to
    follow. Very few readers will be able to penetrate this
    "insular allegory."

7   D. F. G. "The Exile." Boston Evening Transcript
    (17 September), part 6, p. 5.
        The ornamentation and mysticism of The Exile make it a
    very confusing novel. The novel is surely not a "work of
    art because there are terrible lapses in Miss Johnston's
    style."

8   DOUGLAS, DONALD. "Mystic Utopia." New York Tribune
    (11 September), pp. 1-2.
        The Exile is a departure from the best vein of Mary
    Johnston's fiction, a vein marked by the "accuracy" and
    "realism" of works like To Have and to Hold, The Long Roll,
    and Cease Firing. The Exile unfortunately pursues mysti-
    cism and fails to achieve a "willing suspension of disbe-
    lief." Character and "idea" are regrettably polarized from
    each other.

9   DOWD, JEROME. The Negro in American Life. New York: Century
    Company, p. 301.
        Mary Johnston's The Slave Ship "describes life in
    Colonial Virginia, and the transportation of Negroes to
    America."

10 F. H. M. "Mary Johnston's Exile." New York Evening Post
    (15 October), part 3, p. 15.
        The Exile is not in the best tradition of Miss Johnston's
    writing. The protagonist Richard talks in a "pseudo-
    philosophical way of mysticism, reincarnation, changing
    symbols and the Utopian ideal."

11   HUBBELL, JAY B. "Cavalier and Indentured Servant in Virginia
       Fiction." South Atlantic Quarterly, 26 (January), 22-39.
             Mary Johnston makes heavy use of sensational events in
       her novels. Despite her accurate use of "dress and manners,"
       her Virginia settings are not authentic. Her Virginia is,
       in short, a "Utopia of melodramatic romance." On the other
       hand, she was one of the first Virginia novelists to recog-
       nize in fiction the value of "Southern class distinctions."
       Both Audrey and Prisoners of Hope employ class conscious-
       ness as a social barrier between people.

12   PEARSON, EDMUND, ed. "The Book Table." The Outlook, 147
       (5 October), 155-57.
             The Exile is a tale of "imagination and prophesy." The
       author's goals in the novel are so idealistic that the
       reader is not surprised when she fails.

13   WOOLSEY, D. B. "Fiction Notes." The New Republic, 52
       (19 October), 243-44.
             The Exile suffers from "vacuity of situation and charac-
       ter [and] a certain stiff but florid design."

1928 A   BOOKS - NONE

1928 B   SHORTER WRITINGS

 1   MARLEY, HAROLD P. "The Negro in Recent Southern Literature."
       South Atlantic Quarterly, 27 (January), 29-41.
             The Slave Ship is "an excellent modern interpretation of
       the woes of the Negro in the days when he was being
       transplanted."

 2   OVERTON, GRANT MARTIN. The Women Who Make Our Novels.
       New York: Dodd, Mead & Company, pp. 189-201.
             Mary Johnston's works from 1898 to 1918 are accessible
       to all readers. If she had not been a novelist, she would
       have made a great historian or philosopher on the level of
       Santayana. As novelist she is a mystic "in search of a new
       historical method." References are made to To Have and to
       Hold, The Long Roll, Lewis Rand, Foes, Silver Cross, 1492,
       Michael Forth, Sweet Rocket, Croatan, The Slave Ship, and
       The Great Valley.

1930

1930 A   BOOKS - NONE

1930 B   SHORTER WRITINGS

1   JOHNSON, MERLE. "American First Editions: Mary Johnston,
        1870____." Publishers' Weekly, 118 (19 July), 276-77.
        A compilation of Johnston first editions.

2   ODUM, HOWARD W. An American Epoch: Southern Portraiture in
        the National Picture. New York: Henry Holt and Company,
        1930, pp. 15, 301.
        Mary Johnston is a major literary figure in the South.

3   PATTEE, FRED LEWIS. The New American Literature: 1890-1930.
        New York: The Century Company, pp. 98-100.
        Like Mary E. Wilkins Freeman, Mary Johnston was "lyri-
        cal, intense, impulsive, dramatic." Her creation was "the
        lyric drama of the Virginia settlement." To Have and to
        Hold was "verity highly romantic." Although public interest
        waned in historical romance, Miss Johnston continued pub-
        lishing in that genre. Her two most significant Civil War
        novels are The Long Roll and Cease Firing. She achieves in
        these "the very spirit of the great tragedy." Her closest
        rival was Winston Churchill, with whom she is contrasted.

4   RICHARDSON, EUDORA RAMSAY. "The South Grows Up." The Bookman,
        70 (January), 545-50.
        Mary Johnston began her career as a romanticist and pro-
        gressed to realism and finally to mysticism. Her earliest
        fiction reveals "dramatic values and historic verity." The
        Long Roll gave a refreshing view of Jackson, while Hagar
        presented "a civilization that must give place to modernity."

5   WHITE, WILLIAM ALLEN. "A Reader in the Eighties and Nineties."
        Bookman, 72 (November), 229-34.
        Mary Johnston was able to make "historic novels out of
        the wax portraits of the early aristocrats of the Atlantic
        Coast."

1931 A   BOOKS - NONE

1931 B   SHORTER WRITINGS

1   ANON. "Hunting Shirt." The Saturday Review, 8 (19 December),
        399-400.
        Mary Johnston's new novel contains a simple narrative,
        a heavy prose, and a "quasi-heroical interpretation of

Hunting Shirt's experiences." Johnston unfortunately suc-
cumbs to "tricky syntax and odd, implausible idiom." The
strength of the novel lies in its presentation of the
Virginia scene.

2 ANON. "Hunting Shirt." Springfield Republican (18 October),
    p. 7e.
        Hunting Shirt is in the true tradition of Mary Johnston's
    best work, the romance of colonial Virginia. The hero of
    the new work is "engaging," a "paladin in homespun."

3 ANON. "Hymn to the Seasons." New York Times Book Review
    (11 October), part 4, p. 18.
        Hunting Shirt is a "prose poem in praise of the changing
    seasons." The attention to nature, however, is at the ex-
    pense of characterization and narrative. The romance is
    consequently devoid of "vitality" and "realism."

4 ANON. "Johnston, Mary. Hunting Shirt." American Library
    Association Booklist, 28 (December), 151.
        Despite its stilted language, Hunting Shirt is a roman-
    tic story which is, at times, poetically written.

5 ANON. "Mary Johnston, Intense Student of Virginia History,
    Has Long Held Rank Among Foremost American Novelists."
    Richmond Times-Dispatch (6 April), p. 5.
        The "glamour of Virginia history" is "preserved in the
    colorful and romantic novels of Mary Johnston."

6 BUSEY, GARRETA. "A Prose Ballad of Pioneers." New York
    Herald Tribune Books (4 October), p. 2.
        Johnston's Hunting Shirt "links the American pioneer
    with the American Indian, on the one hand, and with his
    Scottish ancestors as they live in the ballads, on the
    other." With considerable romanticism Miss Johnston's
    novel progresses through rather uneven prose.

1932 A BOOKS - NONE

1932 B SHORTER WRITINGS

1 ANON. "Checklist of New Books: Hunting Shirt." American
    Mercury, 25 (January), 24.
        Hunting Shirt is a "sentimental, undistinguished tale."

2 ANON. "Fiction." Wisconsin Library Bulletin, 28 (January),
    29-31.

1932

The new edition of To Have and to Hold is "unusually
handsome." Illustrations are by Frank E. Schoonover.
Hunting Shirt is a "beautifully written and romantic story
for young people."

3   DABNEY, VIRGINIUS. Liberalism in the South. Chapel Hill:
     The University of North Carolina Press, pp. 375, 384-85.
         Mary Johnston's Hagar is a "ringing appeal for women's
     rights."

4   KNIGHT, GRANT C. American Literature and Culture. New York:
     Ray Long and Richard R. Smith, Inc., pp. 295, 446.
         Mary Johnston was able to make life in colonial Virginia
     exciting in To Have and to Hold, a romance hailed by William
     Lyon Phelps as "the best of its kind." Johnston's romances
     are seen as part of a growing discontent with urban life
     of the period.

1933 A   BOOKS - NONE

1933 B   SHORTER WRITINGS

1   ANON. "Civil War Days." New York Times Book Review
     (12 March), part 5, p. 21.
         Mary Johnston's "modern introspective style" is not as
     natural to her as was her romance style. The characters in
     Miss Delicia Allen, for example, do not express themselves
     in a way that persuades the reader of their individuality.
     The earlier part of the novel is "vivid and delightful"
     but the latter half of the novel is episodic and hurried.

2   ANON. "Fiction." Wisconsin Library Bulletin, 29 (April),
     108-112.
         Miss Delicia Allen emphasizes the "serenity" of Southern
     life before the Civil War and the "dignity" with which
     Southerners faced life after the war. The heroine of the
     novel embodies those characteristics which made such de-
     portment possible.

3   ANON. "Johnston, Mary. Miss Delicia Allen." American
     Library Association Booklist, 29 (May), 268.
         Delicia Allen's romance constitutes a "simple, well told
     story."

4   ANON. "Johnston, Mary. Miss Delicia Allen." Pratt
     Institute, Brooklyn Free Public Library Quarterly Booklist
     (Summer), p. 36.

The new Johnston novel is "a picture of life in the
South in the twenty years before the Civil War."

5   ANON. "Miss Delicia." The Saturday Review, 9 (1 April), 516.
        Mary Johnston's novel follows the maturation of the
    heroine but is peopled by lifeless characters, women who
    resemble illustrations from Godey's Lady's Book and men who
    sound more like parody than life. The novel is comprised
    of "stilted, sickly, yet somehow diverting whimsicality."

6   BAGLEY, GERTRUDE. "On the Brink of the Civil War in Virginia."
        Boston Evening Transcript (18 March), part 6, p. 1.
        Miss Delicia Allen presents a view of "the best type of
    plantation life." The suffering of the South during the
    Civil War is seen through the correspondence of the men at
    war and their women at home. The style of the novel is
    "oddly attractive," the events of the narrative being seen
    through Delicia's eyes.

7   GOODE, PETER. "Gallant Ghosts of a Brave Era Live in 'Miss
        Delicia Allen.'" Richmond Times-Dispatch (12 March),
        part 5, p. 7.
        Mary Johnston's new novel contains "pastels of Virginia
    plantation life." The novel presents an interesting element
    of mysticism in addition to a strong plot.

8   LUTZ, MARK. "Latest Mary Johnston Novel Is Invested With
        Familiar Beauty." Richmond News Leader (29 March), p. 18.
        Miss Delicia Allen is a "poetically-told tale" featuring
    a highly romantic protagonist. Miss Johnston, however,
    adds "nothing new to the picture of antebellum plantation
    life."

9   TINKER, EDWARD LAROCQUE. "Miss Delicia Allen." New York
        Herald Tribune (5 March), p. 6.
        The great charm of Mary Johnston's new novel is its
    "serenity and peace." Miss Johnston, moreover, has con-
    siderable talent for implying rather than stating a story,
    for achieving mysticism, and for creating strong unity.
    She attains in the novel a poetic quality that is "detached
    and ethereal."

1934

1934 A BOOKS - NONE

1934 B SHORTER WRITINGS

1   ANON. "Johnston, Mary. Drury Randall." American Library
        Association Booklist, 31 (December), 131.
            Mary Johnston's latest novel is the "story of a man of
        peace in war time." The novel, however, is not up to her
        earlier achievements.

2   BRICKELL, HERCHEL. "The Literary Landscape." North American
        Review, 238 (December), 568-76.
            Drury Randall is a pleasant novel with an "other-worldly
        air that will please some readers and fail to impress
        others because there does not seem a sufficient quantity of
        blood in the veins of the characters."

3   F. B. "Family and Social Life in the Heart of the Old South."
        Boston Evening Transcript (20 October), part 5, pp. 1-3.
            Drury Randall is marked by Mary Johnston's "sensitive--
        even psychic--insight into human nature." Her hero is im-
        bued with considerable Emersonian transcendentalism. All
        will agree on the "beauty and inspiration of the story, and
        the perfection of its craftsmanship."

4   FIELD, LOUISE MAUNSELL. "Civil War Sidelines." New York
        Times Book Review (14 October), part 5, p. 23.
            Characterization, scene painting, and action are weak
        in Drury Randall. The "formal stylized manner" of the
        novel does little to awaken the reader's interest.

5   TINKER, EDWARD LAROCQUE. "Drury Randall." New York Herald
        Tribune Books (21 October), p. 14.
            Drury Randall contains true "spiritual quality," for
        there is extrasensory communication between the characters.
        The novel is a "lovely harmony of opalescent tints."

1935 A BOOKS - NONE

1935 B SHORTER WRITINGS

1   KNIGHT, GRANT C. James Lane Allen and the Genteel Tradition.
        Chapel Hill: The University of North Carolina Press,
        p. 110.
            Mary Johnston made colonial Virginia life "exciting" in
        To Have and to Hold.

MARY JOHNSTON: A REFERENCE GUIDE

1936 A   BOOKS

1   CONSON, VIRGINIA JAMES. "The Virginia History in the Historical Novels of Mary Johnston." M.A. thesis, George Peabody
College for Teachers.
   An examination of the Mary Johnston works set in Virginia. Emphasis is on Miss Johnston's historical accuracy.
The first component of the study concerns the Tidewater,
Virginia novels, those set in time from 1587 to 1763--
Croatan, To Have and to Hold, Prisoners of Hope, Audrey,
and The Slave Ship. The second component of the thesis
studies the frontier works set "before, during, and after
the French and Indian War." The works studied include The
Great Valley, Hunting Shirt, and Lewis Rand. The third
component examines those works set in the period 1837-1882,
including Miss Delicia Allen, The Long Roll, Cease Firing,
and Michael Forth.

1936 B   SHORTER WRITINGS

1   ANON. "Died." Time, 27 (18 May), 52.
   To Have and to Hold was a "swashbuckling romance." The
Long Roll and Cease Firing are "dear to all ex-Confederates."

2   ANON. "1870--Mary Johnston--1936." Richmond Times-Dispatch
(11 May), p. 8.
   At the beginning of her career Mary Johnston was "un-
touched" by the realism of either James or Howells, the
strongest influence on her first work being Tucker's
Hansford. The Long Roll and Cease Firing are the finest
novels ever written about the War Between the States. Miss
Johnston reached the height of her popularity by 1911-1912.

3   ANON. "Mary Johnston, Novelist, Is Dead." New York Times
(10 May), part 2, p. 9.
   From her childhood on, Mary Johnston was marked by a
"lively imagination, a sense of mysticism and an extraor-
dinary faculty for descriptive writing." Her childhood
hours were often spent in reading the classics, including
Shakespeare, Dickens, and Scott. Miss Johnston's philosophy
of life is quoted.

4   ANON. "Mary Johnston." The Saturday Review, 14 (23 May), 8.
   To Have and to Hold "swept the country at the height of
our rediscovery of an aristocratic, honor-seeking America
after the profit-making orgies following the Civil War."
The Great Valley remains "the best story of Indian captivity
and escape" to date.

1936

5 ANON. "Miss Johnston, Noted Author, Is Dead at 64." Richmond
   Times-Dispatch (10 May), p. 1.
       Mary Johnston is primarily remembered as a "word painter
   of Southern history." Her best known novel remains To Have
   and to Hold. Miss Johnston's aesthetic development was always towards a "combination of historical accuracy and
   vivid narrative."

6 ANON. "Miss Mary Johnston." Richmond Times-Dispatch (10 May),
   part 4, p. 2.
       Mary Johnston's name will always be associated in the
   minds of Virginians with the spirit of romanticism, her To
   Have and to Hold remaining "one of the most perfect examples
   of the art of story-telling to be found in American literature." Although a romantic writer, she was a realist in
   her private life, one who struggled for the advancement of
   women.

7 QUINN, ARTHUR HOBSON. American Fiction: An Historical and
   Critical Survey. New York: Appleton-Century-Crofts, Inc.,
   pp. 501-505, 671.
       Prisoners of Hope illustrates the "merits and demerits"
   of all of Mary Johnston's works. As a romancer she recognized the necessity for "vivid contrasts, the continued
   suspense of danger, and the story of a love to which time
   and space are merely incidental impediments." The improba-
   bilities of To Have and to Hold are more "daring" than those
   in Prisoners of Hope. Audrey contains "some reality."
   Lewis Rand contains Johnston's best male character, the
   son of a "'tobacco-roller.'" The Long Roll and Cease Firing,
   Civil War romances, contain action which is undercut by excessive campaign details. Miss Johnston's later novels,
   Michael Forth, Croatan, Hunting Shirt, and Miss Delicia
   Allen, lack the "sweep and vigor" of her earlier works.
   Her romances of foreign life are always weaker than those
   of American life and are filled with "stilted, artificial"
   dialogue.

8 _____. A History of the American Drama From the Civil War to
   the Present Day. 2 vols. New York: Appleton-Century-
   Crofts, vol. 2, p. 137.
       Mary Johnston's play The Goddess of Reason captured the
   "spirit" of the French Revolution. A blank verse play, it
   has "some dramatic moments, especially in the last act."

9 WAGENKNECHT, EDWARD. "The World and Mary Johnston." The
   Sewanee Review, 44 (April-June), 188-206.

To Have and to Hold is a novel of considerable merit.
Sweet Rocket dealt with "the highest kind of spiritual experience" yet was virtually ignored by critics. There are
weaknesses in Miss Johnston's works--poor dialogue, ineffec-
tive "stylistic experiments," and emphasis on history at
the expense of structure. The problem in approaching
Johnston as novelist is that she has "gone so far ahead into
the future that they [the readers] find it impossible to
catch up with her." Wagenknecht's essay includes discussion
of Lewis Rand, Prisoners of Hope, To Have and to Hold,
Audrey, Sir Mortimer, Cease Firing, 1492, and The Fortunes
of Garin.

1938 A BOOKS - NONE

1938 B SHORTER WRITINGS

1   PURCELL, JAMES SLICER, JR. "The Southern Poor White in
     Fiction." M.A. thesis, Duke University, pp. 114-117.
        The protagonist of Lewis Rand is a mixture of "resent-
     ment and ambition." The son of a poor white father and an
     aristocratic mother, he almost rose to real distinction.
     Miss Johnston seems to have believed, however, that "the
     poor white was not incapable of advancement, but he could
     progress just so far."

1941 A BOOKS

1   PATTERSON, DOROTHYA RENTFRO. "Mary Johnston as a Novelist."
     M.A. thesis, Southern Methodist University.
        Recounts Johnston's ancestry, birth, residency, family
     relations, and development as a popular writer. Patterson
     contends that there are five "distinguishable groups" within
     the Johnston corpus: the Virginia historical romances
     (Prisoners of Hope, To Have and to Hold, Audrey, Lewis Rand,
     Croatan, The Great Valley, and Hunting Shirt), the Civil
     War novels, which are largely realistic (The Long Roll and
     Cease Firing), the European romances (Sir Mortimer, The
     Witch, Foes, and 1492), the sociological novel (Hagar, The
     Wanderers, and The Slave Ship), and the mystical or "meta-
     physical" novels (Michael Forth, Sweet Rocket, Silver Cross,
     The Exile, Miss Delicia Allen, and Drury Randall).

1941 B SHORTER WRITINGS - NONE

1942

1942 A BOOKS - NONE

1942 B SHORTER WRITINGS

   1   "Johnston, Mary," in <u>Twentieth Century Authors</u>. Edited by
        Stanley J. Kunitz and Howard Haycroft. New York: The H.
        W. Wilson Company, pp. 732-33.
           Educated, for the most part, at home, Mary Johnston was
        a particularly avid reader of history. <u>To Have and to Hold</u>
        became a best seller. Although successful in sales, <u>Audrey</u>
        did not equal the popularity of the former novel. Her
        books were "thoroughly documented." Her romances have been
        called "romantic novels about history." With the exception
        of <u>Silver Cross</u>, one might say that Miss Johnston "did not
        know how to be uninteresting." <u>The Great Valley</u> is a great
        adventure story.

   2   SHERMAN, CAROLINE B. "Rediscovery of Mary Johnston."
        <u>Southern Literary Messenger</u>, 4 (September), 431-32.
           Americans interested in history will doubtless return to
        the novels of Mary Johnston. A running account of her
        novels is presented: <u>The Long Roll</u>, <u>Cease Firing</u>, <u>Prison-
        ers of Hope</u>, <u>To Have and to Hold</u>, <u>The Slave Ship</u>, <u>Croatan</u>,
        <u>Hunting Shirt</u>, <u>Audrey</u>, etc. She "turned toward the illu-
        sory before other writers began to work more generally in
        realism."

1945 A BOOKS - NONE

1945 B SHORTER WRITINGS

   1   HACKETT, ALICE PAYNE. <u>Fifty Years of Best Sellers: 1895-
        1945</u>. New York: R. R. Bowker Company, p. 16.
           <u>To Have and to Hold</u> was number one on the fiction sales
        list for 1900.

1947 A BOOKS - NONE

1947 B SHORTER WRITINGS

   1   MOTT, FRANK LUTHER. <u>Golden Multitudes: The Story of the Best
        Sellers in the United States</u>. New York: The Macmillan
        Company, pp. 213, 214, 324, 329.
           Although <u>To Have and to Hold</u> passed the half million
        mark, it never "climbed to the topmost rank in distribution"
        (over 750,000 copies).

1951

1948 A   BOOKS - NONE

1948 B   SHORTER WRITINGS

1   COWIE, ALEXANDER. The Rise of the American Novel. New York:
     American Book Company, p. 472.
          Mary Johnston is in the "tradition of Virginia novels
     grounded in picturesqueness and sentiment."

2   VanAUKEN, SHELDON. "The Southern Historical Novel in the
     Early Twentieth Century." Journal of Southern History, 14
     (May), 159-191.
          To Have and to Hold was published during the peak demand
     for historical romance. Mary Johnston's Southern historical
     novels include Prisoners of Hope, Audrey, Sir Mortimer,
     Lewis Rand, The Long Roll, Cease Firing, and To Have and to
     Hold. The Long Roll, Cease Firing, and Lewis Rand comprise
     the trilogy of the Cary family of Albemarle County. Miss
     Johnston strove for "historical exactness and accuracy" in
     her fiction.

1950 A   BOOKS - NONE

1950 B   SHORTER WRITINGS

1   LEISY, ERNEST E. The American Historical Novel. Norman,
     Oklahoma: University of Oklahoma Press, pp. 17-18, 22.
          Leisy makes scattered references to Croatan, To Have and
     to Hold, Prisoners of Hope, Audrey, The Great Valley, Lewis
     Rand, The Long Roll, Cease Firing, and Hunting Shirt.

1951 A   BOOKS - NONE

1951 B   SHORTER WRITINGS

1   GOHDES, CLARENCE. "The Later Nineteenth Century," in The
     Literature of the American People. Edited by Arthur Hobson
     Quinn. New York: Appleton-Century-Crofts, Inc., p. 739.
          Mary Johnston's To Have and to Hold is an example of the
     vogue of the 1890's for historical novels and is "a shallow
     romance of Colonial Virginia written under the aegis of
     Scott and Cooper."

1952

1952 B SHORTER WRITINGS

1 BROOKS, VAN WYCK. The Confident Years: 1885-1915. New York:
E. P. Dutton, pp. 340, 380.
Mary Johnston's Southern romances "continued the line of
John Esten Cooke and his tales about Stonewall Jackson, Lee,
Stuart, and Longstreet."

2 WAGENKNECHT, EDWARD. Cavalcade of the American Novel: From
the Birth of the Nation to the Middle of the Twentieth
Century. New York: Holt, Rinehart and Winson, pp. 197-203,
436, 528b.
Mary Johnston was the most important historical novelist
of the period from the end of the 1890's to the beginning
years of the twentieth century. In her view, "the past
controls the future, and the future remolds the past."
After considerable discussion of such novels as Prisoners
of Hope, To Have and to Hold, Michael Forth, Wagenknecht
concludes that "if the allotrope of the novel exists at all
in our later American literature, it must be among books
as those of Mary Johnston. . . ."

1954 A BOOKS - NONE

1954 B SHORTER WRITINGS

1 HUBBELL, JAY B. The South in American Literature: 1607-1900.
Durham: Duke University Press, pp. 730, 734, 739, 802, 844.
In order to boost the circulation of the Atlantic, Walter
Hines Page printed Mary Johnston's To Have and to Hold in
serial form. The romance typifies the Southern tendency
towards "melodramatic elements." Miss Johnston's Hagar is
a protest against Southern ideals of womanhood, ideals
prevalent in the works of Thomas Nelson Page.

1955 A BOOKS - NONE

1955 B SHORTER WRITINGS

1 SPILLER, ROBERT E. The Cycle of American Literature.
New York: The Macmillan Company, p. 87.
Johnston romances are an expression of Southern ideals.

1956 A BOOKS - NONE

1956 B SHORTER WRITINGS

1   COAN, OTIS W. and RICHARD G. LILLARD. America in Fiction:
    An Annotated List of Novels That Interpret Aspects of Life
    in the United States. Fourth edition. Stanford: Stanford
    University Press, pp. 4, 48, 121, 127, 146.
        Johnston works represented in this annotated list in-
    clude The Great Valley, Lewis Rand, The Slave Ship, Miss
    Delicia Allen, The Long Roll, and Cease Firing.

2   COLEMAN, E. D. "Penwoman of Virginia's Feminists." Virginia
    Cavalcade, 6 (Winter), 8-11.
        Mary Johnston felt intensely that females should be
    given the vote. Hagar marked her the "outstanding penwoman
    of the woman-suffrage movement in Virginia."

3   FISHWICK, MARSHALL W. The Virginia Tradition. Washington,
    D. C.: Public Affairs Press, pp. 20, 40.
        Mary Johnston wrote Hagar to help the feminist movement.

4   HACKETT, ALICE PAYNE. 60 Years of Best Sellers: 1895-1955.
    New York: R. R. Bowker Company, pp. 8, 97, 100, 102, 104,
    109, 113.
        To Have and to Hold was the number one best seller for
    1900.

5   ROBERSON, JOHN R. "Two Virginia Novelists on Woman's Suffrage:
    An Exchange of Letters Between Mary Johnston and Thomas
    Nelson Page." Virginia Magazine of History and Biography,
    64 (July), 286-90.
        Johnston's Hagar was an "attempt to glorify the advo-
    cates of woman's rights."

1957 A BOOKS - NONE

1957 B SHORTER WRITINGS

1   LIVELY, ROBERT A. Fiction Fights the Civil War: An Unfinished
    Chapter in the Literary History of the American People.
    Chapel Hill: The University of North Carolina Press,
    pp. 12, 17, 24, 59, 66, 70, 98, 102, 106.
        A weakness in Mary Johnston's fiction is her belief in
    the necessity for an "actual historical personage" and her
    tendency to allow history to limit the development of her
    narrative. She makes extensive use of battle scenes in

1957

> The Long Roll and Cease Firing. Johnston, Stark Young, and
> Margaret Mitchell are viewed as "unreconstructed rebels."
> In The Long Roll Johnston wrote of Virginians who were
> "still struggling for a reasonable approach to the venture
> of African settlement."

1958 A BOOKS - NONE

1958 B SHORTER WRITINGS

1   LEISY, ERNEST E. "Johnston, Mary," in Dictionary of American
    Biography. Edited by Robert L. Schuyler and Edward T.
    James. New York: Charles Scribner, vol. 22, 349-50.
        Mary Johnston is best known for her works of the colonial
    and Civil War periods. Both To Have and to Hold and Audrey
    were popular works. The Great Valley is one of her best
    works. Lewis Rand demonstrates "improved psychological
    characterization." Her strongest talents were landscape
    description and "story-telling instinct."

1961 A BOOKS - NONE

1961 B SHORTER WRITINGS

1   NELSON, LAWRENCE G. "Mary Johnston and the Historic
    Imagination," in Southern Writers: Appraisals in Our Time.
    Edited by R. C. Simonini, Jr. Charlottesville: The
    University Press of Virginia, pp. 71-102.
        The feminism of both author and heroine are apparent in
    Hagar. Miss Johnston's major concern, however, seems to
    have been, "How shall the visionary or prophetic imagination
    work in harmony with the historic imagination in the making
    of the novel?" Johnston's historic imagination was nour-
    ished by her readings, her "piety," her family tradition,
    and the history of Virginia. Her first romances--Prisoners
    of Hope, To Have and to Hold, Audrey, and Sir Mortimer--are
    "the work of a dreamy girl who has matured into responsible
    adult womanhood." The feeling of tragedy is pronounced in
    these works. Shakespearean tragedy is strong in Lewis Rand.
    Miss Johnston's artistry is even stronger in The Witch, The
    Fortunes of Garin, and The Wanderers. The Slave Ship is a
    "raw, powerful narrative." War in her fiction is viewed as
    a "great beast."

1963 A BOOKS - NONE

1963 B SHORTER WRITINGS

1 HART, JAMES D. <u>The Popular Book: A History of America's
   Literary Taste</u>. Berkeley and Los Angeles: University of
   California Press, p. 199.
       <u>To Have and to Hold</u> is an example of turn-of-the-century
   taste for romance, for romantic tales. Mary Johnston's
   romance anticipates the "Graustarkian theme of the American
   marrying the noble lady and triumphing over decadent foreign
   standards."

2 SIMKINS, FRANCIS BUTLER. <u>A History of the South</u>. Third
   edition. New York: Alfred A. Knopf, pp. 24, 438-39, 442,
   453.
       Mary Johnston was possibly "the most powerful of the
   entire American school of historical romancers." Her début
   as romancer came in 1898 with <u>Prisoners of Hope</u>. <u>To Have
   and to Hold</u> contained just enough of the "picturesque."
   <u>The Long Roll</u> and <u>Cease Firing</u> comprise her Civil War saga.
   <u>Silver Cross</u> was her venture into mysticism. <u>1492, The
   Slave Ship</u>, and <u>The Great Valley</u> subordinated mysticism to
   historical narrative.

3 SPILLER, ROBERT E., et al. <u>Literary History of the United
   States</u>. Third edition revised. New York: The Macmillan
   Company, vol. 2, pp. 610, 1119.
       Miss Johnston was paid in excess of $60,000 royalties
   for publication of <u>To Have and to Hold</u>.

1965 A BOOKS - NONE

1965 B SHORTER WRITINGS

1 HART, JAMES D. <u>The Oxford Companion to American Literature</u>.
   Fourth edition. New York: Oxford University Press, p. 431.
       With her ability to create atmosphere, Miss Johnston was
   the author of twenty-two popular romances. Most of her
   works, however, are "idealistic" and peopled by "stilted"
   characters. Plot summaries of <u>To Have and to Hold</u> and <u>The
   Long Roll</u> are included.

THREE VIRGINIA WRITERS

1966

<u>1966 A   BOOKS</u>

1   CHAPMAN, MARY ELLEN. "Mary Johnston--From Virginian to
    American." M.A. thesis, Longwood College.
        Since she was not an Agrarian, Mary Johnston was fre-
    quently classified a local colorist. Miss Johnston, how-
    ever, represents "the best Southern tradition," and her
    novels have a "timely" message for the contemporary reader.
    Her novel <u>Lewis Rand</u> presents the tragedy of a man unable
    to cope with an evil environment. <u>Hagar</u>, <u>Michael Forth</u>,
    and <u>Sweet Rocket</u> expound the theme that a man may build a
    newer and better order only by building upon the old one.
    <u>Croatan</u>, <u>The Great Valley</u>, <u>The Slave Ship</u>, and <u>Hunting</u>
    <u>Shirt</u> expound the notion that "'through seeking ye shall
    find.'" <u>Prisoners of Hope</u>, <u>To Have and to Hold</u>, <u>Audrey</u>,
    and <u>Lewis Rand</u> expose the "tragedy resulting from a society
    built on a rigid class structure." <u>The Long Roll</u> and <u>Cease</u>
    <u>Firing</u> comprise "one account" of the Civil War. Johnston's
    liberal humanitarianism culminated in <u>Hagar</u>, <u>Michael Forth</u>,
    and <u>Sweet Rocket</u>, all of which were "aimed at setting forth
    her vision of a better world." The frontier spirit per-
    meates a number of her later works--<u>Croatan</u>, <u>The Slave Ship</u>,
    <u>The Great Valley</u>, and <u>Hunting Shirt</u>. A consideration of
    all her works reveals a fundamental theme of justice. Both
    <u>Miss Delicia Allen</u> and <u>Drury Randall</u> contain this theme of
    justice.

<u>1966 B   SHORTER WRITINGS - NONE</u>

<u>1967 A   BOOKS - NONE</u>

<u>1967 B   SHORTER WRITINGS</u>

1   HACKETT, ALICE PAYNE. <u>70 Years of Best Sellers: 1895-1965</u>.
    New York: R. R. Bowker Company, pp. 220, 231.
        Miss Johnston's <u>Sir Mortimer</u> was the number five best
    seller for 1904.

<u>1969 A   BOOKS - NONE</u>

<u>1969 B   SHORTER WRITINGS</u>

1   HERZBERG, MAX J., ed. <u>The Reader's Encyclopedia of American</u>
    <u>Literature</u>. New York: Thomas Y. Crowell Company, p. 551.

MARY JOHNSTON: A REFERENCE GUIDE

1971

Mary Johnston was author of "some of the best of the
historical romances that were so popular at the beginning
of the 20th century." Towards the middle of her career
Miss Johnston grew interested in "mysticism, feminism, and
socialism." Silver Cross reveals those interests.

2   ROUSE, BLAIR. "Mary Johnston (1870-1936)," in A Bibliographi-
     cal Guide to the Study of Southern Literature. Edited by
     Louis D. Rubin, Jr. Baton Rouge: Louisiana State Univer-
     sity Press, pp. 230-31.
        Discusses the scarcity of Johnston scholarly materials
     and her absence from consideration in major critical
     studies. Lists twenty items in the bibliography.

1971 A   BOOKS - NONE

1971 B   SHORTER WRITINGS

1   DABNEY, VIRGINIUS. Virginia: The New Dominion. Garden City,
     New York: Doubleday & Company, Inc., p. 444.
        To Have and to Hold was Mary Johnston's "first best
     seller."

2   DICKINSON, A. T., JR. American Historical Fiction. Third
     edition. Metuchen, New Jersey: The Scarecrow Press,
     pp. 25, 43, 136, 163.
        Contains synopses of Croatan, To Have and to Hold,
     Prisoners of Hope, The Slave Ship, The Great Valley, Hunting
     Shirt, The Long Roll, Miss Delicia Allen, Drury Randall,
     and Michael Forth.

3   EICHELBERGER, CLAYTON L., ed. A Guide to Critical Reviews of
     United States Fiction, 1870-1910. Metuchen, New Jersey:
     The Scarecrow Press, vol. 1, p. 187.
        Lists 34 critical reviews of Johnston fiction.

4   GROSS, THEODORE L. The Heroic Ideal in American Literature.
     New York: The Free Press, pp. 88, 117.
        Mary Johnston was critical of the "idealization of
     Southern womanhood." Hagar reveals that Johnston attitude.

Three Virginia Writers

1972

1972 A BOOKS

1   HANMER, TRUDY J. "A Divine Discontent: Mary Johnston and
     Woman Suffrage in Virginia." M.A. thesis, University of
     Virginia.
          Mary Johnston's decision to join Richmond feminists in
     the fight for suffrage was owed primarily to a "divine dis-
     contentment." In "The Women's War" she "set forth the
     suffragists' objectives." As her concept of female suffrage
     widened, she became increasingly attracted to communism.
     Johnston was urged by Fola Lafollette, Wisconsin suffragette,
     to write "a fictional work for the suffrage movement."
     Hagar complied with that request, for it was a "polemic par
     excellence."

2   HARTLEY, GAYLE MELTON. "The Novels of Mary Johnston: A
     Critical Study." Ph.D. dissertation, University of South
     Carolina.
          An examination of Mary Johnston's works in groups--
     Virginia historical romances, Civil War realistic novels,
     European romances, sociological novels, and mystical fic-
     tion--and as individual compositions. Miss Johnston's de-
     scriptive power is at its best in the Virginia historical
     novels, a group including Prisoners of Hope, To Have and to
     Hold, Audrey, Lewis Rand, Croatan, The Great Valley, and The
     Slave Ship. The Civil War realistic novels include Cease
     Firing and The Long Roll. The European romances, which
     demonstrate "various stylistic techniques," include Sir
     Mortimer, The Witch, The Fortunes of Garin, Foes, and 1492.
     The sociological novels include Hagar, The Wanderers, and
     The Slave Ship. The mystical works, which seek to "relate
     in fictional form the insights she received through her
     extensions of consciousness," include Michael Forth, Sweet
     Rocket, Silver Cross, The Exile, Miss Delicia Allen, and
     Drury Randall.

1972 B SHORTER WRITINGS

1   "Johnston, Mary," in Virginia Authors: Past and Present.
     Edited by W. D. Taylor. Richmond: The William Byrd Press,
     Inc., pp. 66-67.
          The author of twenty-two novels, Mary Johnston learned
     much from her readings in her father's library. Her works
     are patiently researched and carefully documented.

1974 A BOOKS - NONE

1974 B SHORTER WRITINGS

   1   EICHELBERGER, CLAYTON L. A Guide to Critical Reviews of
        United States Fiction, 1870-1910. Metuchen, New Jersey:
        The Scarecrow Press, vol. 2, p. 156.
          Lists 26 reviews of Johnston fiction.

1975 A BOOKS - NONE

1975 B SHORTER WRITINGS

   1   POLK, NOEL. "Guide to Dissertations on American Literary
        Figures, 1870-1910: Part Two." American Literary Realism,
        8 (Autumn), 293.
          Annotated. Includes Gayle Melton Hartley's Johnston
        dissertation (1972.A2).

1976 A BOOKS - NONE

1976 B SHORTER WRITINGS

   1   RUBIN, LOUIS D., JR. William Elliott Shoots a Bear. Baton
        Rouge: Louisiana State University Press, p. 81.
          G. W. Cable's romantic prototypes may also be found in
        Johnston's fiction.

Thomas Nelson Page:
A Reference Guide

Writings about Thomas Nelson Page, 1886-1976

1886 A   BOOKS - NONE

1886 B   SHORTER WRITINGS

1   ANON. "Literary Notes." The Independent, 38 (10 June), 726.
         The dialect of "Meh Lady" is "admirably perfect." The
     realism and pathos of the story are excellent, causing the
     story to rank alongside "Marse Chan."

1887 A   BOOKS - NONE

1887 B   SHORTER WRITINGS

1   ANON. "In Ole Virginia." The Epoch, 1 (17 June), 455.
         "Marse Chan" may be considered "the best story of the
     war for its pathos, humor, and dramatic force." There is
     an aura of "dreamy romance" about all Page stories despite
     their realism. The Negro dialect of all the stories in
     In Ole Virginia is quite good.

2   ANON. "Minor Fiction." The Literary World, 18 (25 June),
     202-03.
         "Marse Chan" and "Meh Lady" are the best stories in In
     Ole Virginia; for the dialect, characterization, and
     "quaint" diction are excellent. Although there is little
     depth in Page's fiction, it is nonetheless "true to the
     laws of universal nature."

3   ANON. "New Books." New York Times (19 June), p. 14.
         Page's In Ole Virginia contains both effective dialect
     and engrossing narratives. "Ole 'Stracted" is a truly
     moving tale.

4   ANON. "Recent Fiction." The Independent, 39 (1 September),
     1102.
         In Ole Virginia presents six studies of plantation life,
     character, and dialect. The stories are "graphic vignettes"

of Virginia life. "Marse Chan" is an excellent story, but "Meh Lady" is the best "'Southern'" or "'dialect'" story to date in America.

5   ANON. "Recent Fiction." Overland Monthly, 10 (July), 104-05.
    In Ole Virginia is bound in a cover "'designed by the Tiffany Art Company.'" Although none of the tales in the collection equal "Marse Chan," the collection does "give fuller play to the genial humor" of the author. The collection, moreover, is prized for its "dramatic vividness, its feeling and intelligence." With the exception of "No Haid Pawn," any of the stories may be taken as "models . . . of the short story."

6   ANON. "Recent Novels." The Nation, 45 (22 September), 236-37.
    Page's In Ole Virginia constitutes an "epic historical and tragic." There is but one central figure in all the stories in the collection, no matter what he may be called; and that one figure is of epic proportions. Page, moreover, is a master of the use of Negro dialect if not of "plain English."

7   ANON. "Reviews." Critic, NS 8 (2 July), 14-15.
    Despite the opinion of some to the contrary, dialect and ethnic character sketching are native to literature. Hence, Burns, Theophrastes, and the Brontës have justified the art form and paved the way for Page. In Ole Virginia is a "series of Black Classics" revealing everyday life in Virginia. The only weakness in the stories is an occasional error in dialect and the sometimes heavy pathos. Page, moreover, may make too much of Negro life.

8   ANON. "Thomas Nelson Page." Book Buyer, 4 (October), 284-85.
    Page has written "the most exquisite story of the war that has yet appeared--'Marse Chan.'" The source for this moving short story was a letter shown to Page by a friend. Page's first publication was the poem "Uncle Gabe's White Folks." "Old 'Stracted" was composed while he watched by the body of the mother of one of his friends. Page himself considers "Unc' Edinburg's Drowndin'" the best of his pictures of life in old Virginia.

9   COLEMAN, CHARLES W. "The Recent Movement in Southern Literature." Harper's New Monthly Magazine, 74 (May), 837-55.
    "Marse Chan" is "the most exquisite story of the war that has yet appeared." In contrast with Joel Chandler Harris, Page tends to "idealize" the Negro, although he seems to have the "advantage" in creating Negro dialect.

"Unc' Edinburg's Drowndin'," "Meh Lady," "Ole 'Stracted," and "Polly" are "variant treatments of the same motif."

1888 A   BOOKS - NONE

1888 B   SHORTER WRITINGS

1   ANON. "New Books." New York Times (20 May), p. 12.
    Befo' de War has "perfect naturalness" in its Negro dialect and a number of moving Negro characterizations.

2   ANON. "Recent Fiction." The Independent, 40 (25 October), 1376-77.
    By using two juvenile protagonists in Two Little Confederates, Page is able to project Southern sentiment without incurring adult censure. The novel has the thrill of a war novel without the horror of one.

3   ANON. "Talk About Books." The Chautauquan, 9 (December), 188-90.
    Two Little Confederates will appeal as much to adults as to children. The novel is "a faithful picture of life on a Virginia plantation during the war, and a story full of stirring incidents, of adventures sometimes pathetic, and of examples of sturdy patriotism and uncomplaining sacrifice."

4   ANON. "Two Little Confederates." The Literary World, 19 (24 November), 417.
    Page's latest novel contains sketches which are "full of life and character, and are worth preserving as well as reading, from their truth and fidelity to nature."

5   ANON. "Two Little Confederates." The Saturday Review (London), 66 (22 December), 754.
    The two little boys in Thomas Nelson Page's new novel are "admirably drawn" and the old Negro Balla is quite "amusing." The book is "delightful" and is much like Twain's Huckleberry Finn.

1889 A   BOOKS - NONE

1889 B   SHORTER WRITINGS

1   WASHINGTON, HUGH V. "Thomas Nelson Page." Literature: An Illustrated Weekly Magazine, 2 (26 January), 225-44.

1889

Page's family estate "Oakland" is the setting for Two Little Confederates. Both Page and Joel Chandler Harris did much to further the development of the Negro dialect story. Page, moreover, is a master of the use of the Negro raconteur especially in "Marse Chan" and "Unc' Edinburg's Drowndin'." Another merit of Page's works is that they "present facts, and facts make history." Whereas Mrs. Stowe presents the darker side of slave life, Page presents the lighter.

1891 A BOOKS - NONE

1891 B SHORTER WRITINGS

1   ANON. "Current Literature." America, 6 (25 June), 360.
     On Newfound River is a "good" novel containing a number of "thrilling scenes." Margaret is "portrayed with rare art."

2   ANON. "New Books." New York Times (26 July), p. 19.
     On Newfound River contains an "antiquated" but "venerable" plot. The conclusion of the novel is exactly what the reader expects.

3   ANON. "Novels of the Week." The Athenaeum, 3329 (15 August), pp. 220-21.
     On Newfound River is not a distinguished performance, even though it contains the customary Page aristocrat and Negro dialect. The plot is typical rather than original. The redeeming moment in the novel is the trial scene at "'Jones's Crossroads.'"

4   ANON. "Recent Fiction." The Critic, 16 (1 August), 51-52.
     On Newfound River is Page's first long work. "Simple and unpretentious," the narrative is "very sweet." Nonetheless, the story fails to equal "Marse Chan" and "Meh Lady."

5   ANON. "Recent Fiction." The Independent, 43 (17 December), 1882.
     Page is a good story teller. In Elsket and Other Stories he "lays on local color with a free hand." The stories are quite natural.

6   ANON. "Recent Fiction." The Independent, 43 (16 July), 1068.
     On Newfound River is a "romance of old-time Southern life sketched in a sincere and pleasing manner; but there

is not a trace of originality, of individuality or a
striking art in it." In general the novel is a "pretty and
pleasing little fiction, quite interesting," but containing
nothing of distinction.

7   ANON. "Recent Fiction." The Nation, 53 (17 December), 470-72.
        Nothing Page wrote was more "touching" than the stories
     in Elsket. In this collection Page is in "the realm of re-
     ality, where his imagination adds force and spirit to the
     things he has seen and known."

8   ANON. "Recent Novels." The Nation, 53 (23 July), 72.
        The most realistically drawn characters in On Newfound
     River are the "'plain neighbors on Newfound,'" not the aris-
     tocrats. Some episodes in the novel should be omitted.

9   ANON. "Recent Publications." New Orleans Daily Picayune
     (25 October), p. 3.
        The five stories comprising Elsket and Other Stories are
     filled with "movement and incident" and strong characteriza-
     tion.

10   ANON. "Recent Publications." New Orleans Daily Picayune
     (21 June), p. 12.
        With "superb" character delineation On Newfound River is
     one of the best novels of the year. Page is admirably
     suited to writing a romance of antebellum Virginia.

11   ANON. "Talk About New Books." The Catholic World, 54
     (October), 138-39.
        On Newfound River is a "very pleasant, well-written,
     thoroughly wholesome story." Unlike a number of Southern
     stories, this one does not suffer from intense sectionalism.
     The characters of the novel are Americans first, aristocrats
     and "'poor white trash'" second. Both Major Landon and his
     son are "lovable" characters. With a naturally developing
     plot, the novel has a style which is "notably free from
     mannerisms and affectation."

12   CLARK, KATE UPSON. "On Newfound River." The Epoch, 9
     (31 July), 415.
        Page's new novel involves a highly conventional love
     story and makes heavy use of coincidence and melodrama.
     The novel would displease William Dean Howells.

13   PAYNE, WILLIAM MORTON. "Recent Books of Fiction." The Dial,
     12 (December), 274-79.

1891

On Newfound River contains the familiar Page plantation
character types and just the right amount of dialect. Elsket and Other Stories contains five very pleasant stories,
the title story of which attains "exquisite sweetness."

1892 A BOOKS - NONE

1892 B SHORTER WRITINGS

1   ANON. "All the Books." Godey's Magazine, 125 (December), 646.
          "Marse Chan" was the most popular of Southern stories to
          deal with the Civil War. The new book edition of the tale
          contains handsome illustrations by W. T. Smedley.

2   ANON. "Briefs on New Books." The Dial, 13 (August), 108-11.
          Page's The Old South flees from "the plain facts of a
          rather crude and prosaic reality." Page's essay "The Negro
          Question" puts forth a logical argument.

3   ANON. "Comment on New Books." The Atlantic Monthly, 69
          (January), 133-39.
          On Newfound River is less successful than Two Little Con-
          federates or In Ole Virginia. The plot of the new novel is
          "threadbare."

4   ANON. "Mr. Page's Southern Essays." New York Times (11 July),
          p. 3.
          Page's essays in The Old South tend to allay "misappre-
          hensions" which many Americans still have about the South.

5   ANON. "New Books and Reprints." The Saturday Review
          (London), 73 (23 April), 493.
          Page's selections in Elsket and Other Stories are
          "stronger and more sympathetic" than his previous works.
          Page's plantation Negro is "a trifle tedious at times."

6   ANON. "Novels of the Week." The Athenaeum, 3362 (2 April),
          434.
          Elsket and Other Stories contains five stories which are
          "genuine in their humour and pathos." "Elsket" and "Run to
          Seed" demonstrate the best of Page.

7   ANON. "The Old South." The Critic, 18 (13 August), 78.
          Page writes "charmingly and with knowledge of its
          [Virginia's] colonial and antebellum aspects, claims,
          civilization, and contributions to society" in The Old
          South.

8   ANON. "Recent Fiction." The Critic, 17 (2 January), 8.
    Among the Camps is a volume of four short stories for
    children, the best of which is "Nancy Pansy," which contains
    "a specimen of child nature that is simply delicious." The
    other three stories are good and entertaining.

9   ANON. "Recent Publications." New Orleans Daily Picayune
    (5 June), p. 14.
    The Old South is a "presentable volume." The essay "The
    Negro Question" is an "able" one.

10 ANON. "Recent Publications." New Orleans Daily Picayune
    (6 November), p. 15.
    "Marse Chan" is told in the "Negro dialect" in which
    Page excels.

11 ANON. Review of "Marse Chan." The Independent, 44
    (22 December), 1835.
    "Marse Chan" is one of the "most charmingly pathetic of
    American dialect short stories." The new edition deserves
    its handsome illustrations.

12 ANON. "The Short Story." The Atlantic Monthly, 69 (February),
    261-70.
    "Elsket" is an excellent story told with "pathos" and
    "restraint."

13 ANON. "Talk About Books." The Chautauquan, 14 (January), 510.
    The heroism in Page's collection Among the Camps is ap-
    propriate for both Northern and Southern children. The
    Elsket collection contains a range of subjects.

14 ANON. "Talk About New Books." The Catholic World, 54
    (January), 609-10.
    Page's recent works in periodicals have been collected
    and republished as two separate volumes. Among the Camps
    contains four of the most pleasant stories ever published
    by Page. The Civil War period is seen here amidst boys
    and girls and the playthings of children. Consequently,
    "the gray lion and the blue lamb lie down together." In
    the title story of Elsket Page demonstrates that "there is
    no way of shutting the tempter out of Eden." "Run to Seed,"
    a better story, is "pathetic and touching." Page always
    writes "agreeably."

15 [TRENT, W. P.] "The Old South." The Sewanee Review, 1
    (November), 90-96.

1892

Page's The Old South: Essays Social and Political will
be read with "pleasure and profit." The only truly political essay in the collection is on the Negro problem, the
last paragraph of which may be taken as one part of a
Southern creed. Page seems to believe a little too much
in the rightness of antebellum Southern life and relies
too heavily upon North-South comparisons as a part of his
reasoning. The collection, nonetheless, is of "rare value
and interest and charm."

1893 A BOOKS - NONE

1893 B SHORTER WRITINGS

1   ANON. "Christmas Books." The Saturday Review (London), 76
    (16 December), 691.
        Negro dialect fans will find "Meh Lady" both interesting
    and entertaining, despite the book's "certain faults of
    taste."

2   ANON. "In Ole Virginia." The Saturday Review (London), 75
    (8 April), 381.
        In Ole Virginia contains stories which will appeal to
    anyone who can grasp their dialect.

3   ANON. "Novel Notes." The Bookman (London), 3 (March),
    189-90.
        In Ole Virginia presents the best side of the era of
    slavery. Page's Southern patriotism is "reasonable" and
    he is a powerful spokesman for his point of view. "Marse
    Chan" is a truly pathetic story.

4   ANON. "Recent Publications." New Orleans Daily Picayune
    (16 July), p. 19.
        All of the selections in Stories of the South are good.

5   ANON. "Thomas Nelson Page's Works." The Critic, 20
    (16 December), 390-91.
        Page made the "Virginia Negroes talk in vocables so mel-
    low and so quaint that, uncouth as they appeared in spell-
    ing, their syllables melted into a music of their own when
    recited by the author or read aloud by one to the manner
    born." Page's work, like that of Hesiod, is tied to his
    own people and his own land.

6   ANON. "What Mr. Page Has Done for Virginia." New York Times
    (8 October), p. 23.

Page's stories contain "exciting" plots, are "humorous"
or "sagely pathetic," and present "ideal" reflections of
life. The dialect of his works is "distinguished."

7   KITTRELL, T. G. "Joel Chandler Harris." Vanderbilt Observer,
    15 (February), 223-28.
        Page's portrayal of the Negro made "little progress be-
    yond one or two stereotyped characters, whose language is
    an invariable dialect throughout."

8   LEE, SUSAN P. Memoirs of William Nelson Pendleton, D.D.
    Philadelphia: J. B. Lippincott Company, p. 476.
        Page writes to his aunt and uncle on 13 July 1881 to ex-
    tend his best wishes on the occasion of their golden wed-
    ding anniversary.

9   M[IMS], E[DWIN]. "Scraps and Fragments." Vanderbilt
    Observer, 15 (February), 247-49.
        Page lectured at Vanderbilt in 1888 and seemed a "typi-
    cal Southern gentleman."

1894 A   BOOKS

1   McCARTHY, CARLTON. Typical Virginia; or, "On Newfound River."
    By Thomas Nelson Page. A Review, in Which the Friend of
    the "Po' Whites" and "Half Strainers" Becomes Indignant
    and Renounces Another Slander of the "First Families of
    Virginia," Their Poor Neighbors, and Hanover County.
    Richmond: J. L. Hill Printing Company, 22pp.
        Questions the "foundation of the prestige of the
    'Landons,'" noting inconsistencies in their characteriza-
    tion and dialogue. McCarthy, moreover, points out Page's
    shallow and inaccurate treatment of a supposedly "typical"
    Virginia community and its inhabitants. Page's treatment
    of non-aristocrats is particularly shallow.

1894 B   SHORTER WRITINGS

1   ANON. "The Burial of the Guns." The Literary World, 25
    (15 December), 455.
        The Burial of the Guns contains Page's customary "cle-
    verness and nerve." The title story is both "powerful and
    pathetic."

2   ANON. "The Burial of the Guns; and Other Stories." The
    Saturday Review (London), 78 (15 December), 645.

1894

Page's new work is a "curious collection of stories with much variety in them."

3   ANON. "Comment on New Books." The Atlantic Monthly, 74 (December), 845-51.
     In Pastime Stories Page has "neither made nor marred his tales in the telling."

4   ANON. "Fiction." The Critic, 22 (28 July), 24.
     Page's Pastime Stories may "stretch the good nature of the critic." The Southern dialect story has "severe limitations," and if "pushed to the extreme of elaboration" tends to degenerate into "gibberish." Page borders on this pitfall in the collection.

5   ANON. "More Fiction." The Nation, 58 (21 June), 472-73.
     Pastime Stories is marked by "the eye for effect, the sense of climax, the love of narration" which constitute the art of storytelling. The stories, nonetheless, have no appeal to "the higher intellectual, moral, or aesthetic instincts."

6   ANON. "Mr. Page's Negro Tales." New York Times (10 June), p. 27.
     Pastime Stories makes delightful reading, Page's Negroes being quite attractive.

7   ANON. "Pastime Stories." Harper's New Monthly Magazine, 89 (June), supplement 3, 162.
     In his Negro stories in Pastime Stories, Page "passes from the major mood to the minor." With faithful rendition of dialect, the stories are quite entertaining.

8   ANON. "'Polly.'" The Critic, NS 22 (24 November), 347.
     "Polly" is an entertaining love story set in old Virginia. The colonel in the story is "painted a trifle too red, like an over-boiled lobster; his juleps and his oaths have an antebellum frequency; and it jars upon refined nerves a little to think that Polly and Bob naturally did play Porphyro and Madeline in their hurry to overcome opposition. . . ."

9   ANON. "Recent Novels." The Nation, 59 (27 December), 483-84.
     The attractively printed Polly: A Christmas Recollection, although entertaining, is lacking at times in both substance and style. The Burial of the Guns is much better workmanship. References are made to "The Burial of the Guns," "The Gray Jacket of 'No. 4,'" "Little Derby," and "My Cousin Fanny."

10   ANON. "Recent Publications." New Orleans <u>Daily Picayune</u>
         (11 November), p. 11.
            <u>Polly</u> is a "charming Christmas story of old Virginia."

11   ANON. "Recent Publications." New Orleans <u>Daily Picayune</u>
         (9 December), p. 10.
            The stories in <u>The Burial of the Guns</u> are "extremely in-
         teresting." The title story is "well told."

12   ANON. "Thomas Nelson Page Once More." <u>New York Times</u>
         (28 October), p. 27.
            Page writes <u>Polly</u> in a "delightful manner."

13   HENNEMAN, J. B. "The Modern Spirit in Literature." <u>The
         Sewanee Review</u>, 2 (August), 500-12.
            Current American tendencies towards romantic feeling and
         richness of description are evident in works like <u>In Ole
         Virginia</u>.

14   HYDE, CLAUDIA. "Fiction." <u>The Literary World</u>, 25 (14 July),
         218-19.
            <u>Pastime Stories</u> is appropriately titled and contains a
         number of "good laughs."

15   McCARTHY, CARLTON. "The Picture Is True?" <u>Religious Herald</u>
         (1 March), p. [1].
            <u>Two Little Confederates</u> is "unfit for use by the children
         of this Commonwealth." McCarthy proposes a number of his-
         torical and quasi-critical weaknesses in the Page novel.
         In particular, McCarthy strenuously objects to Page's ma-
         ligning of Confederate privates and his deification of
         Confederate officers and aristocrats.

16   PAGE, ROSEWELL. "The Picture Is True." <u>Religious Herald</u>
         (15 March), pp. [1-2].
            A rebuttal to Carlton McCarthy's review of <u>Two Little
         Confederates</u> (<u>See</u> 1894.B15). Page was not hostile towards
         Confederate privates, was not writing a history of the War.
         Rosewell Page offers to submit the McCarthy charges against
         <u>Two Little Confederates</u> to a board of arbitration.

17   PAYNE, WILLIAM MORTON. "A Century of Stories." <u>The Dial</u>, 17
         (1 December), 332-34.
            <u>The Burial of the Guns</u> is marked by the usual Page
         "strength, penetration, and feeling." The stories are
         really "studies of character."

1895

1895 A BOOKS - NONE

1895 B SHORTER WRITINGS

1 ANON. "The Burial of the Guns." The Independent, 47
     (10 January), 53.
          The six short stories of Southern life are "pleasantly
     told." The volume, moreover, is handsomely bound, and the
     print is "clear and restful."

2 ANON. "Comment on New Books." The Atlantic Monthly, 76
     (October), 563-69.
          Page's style may always be admired for its "simplicity."
     Page's style is "sincere" and lacks "affectation." Such is
     the case with The Burial of the Guns.

3 ANON. "Fiction." The Literary World, 26 (28 December),
     475-76.
          "Unc' Edinburg's Drowndin'" contains "the charm of high-
     bred Southern society and a genuine true love story of the
     old-fashioned kind, as an old negro saw and had a part in
     it all while following the fortunes of his master."

4 ANON. "Novel Notes." The Bookman (London), 7 (January),
     120-23.
          The Burial of the Guns is a "disappointing" collection,
     for it fails to measure up to "Marse Chan." No lasting im-
     pression is made by any tale in the collection. The strong-
     er tales in the collection are those that have some connec-
     tion with war as in "The Burial of the Guns." The volume
     contains some "pleasant Christmas stories."

5 ANON. "A Sketch of Darky Character." New York Times
     (13 October), p. 27.
          Unc' Edinburg: A Plantation Echo presents accurate
     Negro dialect and a "pretty love story." The nostalgia of
     the story is quite appealing.

6 ANON. "Talk About Books." The Chautauquan, 22 (December),
     379.
          "Unc' Edinburg" is a plantation romance dealing with the
     "mutual affection of master and slave."

7 MANLY, LOUISE. Southern Literature from 1879 to 1895.
     Richmond: B. F. Johnson Publishing Company, pp. 419-22.
          Page's earliest poems and stories were in Negro dialect,
     some of which he wrote jointly with Armistead Churchill
     Gordon. Page "delineates finely" the Virginia Negro. His

work is marked by a "naturalness" of style and "effective
touches of pathos."

1896 A BOOKS - NONE

1896 B SHORTER WRITINGS

1   ANON. "Talk About Books." The Chautauquan, 24 (December),
     376.
        Although Harris, Russell, and Page all present views of
     Southern plantation life, Page's, one hopes, is the most
     truthful, since his view is "graciously and tenderly" drawn.
     "'Marse Chan' and the other tales comprising the dainty
     volume In Ole Virginia are each clear-cut gems in a glitter-
     ing chaplet."

1897 A BOOKS - NONE

1897 B SHORTER WRITINGS

1   ANON. "Book Reviews." Overland Monthly, 30 (August), 191.
        The Old Gentleman of the Black Stock is "a nice little
     story. It is not stupid; for one cannot accuse Thomas Nel-
     son Page of ever writing anything exactly stupid. Yet if
     we did not know that Mr. Page had married rich it is to be
     feared that The Old Gentleman would be styled a pot-boiler.
     However, it can be read in an hour and forgotten nearly as
     soon after."

2   ANON. "Collections of Short Stories." The Literary World, 28
     (6 March), 74-75.
        The new edition of In Ole Virginia contains illustrations
     by "Smedley, Reinhart, Frost, Clinedinst, Howard Pyle, and
     Castaigne" which capture the "fun and pathos" of the text.

3   ANON. "Current Fiction." The Literary World, 28
     (18 September), 324-25.
        The Old Gentleman of the Black Stock is a "refined, quiet
     little story of Southern life." The protagonist and the
     heroine are "delightfully real."

4   ANON. "Mr. Page's Work for Virginia." New York Times,
     Saturday Review of Books and Art (25 December), p. 13.
        Reading Social Life in Old Virginia Before the War is
     "like opening a rose jar," for Page has sought to rescue
     the history of Virginia from oblivion.

1897

5   ANON. "'The Old Gentleman in the Black Stock.'" The Critic,
        NS 28 (27 November), 321.
           The Old Gentleman of the Black Stock is a highly appro-
        priate addition to Scribner's Ivory Series. The moral "love
        is best," is apparent in the protagonist's behavior. Both
        the pathos of the novel and the reticence of the author are
        appealing. In this sense, the novel exemplifies the "manner
        of the old school," i.e., "feeling without mawkishness."
        Page uses two young lovers in the novel to contrast with
        the old gentleman.

6   ANON. "The Old Gentleman of the Black Stock." The Independent,
        49 (19 August), 1085.
           The Old Gentleman of the Black Stock is not a successful
        novel but a "commonplace." Although somewhat entertaining,
        the novel bears "no mark of genius."

7   ANON. "Recent Publications." New Orleans Daily Picayune
        (11 April), p. 25.
           In Ole Virginia is "one of the most beautiful books ever
        written about the south."

8   NELSON, JAMES POYNTZ. "Tom Page's Home: The Country House
        Where His Youth Was Spent." Richmond Dispatch (5 January),
        p. 3.
           A description of "Oakland Plantation" and its furnish-
        ings. The atmosphere of the estate was especially conducive
        to writing. Brief reference is made to Two Little Con-
        federates.

9   WHITTLE, GILBERT S. "Thomas Nelson Page: Sketch of This
        Talented Virginia Author." Richmond Dispatch (3 January),
        p. 3.
           "Unc' Gabe's White Folks" received immediate acclaim for
        its "perfect delineation of the Negro character and speech."
        "Marse Chan," on the other hand, was more widely admired
        once it was published in book form. Page himself considered
        "Unc' Edinburg's Drowndin'" the best picture of Virginia
        life he ever drew. Page's major achievement, however, is
        the presentation of the "delicate vein of sentiment which
        runs through Negro character."

1898 A   BOOKS - NONE

1898 B   SHORTER WRITINGS

1   ANON. "Books and Authors." The Outlook, 59 (7 May), 83-90.
     Page's Two Prisoners, a story about and for little girls,
     is "full of gentle pathos, and is written with taste and
     feeling."

2   ANON. "Collections of Short Stories." The Literary World, 29
     (23 July), 236-37.
     Page's Pastime Stories is built upon "a world of dreams,
     wherein the characters move delicately through a veil of
     tradition and romance." Page's characters are, however,
     realistically drawn.

3   ANON. "Current Fiction." The Literary World, 29 (10 December),
     437-38.
     Page's Red Rock is marked by "charm and individuality"
     and contains "sympathetic illustrations" by B. West
     Clinedinst.

4   ANON. "Mr. Page's Tale of Childhood." New York Times,
     Saturday Review of Books and Art (18 June), p. 404.
     Two Prisoners is a "tender tale of childhood" with ex-
     cellent style and "sympathetic treatment" of subject matter.

5   ANON. "Pastime Stories." The Independent, 50 (16 June), 797.
     Page is able to tell a story "with graceful ease when he
     knows his ground." Although Pastime Stories contains two
     or three stories which epitomize the "Old Virginia flavor
     and savor," Page has nonetheless "gone far out of his usual
     path."

6   ANON. "Recent Publications." New Orleans Daily Picayune
     (5 June), part 2, p. 7.
     Although one knows Page's fiction requires no "foreword,"
     the attractive gray and green binding speaks well for
     Pastime Stories. The stories in the collection are "typi-
     cally Southern" and are pleasantly narrated.

7   ANON. "Recent Publications." New Orleans Daily Picayune
     (1 May), p. 25.
     Page's Two Prisoners is reproduced in "dainty form" and
     is "one of the best the author has ever written for young
     people."

1898

8   ANON. "Recent Publications." New Orleans Daily Picayune
    (27 November), p. 10.
        Red Rock is "the flower of Thomas Nelson Page's mature
    genius, and by far the most important work he has yet given
    to the world." The novel presents finely drawn portraits
    of Southern ladies and gentlemen of the old school.

9   ANON. "Short Sketches of Southern Character." New York Times,
    Saturday Review of Books and Art (28 May), p. 348.
        The selections in Pastime Stories are more "anecdotes"
    than short stories. In their "artistic moderation and
    fineness of workmanship" some of the stories may well repre-
    sent Page at his best. "The Prosecution of Mrs. Dullet" is
    truly entertaining. Page's milieu is the South after the
    Civil War.

10 ANON. "Thomas Nelson Page's Red Rock." New York Times,
    Saturday Review of Books and Art (19 November), p. 773.
        Red Rock is a "historical novel in the highest and best
    sense of that term." The novel, moreover, exposes the
    evils inherent in Reconstruction.

11 ANON. "'Two Prisoners.'" The Critic, NS 30 (July-August),
    105.
        Two Prisoners is a "masterpiece." The story is so
    simple that a child can comprehend it, yet it has a message
    for older readers. The situation in the story is rendered
    without "sensationalism."

12 ARTZ, VICTORINE THOMAS. "Thomas Nelson Page's English." The
    Writer: A Monthly Magazine for Literary Workers, 11 (May),
    69-70.
        Although Page is often described by book reviewers as a
    "'typical Southern gentleman,'" Artz contends that Page's
    language in Red Rock is "entirely different from the lan-
    guage that is written and spoken by typical Southern
    gentlemen."

13 EARLE, MARY TRACY. "A Romantic Chronicle." Book Buyer, 17
    (November), 297-98.
        Written with "the greatest depth of feeling" Red Rock is
    a "story of action, not of reminiscence." The girls Blair
    Cary and Ruth Welsh are endearing characters. In general
    the characters of the novel "show the different types in
    which sincerity and honor embodied themselves at that time
    in the South."

14   LANIER, HENRY WYSHAM. "Fiction, Poetry, and the Lighter Note
     in the Season's Books." American Monthly Review of Reviews,
     18 (December), 723-41.
         A lengthy novel founded on childhood recollections, Red
     Rock compares poorly with "Marse Chan."

15   PAYNE, WILLIAM MORTON. "Recent Fiction." The Dial, 25
     (16 December), 456-59.
         Red Rock is "one of the most satisfactory works of fic-
     tion that the South has ever produced." The novel provides
     real insight into Southern character both before and after
     the Civil War.

1899 A BOOKS - NONE

1899 B SHORTER WRITINGS

1   ANON. "A Few Good Books for the Summer." The Independent, 51
     (8 June), 1565.
         Red Rock is an "engaging romance of the South in recon-
     struction days."

2   ANON. "Mr. Page's Red Rock." Dixie, 1 (June), 655-56.
         In his transition from short story to novel, Page has
     attained the tenderness of "Marse Chan" and "Meh Lady" and
     the strength of a "complex command of material." The major
     purpose of the novel is to contrast the South before and
     after the Civil War. The strongest appeal of the novel is
     its "old world sorrow," its sense of longing for the splen-
     dors of the old South. Yet Page is "none too flattering in
     contrasting the types of gentility represented by the two
     eras." Miss Thomasia becomes the "sampler of gracious
     good-breeding and noble pride." The novel, however, pre-
     sents an overly complicated narrative involving a large
     number of characters.

3   ANON. "Novel Notes." The Bookman (London), 16 (April), 20-26.
         Page is a more devoted speaker for the Southern cause
     than is George Washington Cable. Page's depiction of Re-
     construction life in Red Rock is "hideous," and his villains
     quite genuine. The picture of antebellum life forms quite
     a contrast in the novel, and the reader is apt to be charmed
     by the Grays and the Carys.

4   ANON. "Novels." The Saturday Review (London), 87 (4 March),
     280.

1899

Red Rock contains a number of "dramatic incidents" but is crowded with characters. Page often elaborates where he should suggest.

5   ANON. "Novels of the Week." The Spectator, 82 (28 January), 138-40.
    In Red Rock Page tries to reconcile Northern readers to the South. His "partisanship," however, is apparent. The plot of the novel is "loosely knit, and its working out by no means coherent."

6   ANON. "Recent Novels." The Nation, 68 (2 March), 166-68.
    Page's previous stories concerning the war are "more memorable contributions to fiction" than is Red Rock.

7   ANON. "Red Rock: A Chronicle of Reconstruction." The Critic, NS 31 (January), 83-84.
    With considerable charm Page invites the reader to enjoy the nostalgia of old plantation days in his new novel. Equally pleasant is the thought that Red Rock is an "eloquent protest against the novelistic tendencies of this decadent decade and the school to which true love and holy wedlock are fit subjects of banter and jest." The focus of the novel is on the passing of an era which had much to offer the ladies and gentlemen of the Old South. The "odiousness of the Reconstruction régime has never perhaps been so powerfully brought out as in the overseer and the provost in the story."

8   ANON. "Red Rock by Thomas Nelson Page." The Independent, 51 (16 March), 769-70.
    Page is not as good a novelist in Red Rock as he was raconteur in his Negro sketches. As a novelist Page lacks two necessary strengths--"constructive ability and style-energy." In many instances his new novel drags and his style is "apathetic."

9   ANON. "Some Recent Fiction." The Atlantic Monthly, 83 (April), 518-24.
    Red Rock contains "literary distinction and captivating manner." The novel is without rancour in its indictment of the Reconstruction.

10 ANON. "Tales of Adventure." The Athenaeum, 3720 (11 February), 176.
    Although the story of Red Rock is not compelling reading, the novel should be regarded for its "picture of the Southern states after the war." From this point of view the novel is "well written."

11   ANON. "Talk About Books." The Chautauquan, 28 (January),
     420-21.
         Red Rock is a "delightful" addition to the body of Page's
     work. The novel presents an accurate view of "social con-
     ditions and the lifelike delineation of character." Set in
     the South, the novel makes a powerful contrast between ante-
     bellum prosperity and postbellum "desolation." Although the
     novel is obviously critical of "the scheming Northerner and
     the selfish Southerner," Page indicates that "the best
     people of the two sections come at length to understand and
     appreciate each other." When Northerner and Southerner
     intermarry in the novel, one is assured that "the era of
     good will has come to remain." B. West Clinedinst's illus-
     trations capture the "spirit" of the novel.

12   ANON. "The Year's Fiction." The Independent, 51 (23 November),
     3171.
         Red Rock "still claims strong attention for its sterling
     qualities."

13   DUKE, R. T. W. "Red Rock." Conservative Review, 1 (May),
     339-46.
         Page's new novel marks an "epoch in Southern fiction"
     and is superior to Uncle Tom's Cabin with which it has been
     compared. Page himself was an aristocrat. Since Southern
     aristocrats were often close to the Negro, Page has a
     genuine understanding of the Negro. His Negroes conse-
     quently are "wonderfully drawn." Although the plot of the
     novel is not "very original," there is enough narrative in
     the work to retain the reader's attention. The novel will
     undoubtedly be remembered among works of history, for much
     of the "splendor" of the old South has been preserved within
     its pages.

14   HIGGINSON, THOMAS WENTWORTH. "The Case of the Carpet-Baggers."
     The Nation, 68 (2 March), 162-63.
         Although Page sought to be impartial in Red Rock, he
     failed to consider two major points concerned with Recon-
     struction. First, Negro suffrage was a necessity in order
     to insure loyal American Blacks of their "most ordinary
     rights." Secondly, influential Southern whites refused to
     accept socially the better class American whites during
     Reconstruction.

15   HINCKLEY, HENRY BARRETT. "A Brief for the South." The
     Bookman, 9 (March), 44-47.
         Page's "plea for the injured South" sometimes takes
     precedence over the demands of art in Red Rock. The novel,

1899

despite this weakness, contains "humor and pathos." Page
frequently writes as "an advocate with a brief for the
plaintiff aristocracy of Virginia, and not as a judge."

16   [MABIE, HAMILTON W.]. "In the Field of Fiction." The Outlook,
      63 (2 December), 771-78.
            Using a traditional Dickens' theme, Page revived the old-
      fashioned Christmas tale with Santa Claus's Partner, a story
      filled with "charm" and "sincerity."

1900 A BOOKS - NONE

1900 B SHORTER WRITINGS

1   ANON. "Current Fiction." The Literary World, 31
     (20 January), 26-27.
           Santa Claus's Partner, a "lovely story," contains the
     "meaning of the true spirit of Christmas." The "family
     life of the hard-worked clerk is true and sweet." Color
     illustrations by W. Glackeno are excellent.

2   ANON. "Recent Publications." New Orleans Daily Picayune
     (14 January), part 2, p. 7.
           Santa Claus's Partner appeals to the "universal human
     heart." In both "manner and tenderness" the tale is similar
     to "Marse Chan."

3   ANON. "'Santa Claus's Partner.'" The Critic, 36 (January),
     91.
           The story is truly "charming," for Page's style is "at
     its best."

4   CABLE, GEORGE W. "A Charming Old Gentleman." Book Buyer, 21
     (December), 378-80.
           The Old Gentleman of the Black Stock is "a love story of
     the simplest sort." Dealing with life known to many men,
     the novel raises that life to "its highest spiritual pulsa-
     tion." The novel is a success because it presents "one of
     the problems that began with the human heart, and will be
     a problem to every human heart while the world endures."
     The new novel is also marked by strong Southern local color
     and "clear and winsome character-drawing."

5   POND, J. B. Eccentricities of Genius. New York: G. W.
     Dillingham, pp. 227, 482, 508, 521-23.
           Mentions a quip from Clemens regarding Page, and a dinner
     party at Page's Washington home. In his two-page essay on

Page, Pond notes that the author conveyed in fiction "all that is best in a character." Notes the beginning of Page's public appearances and the glamor of his Washington life.

1901 A BOOKS - NONE

1901 B SHORTER WRITINGS

1   ANON. "Current Fiction." The Literary World, 32 (1 May), 71.
     The Old Gentleman of the Black Stock is a book of "pure
     fresh air." Elizabeth Dale is a "womanly creature."

2   ANON. "The Old Gentleman of the Black Stock." The Critic, 38
     (March), 279.
         Page's "charming tale" of the old gentleman has been en-
     larged and included in this new edition. Howard Chandler
     Christy's illustrations are quite effective.

3   HALSEY, FRANCIS WHITING. American Authors and Their Homes.
     New York: James Pott and Company, pp. 175-86.
         Because Page himself knew poverty, he has never lost
     sympathy with the unfortunate. In his interview with Page,
     Halsey gives a full description of Page's Washington, D. C.
     home, noting a number of Page's personality traits and his
     reading habits (viz. Scott). The interviewer notes that
     Red Rock underwent a number of revisions, the finished novel
     requiring approximately two years to write.

1902 A BOOKS - NONE

1902 B SHORTER WRITINGS

1   ANON. "Mr. Page's Christmas Story." New York Times,
     Saturday Review of Books and Art (22 November), p. 807.
         A Captured Santa Claus is lacking in originality, and
     its "idea is hackneyed." The work, however, is marked by
     "delicacy," "quaintness," "tenderness," "pathos," and
     "humor."

2   ANON. "Short Stories." The Athenaeum, 3871 (4 January),
     15-16.
         Page's "quaint phraseology" in several stories in In Ole
     Virginia deserves careful consideration. Page's style has,
     moreover, the virtue of simplicity. The narratives of the
     stories in this new edition of Page's old collection are
     quite good.

Three Virginia Writers

1903

<u>1903 A   BOOKS - NONE</u>

<u>1903 B   SHORTER WRITINGS</u>

1   ANON. "Books and Authors: Comment and Gossip." Richmond
     <u>Times-Dispatch</u> (12 April), p. 10.
          Page's forthcoming novel <u>Gordon Keith</u> promises much that
     is pleasant.

2   ANON. "Bret Harte and Sundry Novels." <u>The Nation</u>, 77
     (6 August), 117-18.
          Page is the major Southern historian, his early tales
     constituting an "idyll of the old South." Whereas <u>Red Rock</u>
     concerns the Reconstruction era, <u>Gordon Keith</u> deals with a
     commercial and industrial South. The latter, despite its
     admirable purpose, is unaccountably dull.

3   ANON. "Current Books." <u>Overland Monthly</u>, 41 (January), 79-80.
          Page's "A Captured Santa Claus" is set in Civil War Vir-
     ginia. The story is written in Page's "usual felicitous
     manner." Illustrations are by W. L. Jacobs.

4   ANON. "<u>Gordon Keith</u>." <u>The Literary World</u>, 34 (July), 168-69.
          Ferdy Wickersham is "one of the most conscientious and
     painstaking villains on record." Page's pictures of North-
     ern financiers in <u>Gordon Keith</u> are stereotypes nearly as
     allegorical as those in <u>Pilgrim's Progress</u>. All of the
     women characters are unconvincing.

5   ANON. "Mr. Page's <u>Gordon Keith</u>." <u>World's Work</u>, 6 (July),
     3702.
          The new novel presents an effective North-South contrast,
     but it is poorly constructed. One would expect better from
     the best American short story writer since Poe or Bret
     Harte.

6   ANON. "Mr. Page's Latest Story." <u>New York Times</u>, <u>Saturday
     Review of Books and Art</u> (6 June), p. 390.
          <u>Gordon Keith</u> "savors of biography rather than of fic-
     tion." Although the novel is inconsistent in its narrative
     and relies a bit heavily on coincidence, it is written with
     "sincerity and strength."

7   ANON. "Mr. Page's Novel." <u>The Independent</u>, 55 (20 August),
     1993-94.
          <u>Gordon Keith</u> is a strong story of Reconstruction life,
     for it contains little sentimentality. The protagonist of
     the novel commands the reader's sympathy. The insistence

upon the superiority of the Southern gentleman over all
other Americans, however, becomes wearisome--the old theme
of "pedigree, pride, and power."

8   ANON. "New Novels." The Athenaeum, 3957 (29 August), 280-82.
     The author of Gordon Keith is too "prolix."

9   ANON. "Novels." The Saturday Review (London), 96 (3 October),
     432.
          Page seems obsessed by the idea that his hero in Gordon
     Keith is a "'gentleman.'" The large number of characters
     in the novel were apparently added merely to lengthen the
     work.

10 ANON. "Page--Gordon Keith." The Critic, 43 (October), 380.
          Although Gordon Keith is more "pretentious" than most
     Page novels, it is "masterfully handled and never dull."
     The novel, moreover, although somewhat melodramatic, in-
     troduces a refreshing "sarcasm."

11 ANON. "Page--Two Prisoners." The Critic, 43 (October), 579.
          Two Prisoners is not particularly original and consti-
     tutes a "survival of an outgrown school."

12 ANON. Review of Gordon Keith. The Saturday Review (London),
     96 (15 August), 212.
          Page's "control of the perspective of construction" in
     Gordon Keith is quite poor. Page seems unable to handle
     the length that the novel demands.

13 ANON. "Thomas Nelson Page's Washington Residence." Richmond
     Times-Dispatch (1 February), p. 6.
          Page has been regarded as "one of the best interpreters
     of Southern life and conditions 'after the war.'"

14 ANON. "Three Novels: Mr. Page's Latest Study of Southern
     Life." New York Daily Tribune (27 June), p. 10.
          Gordon Keith, unlike a number of current Southern
     stories, merely alludes to the Civil War and consequently
     avoids the vogue for Civil War battle scenes. Page, on the
     other hand, stresses beyond endurance the hero's status as
     gentleman. The strongest part of the novel is its pre-
     sentation of a young man's struggle for success.

15 HARRIS, MRS. L. H. "Heroes and Heroines in Recent Fiction."
     The Independent, 55 (3 September), 2111-2115.
          The goal of most current Southern writers is apparently
     "to maintain a defunct ideal of aristocracy and to preserve

1903

in the hero the mind, manners, and spirit of an antebellum past." Page exemplifies that very goal in Gordon Keith.

16 HENNEMAN, JOHN BELL. "The National Element in Southern Literature." The Sewanee Review, 11 (July), 345-66.
Red Rock was part of the 1898 American vogue for romance.

17 MIMS, EDWIN. "The Function of Criticism in the South." The South Atlantic Quarterly, 2 (October), 334-345.
Red Rock gives graphic representation of "the terrible experiences of the Southern people in reconstruction times, but there is a moderation about it. . . ."

18 _____. "Thomas Nelson Page," in Southern Writers: Biographical and Critical Studies. Edited by William Malone Baskervill. 2 vols. Nashville, Tennessee: Publishing House of the M. E. Church South, Bigham & Smith Agents, 1903, vol. 2, pp. 120-51.
Page is a Southern romancer who looks to the past for his inspiration. Because of his background, Page was thoroughly attuned to antebellum Southern life. Page's ancestry, childhood, education, and lifestyle are examined in some detail. References are made to Two Little Confederates, The Old Gentleman of the Black Stock, "Unc' Gabe's White Folks," "Marse Chan," The Burial of the Guns, and Santa Claus's Partner. Page admittedly lacks the irony of Hawthorne or the "sarcasm" of Thackeray; moreover, he demonstrates little insight into Southern problems in his essays. Like Irwin Russell, however, he recognized "the literary capabilities of the Negro" as a point of view character.

19 PAYNE, WILLIAM MORTON. "Recent Fiction." The Dial, 35 (1 August), 63-67.
Gordon Keith suffers from comparison with Red Rock, for "its interest is more scattered, and its plan does not have so definite a historical background." The novel makes use of innumerable characters and several changes of scene.

1904 A BOOKS - NONE

1904 B SHORTER WRITINGS

1 ANON. "Bred in the Bone." The Independent, 57 (14 July), 100-01.
Page is obviously the "literary expounder of blood and pedigree in this country" as in Bred in the Bone. Despite

the dogma of his work, Page's stories contain both "art" and "charm."

2   ANON. "Bred in the Bone." The Literary World, 35 (July), 205.
    Page "knows his South and loves it" so much that setting often becomes of major interest to the reader. Such is the reaction to Bred in the Bone, a novel written with both humor and understanding.

3   ANON. "Mr. Page's Novel." New York Times, Saturday Review of Books and Art (25 June), p. 439.
    The stories in Bred in the Bone will come as a disappointment to those who remember In Ole Virginia or Red Rock. The new stories seem a bit too long and lack the usual Page humor and pathos.

4   ANON. "The Negro Problem: A Survey of the Matter by Thomas Nelson Page Setting Forth the Most Conservative Southern Estimates." New York Times, Saturday Review of Books and Art (10 December), p. 874.
    Despite the "temperateness" with which Page undertakes his study of the Negro in The Negro: The Southerner's Problem, he does write with a "Southern point of view." The book will appeal to all Southerners and "most good Americans."

5   ANON. "Successful Fiction of 1903." The Bookman, 18 (January), 481–84.
    Gordon Keith "forged far to the front" in sales for August 1903 and remained first for September 1903.

6   M. J. M. "Bred in the Bone." The Reader Magazine, 4 (August), 347–48.
    Because of his deep knowledge of Southern life, every Page story contains "perfect" atmosphere. Bred in the Bone unfortunately suffers from "unevenness," for the stories in the collection seem to have been written to present "isolated phases of humanity." The collection, however, presents a "decided Southern atmosphere." The collection shows Page's "absolute control of local color; the maturity of his views of human nature; but as stories, the seven in the book leave much to be desired."

7   ORMOND, JOHN RAPER. "Some Recent Products of the New School of Southern Fiction." The South Atlantic Quarterly, 3 (July), 285–89.
    Gordon Keith represented a "woful [sic] seeking for light where none was to be found."

1905

1905 A BOOKS - NONE

1905 B SHORTER WRITINGS

1   ANON. "Book Department." The Annals of the American Academy
     of Political and Social Science, 25 (March), 335-[356].
          The Negro: The Southerner's Problem is "considerate,
     conservative, yet hopeful." Page discusses racial rela-
     tions in terms of history. Although Page offers no new
     perspective on the racial problem in the work, his treat-
     ment of it is commended as an example of how "the intelli-
     gent South views the problem."

2   ANON. "Modern American Problems." The American Monthly
     Review of Reviews, 31 (January), 127-28.
          The Negro: The Southerner's Problem is a "temperate
     discussion of the race question from the Southerner's point
     of view." Page argues in the work for practical education
     for the Negro.

3   ANON. "Mr. Page's Book on the Negro." The Sewanee Review,
     13 (April), 237-38.
          Although Page's The Negro: The Southerner's Problem may
     not solve the Negro problem, the work suggests avenues of
     exploration. With optimism and pride Page holds that the
     two races must remain "distinct, each developing under con-
     ditions with substantial justice to both."

4   ANON. "Page--Bred in the Bone." The Critic, 46 (February),
     189.
          Page's real talent in Bred in the Bone is not the con-
     struction of a short story but the portrayal of "certain
     types of Southern character." His proclivity towards sen-
     timentality is compensated for by his "sincerity and
     sympathy."

5   EATON, ISABEL. "The Negro: The Southerner's Problem."
     International Journal of Ethics, 15 (July), 518-22.
          Page's study of the Negro is written in a pleasant style,
     but in a work of its kind substance is of far more im-
     portance than style. Page expounds three points: (1) the
     Negro is the concern of the South, not the North, (2) a
     race may be judged by its "rank and file," and (3) the
     Negro is incapable of improvement. Eaton points out that
     the Negro is a national concern, that a race must be judged
     on the basis of both its strengths and weaknesses, and that
     the Negro has demonstrated considerable potential through-
     out history.

6   M[IMS], E[DWIN]. "Book Reviews." The South Atlantic
     Quarterly, 4 (April), 192-95.
          In his review of Thomas Dixon Jr.'s The Clansman, Mims
     notes that Dixon is not a "successful novelist" if compared
     with Joel Chandler Harris or Thomas Nelson Page, both of
     whom had "artistic power" and "purpose in view."

7   ORMOND, J. R. "Book Reviews." The South Atlantic Quarterly,
     4 (January), 96-98.
          The title story of Bred in the Bone is Page's real
     milieu. The narrative is "in the style . . . [of] 'Edin-
     burg's Drowning [sic].'"

1906 A BOOKS - NONE

1906 B SHORTER WRITINGS

1   ANON. "Recent Fiction." The Nation, 83 (18 October), 332-34.
          Although a moonlight and roses Southern story, On New-
     found River contains a love story that is "young, Arcadian,
     rough-running, happily arriving."

2   ANON. "The Works of Thomas Nelson Page." The Independent,
     61 (6 December), 1351-52.
          Page is the "preeminent" writer of Southern life, "Meh
     Lady" and "Marse Chan" being his best works. The Planta-
     tion Edition demonstrates "the variety of Mr. Page's art."
     In Ole Virginia remains superior to Bred in the Bone.

3   ELLWOOD, CHARLES A. "The Negro: The Southerner's Problem."
     The American Journal of Sociology, 11 (March), 698-99.
          Page's The Negro: The Southerner's Problem is marked by
     impartiality and genuine concern. If what Page presents in
     his study represents the attitudes of most Southern whites,
     the Negro problem may soon be solved.

4   HALLIDAY, CARL. A History of Southern Literature. New York:
     The Neale Publishing Company, pp. 366, 369, 390.
          The Negro is the primary source of Page's fame. His
     "most popular work has been his Negro dialect stories."
     The majority of his fiction--Two Little Confederates, On
     Newfound River, The Old South, and Social Life in Old Vir-
     ginia--is an "elaborate and effective defense of the ante-
     bellum system and institutions." In Ole Virginia is "free
     from all taint of sentimentality" and comes close to
     artistic perfection.

1906

5   HARKINS, EDWARD FRANCIS. Famous Authors (Men). Boston:
      L. C. Page and Company, pp. 201-14.
         "Marse Chan" brought Page a national reputation. The
      source for the short story is discussed. Page himself be-
      lieved, however, that "Unc' Edinburg's Drowndin'" was his
      "best picture of Virginia life." Page's fiction has re-
      vealed the "lighter side" of slavery days, Stowe's the
      "harsher." Red Rock did much to effect a North-South
      reconcilliation.

1907 A   BOOKS - NONE

1907 B   SHORTER WRITINGS

1   ANON. "Notes on New Books." The Sewanee Review, 15
      (January), 121-28.
         Page's On Newfound River is filled with "sentiment and
      love." The Coast of Bohemia is Page's collection of "seri-
      ous" and "dialect" poems.

2   ANON. "On New Found River." The Independent, 62 (21 March),
      62.
         On Newfound River is a "disappointing" novel. To roman-
      tics interested in older civilizations, the novel will have
      some appeal.

3   ANON. "Recent Poetry." Current Literature, 42 (January),
      104-11.
         The Coast of Bohemia is in imitation of Marlowe, Milton,
      Keats, and Shelley. The best poems in the collection are
      patriotic ones. There is nothing "compelling" in Page's
      poetry.

4   ANON. "The Waning Influence of Thomas Nelson Page." Current
      Literature, 43 (August), 171-72.
         Page has concluded his major work, a fact supported by
      the recent publication of the Plantation Edition of his
      works. His best work, In Ole Virginia, was, ironically,
      his downfall as he later sought to imitate it. His down-
      fall is also owed in part to the coming of age of the new
      South, one uninterested in the old codes.

5   DUKE, R. T. W., JR. "Dr. Thomas Nelson Page." Corks and
      Curls, 20, 3-5.
         "Marse Chan" brought Page his earliest important atten-
      tion. On Newfound River proved that he was equally tal-
      ented at the novel. Red Rock was presented in "a most

conservative and yet truthful manner." Page had great
understanding of "negro character."

6   KENT, CHARLES W. "Thomas Nelson Page." The South Atlantic
    Quarterly, 6 (July), 263-71.
        A review of the Plantation Edition of Page's work. Kent
    praises Page's realism, concluding that his short stories
    constitute "the highest exercise of his creative power."

7   [MABIE, HAMILTON W.] "Thomas Nelson Page: Two Recent Books."
    The Outlook, 87 (30 November), 742-43.
        Page is an "idealist in prose." As social historian of
    Virginia, he is well known for "Meh' Lady" and "Marse Chan."
    Page, moreover, is often recognized for his disdain of the
    "ultra-fashionable set" and for his attacks on the evils of
    Reconstruction. Under the Crust contains Page's character-
    istic idealism, for the characters in these stories "live
    in the world as if life were still a matter of the spirit
    and not a matter of physical luxury." The Coast of Bohemia
    contains poems which are "unaffected and sincere." The
    spirituality of these poems comes at a time when spiritual-
    ity is no longer in fashion.

8   MIMS, EDWIN. "Thomas Nelson Page." The Atlantic Monthly, 100
    (July), 109-15.
        Page presented Southern antebellum life with "some
    degree of fulness." His concept of the Southern aristocrat
    varies from novel to novel. His favorite medium for fic-
    tion is the old Negro. Discussion includes "Polly," Red
    Rock, Burial of the Guns, "Marse Chan," "Meh Lady," "Unc'
    Edinburg's Drowndin'."

9   PAINTER, F. V. N. Poets of Virginia. Richmond: B. F.
    Johnson Publishing Company, pp. 242-43.
        Befo' De War was Page's earliest collection of poetry.
    The work was co-authored by Armistead C. Gordon. Poems
    like "Unc' Gabe's White Folks," "Little Jack," and "Marse
    Phil" are akin to Page's fiction. Such poems employ the
    dramatic monologue of Browning.

10 RUTHERFORD, MILDRED LEWIS. The South in History and Litera-
    ture: A Handbook of Southern Authors. Atlanta, Georgia:
    The Franklin-Turner Company, pp. 522-528.
        Two Little Confederates describes "the home and boyhood
    of Thomas Nelson Page." "Unc' Gabe's White Folks" achieved
    "perfect delineation of the Negro character and dialect."
    "Marse Chan" is thought to be "the best story that has been
    written about the War Between the States." Page's essays

1907

> in The Old South are greatly admired by Southerners. Red
> Rock is "a historical novel in the highest sense of the
> word." Page's works represent "what is best in the litera-
> ture of the South."

1908 A BOOKS - NONE

1908 B SHORTER WRITINGS

1   ANON. "Current Fiction." The Nation, 86 (23 January), 83-85.
>   With "conventional sentiment," Under the Crust has con-
>   siderably less appeal than "Marse Chan."

2   ANON. "Robert E. Lee the Southerner." Richmond Times-Dispatch
>   (29 November), p. 5.
>   Page sought in Robert E. Lee to "estimate" the "charac-
>   ter and ability" of the subject.

3   ANON. "Tommy Trot's Visit to Santa Claus." Richmond Times-
>   Dispatch (22 November), p. 5.
>   Tommy Trot's Visit to Santa Claus is written with a
>   "very charming feeling for the generous spirit of that
>   day." Page's style is "particularly successful."

4   DODD, WILLIAM E. "The Old Dominion: Her Making and Her
>   Manners." American Historical Review (October), 182-83.
>   The Old Dominion is a "collection of the by-products of
>   a literateur." The work contains "nothing new or fresh."
>   The traditional Page weakness mars this new work: charac-
>   ter is "absolutely determined by status."

5   ORGAIN, KATE ALMA. Southern Authors in Poetry and Prose.
>   New York: Neale Publishing Company, pp. 228-30.
>   Few writers have equalled Page as a "delineator of
>   negro dialect and character;" he also has "absolute per-
>   fectness of finish as to style and rhetoric."

1909 A BOOKS - NONE

1909 B SHORTER WRITINGS

1   ANON. "Current Fiction." The Nation, 89 (2 December), 540-41.
>   John Marvel, Assistant is written in a "florid and in-
>   genuous" style. Glavé's primary motivating characteristic
>   is his belief that he is a gentleman. The novel provides
>   a "kaleidoscopic" if not "panoramic" view of contemporary
>   life in America.

1909

2   ANON. "General Lee: Man and Soldier." The Spectator
       (London), 102 (20 March), 467.
          Lee's professional and personal strengths made him an
       historical figure almost without equal. Page's new study
       (English edition) is written with considerable "spirit."
       One must question, however, Page's historical judgments es-
       pecially in the last chapter "The Heritage of the South."

3   ANON. "A Guide to the New Books." The Literary Digest, 39
       (27 November), 959-70.
          Page's John Marvel, Assistant grapples with a number of
       "modern" problems. The somber nature of the story is re-
       lieved by a pleasant love story. Although the unity of the
       novel is badly marred, one must admire the sound charac-
       terization.

4   ANON. "John Marvel, Assistant." New York Times (23 October),
       part 2, p. 648.
          Page's new novel is an "interesting and straightforward
       story." Page seems, however, a little more concerned with
       certain social problems than he is with storytelling in the
       novel. There is strength in the scenepainting and charac-
       terization, despite a tendency towards melodrama.

5   ANON. "John Marvel, Assistant." Richmond Times-Dispatch
       (17 October), p. 7.
          Page presents many types of characters in John Marvel
       but each is skillfully "individualized." The new novel is
       the most "American" of his works.

6   ANON. "The New Books." The Outlook, 93 (30 October), 514-16.
          Page makes effective use of melodrama in John Marvel,
       Assistant. The story is the best Page story to appear
       lately.

7   ANON. "Page, Thomas Nelson. Robert E. Lee: Man and Soldier."
       American Library Association Booklist, 5 (February), 47.
          Robert E. Lee: Man and Soldier is interesting eulogy
       but "negligible" biography. The work focuses on Lee's
       military genius.

8   CABLE, GEORGE W. "A Study in Reminiscence and Appreciation."
       Book News Monthly, 28 (November), 139-41.
          Page seeks to present "the truth and beauty of the
       things he knows best . . . to make the ways of life clearer
       and smoother for whoever, from North or South, looks upon
       his pictures."
          In his work art and public interest become one.

1909

9   KENT, CHARLES W. "Thomas Nelson Page," in Library of Southern
    Literature. Edited by Edwin Anderson Alderman, et al. 17
    volumes. Atlanta: Martin & Hoyt Company, vol. 9, 3849-87.
        A biographical entry emphasizing Page's Romantic disposi-
    tion. Kent sees In Ole Virginia as Page's real métier and
    judges him "among the best known and most admired of
    America's living writers."

10 PAYNE, WILLIAM MORTON. "Recent Fiction." The Dial, 47
    (16 November), 384-87.
        Page has fallen "victim of the Zeitgeist" in John Marvel,
    Assistant. He uses familiar character types but does not
    fall victim to melodrama or pathos.

11 QUINN, ARTHUR HOBSON. "Mr. Page in Fiction and Poetry."
    Book News Monthly, 28 (November), 142-44.
        Page is a major figure in the renaissance of the South.
    Although John Marvel, Assistant is evidence of Page's com-
    mand of the possibilities of the novel, his real achievement
    lies in short stories like "Marse Chan," "Meh Lady," "No
    Haid Pawn," "Little Darby," "Run to Seed," and "Elsket."
    The great power of these stories is their effect, which is
    owed, in part, to his use of the theme of loyalty. Heredity
    is a frequent note in his fiction. In Gordon Keith and
    John Marvel there is a "hint" of melodrama, and cause and
    effect are strained. Red Rock is undoubtedly Page's most
    appealing novel. "Fancy" rather than "imagination" seem to
    have inspired his poetry. Although "A Message" and "The
    Coast of Bohemia" are good poems, Page's best poetry is his
    dialect poetry like "Little Jack" and "Unc' Gabe's White
    Folks." He succeeded in bringing together the vernacular
    language and poetry. Elsket indicates that Page was no
    mere provincial writer.

12 STANTON, THEODORE. A Manual of American Literature. New York:
    G. P. Putnam's Sons, pp. 250-51, 257, 270, 497.
        Page's "Marse Chan" met with considerable popularity.
    His general subject was antebellum and postbellum Virginia
    life. His depiction of aristocrats and Negroes is quite
    vivid.

13 WILLEY, DAY ALLEN. "Literary Life in Washington, D. C."
    Book News Monthly, 28 (November), 145-48.
        Page's works may be regarded as "word-pictures of life
    in the South."

1910 A BOOKS - NONE

1910 B SHORTER WRITINGS

1 ANON. "Fairyland." Bookman (London), 39 (December), 145-48.
   Page's Santa Claus's Partner is so "delightful" that one
   might rank it alongside Dickens' "The Christmas Carol."
   The work contains "the true spirit of Christmas."

2 COOPER, FREDERICK TABER. "The Permanent Interest and Some
   Recent Fiction." The Bookman, 30 (January), 510-15.
   John Marvel, Assistant is concerned with a growing
   American problem, the problem caused by immigration and
   "seething intermixture." The novel exposes "many of the
   weak points of our social and economic system."

3 MOSES, MONTROSE J. The Literature of the South. New York:
   Thomas Y. Crowell & Company, pp. 249, 471.
   Page is "the successor in the presentation of a passing
   atmosphere" to John Pendleton Kennedy. Page's poetry and
   essays are favorably judged.

1911 A BOOKS - NONE

1911 B SHORTER WRITINGS

1 ANON. "The New Books." The Outlook, 99 (30 December),
   1070-73.
   Page's thesis for Robert E. Lee: Man and Soldier was
   that Lee was a "great captain without reservation or
   limitation."

2 HEYDRICK, BENJAMIN A. "II. The Novel." The Chautauquan, 64
   (October), 165-84.
   John Marvel, Assistant is discussed in the context of
   the novel of protest.

3 TOULMIN, HARRY AUBREY, JR. Social Historians. Boston: R. G.
   Badger, pp. 1-34.
   Page undertook the writing of "Virginia and things Vir-
   ginian." Social Life In Old Virginia Before the War testi-
   fies to Page's keenness in sketching. "Marse Chan" had an
   unusual origin. In his discussion of Page's talents as
   writer, Toulmin refers to "Meh Lady," "Unc' Edinburg's
   Drowndin'," "Ole 'Stracted," "Polly," "No Haid Pawn," Red
   Rock, John Marvel, Gordon Keith, "The Old South," and The
   Negro: the Southerner's Problem. Red Rock and On Newfound
   River are "masterpieces of character and setting."

1912

1912 A BOOKS - NONE

1912 B SHORTER WRITINGS

1   ANON. "Book Department." The Annals of the American Academy
     of Political and Social Science, 44 (November), 145-203.
          Robert E. Lee, Man and Soldier suffers from its Southern
     point of view. Page lacks the "impartial and judicial at-
     titude" of General Lee himself. In general the book is
     never dull, the portrait of Lee after the war being "ad-
     mirably drawn."

2   ANON. "Lee's Triumphs and Failures." New York Times
     (4 February), part 6, p. 52.
          The reviewer of Page's Robert E. Lee: Man and Soldier
     notes that Lee is quite comparable in integrity to Washing-
     ton. Page is a biographer who is willing to take a stand
     on interpretations of history. The biography is a "fine
     and thrilling picture of a splendid American," informative
     as well as gracefully written.

3   ANON. "Mr. Page's Robert E. Lee." The Literary Digest, 44
     (6 April), 696.
          In Robert E. Lee: Man and Soldier, Page dwells upon
     Lee's religiosity and gentlemanly ways. He points out that
     Lee was never personally defeated.

4   ANON. "New Books on the Civil War." The Independent, 73
     (15 August), 384-86.
          While Page's Robert E. Lee: Man and Soldier is "de-
     lightful reading," it is nonetheless indiscriminate in its
     use of evidence. The best section of the biography is con-
     cerned with Lee's relationship with civil authority.

5   ANON. "Page, Thomas Nelson. Robert E. Lee: Man and Soldier."
     American Library Association Booklist, 8 (April), 338.
          Page's biography is "sympathetic and in the main non-
     partisan." The "spirit and color" of the work make it in-
     teresting if not well-documented reading.

6   ANON. "Robert E. Lee: Man and Soldier." The Catholic World,
     95 (July), 528-30.
          Robert E. Lee is marred by historical inaccuracy and
     Page's own contradictions. The work is comprised of
     "apostrophies and rhapsodies of words."

7   ANON. "Robert E. Lee: Man and Soldier." The North American
     Review, 195 (March), 427-30.

None of the acceptable three measures of biography can be applied to Page's Lee. The major point of the new biography is to bring Northerners to a more sympathetic attitude towards Lee.

8   ANON. "Two Books About the Civil War." The American Review of Reviews, 45 (February), 254.
Robert E. Lee: Man and Soldier is a sympathetic study of Lee's character.

9   ANON. "Two Books on General Lee." The Nation, 95 (4 July), 13.
Gamaliel Bradford's Lee the American, like Page's Robert E. Lee: Man and Soldier, testifies to the nobility of Lee's character. Page's biography underscores the aristocratic society that shaped him.

10   CAIRNS, WILLIAM B. A History of American Literature. New York: Oxford University Press, pp. 464, 475.
Page is a writer of "delightful stories" which employ antebellum Negroes as major characters.

11   GREEVER, GARLAND. "A Heritage of American Personality." The Dial, 52 (1 March), 159-62.
Robert E. Lee: Man and Soldier is marred by a number of stylistic weaknesses. Page obviously seeks here to exalt both Lee and the state of Virginia.

1913 A   BOOKS - NONE

1913 B   SHORTER WRITINGS

1   ANON. "American Appointments." The Times (18 June), p. 7b.
President Wilson has sent the senate his nomination of Page as ambassador to Italy.

2   ANON. "The American Embassy in London." The Times (17 March), p. 39d.
Page is a likely candidate for appointment to the London Embassy.

3   ANON. "Court Circular." The Times (22 September), p. 25a.
Page has left Claridge's Hotel on his way to Rome.

4   ANON. "Critical Reviews of this Season's Latest Books." New York Sun (26 April), p. 9.

1913

The seven short stories in The Land of the Spirit are
written with "grace and skill" despite the fact that they
are not "characteristic of the author." The one long story
in the collection is a "tragedy such as Hawthorne might
have imagined." Three of the stories in the collection
"follow the new fashion of bringing the Saviour into common
life,"

5   ANON. "Current Fiction." The Nation, 97 (28 August), 187-88.
    The stories in The Land of the Spirit contain the "senti-
ment of the Victorian fathers." The only real appeal of the
collection is perhaps "the style of a Southerner 'of the
old school.'"

6   ANON. "Fiction." The Athenaeum, 4480 (6 September), 227-29.
    The Land of the Spirit contains "charming short stories,"
some of which have unfortunately abrupt endings. One's
"curiosity is aroused, but not satisfied."

7   ANON. "The Land of the Spirit." The Independent, 75
    (3 July), 46.
    With considerable "literary charm" and an appealing
spiritual quality, the stories in The Land of the Spirit
are quite pleasant.

8   ANON. "Lord Haldrane's Return: The Lusitania in a Gale."
    The Times (9 September), p. 4e.
    Page arrives at Fishguard aboard the Lusitania on his
return from the U. S. A.

9   ANON. "More Lines to T. N. P." The Bookman, 38 (September),
    114.
    John Kendrick Bangs is reputed to have written the poem
which honors Page, reprinted herein.

10 ANON. "Thomas Nelson Page Receives Degree." The Times
    (20 June), p. 7c.
    Harvard University has conferred an honorary doctorate
on Page.

11 ANON. "Reviews of New Books." The Literary Digest, 47
    (18 October), 686-98.
    The Land of the Spirit contains "a finished style and
worthy subjects." The collection centers on "divine com-
mandments." The themes of the stories are serious, and
the characterization is "true."

12   ANON. "United States Diplomatic Appointments." The Times
     (7 June), p. 7e.
          Gossip has it that Page and Fréderick C. Penfield will
     be appointed to the Rome and Vienna embassies respectively.

13   ANON. "United States Embassies: The London Appointment."
     The Times (8 March), p. 5e.
          Page is among those rumored being considered for appoint-
     ment to the London Embassy.

14   BRIDGES, ROBERT. "Marse Tom at Co'te." The Bookman, 37
     (August), 605.
          Bridge's dialect poem is imitative of Page. The poem
     honors Page as he leaves to accept the diplomatic appoint-
     ment to Italy. The poem alludes to a number of well-known
     Page characters.

15   CHAMBERLAYNE, LEWIS PARKE. "Two Recent Books on Lee." The
     Sewanee Review, 21 (January), 108-18.
          Lee is the ideal in Southern character in Page's Robert
     E. Lee: Man and Soldier. The biography lacks, however,
     "totality of effect" and has little to add to military
     history.

16   EDGETT, EDWIN FRANCIS. "A New Thomas Nelson Page: Venturing
     Untried Paths in The Land of the Spirit." Boston Evening
     Transcript (23 April), p. 24.
          For years Page was known as a writer who often focused
     on the Southern "sectional relationships." That interest
     is exemplified by In Ole Virginia, "Marse Chan," The Old
     Gentleman of the Black Stock, and The Old Dominion. The
     Land of the Spirit is quite a departure from such a métier.
     Page's retelling of old Christian allegories borders at
     times on "sacrilege." "The Old Planters" is probably the
     best tale in the collection. Page should continue to write
     of Virginia life since the new collection has so little to
     recommend it.

17   GRAVES, JOHN TEMPLE. "A Gentleman at Rome." Cosmopolitan,
     56 (December), 85-87.
          Throughout the history of Virginia, there has always
     been a member of the Page family to "illustrate" the his-
     tory of their native state. Page's formative years were
     spent during the war years and postbellum period of Hanover
     County, an influence which lent "force" to the development
     of his inclination for writing.

1913

18   THOMPSON, HUGH. "Personal Portraits: Thomas Nelson Page."
      The Bookman, 38 (September), 25-26.
           Page did for Virginia what Garland, Mary E. Wilkins
      Freeman, and James Lane Allen did for their respective re-
      gions. He is the "Boswell of the old-time negro." His
      "Marse Chan" is said to have been written after his day in
      his office was over.

1914 A   BOOKS - NONE

1914 B   SHORTER WRITINGS

1   METCALF, JOHN CALVIN. American Literature. Richmond: B. F.
     Johnson Publishing Company, pp. 336-39.
          "Marse Chan," "Meh Lady," and "Unc' Edinburg's Drowndin'"
     are "classics." Page's permanent fame rests upon his fic-
     tion dealing with Southern life before and after the Civil
     War, eras he was ideally suited to depicting. The old
     Negro retainer is Page's best point of view character, and
     pathos and humor are the author's hallmarks. Red Rock
     exemplifies much of the best of Page's work, yet his most
     "pleasant" reconstruction of aristocratic life is found in
     his short fiction.

2   O'CONNOR, ELIZABETH PASCHAL (MRS. T. P.). My Beloved South.
     New York: G. P. Putnam's Sons, p. iii.
          Mrs. O'Connor notes in the dedication of her book that
     both she and Page must continue to recall the beauties of
     the Old South lest the younger generation forget.

1916 A   BOOKS - NONE

1916 B   SHORTER WRITINGS

1   ANON. "Court Circular." The Times (17 July), p. 11b.
          Page and his wife have arrived in London from Rome.

2   ANON. "Imperial and Foreign News Items." The Times
     (20 September), p. 7e.
          Page, ambassador to Italy, has made a visit to the
     entire Italian front.

3   ANON. "The Shepherd." New York Times (24 December), part 6,
     p. 566.
          The protagonist of The Shepherd Who Watched By Night is
     a minister who has outgrown his congregation in "spiritual

truth." The novel is distinguished by Page's "usual
finished style and clear English."

4   PAINTER, FRANKLIN VERZELIUS NEWTON. <u>Introduction to American</u>
     <u>Literature</u>. Boston: Sibley & Company, p. 319.
          Page is a "novelist of Southern life."

5   PATTEE, FRED LEWIS. <u>A History of American Literature Since</u>
     <u>1870</u>. New York: The Century Company, pp. 265-269.
          Page was "the first writer really to picture the South
     from the heart outward, to show it not as a picturesque
     spectacle but as a quivering section of human life." Page's
     impressionable years were spent amid the Civil War battle
     scenes near his home. He was greatly indebted to Irwin
     Russell's Mississippi Negro dialect poetry. <u>In Ole Virginia</u>
     was Page's major work and remains his major claim to fame.
     <u>Red Rock</u> began Page's "period of long romances." Federal
     mistreatment of the South is so strong in the novel that it
     detracts from the artistry. The novel is "primarily a
     treatise, a bit of special pleading."

6   ROLLINS, HYDER E. "The Negro in the Southern Short Story."
     <u>The Sewanee Review</u>, 24 (January), 42-60.
          Page has idealized the Southern slave just as he ideal-
     ized Southern ladies. Page's Negroes have traits normally
     attributed to Southern aristocrats. Sam ("Marse Chan") and
     Uncle Billy ("Meh Lady") are Negro "paragons."

<u>1917 A   BOOKS - NONE</u>

<u>1917 B   SHORTER WRITINGS</u>

1   ANON. "Court Circular." <u>The Times</u> (20 July), p. 9b.
          Page has arrived in London on leave and will remain in
     England several weeks.

2   ANON. "Imperial and Foreign News Items." <u>The Times</u>
     (24 February), p. 7e.
          Page commemorated Washington's birthday by delivering
     an address at the American Embassy in Rome on "what Ameri-
     cans had done for liberty and civilization."

3   ANON. "Italy and Austria's New Enemy." <u>The Times</u>
     (11 December), p. 5b.
          On December 10, 1917, Ambassador Page addressed Italian
     demonstrators, expressing his admiration for their re-
     sistance in the war.

1917

4   CUNLIFFE, JOHN W. and ASHLEY H. THORNDIKE, eds. The Warner
     Library, vol. 18. New York: The Knickerbocker Press,
     pp. 10937-39.
          Page was lucky insofar as the time and place of his
     birth are concerned. By 1883 Page had collaborated with
     A. C. Gordon on Befo' De War, which contains his lovely bal-
     lad "My Boy Cree." Page's best work, such as that in In Ole
     Virginia, contains "pictures of Virginia life before, or
     during the Civil War." His most "characteristic" novels
     are Red Rock, Gordon Keith, and John Marvel, Assistant.
     Much of Page's writing is owed to the environment in which
     he lived and his readings in the family library. A good
     part of his charm lies in his use of the loyal Negro ser-
     vant as the point-of-view character. Page was equally good
     in presenting the "poor white" of the old South.

5   DALY, JOSEPH FRANCIS. The Life of Augustin Daly. New York:
     Macmillan Company, p. 697.
          Page "conceived a dramatic idea to be incorporated into
     a play which he intended to call In Old Virginia." Page
     wrote to Daly on 14 November 1892 asking him to read the
     play and telling him that he planned to be in New York on
     18 November 1892.

6   DAVIS, CHARLES BELMONT, ed. Adventures and Letters of Richard
     Harding Davis. New York: Charles Scribner's Sons, p. 550.
          In his letter of 16 May 1897 Davis mentions that he went
     to visit the Pages in Rome and that they showed him "Rome
     by moonlight in one hour. It was like a cinematograph."

1918 A BOOKS - NONE

1918 B SHORTER WRITINGS

1   ANON. "Court Circular." The Times (6 September), p. 9b.
     Ambassador Page has left London for Leicester.

2   ANON. "Court Circular." The Times (31 August), p. 9a.
     Ambassador Page has left London for Leicester.

3   ANON. "Imperial and Foreign News Items." The Times (5 July),
     p. 5e.
          Ambassador Page has accepted a gift for the American Red
     Cross from the Civil Organization Committee.

4   SMITH, C. ALPHONSO. "Dialect Writers," in The Cambridge
     History of American Literature. Edited by John Erskine,

Stuart P. Sherman, and Carl Van Doren. New York: G. P.
Putnam's Sons, vol. 2, pp. 86, 89, 312.
    Page recognized his indebtedness to Mississippi dialect
poet Irwin Russell. The Negro dialect of Tidewater Virginia
is best represented in Page's fiction.

1919 A BOOKS - NONE

1919 B SHORTER WRITINGS

    1   ANON. "U. S. Ambassador at Rome." The Times (29 April),
            p. 11b.
            Ambassador Page has left Rome for Paris.

1920 A BOOKS - NONE

1920 B SHORTER WRITINGS

    1   ANON. "Literary Notes." Springfield Republican (4 December),
            p. 6.
            Using "personal observation and experience," Page de-
        fends Italy in Italy and the World War.

    2   LITTLEFIELD, WALTER. "Ambassador Page On Italy's Part in the
            War." New York Times, Review of Books (28 November),
            part 3, p. 3.
            Italy and the World War is marked by Page's "literary
        genius, the results of six years of residence in the penin-
        sula--years of careful observation into the life of the
        people. . . ."

1921 A BOOKS - NONE

1921 B SHORTER WRITINGS

    1   ANON. "Echoes of the Great War." The American Review of
            Reviews, 63 (February), 222-23.
            Page is well qualified to write of Italy's participation
        in the World War in Italy and the World War. Page's account
        is written with considerable sympathy for Italy.

    2   ANON. "Italy and the War." Times Literary Supplement
            (24 March), p. 188.
            Page was quite right in devoting a good part of Italy
        and the World War to the history of Italy, for the histori-
        cal context throws much light on Italy's struggles with

1921

the "Central Powers." Page, moreover, has considerable
sympathy for the Italian people. His attempt, however, to
glorify the Italian people may ultimately prove a disser-
vice to them.

3   ANON. "Page, Thomas Nelson. Italy and the World War."
     American Library Association Booklist, 17 (January), 149.
         Italy and the World War is a "first-hand, sympathetic
     study of Italy's motives and conduct."

4   McFEE, WILLIAM. "Ambassadorial Style." New York Evening Post
     (29 January), part 3, p. 4.
         Italy and the World War reveals little about the subject
     matter that one could not gain from the newspapers and an
     atlas. The "genius" underlying Tommy Trot's Visit to Santa
     Claus is not present in this new work. Page's style is
     marked by "ambiguous syntax and inaccurate allusions."

1922 A BOOKS - NONE

1922 B SHORTER WRITINGS

1   ANON. "Admiring Dante." Springfield Republican
     (19 November), p. 7a.
         Dante and His Influence is a "decided disappointment."
     The work is a combination of "quoted criticism, personal
     reminiscence and glorification of Italy."

2   ANON. "Brief Book Notes." The Independent, 109
     (11 November), 283-84.
         Dante and His Influence contains nine lectures originally
     delivered at the University of Virginia.

3   ANON. "Thomas Nelson Page." The American Magazine of Art,
     13 (December), 548.
         In every way a "Christian gentleman" Page was a strong
     supporter of the American Federation of Arts. His "pic-
     turesque" writings were marked by appealing "sentiment"
     and "artistic feeling."

4   ANON. "Thomas Nelson Page." The Outlook, 132 (15 November),
     468-69.
         Page's Italy and the World War contained "restraint, a
     high sense of loyalty, and a passion for fairness." Page's
     novels like Gordon Keith and Red Rock did not have the ap-
     peal of his antebellum stories like "Marse Chan," "Unc'
     Edinburg's Drowndin'," or "Meh Lady." A significant

strength in Page's stories was his natural use of Negro
dialect.

5   CHEW, SAMUEL C. "Two Studies of Dante." The Nation, 115
    (20 December), 695.
        Despite Page's social and political prominence and de-
    spite his many public lectures, university students deserve
    a better book than Page's loose "'appreciation,'" Dante and
    His Influence.

6   HUBBELL, JAY BROADUS. Virginia Life in Fiction. New York:
    New York Public Library, pp. 27-29.
        Page is a novelist of "the old régime." Page's success
    was owed to his ability to express "the spirit of the old
    South." His choice of setting coincided with prevailing
    popular taste for local color stories.

1923 A   BOOKS

1   PAGE, ROSEWELL. Thomas Nelson Page: A Memoir of a Virginia
    Gentleman. New York: Charles Scribner's Sons, 210 pp.
        The thesis for this study is that "few men ever had a
    fuller or happier life than Thomas Nelson Page." The bi-
    ographer Rosewell Page was brother to the subject. The
    study begins with an exploration of Page's ancestry, which
    includes a citation of the family's contributions to Ameri-
    can life. "Oakland Plantation" is described. A number of
    sources for the settings in Page's fiction are discussed,
    and Page's childhood contacts with Civil War battle scenes
    are presented. Considerable attention is devoted to anec-
    dotes revealing the formation of Page's character and the
    nature of his education. Particular attention is paid to
    Page's university days and the years during which he prac-
    ticed law in Richmond. Rosewell Page's exploration of the
    literary genesis of his brother includes a discussion of
    "Unc' Gabe's White Folks" and "Marse Chan." A discussion
    of Page's short stories includes references to "Marse Chan"
    and "Meh Lady." Some attention is devoted to Page's ex-
    periences abroad, his career as lecturer, his time spent in
    Washington, his friendships with well-known men and women,
    and his relationships with Negroes. The biographer dis-
    cusses Page's method of composition, his love of good
    writing, and his attention to revision.

1923

1923 B SHORTER WRITINGS

1 ALDERMAN, EDWIN ANDERSON. "A Personal Reminiscence." The
      University of Virginia Alumni Bulletin, 16 (January), 1-3.
         In this personal tribute to the memory of Page, Alderman
      alludes to "Marse Chan" and the "new comprehension of the
      old life of the South" it seemed to offer readers.

2 ANON. "Page, Thomas Nelson." The Booklist, 19 (January), 115.
         Dante and His Influence is written from the "standpoint
      of an enthusiastic admirer rather than of an unemotional
      critic."

3 ANON. "Recent Books in Brief Review." The Bookman, 56
      (February), 770.
         Page's admiration for Dante in Dante and His Influence
      is strong. The work contains "enthusiasm supported by
      scholarly research."

4 ANON. "Thomas Nelson Page." The Journal of the National
      Education Association, 12 (February), 59.
         According to this obituary, Page's "Unc' Edinburg's
      Drowndin'," "Meh Lady," etc., attracted little attention
      until placed in In Ole Virginia. Page, like Craddock and
      Harte, sought to create "a new type of dialect literature."
      No one has equalled Page's idealistic treatment of planta-
      tion life. Although Red Rock and Two Little Confederates
      achieved "distinction," Page is not as adept at characteri-
      zation in his novels as he is in his shorter fiction.

5 ANON. "With the Makers of Books in America. II. The House
      of Scribner." The Literary Digest International Book
      Review, 1 (June), 51.
         Page's fiction is representative of the type published
      by Charles Scribner's Sons.

6 FULLER, HENRY B. "Thomas Nelson Page." The Freeman, 7
      (18 July), 450-52.
         In this review of Rosewell Page's Thomas Nelson Page,
      Fuller discusses with some thoroughness the implications of
      the term gentleman and Page's role as ambassador to Italy.
      Page's major contribution to American life, however, was
      his attempt at reconciliation of North and South.

7 GORDON, ARMISTEAD C. "Thomas Nelson Page: An Appreciation."
      Scribner's Magazine, 73 (January), 75-90.
         Page was the product of both heredity and environment.
      His first published prose piece "Old Yorktown" contains the

romance marking his later career. "Marse Chan" was renowned for its "charm of sentiment and fidelity to nature."
Page's "devotion to his state was a part of his larger love
for America and of a catholicity of spirit that was more
than cosmopolitan."

8 ____. "Thomas Nelson Page: An Appreciation." The University
of Virginia Alumni Bulletin, 16 (January), 10-19.
Reprint of 1923.B7.

9 ____. Virginian Writers of Fugitive Verse. New York:
James T. White & Co., pp. 115, 127, 335.
According to Thomas Nelson Page, the South stood for
three things in 1861: "'devotion to duty, the sense of
honor, and a passion for free government.'" Page's best
poetry includes Befo' de War, The Coast of Bohemia, "The
Vision of Raleigh," and "At Pilot's Judgment Seat."

10 HANEY, JOHN LOUIS. The Story of Our Literature. New York:
Charles Scribner's Sons, pp. 179-80, 362.
Page was probably the best of the American writers to
try to depict Negro character. Consequently, In Ole Virginia is his best collection. Page's view of plantation
life was "idealized."

11 JOHNSON, ROBERT UNDERWOOD. Remembered Yesterdays. Boston:
Little, Brown and Company, pp. 121-22, 406, 513.
"Marse Chan" was "one of the very best negro-dialect
stories ever written" and a veritable boon to the publishers. It was Johnson who suggested the motif of "Meh Lady"
to Page (it is from Lessing's "Minna von Barnheim"). The
hero and heroine of that piece are Prussian and Saxon, and
their marriage serves the cause of national unification.

12 METCALF, JOHN CALVIN. "Thomas Nelson Page, Man of Letters."
The University of Virginia Alumni Bulletin, 16 (January),
20-26.
Early Page stories collected into In Ole Virginia present "the loyal attachment of the negro to his master and
his family in reverses which the tragic fortunes of war had
brought to them." The faithful Black retainer is "the real
hero" in the best of such stories. It was in these early
"dramatic monologues" that Page found his true "métier":
the manners of antebellum Southern society. Two Little
Confederates, Elsket, Among the Camps, and Pastime Stories
are "sketchy studies" which do not equal in quality the
stories in In Ole Virginia. Red Rock is an "uneven book,
more artistic in the earlier chapters than in the middle

1923

and end." There is a "dual motif" in Page's books--"a looking backward toward a romantic past whose crimson sunset had caught him in its gorgeous afterglow; and a looking forward with confidence to complete national unity and, as his latest writings show, international good will formally organized."

13 PATTEE, FRED LEWIS. The Development of the American Short Story: An Historical Survey. New York and London: Harper Brothers, pp. 170, 269, 284-86.
    Page's early stories--"Marse Chan," "Unc' Edinburg's Drowndin'," "Meh Lady," and "Polly"--were written "painstakingly and feelingly" and were never equalled by his later works. Emphasis on heredity is obvious in Page's works. His greatest strength, however, is his point of view, his use of the "negro survivors of the tragedy." In this sense "Marse Chan" is one of the "great American short stories."

14 THORNTON, WILLIAM MYNN. "Thomas Nelson Page." The University of Virginia Alumni Bulletin, 16 (January), 4-9.
    Pathetic figures like the narrator of "Marse Chan" were born from the "treasury of a child's legends of loveliness, a boy's dream of romance." The Italian period in Page's life bore fruit in Italy and the World War and Dante and His Influence.

15 TOOKER, L. FRANK. The Joys and Tribulations of an Editor. New York: The Century Company, pp. 202-03.
    "Marse Chan" received instant praise from the reading public. It was a "conventional, sentimental tale of the old South, with the typical family feud as the one serpent in that Garden of Eden." "Meh Lady" was a "monologue in Negro dialect."

16 TREE, RONALD. "Thomas Nelson Page." The Forum, 69 (January), 1137-42.
    An account of Page's service to Italy and his sometimes troubled relationship with President Wilson.

17 WILSON, JAMES SOUTHALL. "'In Ole Virginia' With Thomas Nelson Page." The University of Virginia Alumni Bulletin, 16 (January), 27-35.
    "The spirit of old Virginia" lives on in the romances of Page, a writer who was "never a realistic seeker after 'local color.'"

1924 A   BOOKS - NONE

1924 B   SHORTER WRITINGS

1   ANON. "The New Books." The Outlook, 138 (5 November) 376-80.
         The posthumously published The Red Riders contains the
         usual Page Negro dialect, and the Reconstruction scenes are
         "painful but true."

2   ANON. "Posthumous Work of Thomas Nelson Page." New York Times
         Review of Books (21 September), part 3, p. 8.
         The Red Riders is "not as good as the early work of
         Thomas Nelson Page." Despite its "temperate tone" the novel
         suffers from diffuseness.

3   ANON. "Shorter Notices." The New Statesman (22 March),
         710-14.
         Page's account of the origins of Washington, its history,
         and social life in Washington and Its Romance is "well
         told."

4   ANON. "Uninspired." New York Herald Tribune (14 December),
         p. 11.
         The posthumous publication of The Red Riders will add
         nothing of value to Page's reputation. Although "smoothly
         moving" and "straightforward," the new novel is "uninspired."

5   ANON. "Washington and Its Romance." Times Literary Supplement
         (21 February), p. 114.
         Page speaks "enthusiastically" in this new work. The
         work is typical of Page's "bent towards historical, social,
         and topographical studies."

6   BALDWIN, CHARLES C. The Men Who Make Our Novels. New York:
         Dodd, Mead and Company, 1924, pp. 415-18.
         Page seemed to believe that "good things grew on trees,"
         that the good in life would be rewarded. He regarded the
         end of the old order a tragedy. Although "Marse Chan,"
         Page's first work, was "sentimental and silly," it had an
         interesting source. The story marked the beginning of a
         literary career in which there was very little artistic
         growth.

7   BECKWITH, E. C. "A Red Ku Klux." Literary Review of New York
         Evening Post (27 September), p. 14.
         The inappropriateness of style towards the end of The
         Red Riders is apparently owed to Rosewell Page who completed
         and published his brother's manuscript after the famous

author's death. Employing a "direct surface narrative of
the simplest kind," the novel is apparently meant for adol-
escent readers and is replete with "black mammies, vener-
able, proud Southern colonels, despicable conniving scala-
wags and other fictional relics."

8   FULLER, HENRY C. "The Old Order." The Saturday Review, 1
    (4 October), 160.
        Page seeks in The Red Riders to help bring an end to
    "the wounds of civil strife." Although his brief portrait
    of Lincoln matches the national image, the villain
    "'Grease'" seems unfinished. The work should perhaps be
    remembered more as "historical documentation" than as a
    novel.

9   GAINES, CLARENCE H. "Some Philosophers in Fiction." The
    North American Review, 220 (December), 375-84.
        The Red Riders is "sweet in spirit--not lacking in humor,
    just and sincere, with no undue attachment to the old or-
    der." Page, nonetheless, fails in the novel to write a
    "stirring narrative."

10 GAINES, FRANCIS PENDLETON. The Southern Plantation: A Study
    in the Development and the Accuracy of a Tradition.
    New York: Columbia University Press, pp. 77-78.
        Page contributed works to the plantation tradition which
    were "considerable in quantity and marked by high artistic
    ability." Unlike other plantation writers, he gave the
    "supreme glorification of the old regime." "Unc' Edin-
    burg's Drowndin'," for example, contains "all the signifi-
    cant elements of the social rapture which marked the old
    epoch." His greatest contribution to the plantation tradi-
    tion is the portrayal of racial harmony. Page's linking of
    master and slave "softens the inevitable hardship of
    slavery."

11 GORDON, ARMISTEAD CHURCHILL. Virginian Portraits: Essays in
    Biography. Staunton, Virginia: McClure Company, p. 125.
        Page's life and character were, in large part, the re-
    sult of his aristocratic heredity and environment. Gordon
    points out a number of biographical influences on Page's
    work.

1925 A BOOKS - NONE

1925 B SHORTER WRITINGS

1   D. L. M. "The Red Riders of the South: A Posthumous Novel by
    Thomas Nelson Page." Boston Evening Transcript (3 January),
    p. 5.
        It is quite appropriate that The Red Riders, Page's last
    novel, should be set in the South. Page would undoubtedly
    admit that the Ashleys represent Southerners "at their very
    best." The novel "mirrors the romance of the South at its
    best."

2   JACOBS, ELIZABETH McDOWELL. "The Red Riders." The Literary
    Digest International Book Review, 3 (January), 140.
        The Red Riders, although set in South Carolina, is quite
    similar to Page's many works about Virginia life. The post-
    humously published novel contains "accuracy of description
    and anecdote," much history, and a sympathy for both North
    and South. The novel, although lacking the sentiment of
    "Marse Chan," contains realism and the "atmosphere of the
    old South."

3   JOHNSON, ROBERT UNDERWOOD, BLISS PERRY, and CHARLES A. PLATT.
    Commemorative Tributes to Page, Wilson, and Bacon.
    New York: American Academy of Arts and Letters, pp. 1-10.
        It was Mrs. Sophie Bledsoe Herrick at Scribner's Monthly
    who enthusiastically forwarded the manuscript of "Marse
    Chan" to Robert Underwood Johnson. Redundancy was the only
    weakness of the story, which proved to be one of the best
    of postbellum short fiction. "Marse Chan" is typical of
    Page in two ways. First, the work, in taking up "sectional
    prejudices," has "generous candor." Secondly, Page's atti-
    tude towards women borders on chivalry, for he displays
    love as "principle" and not as "passion." "Meh Lady" under-
    takes the "reconciliation of prejudiced foes." As a spokes-
    man, Page in this selection seems an "exponent of Virginia
    aristocracy turned democrat." His works in general display
    "homogeneity rather than diversity, but they never fail of
    ease or charm of atmosphere." Italy and the World War is
    a "tour de force of narrative--comprehensive, temperate,
    judicial, well-balanced. . . ."

4   QUINN, ARTHUR HOBSON. "Passing of a Literary Era." The
    Saturday Review, 1 (21 March), 609-10.
        The deaths of G. W. Cable and James Lane Allen coming
    so soon after that of Page mark the end of "one of the most
    significant chapters in our literary history." Page as

1925

artist represented the "patrician striving to be the demo-
crat," the appeal of his stories being in his "artistic
handling of the theme of loyalty" as in "Marse Chan" or
"Little Darby."

1926 A BOOKS - NONE

1926 B SHORTER WRITINGS

1   MIMS, EDWIN. The Advancing South: Stories of Progress and
    Reaction. Garden City, New York: Doubleday, Page &
    Company, pp. 23-27, 202, 218.
       Page was a romantic who saw antebellum life as a "golden
    age."

2   PAGE, ROSEWELL. Hanover County: Its History and Legends.
    Richmond: Rosewell Page, pp. 117, 130.
       Page was "a regular practicioner at the Hanover Bar un-
    til his literary works overshadowed his fine gifts as a
    lawyer." "Oakland Plantation" was the scene for Two Little
    Confederates. Although "Oakland" was located near Helltown,
    publishers insisted that Page substitute Hall-town for
    Helltown.

1927 A BOOKS

1   McFADIN, MAUDE A. "Thomas Nelson Page As A Short Story
    Writer." M.A. thesis, University of Kansas.
       In his antebellum stories ("Marse Chan," "Meh Lady,"
    "Unc' Edinburg's Drowndin'," "The Long Hillside, A Christ-
    mas Hare-Hunt in Old Virginia," and "George Washington's
    Last Duel"), Page created nine character types, writing
    almost exclusively of two classes--aristocrats and slaves.
    In his Reconstruction short fiction (Two Little Confeder-
    ates, "The Old Planters," "How the Captain Made Christmas,"
    "The Christmas Peace," "Gray Jacket of 'No 4'," "Miss
    Goodwin's Inheritance," "Leander's Light," "Run to Seed,"
    "The New Agent," "Bred in the Bone," "The Trick Doctor,"
    "A Story of Charlie Harris," "Mam Lyddy's Recognition,"
    "How Andrew Carried the Precinct," "Old 'Stracted," and
    "The Spectre in the Cart"), Page's characters are "victim-
    ized, dethroned." Page's legal experience, his residency
    in Washington, and his foreign travel furnished him with
    materials for fiction dealing with "law and the courts,
    humorous stories of Negroes and mules, stories of foreign
    lands, stories of successful people, and stories of the
    'spirit.'"

118

1927 B   SHORTER WRITINGS

1   DOWD, JEROME. <u>The Negro in American Life</u>. New York: Century
Company, p. 285.
Page is the "outstanding literary exponent" of the Virginia Negro; he provides an "account of the patriarchal
character of slavery in Virginia."

2   HAZARD, LUCY LOCKWOOD. <u>The Frontier in American Literature</u>.
New York: Thomas Crowell Company, pp. 73, 74, 85.
Page and others "dwelt lovingly on the gentle and pathetic figure of the Civil War Colonel" and the panorama of
the passing of an old order. His Old Virginia is comprised
of "reverently preserved if somewhat stiffly posed daguer-
rotypes."

1928 A   BOOKS - NONE

1928 B   SHORTER WRITINGS

1   HAWKINS, SIR ANTHONY HOPE. <u>Memories and Notes</u>. Garden City:
Doubleday, Doran and Company, p. 209.
Hawkins first met Theodore Roosevelt at Page's home.

1929 A   BOOKS - NONE

1929 B   SHORTER WRITINGS

1   JOHNSON, MERLE. <u>American First Editions: Bibliographic Check
Lists of the Works of One Hundred and Five American Authors</u>.
New York: R. R. Bowker Company, pp. 404-07.
Lists first editions of Page's works. Page is a member
of the "southern school of writers;" his major volume was
<u>In Ole Virginia</u>.

2   LEISY, ERNEST ERWIN. <u>American Literature: An Interpretive
Survey</u>. New York: Thomas Y. Crowell Company, p. 185.
<u>In Ole Virginia</u> was "a group of artistic tales, told by
a negro slave, to show how loyal such persons had been. . . ."

1930

1930 A   BOOKS - NONE

1930 B   SHORTER WRITINGS

   1   PATTEE, FRED LEWIS. The New American Literature: 1890-1930.
        New York: The Century Company, p. 255.
           Page's fiction presented "Cavalier chivalry completely
        destroyed by the war, blooded aristocracy like Old World
        nobility forever gone."

   2   RICHARDSON, EUDORA RAMSAY. "The South Grows Up." The Bookman,
        70 (January), 545-50.
           Page, "in the delightful inanity of his singing optimism,"
        presented pictures of a Southern life that never really
        existed.

1931 A   BOOKS

   1   DAVIS, MARY MOORE. "Children in Thomas Nelson Page's Stories
        of Children." M.A. thesis, George Peabody College for
        Teachers.
           An examination of seven Page stories concerning children:
        "Two Little Confederates," "A Captured Santa Claus,"
        "Kittykin and the Part She Played in the War," "Nancy
        Pansy," "Jack and Jake," "Tommy Trot's Visit to Santa
        Claus," "Santa Claus's Partner," "The Long Hillside," and
        "Two Prisoners." Chapter one concerns the occupations and
        pastimes of Page's child characters. Chapter two deals
        with the "character of the children--how they act, whether
        fearlessly or timorously; whether they show love or hate;
        and what other characteristics they display in definite
        situations." Chapter three deals with the rapport children
        have with the adult world. The thesis concludes that many
        of Page's own experiences as a child were used in some of
        his stories about children.

   2   MOORE, EVA LURA. "Two Virginia Regionalists: A Comparison
        of the Materials and Methods of Thomas Nelson Page and
        Ellen Glasgow." M.A. thesis, University of Missouri.
           Page's depiction of Virginia is romantic, Miss Glasgow's
        realistic. Points of comparison include use of materials
        available to the two authors and their manner of presenta-
        tion. The opening chapters discuss the kinds of materials
        available to Virginia regionalists (geography, native char-
        acter, social classes, and racial elements) and a brief
        history of Virginia as that history relates to the charac-
        ter of Virginians. References to Page works include: Two

Little Confederates, In Ole Virginia, Elsket, The Burial of
the Guns, Bred in the Bone, On Newfound River, The Old
Gentleman of the Black Stock, Red Rock, Gordon Keith, and
John Marvel, Assistant.

1931 B SHORTER WRITINGS

1 HEXMAN, DAVE. "Thomas Nelson Page, American Ambassador to
   Italy, One of Most Popular Writers South Has Ever Produced."
   Richmond Times-Dispatch (3 May), p. 5.
      Page was instrumental in creating the plantation tradi-
   tion in writing. His dialect poetry is "particularly
   striking," his subjects "natural and interesting."

1932 A BOOKS

1 HOWARD, HELEN EUGENE. "The Negro in the Fiction of Thomas
   Nelson Page." M.A. thesis, George Peabody College for
   Teachers.
      An examination of sixteen Page works which include the
   Negro. Treats in part the "change which took place in the
   negro's attitude toward the white people during the ante-
   bellum, the Reconstruction and the post-Reconstruction
   periods." The Negro, moreover, is analyzed both socio-
   logically and racially as he appears in Page fiction.
   References include On Newfound River; Red Rock; The Red
   Riders; The Old Gentleman of the Black Stock; Gordon Keith;
   John Marvel, Assistant; Two Little Confederates; Two
   Prisoners; Among the Camps; Bred in the Bone; Elsket; In
   Ole Virginia; Pastime Stories; The Burial of the Guns; The
   Land of the Spirit; and Under the Crust.

1932 B SHORTER WRITINGS

1 DABNEY, VIRGINIUS. Liberalism in the South. Chapel Hill:
   The University of North Carolina Press, pp. 104-05, 223,
   380.
      Page's works are "compounded wholly of the traditional
   moonlight and magnolias."

2 KNIGHT, GRANT C. American Literature and Culture. New York:
   Ray Long and Richard R. Smith, Inc., p. 349.
      Page is largely responsible for the public's romantic
   view of Virginia life. He seemed to hold that the aristocracy tended to beget noble character.

1933

1933 A BOOKS

1   ABERNATHY, ROBERT. "The Southern Planter Portrayed in Fiction
     of Thomas Nelson Page." M.A. thesis, George Peabody College
     for Teachers.
          A study of the concept of "Southern planter" as evinced
     in Gordon Keith; John Marvel, Assistant; The Old Gentleman
     of the Black Stock; On Newfound River; The Red Riders; Red
     Rock; Two Little Confederates; Two Prisoners; Among the
     Camps; Bred in the Bone; The Burial of the Guns; Elsket;
     The Land of the Spirit; In Ole Virginia; and Pastime
     Stories. The study is comprised of "a careful collecting
     of every reference to the occupations, homes, religion, edu-
     cation, and recreation of the planter." On the basis of
     materials examined, Abernathy concludes that Page was
     familiar with the life of the Southern planter and that
     many of the events in his own life underlay his fiction.
     Page, moreover, presented his planter amidst three major
     periods of Southern history: antebellum, Civil War, and
     Reconstruction. The antebellum fiction reveals an ideal
     planter life style, and the Civil War fiction reveals a
     period of decay that is very nearly total in the Reconstruc-
     tion fiction.

2   ALLBRITTEN, GERALDINE. "The Conception of the Southern
     Aristocracy in the Fiction of Thomas Nelson Page." M.A.
     thesis, University of Kansas.
          Attempts to explain why Page viewed the South the way
     he did. Page was a firm believer in the gentleman's "code
     of honor." His concept of the Southern lady was equally
     rooted in moral idealism. He attempted, moreover, to be
     "realistic" in his presentation of master-slave relation-
     ships. In general, he saw the South as "unique as it was
     distinct, the joint product of chivalry and Christianity."
     Discussions include In Ole Virginia, Two Little Confeder-
     ates, The Old Gentleman of the Black Stock, Among the Camps,
     On Newfound River, Elsket and Other Stories, Bred in the
     Bone, The Land of the Spirit, Gordon Keith, The Burial of
     the Guns, and Red Rock.

3   BRIDGERS, FRANK ERNST, JR. "Thomas Nelson Page's Treatment of
     Southern Plantation Life." M.A. thesis, Duke University.
          The opening chapter is devoted to a sketch of Page's
     life.
          Chapter two is devoted to the plantation home or great
     house as it appeared before and after the Civil War. Al-
     though Page sometimes refers to other types of houses, such
     reference serves merely to emphasize the "significance" of

the manor house. Social life on the plantation is also
analyzed.

Chapter three is an analysis of Page's Southern white
plantation types amidst antebellum, war, and postbellum
times. The types include "master, mistress, old master,
old mistress, young mistress, young master, aunts, cousins,
and friends." Other types make their appearance in Red Rock
and Gordon Keith.

Chapter four is devoted to Page's creation of black plantation types--the mammy, the butler, the carriage-driver,
gardeners, personal maids, and the body servant. Black
plantation types are analyzed in terms of Page's antebellum,
war, and Reconstruction works. References include Two
Little Confederates, In Ole Virginia, The Burial of the
Guns, Pastime Stories, On Newfound River, The Red Riders,
The Old South, Befo' De War, and John Marvel, Assistant.

4   RANDALL, HELEN LESLIE. "Thomas Nelson Page and Ellen Glasgow
     as Interpreters of Southern Women." M.A. thesis, State
     University of Iowa.

     "The scope and strength of Miss Glasgow's work can be
shown better by comparing her writings with those of Thomas
Nelson Page, an exponent of the more traditional manner of
dealing with the Southern woman in fictional literature."
Glasgow, moreover, has more nearly approached doing justice
to the Southern woman than has Page because of the "wider
range of types in her stories and because of her more realistic portrayal." Although major attention in this thesis
is devoted to Glasgow, references are made to Social Life
in Old Virginia Before the War, Gordon Keith, Red Rock,
"Marse Chan," "Unc' Edinburg's Drowndin'," and John Marvel,
Assistant. In general, Page seems to have viewed the Southern female as "southern gentlewoman," an idealistic view
owed to the "circumscribed limits of the romantic tradition."

1933 B SHORTER WRITINGS - NONE

1935 A BOOKS - NONE

1935 B SHORTER WRITINGS

1   KNIGHT, GRANT C. James Lane Allen and the Genteel Tradition.
     Chapel Hill: The University of North Carolina Press,
     pp. 49, 86, 94, 149, 196.

     Allen was perhaps aware of the kind of attention being
given by magazines to local colorists like Page.

THREE VIRGINIA WRITERS

1936

1936 A BOOKS

1   SMITH, MRS. L. H. (MARY POPE SAUNDERS). "Thomas Nelson Page:
     The Literary Interpreter of Ole Virginia (1850-1880)."
     M.S. thesis, Alabama Polytechnic Institute.
        Page became the primary literary spokesman of the South
     during its antebellum, Civil War, and Reconstruction peri-
     ods. Page's concept of life in these eras is most clearly
     delineated in The Old South, Two Little Confederates, In
     Ole Virginia, and Red Rock. As social historian Page "did
     what he urged others to do--recorded in literary form the
     history of Southern life and times." Page's best view of
     antebellum life is found in his volume of essays The Old
     South. An examination of this volume provides insight into
     antebellum mansions, gardens, class distinctions, recrea-
     tion, labor, and social life. The best view of the Civil
     War is found in Page's Two Little Confederates. Red Rock
     is the "most typical" of Page's novels to deal with Recon-
     struction life. An examination of this volume provides in-
     sight into Reconstruction "community gatherings," black-
     white relationships, etc. Page's Negro "lived for his mas-
     ter and for his master's family with no thought of self or
     family. He was loyal, devoted, sympathetic. . . ." The
     concept of the Negro is examined in "Meh Lady," "Unc' Edin-
     burg's Drowndin'," and "Marse Chan." The dialect of Joel
     Chandler Harris' Negro characters is contrasted with that
     of Page's.

1936 B SHORTER WRITINGS

1   FULLERTON, B[RADFORD] M[ORTON]. Selective Bibliography of
     American Literature 1775-1900. New York: Dial Press,
     p. 211.
        A brief sketch of Page's origin and development. Page
     is "the most idealistic and at the same time the most ar-
     tistic portrayer of the 'Old Régime.'" Three Page works
     are cited in the bibliography.

2   QUINN, ARTHUR HOBSON. American Fiction: An Historical and
     Critical Survey. New York: Appleton-Century-Crofts, Inc.,
     pp. 321, 357-62, 372, 379, 381-82, 494, 507.
        Page was to Virginia as George Washington Cable was to
     Louisiana. A keynote in Page's fiction is the "fidelity of
     a Negro to his master" as in "Unc' Gabe's White Folks" and
     "Marse Chan." The general appeal of In Ole Virginia is en-
     hanced by the dialect. A favorite Page theme is the "per-
     sistence of hereditary characteristics" as in "Little

124

Darby," "Bred in the Bone," and "Run to Seed." Reference
is made to the source of "Marse Chan." The strongest quality of Page's fiction is always the effect that it achieves.
On Newfound River is a "Montague-Capulet story of Virginia
before the War." Red Rock, a much better novel, deals with
events of the Reconstruction era. The Old Gentleman of the
Black Stock is based on "a profound reality." Gordon Keith
presents a comparison of a Southerner and a Northern
"parvenu."

1937 A   BOOKS - NONE

1937 B   SHORTER WRITINGS

1   BRODIN, PIERRE. Le Roman Régionaliste Américain. Paris:
     G. P. Maisonneuve, p. 97.
        Page's works are best known for their presentation of
     the atmosphere of antebellum Virginia life, an atmosphere
     treated humorously by F. Hopkinson Smith in Colonel Carter
     of Cartersville (1891).

2   BUCK, PAUL H. The Road to Reunion: 1865-1900. Boston:
     Little, Brown and Company, p. 224.
        In Ole Virginia placed Page at the head of those who
     "painted the mellowed tradition of the plantation." Page's
     Negroes were used "primarily as accessories to heighten the
     effect of pathos emanating from the departed grandeur of
     plantation days."

3   HARRINGTON, F. H. "Literary Aspects of American Anti-
     Imperialism." New England Quarterly, 10 (December), 650-67.
        Page was one of the "exponents" in American history of
     the "'manifest destiny'" theory, a position that accorded
     with the notion of the "'white man's burden.'"

1938 A   BOOKS - NONE

1938 B   SHORTER WRITINGS

1   "Page, Thomas Nelson," in American Authors 1600-1900. Edited
     by Stanley J. Kunitz and Howard Haycroft. New York: The
     H. W. Wilson Company, pp. 587-88.
        An account of Page's birth, ancestry and political dis-
     tinctions. Page was a "typical Virginia aristocrat of the
     old school" who saw antebellum Virginia as a "paradise of
     benevolent feudalism." His greatest strength was his ren-
     dition of dialect.

THREE VIRGINIA WRITERS

1938

2   PURCELL, JAMES SLICER, JR. "The Southern Poor White in
      Fiction." M.A. thesis, Duke University, pp. 99-102.
          Page's "Little Darby" holds a significant place in the
      development of the Southern "poor white" in fiction. The
      story focuses on "two heroic characters, Vashti Mills and
      Little Darby," both Virginia poor whites and both exempli-
      fying considerable courage during the Civil War. Darby was
      the "Marse Chan of the poor whites."

1939 A BOOKS - NONE

1939 B SHORTER WRITINGS

1   BROWN, STERLING A. "The American Race Problem as Reflected in
      American Literature." Journal of Negro Education, 8
      (July), 275-90.
          Page is a major "glorifier" of the old Southern order.
      "In Ole Virginia is a plaintive cry for the lost heaven;
      Red Rock is a turgid description of the new hell."

2   McILWAINE, SHIELDS. The Southern Poor-White from Lubberland
      to Tobacco Road. Norman, Oklahoma: University of Oklahoma
      Press, pp. 76, 77, 79, 105, 106.
          Since the aristocracy was "the highest development of
      Southern culture," it was the first social stratum to be
      glorified by writers like Page.

1940 A BOOKS - NONE

1940 B SHORTER WRITINGS

1   LONG, FRANCIS TAYLOR. "The Life of Richard Malcolm Johnston
      in Maryland, 1867-1898. II. Some Literary Friendships--
      The Lecture Platform, 1882-1889." Maryland Historical
      Magazine, 35 (September), 270-86.
          Page and Richard Malcolm Johnston sought to arrange a
      lecture tour.

1941 A BOOKS - NONE

1941 B SHORTER WRITINGS

1   BANGS, FRANCIS HYDE. John Kendrick Bangs: Humorist of the
      Nineties; the Story of an American Editor--Author--Lecturer,
      and His Associations. New York: Alfred A. Knopf, pp. 114,
      119, 185, 190, 257.

126

For two years Page was "Conductor" of Harper's "The Editor's Drawer," his contributions being mostly Negro dialect sketches which were later collected into Pastime Stories.

2   CASH, W. J. The Mind of the South. New York: Alfred A. Knopf, Inc., pp. 130, 147, 333, 390.
    The legend of the Old South is "perfectly rendered" in Page's works.

3   WARFEL, HARRY R. and G. HARRISON ORIANS, eds. American Local-Color Stories. New York: American Book Company, p. 447.
    Negro slaves become the main spokesmen in Page's fiction. Since they are "almost exclusively house servants, [they] live only to serve the white people near them."

1943 A   BOOKS - NONE

1943 B   SHORTER WRITINGS

1   NELSON, JOHN HERBERT. "Page, Thomas Nelson," in Dictionary of American Biography. Edited by Dumas Malone. New York: Charles Scribner, vol. 14, pp. 141-42.
    "Marse Chan," Page's "dialect story," marked the beginning of his literary career. The majority of his fiction dealt with antebellum or postbellum Southern life. He was primarily a romancer of Southern "feudalistic splendor."

1944 A   BOOKS

1   CRAVER, SADIE B. "Thomas Nelson Page." M.A. thesis, Southern Methodist University.
    Page's ancestry, childhood, education, legal career in Richmond, marriages, and career as a diplomat are recounted. His views of antebellum Southern society in Red Rock, Two Little Confederates, Social Life in Old Virginia, On Newfound River, In Ole Virginia, and The Old Gentleman of the Black Stock are examined. His most notable children's works are Two Little Confederates and "Kittykin and the Part She Played in the War." The children in such works are generally idealistically drawn. Page's works often deal with social problems as in The Old South, Red Rock, "How Andrew Carried the Precinct," "Mam' Lyddy's Recognition," "The Spectre in the Cart," and John Marvel, Assistant.

1944 B   SHORTER WRITINGS - NONE

1945

<u>1945 A   BOOKS</u>

1   BITTINGER, MARY SHIRKEY. "The Historical Validity of
        Representative Short Stories of Thomas Nelson Page." M.A.
        thesis, Vanderbilt University.
            Page's fame is owed primarily to his success in short
        fiction. That success is, in turn, owed to strengths in
        presentation of Negro dialect and depiction of his native
        region. In <u>In Ole Virginia</u> he wrote of Virginia life and
        manners with "historical accuracy." Page, moreover, em-
        phasized the "chivalric relation which existed between the
        slave and the Southern planter's family in the idealized
        life before the war, during the days of poverty in war
        times, and in the years following Lee's surrender. . . ."
        His stories in <u>In Ole Virginia</u> involve "dramatic situations
        and interactions of characters which give room for subtle
        character analyses and delineations."

<u>1945 B   SHORTER WRITINGS</u>

1   BAKER, RAY STANNARD. <u>American Chronicle: The Autobiography</u>
        <u>of Ray Stannard Baker</u>. New York: Charles Scribner's Sons,
        pp. 153, 369, 370, 448.
            Baker mentions travelling from Rome to Paris in 1918
        with Page and Guglielmo Marconi. Baker was Ambassador
        Page's guest at "a jolly dinner . . . in the little hotel
        in the frontier town of Modane." Baker once again encoun-
        tered Page at Colonel House's "farewell conference."

2   BLACKFORD, W. W. <u>War Years with Jeb Stuart</u>. New York:
        Charles Scribner's Sons, p. 256.
            Blackford identifies the protagonist of "My Cousin
        Fanny" as Fanny Minor of "Edgewood," Hanover County,
        Virginia.

<u>1946 A   BOOKS - NONE</u>

<u>1946 B   SHORTER WRITINGS</u>

1   BURLINGAME, ROGER. <u>Of Making Many Books: A Hundred Years of</u>
        <u>Reading, Writing, and Publishing</u>. New York: Charles
        Scribner's Sons, pp. 52, 110, 111, 132, 211.
            Discusses Page's letter to Charles Scribner asking
        Scribner himself to check for a possible error in <u>Red Rock</u>.
        No matter how "fondly" one remembers the fiction of Page,
        one cannot view it as "serious literature."

Thomas Nelson Page: A Reference Guide

2   HOLMAN, HARRIET R. "A Letter from Henry W. Grady Regarding
    Southern Authors and the Piedmont Chautauqua." Georgia
    Historical Quarterly, 30 (December), 308-11.
        In his letter to Page, Henry W. Grady "enthusiastically
    explained" his plans for the building of the Piedmont Chau-
    tauqua, hoping that Page would be available for a reading
    or a lecture.

1947 A BOOKS

1   HOLMAN, HARRIET. The Literary Career of Thomas Nelson Page,
    1884-1910. Ph.D. dissertation, Duke University.
        Begins with a biographical account of Page's life. His
    success as lawyer, statesman, family man, and author "ac-
    complished major objectives on which he had set his heart.
    . . ." The fact that he was both "raconteur" and "South-
    erner" accounts for his becoming the writer he was. Page
    was fortunate in having a reading audience which had "a
    well-developed taste for local color. . . ." A large number
    of his stories had distinct sources--"Marse Chan," "Little
    Darby," and "Meh Lady," even the novel Red Rock. The novel
    Gordon Keith represents a departure from Page's plantation
    tradition in fiction.
        Miss Holman analyzes Page's use of the Negro in his fic-
    tion, and in nonfiction work like The Negro: The Southern-
    er's Problem. John Marvel, Assistant, his last novel, is
    a "grab-bag of most of the ideas which interested Page in
    the first decade of the century."
        In her critical estimate of his work, Miss Holman notes
    that Page believed that the writer should "present things
    as they ought to be. . . ." He consequently never wrote
    "'an impure line.'" In his own day he was seen as some-
    thing of an "idealist." His idealism tended to impel the
    removal of impurities from his realistic fiction. A favor-
    ite technique is the use of the old Negro servant as the
    raconteur of a narrative as in "Unc' Gabe's White Folks,"
    "Marse Chan," "Meh Lady," and "Unc' Edinburg's Drowndin'."
        The structure of Gordon Keith, on the other hand, is
    very weak, the novel essentially episodic. John Marvel is
    the result of "hasty composition, The Red Riders "a weak
    repetition of Red Rock." Two Little Confederates, accord-
    ing to Miss Holman, was Page's "most successful juvenile,
    the only one which remains readable today." Among the
    Camps was "written out of his imagination in the pattern of
    the priggish stories then foisted off on children."
        Page's poetry is of far less consequence than his fic-
    tion. He himself saw his poetry as "'frail'" and "'middling

1947

verse.'" Miss Holman concludes that Page was "more than
the defendant and historian of the Old South, looking always
to the past; but it was that work which he did most effectively, and it is that which will preserve his modest
measure of fame."

1947 B SHORTER WRITINGS

1   PAINE, GREGORY. Southern Prose Writers. Freeport, New York:
     American Book Company, pp. 305-07.
          Page's literary recognition began with "Marse Chan" and
     not with earlier works like "Uncle Gabe's White Folks" and
     "Old Yorktown." All of the stories collected into In Ole
     Virginia are drawn from life in Hanover County, Virginia.
     Red Rock is perhaps Page's best novel. His stories are ad-
     mired for "their vivid characterization, well-organized
     plots, and skillful use of Negro dialect." His "Negro
     stories" are comparable to those of Harris, while his de-
     piction of Virginia life stands in contrast to that of
     Ellen Glasgow. His view of antebellum plantation life is
     not "inaccurate" but is "incomplete and fragmentary."

1948 A BOOKS - NONE

1948 B SHORTER WRITINGS

1   COWIE, ALEXANDER. The Rise of the American Novel. New York:
     American Book Company, pp. 261, 472, 536, 592.
          Page's work is in the tradition of "Virginia novels
     grounded in picturesqueness and sentiment."

2   GLOSTER, HUGH M. Negro Voices in American Fiction. New York:
     Russell & Russell, Inc., pp. 7-10, 12, 23, 24, 25, 34, 35,
     38, 46-47, 54, 98, 99, 109, 252.
          Sees Page as the major spokesman for the plantation tra-
     dition in the novel. Page's gentlemen are idealistically
     drawn; the devotion of servants to their masters is ex-
     cessive. Gloster agrees with Francis Pendleton Gaines that
     Page wrote "'the epitaph of a civilization.'" Page saw the
     Negro as "simple, contented, comic, credulous, picturesque
     . . . gifted in singing, dancing, tale-telling, and re-
     uniting white lovers." He was also a "defender of the
     patriarchal South" and helped bring about many restrictions
     on Negroes. Page admired Booker T. Washington, and the
     black American poet Paul Laurence Dunbar followed in the
     plantation tradition created by Page.

3   VanAUKEN, SHELDON. "The Southern Historical Novel in the
    Early Twentieth Century." Journal of Southern History, 14,
    159-91.
        Red Rock was the "progenitor of many novels on Recon-
    struction." Gordon Keith presents the Southern gentleman
    as superior to the "Yankee parvenu."

1950 A BOOKS

1   BROWN, DOROTHY WARE. "The Negro Problem in the Fiction of
    Thomas Nelson Page, Joel Chandler Harris, and George Wash-
    ington Cable: 1880-1900." M.A. thesis, Texas Christian
    University.
        Page's major contribution to American literature lies
    within the plantation tradition. His background, education,
    and general lifestyle made him an ideal spokesman for the
    Old South. The most convincing manifestation of an Old
    South tradition in Page's fiction is his presentation of
    Negro servants who are loyal to their white masters before,
    during, and after the Civil War. Noteworthy are Old Sam,
    Unc' Edinburg, Ole Billy, and Ole 'Stracted.
        In contrast to the loyal servant is the "villainous
    Negro." Noteworthy here is the runaway slave in "No Haid
    Pawn." A departure from the plantation tradition is evi-
    dent in Page's use of the freed slave. Polly and Ephraim
    in "Ole 'Stracted" are good examples of freed blacks capable
    of adjusting to freedom.
        An examination of white attitudes towards blacks in
    Page's works reveals more of the plantation tradition.
    Most white masters, for example, are "loving and kind to
    their slaves." "Marse Chan" and "Polly" exemplify this
    attitude. The Old Gentleman of the Black Stock and Red
    Rock are also included in this study of Page's view of
    Negroes. The Negro: The Southerner's Problem is a culmin-
    ation of Page's attitude towards the Negro.

1950 B SHORTER WRITINGS - NONE

1951 A BOOKS - NONE

1951 B SHORTER WRITINGS

1   GOHDES, CLARENCE. "The Later Nineteenth Century," in The
    Literature of the American People. Edited by Arthur Hobson
    Quinn. New York: Appleton-Century-Crofts, Inc., pp. 638,
    652, 656, 657, 739.

1951

> The major significance of "Unc' Gabe's White Folks" is
> its use of materials which are "authentically American."
> *In Ole Virginia* portrays plantation life with "attractive
> excess." The "moonlight and magnolias" tradition so well
> exemplified by Page continued to attract later American
> writers.

1952 A BOOKS - NONE

1952 B SHORTER WRITINGS

1   WAGENKNECHT, EDWARD. *Cavalcade of the American Novel: From
     the Birth of the Nation to the Middle of the Twentieth
     Century*. New York: Holt, Rinehart and Winston, pp. 191-93.
     Page was a true Southern gentleman. His short stories
     like *In Ole Virginia* are admittedly indebted to George W.
     Bagby. *Red Rock*, Page's study of the Reconstruction era,
     was his most important novel. His second most important
     novel was *John Marvel, Assistant*, the characters of which
     seem "machine-made."

1953 A BOOKS - NONE

1953 B SHORTER WRITINGS

1   ANON. "Centennial Events Honor Writer of Southern Stories."
     Richmond *News Leader* (23 April), p. 56.
     Two Little Confederates remains one of Page's "most
     popular novels."

2   ANON. "Dr. Gaines Praises Work of Thomas Nelson Page."
     Richmond *Times-Dispatch* (24 April), p. 7.
     Dr. Francis Pendleton Gaines in his centennial address
     on Page states that Page "glorified and he veneered with
     sentiment an epoch of history that we have not yet examined
     with sincerity." Page, nonetheless, was gifted in recall-
     ing the mood and pageantry of a bygone era.

3   ANON. "Salute to a Southern Writer: Virginians Plan to Ob-
     serve Centennial of Page's Birth." Richmond *News Leader*
     (20 March), p. 13.
     Page's fame is owed primarily to his novels set in the
     Civil War and Reconstruction South.

4   BROOKS, VAN WYCK. *The Confident Years: 1885-1915*. New York:
     E. P. Dutton & Company, pp. 43-46, 49, 89, 230, 345, 347,
     348, 545, 546.

Page undertook to present to the world those traits
which he believed distinctively Southern. In Ole Virginia
presents Southerners yearning for their "lost régime." The
characters in Red Rock are somewhat "real."

5 FISHWICK, MARSHALL. "Virginia Honors Thomas Nelson Page in
    Centennial." Commonwealth, 20 (April), 39, 52.
        Page is remembered as "the writer who conveyed to the
    New South the glory and tradition of the Old South." Even
    "debunkers" have had to admit that he wrote with "sincerity
    and naturalness." His works after 1900 (viz. Gordon Keith
    and John Marvel) took on broader themes and settings.

6 PERRINI, ALBERTO. "Sinfonia americana: È la storia della
    nostra crudeltà? Della nostra miopia?" La Fiera Letteraria,
    8 (9 August), 4.
        Notes that George Nelson Page is from the same old and
    noble Virginia family that produced Thomas Nelson Page,
    American ambassador to Italy from 1913 to 1919.

7 RACHAL, WILLIAM M. E. "Some Letters of Thomas Nelson Page."
    Virginia Magazine of History and Biography, 61 (April),
    179-85.
        Includes a brief sketch of Page's literary evolution,
    noting that "publication of 'Marse Chan' in the Century
    Magazine started Page on his career as an author." The let-
    ters printed in the article are in the collection of the
    Virginia Historical Society.

8 SCRIBNER, ROBERT L. "'In Ole Virginia': Too Young to Defend
    the Old South With His Sword, Thomas Nelson Page Revived It
    With His Pen And So Gave Point to An Ancient Adage."
    Virginia Cavalcade, 3 (Summer), 4-9.
        Includes a largely biographical tribute and notes the
    initial public reaction to "Marse Chan," Page's tendency
    towards realism, and his similarity to Sir Walter Scott.

1954 A   BOOKS - NONE

1954 B   SHORTER WRITINGS

1 HUBBELL, JAY B. The South in American Literature: 1607-1900.
    Durham: Duke University Press, pp. 795-804.
        During the period of the New South, Page was the leading
    spokesman for the old order. It was in "Unc' Gabe's White
    Folks" that he discovered the mouthpiece for his later fic-
    tion. His stories employ a number of recurrent themes.

1954

His novel Red Rock is something of a failure. Gordon Keith,
although a popular success, elicited considerable unfavor-
able comment. Page's reading habits at "Oakland" and his
dependency upon Northern editors and publishers for revi-
sions of his work are mentioned. To his Southern readers,
Page's "Marse Chan," "Meh Lady," and Red Rock were not only
entertaining stories but "historical documents" justifying
the plantation system.

2   LOGAN, RAYFORD W. The Negro in American Life and Thought: The
     Nadir: 1877-1901. New York: The Dial Press, pp. 162, 240,
     243, 244, 252-53, 261-62, 266, 268.
          Page "glorified the plantation tradition in Harper's
     more effusively than did any other writer." The plantation
     tradition is epitomized in "Ole 'Stracted" and "Unc' Edin-
     burg's Drowndin'."

1955 A BOOKS - NONE

1955 B SHORTER WRITINGS

1   SPILLER, ROBERT E. The Cycle of American Literature.
     New York: The Macmillan Company, pp. 87, 163.
          Page's romances are an expression of the Southern ideal,
     in which the Civil War signifies "the sad passing of an
     agrarian and aristocratic way of life."

1956 A BOOKS - NONE

1956 B SHORTER WRITINGS

1   COAN, OTIS W. and RICHARD G. LILLARD. America in Fiction:
     An Annotated List of Novels That Interpret Aspects of Life
     in the United States. Fourth edition. Stanford: Stanford
     University Press, pp. 49, 128, 168.
          Cites In Ole Virginia and Red Rock.

2   FISHWICK, MARSHALL W. The Virginia Tradition. Washington,
     D. C.: Public Affairs Press, pp. 6, 36, 90.
          Antebellum Virginia Negroes must have had tremendous de-
     sire for their freedom and "were far different from the
     Thomas Nelson Page stereotypes."

3   ROBERSON, JOHN R. "Two Virginia Novelists on Woman's Suffrage:
     An Exchange of Letters between Mary Johnston and Thomas
     Nelson Page." Virginia Magazine of History and Biography,
     64 (July), 286-90.

Mary Johnston, active in women's rights movements, wrote to Page to enlist his support for the rights of women.

4   TAYLOR, WALTER FULLER. The Story of American Letters. Chicago: Henry Regnery Company, p. 235.
         Page was to old Virginia as Bret Harte was to the far West.

1957 A   BOOKS - NONE

1957 B   SHORTER WRITINGS

1   LIVELY, ROBERT A. Fiction Fights the Civil War: An Unfinished Chapter in the Literary History of the American People. Chapel Hill: The University of North Carolina Press, pp. 42, 48, 53, 57, 60, 66, 68, 70, 101, 109, 130.
         Page's work is classed as "loving recollections." His Negro is "loyal during the war to his masters; shrewd, with the wisdom of a contented and rooted peasant; and carefree, happily confident in his security under the plantation system." Uncle Billy in "Meh Lady" is a good example of this concept. Page and other Southern writers discovered that "a culture which in its life was anathema to the North could in its death be honored."

2   ROBERSON, JOHN R. "The Manuscript of Page's 'Marse Chan.'" Studies in Bibliography, 9, 259-62.
         Roberson's collation of the Century Magazine, In Ole Virginia, and Plantation Edition printings of Page's "Marse Chan" reveals that "the editors of the Century made considerable revisions before the first publication, and that almost without exception Page let their changes stand when he brought out the story in book form." An account of the preparation of the manuscript of the story is included. Page's revisions and deletions are discussed.

1959 A   BOOKS - NONE

1959 B   SHORTER WRITINGS

1   COWAN, LOUISE. The Fugitive Group: A Literary History. Baton Rouge, Louisiana: Louisiana State University Press, p. 40.
         Page is a novelist of the Old South and regresses to the golden age of the past.

1959

2   FISHWICK, MARSHALL W.   "Civil War II."   <u>Texas Quarterly</u>, 2
(Summer), 109-18.
Page "saw the old régime in his most impressionable years
and idealized it all the rest of his life." "Before the
war" acquired a special meaning for him. In the tradition
of Russell, Cable and Harris, he pioneered as local color-
ist. As a chronicler of the Old South, he developed the
"'blood will tell'" formula. In a sense, in his view,
"character is determined by status." <u>In Ole Virginia</u> is
"pre-eminently the Virginia classic. Anyone who wants to
understand the working of the Virginia mind and the per-
sistence of certain attitudes into the twentieth century
should read it."

3   _____.   <u>Virginia: A New Look at the Old Dominion</u>.   New York:
Harper and Brothers, pp. 158, 216, 258, 266.
Page's poems extolled the virtues of slavery. His books
are "Virginian to the core." He equates character with
status, and his view of the poor white is an unflattering
one.

<u>1960 A   BOOKS - NONE</u>

<u>1960 B   SHORTER WRITINGS</u>

1   HUBBELL, JAY B.   <u>Southern Life in Fiction</u>.   Athens: University
of Georgia Press, pp. 56-57.
Emphasis upon heredity is strong in <u>Gordon Keith</u>. Page
used the same story in "Little Darby" that he had used in
"Marse Chan."

2   JOHNSON, GERALD W.   "To Live and Die in Dixie."   <u>The Atlantic
Monthly</u>, 206 (July), 29-34.
Page, like John Pendleton Kennedy, helped deceive the
South. <u>Red Rock</u>, for example, creates another Camelot.

3   TURNER, ARLIN, ed.   <u>Southern Stories</u>.   New York: Holt,
Rinehart and Winston, Inc., p. 137.
Page is preeminent among writers of the plantation tra-
dition. Characteristic stories like "Unc' Edinburg's
Drowndin'" employ a Negro spokesman who yearns for ante-
bellum life.

1961 A BOOKS - NONE

1961 B SHORTER WRITINGS

1 FISHWICK, MARSHALL W. <u>Gentlemen of Virginia</u>. New York: Dodd,
   Mead & Company, pp. 188, 210-26.
      Page's writing blossomed in the Old South despite the
   fact that he himself lived in the New South. His youth was
   the source of his writing, and dialect stories were his
   real forte. Like Lee, the man he most revered, Page hoped
   to reconcile North and South. He was sickened by the
   <u>nouveau riche</u> of the day. The gentlemen of the old order,
   on the other hand, were quite real to him. References to
   works include <u>Red Rock</u>, <u>Santa Claus's Partner</u>, <u>Gordon Keith</u>,
   and <u>John Marvel, Assistant</u>.

2 GROSS, THEODORE. "The Negro in the Literature of Reconstruction." <u>Phylon</u>, 22 (Spring), 5-14.
      Reconstruction Southern writers were more interested in
   propaganda than in art. There is an implied "racist note"
   in everything Page wrote. He was unable to understand and
   therefore unable to sympathize with freed Blacks. Novels
   like <u>Red Rock</u> and <u>The Red Riders</u> are consequently peopled
   by stereotypes.

3 GROSS, T. L. "Thomas Nelson Page: Creator of a Virginia
   Classic." <u>Georgia Review</u>, 20 (Fall), 338-51.
      Page is more often than not associated with the planta-
   tion tradition in literature. He was the father of a myth
   that recalled only those segments of antebellum life that
   he wished to remember. His portrayal of that myth in his
   fiction "persuaded a generation of readers of their author's
   accuracy." As a conservative Southern spokesman, Page
   sought the reconciliation of the North and the South.
      Page's significance today is of two sorts. For one, he
   is the creator of a number of stories which bring to life a
   vision of the Old South as it might have been. For another,
   he is "the most lucid and impressive chronicler of a myth
   of heroism that champions the Southern gentleman, the Southern lady, and inevitably the Southern way of life."
      Included in the article are discussions of Page's birth
   and education, "Marse Chan" and the Page myth, "Unc' Edinburg's Drowndin'," "Ole 'Stracted," "No Haid Pawn," and
   "Polly: A Christmas Recollection."

4 SOWDER, WILLIAM J. "Gerald W. Johnson, Thomas Nelson Page,
   and the South." <u>Mississippi Quarterly</u>, 14 (Fall), 197-203.

1961

Despite Gerald W. Johnson's thesis (See 1960.B2), Page "deplored sectional extremism." He even went so far as to place part of the blame for dissolution of the union on the "fire eating Cotton States" as in "Polly: A Christmas Recollection." Page, moreover, had little but "scorn for Southern rabble." In works like On Newfound River and "Meh Lady: A Story of the War" the "irresponsible aristocrat" is criticized. References are also made to Red Rock, Gordon Keith, and John Marvel.

5   TAYLOR, WILLIAM R. Cavalier and Yankee: The Old South and American National Character. New York: George Braziller, pp. 145, 157, 159, 162, 163, 307.
     Fictional treatments of plantation life tend to place the female at the head of the household, as she is in Page's stories.

1962 A   BOOKS - NONE

1962 B   SHORTER WRITINGS

1   SOWDER, WILLIAM J. "Thomas Nelson Page: The Bewildered Voice of a Reconstructed Rebel." High Point College Studies, 2 (Spring), 19-40.
     An account of how Page "came to reject the South and what this rejection cost him as a Southerner." In early works, like In Ole Virginia, for example, Page was "critical of early Southern culture." He treated "many of the themes that Faulkner has used: the irresponsibility of the Southern aristocracy, defects in the aristocratic code, the loyalty and endurance of the Negro, the interlocking fates of the Southern white and black man, and Southern antipathy toward Northern meddlesomeness." References are made to In Ole Virginia, Two Little Confederates, On Newfound River, Elsket and Other Stories, Among the Camps, The Old South, The Burial of the Guns, Pastime Stories, The Old Gentleman of the Black Stock, Social Life in Old Virginia, Red Rock, John Marvel, and The Land of the Spirit.

2   STONE, EDWARD. "William Faulkner's Two Little Confederates." Ohio University Review, 4, 5-18.
     Five William Faulkner short stories published 1934-1936 in the Saturday Evening Post bear considerable resemblance in dramatic situation, theme, and plot to Two Little Confederates.

Thomas Nelson Page: A Reference Guide

3   WILSON, EDMUND. _Patriotic Gore_. New York: Oxford University
     Press, pp. 613-14.
         Page's fiction fulfilled a Northern demand for literary
     portrayals of the South and expressed his hope for North-
     South reconciliation. His _The Negro: The Southerner's
     Problem_ may have been a rebuttal to George Washington Cable.
     Red Rock was his "most ambitious novel." References to
     other works include _Two Little Confederates_ and "The Gray
     Jacket of No. 4."

1963 A   BOOKS - NONE

1963 B   SHORTER WRITINGS

1   SPILLER, ROBERT E., et al. _Literary History of the United
     States: History_. Vol. 2, third edition revised. New York:
     The Macmillan Company, pp. 613, 791, 849-50, 1468.
         The basic Page formula underlies the stories collected
     into _In Ole Virginia_: former slaves pine for the securities
     and benefits of antebellum plantation life. Despite his
     weaknesses, Page had real talent for description, detail,
     and dialect.

1964 A   BOOKS

1   KING, JAMES KIMBALL. "George Washington Cable and Thomas
     Nelson Page: Two Literary Approaches to the New South."
     Ph.D. dissertation, University of Wisconsin.
         Page eulogized Southern life. His views owe much to his
     background, his religious preferences, and his readings of
     the eighteenth century English essayists and poets. His
     plot structures owe much to the example of Sir Walter
     Scott.
         Page's readings of Poe and other writers of the South
     heightened his interest in "national literature and pro-
     vided him with popular fictional themes." References are
     made to _On Newfound River_, _Two Little Confederates_, _Gordon
     Keith_, _In Ole Virginia_, _Bred in the Bone_, _Burial of the
     Guns_, _Under the Crust_, and _John Marvel_.
         Page, to a large extent, accepted the attitudes of his
     family, especially their belief in an "hierarchial society
     and a fixed order in the universe." References include
     Two Little Confederates, _The Burial of the Guns_, _Bred in
     the Bone_, _The Old South_, _The Red Riders_, _In Ole Virginia_,
     Under the Crust, _Gordon Keith_, _The Old Dominion_, "The
     Lynching of Negroes--Its Cause and Prevention."

1964

Page's most stereotyped characters are the "'white trash,'" his most realistic ones the Northern socialites. References include In Ole Virginia, Red Rock, Pastime Stories and Poems, Bred in the Bone, Burial of the Guns, Gordon Keith, Robert E. Lee, The Red Riders, and John Marvel, Assistant.

1964 B   SHORTER WRITINGS - NONE

1965 A   BOOKS - NONE

1965 B   SHORTER WRITINGS

1   BERTHOFF, WARNER. The Ferment of Realism: American Litera-
     ture: 1884-1919. New York: The Free Press, p. 9.
         Ellen Glasgow is not "a great deal more seriously read-
     able than the costume romancers like Thomas Nelson Page
     whom she meant to displace."

2   HART, JAMES D. The Oxford Companion to American Literature.
     Fourth edition. New York: Oxford University Press, p. 629.
         Page is a sentimental writer of the "aristocratic Old
     South" and a "leader of the local-color movement." In-
     cluded are plot summaries of the six stories in In Ole
     Virginia.

3   KING, KIMBALL. "Regionalism in the Three Souths." Trans-
     actions of the Wisconsin Academy of Sciences, Arts and
     Letters, 54, 37-50.
         Despite the great popularity of nineteenth century "nos-
     talgic eulogies" of a lost Southern order, Southern litera-
     ture is "not the product of one, but of three regions: the
     Tidewater and Atlantic coastal South, the mountaineers'
     South, and the deep South." Page and George W. Bagby,
     however, did much to emphasize the plantation tradition in
     literature. Page's "Unc' Gabe's White Folks" found an
     audience already "eager" to learn of life in a defeated
     South. His works, moreover, carried with them a desire
     for North-South reconciliation. Although one recognizes
     the "romantic stereotypes" of Page's noble characters, his
     heroes are "cast in the image of Robert E. Lee." The pa-
     ternalism of Page's works is two dimensional: "Negroes re-
     main loyal to their masters after the Emancipation, and the
     masters offer their protection and trust in return." "Meh
     Lady" and "Marse Chan" exemplify this attitude.

4   ____. "Satirical Portraits by Thomas Nelson Page."
       Mississippi Quarterly, 18 (Spring), 74-81.
            Both Gordon Keith and John Marvel, Assistant are satiri-
       cal of "American mores following the Civil War." Although
       these two novels are not as "memorable" as some other Page
       works, they contain rather candid and witty criticisms of
       "high society in general, especially its rich women and
       fashionable clergymen." There is no conflict between Page's
       personal lifestyle and the nature of his satirical criti-
       cisms. He seemed to believe that "America's upper class
       was forgetting its moral obligations."

5   PAGE, RICHARD CHANNING MOORE. Genealogy of the Page Family in
       Virginia. Bridgewater, Virginia: C. J. Carrier Company,
       p. 88.
            An account of Page's ancestry on his father's side.

1967 A BOOKS

1   GROSS, THEODORE L. Thomas Nelson Page. New York: Twayne
       Publishers, Inc., 175 pp.
            Studies the "myth of Southern heroism" underlying In Ole
       Virginia, Page's "lasting contribution to American litera-
       ture." Gross argues that Page, like most local colorists,
       draws heavily from "real life" to create his best fiction.
       In an analysis of his non-fiction works, Gross considers
       Social Life in Old Virginia Before the War an "index to
       Page's mind." "The Race Question" sheds light on his view
       of Negro equality. The Negro: The Southerner's Problem
       and The Old Dominion: Her Making and Her Manners are
       "representative" of his "basic attitudes." Two Little Con-
       federates is his "most elaborate recollection of experiences
       during the war." On Newfound River, on the other hand, is
       a "more explicit" local color exploration of old Virginia.
       Familiar Page techniques, themes, and attitudes are preva-
       lent in "The Burial of the Guns," "Little Darby," and "The
       Old Gentleman of the Black Stock." Red Rock, although "not
       a successful novel," is an attempt at an "objective render-
       ing" of the Reconstruction era. "Bred in the Bone" dis-
       plays Page's emphasis on pedigree, whereas Gordon Keith is
       a departure from local color to the "'novel of manners.'"
       John Marvel, Assistant describes the world in which the
       author was living rather than the world which he remembered.
       Robert E. Lee: Man and Soldier is more "hagiography" than
       biography. Page led "'an ideal life,'" Gross concludes,
       and became the chauvinistic champion of antebellum Southern
       life. Even as historian, he allowed his work to be strongly

1967

colored by his idealism. Nonetheless, the stories of In
Ole Virginia are artistically "superb."

1967 B SHORTER WRITINGS

1   GROSS, THEODORE L. "Thomas Nelson Page (1853-1922)."
    American Literary Realism, 1 (Fall), 90-92.
        A discussion of secondary sources on Page. The most
    valuable are Jay B. Hubbell's The South in American Litera-
    ture (1954), Edmund Wilson's Patriotic Gore (1962), Harriet
    Holman's The Literary Career of Thomas Nelson Page: 1884-
    1910 (1947), and Theodore L. Gross' Thomas Nelson Page
    (1967).

2   MARTIN, JAY. Harvests of Change: American Literature:
    1865-1914. Englewood Cliffs, New Jersey: Prentice-Hall,
    Inc., pp. 18, 88, 193.
        Page's work is essentially that of a daydreamer and con-
    trasts sharply with that of Ambrose Bierce. "Marse Chan"
    presents an ideal view of the plantation myth, a myth that
    persisted for generations. When he did not use the Southern
    myth, Page turned to the Santa Claus myth.

1968 A BOOKS

1   MAIDEN, EMORY V., JR. "A Comparison of the Negro Dialect
    Poetry of Irwin Russell and Thomas Nelson Page." M.A.
    thesis, University of Virginia.
        The strong popularity in the past of antebellum planta-
    tion literature was owed to "the charm of Negro dialect
    poetry that bespeaks a simpler, more elegant life than that
    of the Northern reader in the nineteenth century." The
    faithful family retainer is examined, and particular atten-
    tion is paid to The Coast of Bohemia. The narrators of
    Page's poetry remain indistinguishable. His Negro dialect
    poetry fails to "rise above sentimental romanticism" and
    is "predicated on the belief that one man is inherently
    superior to another."

1968 B SHORTER WRITINGS

1   LOGAN, RAYFORD W. The Betrayal of the Negro from Rutherford
    B. Hayes to Woodrow Wilson. New York: Collier Books,
    pp. 243, 245, 247, 255-56, 264, 268, 270, 354, 374, 377.

Page "glorified the plantation tradition in Harper's more effusively than did any other writer."

2   "Thomas Nelson Page," in The Literature of the South. Edited by Thomas Daniel Young, Floyd G. Watkins, and Richmond Croom Beatty. Revised edition. Glenview, Illinois: Scott, Foresman and Company, pp. 449-50.
    Notes Page's purpose as social historian. In Ole Virginia and Red Rock are "still held in high critical esteem," and Page is still admired for his plots and use of dialect.

1969 A   BOOKS - NONE

1969 B   SHORTER WRITINGS

1   HERZBERG, MAX J., ed. The Reader's Encyclopedia of American Literature. New York: Thomas Y. Crowell Company, pp. 844-45.
    Page was a product of the chivalry of old Virginia. Red Rock "thrilled readers with its picture of the Southern revolt against Reconstruction. . . ."

2   HOLMAN, HARRIET R., ed. "Thomas Nelson Page's Account of Tennessee Hospitality." Tennessee Historical Quarterly, 28 (Fall), 269-72.
    Page's 1893 visit to McMinnville, Tennessee left the warmest impressions upon him. Miss Holman reprints here Page's "penciled account" of his reception.

3   KING, KIMBALL. "Introduction" to In Ole Virginia. Southern Literary Classics Series. Chapel Hill, North Carolina: The University of North Carolina Press, pp. i-xxxvi.
    Notes Page's importance as part of the plantation literary tradition, the climate of his publication, his traditional values, his "epic theme," and the influences on his work. Includes analyses of stories in In Ole Virginia.

4   _____. "Thomas Nelson Page (1853-1922)," in A Bibliographical Guide to the Study of Southern Literature. Edited by Louis D. Rubin, Jr. Baton Rouge: Louisiana State University Press, 254-55.
    Page was "chief spokesman for the plantation literary tradition." Lists 14 items in the bibliography.

1970

1970 A BOOKS - NONE

1970 B SHORTER WRITINGS

1   HOLMAN, HARRIET R. "Attempt and Failure: Thomas Nelson Page
        As Playwright." Southern Literary Journal, 3 (Fall), 72-82.
          Page did not like the 1915 film version of "The Outcast."
        His interest in drama, including his relationship to Augus-
        tin Daly is discussed. Preston Gibson, Mrs. Florence Page's
        son-in-law, tried revamping Page's dramatic version of In
        Ole Virginia and Red Rock but to no avail. Dramatic writing
        was not among Page's literary talents.

2   _____. "The Kentucky Journal of Thomas Nelson Page."
        Register of the Kentucky Historical Society, 68 (January),
        1-16.
          Page returned to Kentucky three times in 1891. He had
        served in 1872-1873 as tutor in the home of Theodore Brown.
        On 13 April 1891 Page addressed the people of Louisville in
        a speech entitled "The Want of a History of the Southern
        People." Reconciliation of North-South was one of his fre-
        quent themes. Page's Kentucky journal for the 1891 visits
        suggests that his experience there was "augury of all that
        was to come." He saw in his journal a "record of himself,
        of persons and places he had known, and more than a hint of
        the emotional response they elicited from him."

3   _____. "Of John Fox and Tom Page and the Record," in John
        Fox and Tom Page As They Were. Edited by Harriet R. Holman.
        Coconut Grove, Miami, Florida: Field Research Projects,
        pp. 1-9.
          Page and John Fox became good friends. Both men were
        "delightful human beings and conscientious writers."

4   SLOANE, DAVID E. E. "Notes: David Graham Phillips, Jack
        London, and Others On Contemporary Reviewers and Critics,
        1903-1904." American Literary Realism, 3 (Winter), 67-71.
          In 1903 the New York Bookman sampled a number of Ameri-
        can writers concerning their judgments of current newspaper
        and magazine criticism. Page's major complaint regarding
        criticism was "over-stated praise and censure." Page noted
        in his response that his goal as writer was to present life
        as he knew it and liked it.

Thomas Nelson Page: A Reference Guide

1971 A BOOKS - NONE

1971 B SHORTER WRITINGS

1   DABNEY, VIRGINIUS. <u>Virginia: The New Dominion</u>. Garden City,
    New York: Doubleday & Company, Inc., pp. 243, 269, 404,
    407, 419.
        Page's work was "ardently pro-Southern" and helped create
    in the minds of American readers an extremely favorable
    view of antebellum Southern life.

2   DICKINSON, A. T., JR. <u>American Historical Fiction</u>. Third
    edition. Metuchen, New Jersey: The Scarecrow Press,
    p. 148.
        Brief synopsis of <u>Red Rock</u>.

3   EICHELBERGER, CLAYTON L., ed. <u>A Guide to Critical Reviews of
    United States Fiction, 1870-1910</u>. Metuchen, New Jersey:
    The Scarecrow Press, vol. 1, pp. 236-38.
        Lists 68 reviews of Page's works.

4   GROSS, THEODORE L. <u>The Heroic Ideal in American Literature</u>.
    New York: The Free Press, pp. 44, 88, 89, 102, 104, 105-18,
    119, 120, 121, 128, 131, 138, 248, 293.
        Page's fiction is filled with a "perpetuation of Southern
    chauvinism" and the "dedication to an idealization of the
    code of Southern heroism." The sentimental romance is
    joined in Page's work to a "glorification of the Southern
    past." Page's best fiction, the stories of <u>In Ole Virginia</u>,
    insist upon the following of a code. His worst fiction
    tends to play up the code at the expense of plot and charac-
    ter. The only plausible character in "Marse Chan" is the
    Negro, since the other characters in the story are mythical
    in nature. References to other Page works include <u>Gordon
    Keith</u>, <u>In Ole Virginia</u>, <u>John Marvel</u>, "Marse Chan," "The Old
    South," <u>Red Rock</u>, and <u>The Red Riders</u>.

1972 A BOOKS - NONE

1972 B SHORTER WRITINGS

1   TAYLOR, W. D. "Page, Thomas Nelson," in <u>Virginia Authors:
    Past and Present</u>. Edited by W. D. Taylor. Richmond: The
    William Byrd Press, Inc., p. 89.
        Although quite successful as a diplomat, Page is primar-
    ily remembered as the author of "Marse Chan" and, in general,
    as the writer of romantic stories like "Meh Lady" and
    "Polly," all appearing during a realistic age.

1973

1973 A   BOOKS - NONE

1973 B   SHORTER WRITINGS

    1   HOLMAN, HARRIET R.   "Magazine Editors and the Stories of
        Thomas Nelson Page's Late Flowering," in Essays Mostly on
        Periodical Publishing in America.   Edited by James Wooddress.
        Durham: Duke University Press, pp. 148-61.
           Page's eleven stories from his "late flowering" employed
        what was, for him, "atypical" substance and style.   The
        stories, which were included in Under the Crust, the Planta-
        tion Edition of his works, and The Land of the Spirit, were
        not what Page's "prescriptive" publishers preferred.   The
        eleven stories are "social commentary verging upon protest,
        all attack inhumanity to man, and all imply criticism of
        whole castes, if not classes, in the American social struc-
        ture."   The stories, by nature, resemble the protests of a
        young Garland or Norris.   Page's shift, however, from
        stories dealing with the antebellum South to those taking
        up similar ideals set in the contemporary world was not
        pleasing to magazine editors, who insisted upon "more
        Southern material of the kind he had been writing twenty
        years before."

    2   OSTERWEIS, ROLLIN G.   The Myth of the Lost Cause: 1865-1900.
        Hamden, Connecticut: Archon Books, pp. 33, 39, 42, 49-50,
        55, 61, 146, 152.
           Page's "Marse Chan" stories are major contributions to
        the "Myth of the Lost Cause."   Page's stories supplied "the
        appealing stereotypes of the chivalric young cavalry offi-
        cer, of the beautiful, magnolia-scented Southern belle, and
        of the devoted, loyal Negro slave."

    3   TURNER, ARLIN.   "Comedy and Reality in Local Color Fiction:
        1865-1900," in The Comic Imagination in American Literature.
        Edited by Louis D. Rubin, Jr.   New Brunswick, New Jersey:
        Rutgers University Press, p. 163.
           The essay refers to Page's use of dialect in his local
        color writings, his debt to Irwin Russell, and the reluc-
        tance of the editor of Century Magazine to print "Marse
        Chan."

Thomas Nelson Page: A Reference Guide

1974 A   BOOKS - NONE

1974 B   SHORTER WRITINGS

   1   EICHELBERGER, CLAYTON L.   A Guide to Critical Review of United
      States Fiction, 1870-1910.   Metuchen, New Jersey: The
      Scarecrow Press, Inc., vol. 2, pp. 205-06.
         Lists 60 critical reviews of Page works.

1975 A   BOOKS - NONE

1975 B   SHORTER WRITINGS

   1   POLK, NOEL.   "Guide to Dissertations on American Literary
      Figures, 1870-1910:   Part Two."   American Literary Realism,
      8 (Autumn), p. 320.
         Annotated.   Includes Harriet R. Holman's and James
      Kimball King's dissertations on Page.

1976 A   BOOKS - NONE

1976 B   SHORTER WRITINGS

   1   RUBIN, LOUIS D., JR.   William Elliott Shoots a Bear.   Baton
      Rouge: Louisiana State University Press, pp. 20-21, 77,
      92-93, 323-33.
         Notes that Page had observed that writing was considered
      "suspect" in the antebellum South and that he was unable to
      see the interests of plantation master and slave as diver-
      gent.   Page never realized that he "might not" understand
      the Negro.

   2   SIMMS, L. MOODY, JR.   "Walter Hines Page on Southern Litera-
      ture."   Resources for American Literary Study, 6 (Spring),
      70-79.
         Notes that the Northern critical standards by which
      Southern writers like Page were judged were not "very high."

Amélie Rives Troubetzkoy:
A Reference Guide

Writings about Amélie Rives Troubetzkoy, 1887-1974

1887 A BOOKS - NONE

1887 B SHORTER WRITINGS

1   COLEMAN, CHARLES W. "The Recent Movement in Southern
     Literature." Harper's New Monthly Magazine, 74 (May),
     837-55.
         "A Brother to Dragons" demonstrated "an imaginative
     power unequalled in contemporary fiction." The story was
     characteristically Elizabethan in its "bold yet delicate
     quaintness."

2   PAGE, WALTER HINES. "Literature in the South." Critic, 10
     (25 June), 322-24.
         In his discussion of the absence of Southern literary
     criticism and the lack of publishing houses in the South,
     Page observes that it was Northern editors who discovered
     Rives.

1888 A BOOKS

1   DeLEON, T. C. The Rock or the Rye? 23rd edition. Mobile,
     Alabama: Gossip Printing Company, 34 pp.
         DeLeon claims to have written this parody of The Quick
     or the Dead? long before other "scurrilous critiques had
     appeared." His parody is aimed at the "verbal mannerisms
     and overstrained emotions" of Miss Rives's novel. The
     parody attacks both the substance and style of the novel.

2   STEARNS, FREDERICK A. Be Quick and Be Dead: A Parody with
     Apologies to Amélie Rives. New York: M. J. Ivers & Co.,
     192 pp.
         Attacks both the substance and style of The Quick or the
     Dead? Even the original Rives portrait is parodied in this
     satire with a portrait of Ophélia Hives—obese, middle-aged,
     sensuous. Hives notes that, "My purpose is simply to write
     a romance which shall sort of revolutionize things in a

1888

quiet, unostentatious sort of way, and make the reader wonder when he gets through why he was ever born, any way." The parody is set in New York, the opening scene a Lexington Avenue apartment. The heroine Gabriella Pompoon is scheming, desperate, insincere.

1888 B SHORTER WRITINGS

1   ANON. "Amélie Rives's Work." New York Times (14 May), p. 3.
    "A Brother to Dragons" does not deserve the excitement it has generated since its first publication in the Atlantic. The title story in the new collected edition is artificial at best and occasionally guilty of "literary vulgarity." "Nurse Crumpet Tells the Story" shares similar defects. "The Farrier Lass o' Piping Pebworth" is the best story in the new collection.

2   ANON. "The American Widow--New Style." The Saturday Review (London), 66 (17 November), 570-71.
    The Quick or the Dead?, which generated much excitement in America, will come as nothing new to British readers accustomed to such romances. Miss Rives has possibly outdone Ouida or Miss Braddon, however, in describing the many dresses of the heroine.

3   ANON. "Fiction." The Literary World, 19 (13 October), 343-44.
    The usual elements of Rives's style--"brilliance and impulse," "charm of expression," "exuberance of feeling," "freshness and candor," "Love of out-of-door life," and "audacity and passion"--are present in Virginia of Virginia. Miss Rives demonstrates great promise if she can only "temper" the "fervor" of her works.

4   ANON. "Fiction." The Literary World, 19 (12 May), 153-55.
    A Brother to Dragons and Other Old-Time Tales indicates the "freshness, the fervor, and the excess of an undisciplined imagination." The characters in the stories are merely superficially true to their respective eras. They, nonetheless, have "flesh and blood" appeal about them. "The Farrier Lass O' Piping Pebworth" is the best story in the collection.

5   ANON. "Miss Amélie Rives's first Book." The Epoch, 3 (20 April), 217.
    A Brother to Dragons and Other Old-Time Tales contains three stories which are "original both in matter and manner." The collection, on the other hand, bears a "certain

'staginess,' almost inevitably resulting from her early and
lightly-won popularity." "A Brother to Dragons" is the
best story in the collection and contains some excellent
description despite occasional weaknesses in taste.

6   ANON. "Miss Amélie Rives's Short Stories." The Critic, 9
     (12 May), 228-29.
         The characters of A Brother to Dragons and Other Old-
     Time Tales have "some nobility of motive, some dignity of
     carriage." Miss Rives nonetheless can do better work. The
     Elizabethan English, for example, has been handled "with
     only partial success," for the idiom is strained and inac-
     curate. A more serious defect is her inability "to sustain
     throughout the individuality of the narrator." "The Farrier
     Lass" is the best of the three stories.

7   ANON. "Notices." New York Times (18 November), p. 4.
         The Quick or the Dead? is enjoying "enormous" English
     sales, and English critic Andrew Lang has composed a
     "'scathing criticism of the author's style.'" One wonders
     why the English would even bother to read "ridiculous trash"
     like The Quick or the Dead?

8   ANON. "Recent Fiction." The Independent, 40 (23 August),
     1073.
         Virginia of Virginia is Miss Rives's "strongest and cer-
     tainly most creditable claim to literary compliment." The
     "sketch" is moving and "powerful." The story, moreover, is
     revealed with "nice realism" as a "series of pictures" and
     is free of those elements which formerly provoked moral
     censure of Rives's work.

9   ANON. "Recent Novels." The Nation, 47 (4 October), 272-75.
         The incidents in Virginia of Virginia are "cheaply sen-
     sational," and the heroine offends one's good taste. The
     language is "extravagant."

10 ANON. "Talk About New Books." The Catholic World, 47
     (August), 694.
         A Brother to Dragons and Other Old-Time Tales contains
     three stories written in Renaissance English dialect, or
     what Miss Rives believes that dialect to have been. Each
     of the three tales is narrated by a lower-class person in
     order that the author may have considerable excuse for her
     "verbal licenses that border on indecency." Although the
     tales have some strength, they offer little in the way of
     a future for Rives. The stories, moreover, contain "the
     Frenchiest of the French novels of to-day." The Quick or

153

1888

the Dead? caused a sensation of a sort, and Rives unfortunately allowed herself to be identified with the heroine.

11   ANON. "Virginia of Virginia." The Critic, 10 (15 September),
     122-23.
        Virginia of Virginia is "simple in motive, direct in
     treatment, profuse in incident and devoid of plot." Rives,
     however, sees nature "with the eye of a painter, and de-
     scribes it with the voice of a poet." The characters of
     the novel are unfortunately "wooden as usual." Nonetheless
     there is a strong "poetico-theatrical" quality to the novel.
     Swedenborgianism is "impressed into literary service."

12   ANON. "Virginia of Virginia." New York Times (30 July), p. 3.
        Miss Rives's new novel, her best to date, creates an
     effective portrait of female jealousy. The unattractive
     sensual qualities which permeated The Quick or the Dead?
     are held in check in this new work.

13   HURRELL, J. D. "Some Days With Amélie Rives." Lippincott's
     Monthly Magazine, 42 (April), 531-36.
        Recounts the circumstances of Amélie Rives's birth, her
     upbringing, her fondness for "Castle Hill," her youthful
     attempts at painting, and her love of reading. Heavy em-
     phasis is placed on a description of the room in which she
     did her writing. Notes the picturesque nature of Rives's
     Albemarle County environment and the close relationship
     she had with her father.

14   HUTTON, LAURENCE. "Literary Notes." Harper's New Monthly
     Magazine, 76 (April), 1-2.
        Despite the error in its title, "A Brother to Dragons"
     is a pleasant tale if not authentically Elizabethan in na-
     ture. The story, moreover, is "free from anachronisms."
     "Nurse Crumpet Tells the Story" is equally well told if not
     as "cheerful."

15   PAYNE, WILLIAM MORTON. "Recent Fiction." The Dial, 9 (July),
     65-69.
        "A Brother to Dragons" elicited attention owing to its
     "singular title and antique style." Upon closer examina-
     tion one recognized that its characterization was "senti-
     mental" and its manner "affected." A Brother to Dragons
     and Other Old-Time Tales indicates promise but does not go
     beyond the promise of talent, for it is filled with the
     "crudities, the mannerisms, and the undisciplined fancy of
     . . . [Rives's] first effort."

1889 A BOOKS - NONE

1889 B SHORTER WRITINGS

1 AÏDÉ, HAMILTON. "The Quick or the Dead? and Virginia of
   Virginia." Nineteenth Century Magazine, 25 (February),
   228-30.
      The Quick or the Dead? is "unhealthy in tone, false in
   morality, and strangely coarse in parts." The novel, nevertheless, demonstrated a promise of talent fulfilled in Miss
   Rives's later fiction. Virginia of Virginia reflected a
   growth in the author's ability to edit her work and was
   "original in conception, and singularly fresh in treatment."
   Herod and Mariamne indicated, however, a failure in style,
   especially in repetition of words for the sake of emphasis.

2 ANON. "In the Library." Cosmopolitan, 7 (May), 101-04.
      The Witness of the Sun indicates Miss Rives's own lack
   of real suffering in life and, hence, the lack of wisdom
   necessary to novel writing.

3 ANON. "Literary Notes." America, 2 (4 April), 24.
      The Witness of the Sun is less decadent and less power-
   ful than The Quick or the Dead? Fortunately the new novel
   is set in Italy and focuses on a Russian novelist and an
   Italian princess, people Americans know little about.

4 ANON. "Miss Amélie Rives's Novels." The Saturday Review
   (London), 67 (22 June), 765-66.
      No true critic could have judged The Quick or the Dead?
   a "good book." Virginia of Virginia, however, has some
   good scenes of Virginia life, despite its stylistic weaknesses. The Witness of the Sun bears the influence of
   Ouida. Despite its dramatic force, however, the new novel
   is lacking in realism. At best, it is a "clever pastiche."

5 ANON. "New Books and Reprints." The Saturday Review
   (London), 67 (30 March), 393.
      The "'author's copyright edition'" of The Quick or the
   Dead? contains Miss Rives's denial that she is Barbara
   Pomfret. Barbara, according to this English critic, was
   an "exceedingly uncomfortable person."

6 ANON. "Novels of the Week." Athenaeum (London), 3214
   (1 June), 693-94.
      The Witness of the Sun has the "convulsive, passionate"
   style of The Quick or the Dead? The narrative is "rather
   affected and showy." Virginia of Virginia, a superior work,

1889

has "something genuine." Miss Rives is "freer" in her
characterization here than in The Witness of the Sun. The
heroine of the new novel and her father are the best characters in the book. A Brother to Dragons contains three
stories which are "not worth reprinting."

7   ANON. "Novels of the Week." Athenaeum (London), 3203
    (16 March), 341-42.
        The Quick or the Dead? is written in a style too "luxuri-
    ant" and too "frank" for American readers. The author's
    preface does the novel a disservice. There is nothing par-
    ticularly shocking in the novel, but there is a "vigorous
    appreciation of a piece of character." Miss Rives's major
    weakness is her lack of training.

8   ANON. "Recent Novels." The Nation, 48 (27 June), 529-30.
        "The sun never shone on the land which Miss Rives de-
    scribes" in The Witness of the Sun. The novel owes much to
    the novels of Ouida.

9   CLARK, KATE UPSON. "Amélie Rives' Latest Novel." The Epoch,
    5 (19 April), 180.
        The guidance of Henry M. Alden or Thomas Bailey Aldrich
    could have helped Miss Rives attain the literary competency
    promised by her collection A Brother to Dragons. The Wit-
    ness of the Sun unfortunately is "one of the most revolting,
    in its way, of anything in modern fiction." The novel is
    an "inartistic and unsatisfactory little work."

10 DIDIER, EUGENE L. "Amélie Rives." Literature: A Weekly
    Magazine, 2 (2 March), 325-27.
        This largely biographical sketch asserts that Miss Rives
    was a "gifted" writer as a child. Having "fastidious
    literary taste" she destroyed, like Hawthorne, many of her
    early manuscripts. The curious publication of "A Brother
    to Dragons" is recounted. Didier has brief praise for "The
    Farrier Lass O' Piping Pebworth," "Nurse Crumpet Tells the
    Story," "Grief and Faith," "Story of Arnon," Virginia of
    Virginia, The Quick or the Dead? and Herod and Mariamne.

11 FAWCETT, EDGAR. "The Quick or the Dead?" Literature: A
    Weekly Magazine, 2 (2 March), 329-30.
        Notes that the repercussions from The Quick or the Dead?
    were due to the fact that Miss Rives "steeped a love-story
    in realism."

12 FIELDING, HOWARD. Col. Evans from Kentucky and Other Humorous
    Sketches. New York: Manhattan Therapeutic Company, p. 10.

Notes: "I have seen Amelia [sic] Rives dance on the
Virginia dialect in a moment of unbridled passion."

13   TIMSOL, ROBERT. "Carping Criticism." Literature: A Weekly
      Magazine, 2 (2 March), 327-29.
         Points out in his defense of Miss Rives that her often-
      times shocking reception has been owed to human jealousy.
      The fact that she is an attractive, talented writer who has
      achieved considerable attention has provoked innumerable
      character assassinations.

1891 A   BOOKS - NONE

1891 B   SHORTER WRITINGS

1   ANON. "According to St. John: Amélie Rives Tells the Herald
     About Her New Book and of Her Impressions of the Continent."
     New York Herald (31 July), n.p.
        Miss Rives states that she looks forward to her return
     to the tranquility of her Virginia home. Paris, she admits,
     has done much for her. According to St. John is her "dif-
     ferent impressions of Paris" and will offend fewer readers
     than some of her earlier works.

2   ANON. "Amélie Rives's According to St. John." The Critic, 16
     (14 November), 260.
        According to St. John contains "unflinching realism; and
     it is because the leaders of artistic thought in France in-
     sist that one subject is as good as another, provided the
     treatment be truthful, that her [Rives's] warmest friends
     must acknowledge her decadence." Both tone and subject
     matter are lacking in good taste.

3   ANON. "Mrs. Chanler Back." Richmond Dispatch (25 August),
     n.p.
        An account of the Chanlers' stay in Europe. Mrs. Chan-
     ler notes that she intends studying art and literature at
     "Castle Hill." According to the interview, she will con-
     tinue her studies in art under Charles Lasar.

4   ANON. "New Books." New York Times (20 December), p. 19.
        According to St. John is "one of the poorest, trashiest
     things by a young writer of decided talents whose head the
     publishers and magazine editors have turned." Although
     Miss Rives provides excellent description of Paris street
     scenes, her heroine is "untrue to nature."

1891

5   ANON. "Novels of the Week." The Athenaeum, 3346
(12 December), 797-98.
      According to St. John has a great deal more restraint
than The Quick or the Dead? Rives obviously understands
women and is quite adept at description. Nonetheless, she
is "less amusing as she approaches nearer to mediocrity."

6   ANON. "Recent Fiction." The Nation, 53 (17 December), 470-72.
      According to St. John is a "foolish novel." Miss Rives
tries hard to be "virtuous" here but is quite confused in
her morals. The "nastiness" of Mme. Cici does credit to
the "French naturalists."

7   ANON. "Recent Publications." New Orleans Daily Picayune
(18 October), p. 16.
      According to St. John is one of Miss Rives's oddest
books. The novel, moreover, misuses the injunction of St.
Paul implicit in its title. The work, well written, is
"nonetheless absurd."

8   ANON. Review of According to St. John. The Saturday Review
(London), 72 (21 November), 589.
      Jean Carter in According to St. John has a "capacity for
self-torture not less fruitful and ingenious than
Rousseau's."

1892 A BOOKS - NONE

1892 B SHORTER WRITINGS

1   ANON. "Amélie Rives's New Story." New York Times
(13 November), p. 19.
      Barbara Dering, a sequel to the offensive novel The
Quick or the Dead?, is marked by "fleshiness and an over-
wrought sensuousness." Barbara Dering fails to act like a
proper young lady.

2   ANON. "Barbara Dering." The Literary World, 23 (19 November),
403-04.
      Miss Rives's characters often skirt "the verge of posi-
tive indecency" and such is the case in Barbara Dering, a
novel concerning Rives's notions of marriage.

3   ANON. "Novels of the Week." The Athenaeum, 3396
(26 November), 736-37.
      Barbara Dering, a sequel to The Quick or the Dead?, is
something of an improvement on the latter novel. Despite

her questionable choice of subjects, Miss Rives often writes "novels of clever impressions of character and intense phases of feeling." She is one of the first Americans to give "the feminine outlook and taste in matters of love and love-making" as is evident in the new novel. Unfortunately Barbara Dering contains "lapses in good taste."

4 ANON. "Recent Publications." New Orleans Daily Picayune (27 November), p. 22.
Barbara Dering is a sequel to The Quick or the Dead? and "supposedly expresses her [Rives's] ideas of the proper relations of the sexes." The two lovers in the novel are deservedly unhappy.

5 RIVES, AMÉLIE. "Innocence Versus Ignorance." The North American Review, 155 (September), 287-92.
Miss Rives's self-defense consists here of her quoting of Browning, "'Ignorance is not innocence, but sin.'"

1893 A BOOKS - NONE

1893 B SHORTER WRITINGS

1 ANON. "All the Books." Godey's Magazine, 126 (January), 104.
The two married couples in Barbara Dering stand in sharp contrast to each other. If the author had studied marriage in greater depth, she "might have made a strong story instead of a bundle of able sketches of people merely exasperating."

2 ANON. "All the Books." Godey's Magazine, 126 (June), 770.
The story of Athelwold is told "strongly and dramatically." Miss Rives "has no equal at drawing women who are at once proud, selfish, handsome, alluring, lacking in womanly delicacy and, above all things, desperately self-absorbed and inconceivably mean, but in Athelwold she has excelled herself in the depicting of this interesting type of character."

3 ANON. "Amélie Rives's Play." New York Times (26 March), p. 19.
Athelwold contains an old story and a strong dramatic structure. Female conversation is a bit too sensuous.

4 ANON. "Barbara Dering." The Critic, 19 (11 March), p. 140.
Barbara Dering is a sequel to The Quick or the Dead? and is the best work the author has done to date. Nature

1893

descriptions are particularly good in the novel. Although many readers will dislike the outspoken quality of the work, "the fact remains that few women could have written it."

5   ANON. "Comment on New Books." The Atlantic Monthly, 72 (July), 125-132.
     Barbara Dering demonstrates an "advance in maturity of reflection" but does not demonstrate any artistic growth. The novel deals more with problems than with people.

6   ANON. "Fiction." The Literary World, 24 (21 October), 351.
     Tanis the Sang-Digger is a "story of the Warm Springs Valley." Notes that "Mrs. Rives-Chanler's descriptions of kisses and embraces ad libitum may be imagined."

7   ANON. "New Novels." The Athenaeum, 3449 (2 December), 766-68.
     Tanis the Sang-Digger contains a vivid contrast between the primitive mountain heroine and the lovely Southern lady. The dialect may be tedious to many.

8   ANON. "Recent Fiction." The Independent, 45 (7 December), 17.
     Tanis the Sang-Digger, a "strong but singularly dis-agreeable story," employs a heroine who is "among the lowest that the Southern mountains can offer." The reviewer notes two flaws in the novel insofar as realism is concerned—dialect and folk dress. Drama and "poetical energy," on the other hand, save the novel.

9   ANON. "Talk About New Books." The Catholic World, 56 (January), 579-80.
     Rives comes to the defense of The Quick or the Dead? in her new novel Barbara Dering. Having remained loyal to the memory of her deceased husband for two years, Barbara now marries Val, "amidst much rapturous love-making which both precedes and follows the nuptial ceremony." Barbara Dering now makes the point that both she and the author are indeed "very spiritual" women despite the fact that they burn with "clear, pure fires." Miss Rives might well learn a lesson in serious writing from Ursula N. Gestefeld's The Woman Who Dares, which undertakes a similar task.

10   HUTTON, LAURENCE. "Literary Notes." Harper's New Monthly Magazine, 76 (May), 2.
     Athelwold is "less estimable than interesting." Miss Rives's play is one of many to treat the legend of Athel-wold. Her play unfortunately has "neither thought, design nor expression resembling those of the older tragedies upon the same subject which have preceded it." Hume is Rives's historical source.

1894 A BOOKS - NONE

1894 B SHORTER WRITINGS

1   ANON. "Comment on New Books." The Atlantic Monthly, 73
        (January), 133-38.
            The protagonist of Tanis is "of wonderful physical vigor
        and beauty." The dialect is, however, "distressful."

1895 A BOOKS - NONE

1895 B SHORTER WRITINGS

1   MANLY, LOUISE. Southern Literature from 1579 to 1895.
        Richmond: B. F. Johnson Publishing Company, pp. 431-37.
            Miss Rives's early stories were in a Shakespearean vein,
        the best of which was "The Farrier Lass O' Piping Pebworth."
        Her real forte is poetry and drama.

1896 A BOOKS - NONE

1896 B SHORTER WRITINGS

1   ANON. "Amélie Rives: Now She Is A Princess." The Colon
        Telegram (28 February), n.p.
            An account of Miss Rives's marriage to Prince Pierre
        Troubetzkoy. Present at the ceremony at "Castle Hill" were
        Colonel and Mrs. Rives, the Misses Gertrude and Landon
        Rives, Miss Julia Magruder, and Allan Potts.

2   ANON. "Amélie Rives' Romance and Its Sequel." Cleveland
        Plain-Dealer (22 March), n.p.
            Both The Quick or the Dead? and Barbara Dering are
        highly autobiographical. The former reveals an "impetuous"
        young country girl, the latter a sophisticated woman of the
        day. The Chanler marital relationship may be inferred from
        the events of the two novels.

3   ANON. "Beauty Rules of a Princess." Milwaukee Sentinel
        (29 March), n.p.
            Noting that "no one is more beautiful than the newly-
        married princess," the account concerns Miss Rives's cos-
        metic practices.

4   ANON. "Gives Her Heart-Diary in Detail." New York World
        (23 February), n.p.

1896

The marriage of Miss Rives to Prince Pierre Troubetzkoy created quite a stir among Albemarle County, Virginia natives. According to this reporter, both The Quick or the Dead? and Barbara Dering may be read as autobiography, the two novels thus ranking alongside Rousseau's Confessions. Despite the traditions which nurtured her, this account argues, Rives became quite unconventional. The history of Miss Rives's courtship and marriage to John Armstrong Chanler is revealed in the relationship of Jock Dering and Barbara Pomfret of The Quick and the Dead?

5   ANON. "A Poetess Weds a Prince." Richmond Times (19 February), n.p.
A detailed description of the wedding of Miss Rives to Prince Pierre Troubetzkoy at "Castle Hill" on 18 February 1896. Among the attendants in the wedding was Julia Magruder, the popular Virginia authoress. Reference is made to Miss Rives's marriage to John Armstrong Chanler and its termination due to "incompatibility of temperament." A brief sketch of Prince Troubetzkoy is included.

1897 A   BOOKS - NONE

1897 B   SHORTER WRITINGS

1   ANON. "Books and Authors." New York Times, Saturday Review of Books and Art (4 December), p. 10.
Yovanne in A Damsel Errant is "half Atlanta, half Artemis."

2   ANON. "A Damsel Errant." The Critic, NS 28 (27 November), 319.
There is much to admire in the charming love story, A Damsel Errant. The characterization of Lady Yovanne de Savaré is quite good. The waterfowl in the novel suggests "The Ancient Mariner." The novel is marred, however, by some inconsistency in diction.

3   ANON. "A Damsel Errant." The Independent, 49 (2 December), 1583.
A Damsel Errant is a highly seasoned, suspenseful romance of medieval France. The romance, however, reveals the author's "superficial knowledge" and is told "to charm the savage ear."

1898 A   BOOKS - NONE

1898 B   SHORTER WRITINGS

1   ANON. "A Damsel Errant." Godey's Magazine, 136 (January),
    104.
        Despite some of the negative criticism she has received,
    Miss Rives has an "individuality" that is "intense and full-
    blooded." A Damsel Errant is marked by both archaic lan-
    guage and occasional moments of poetry.

2   ANON. "New Novels." The Athenaeum, 3687 (25 June), 816-17.
        Miss Rives's Meriel is unlike anything she ever wrote
    and has very little to recommend it.

1900 A   BOOKS - NONE

1900 B   SHORTER WRITINGS

1   ANON. "Chanler Escapes: Amélie Rives' First Husband Is Out
    of Asylum." New York Herald (5 December), p. [1].
        Report of Chanler's escape from Bloomingdale Asylum and
    subsequent residence at "Castle Hill." Passing reference
    is made to The Quick or the Dead?, the courtship and mar-
    riage of Miss Rives and Chanler, and their divorce.

1903 A   BOOKS - NONE

1903 B   SHORTER WRITINGS

1   PRICE, WARWICK J. "Agnes Repplier in Philadelphia," in Women
    Authors of Our Day in Their Homes. Edited by Francis
    Whiting Halsey. New York: James Pott and Company, p. 49.
        In speaking of Thomas Bailey Aldrich, Agnes Repplier
    notes that it was Thomas Bailey Aldrich who discovered and
    helped both Elizabeth Robbins (Mrs. Pennell) and Amélie
    Rives. According to Repplier, Aldrich once said of "A
    Brother to Dragons" that "'Miss Rives will never do any-
    thing better than this.'" Repplier adds, "She never did
    anything quite so good."

1905

1905 A   BOOKS - NONE

1905 B   SHORTER WRITINGS

   1   ANON. "Dramatic Verse: Recent Works by E. D. Schoonmaker and
          the Princess Troubetzkoy." New York Times, Saturday Review
          of Books and Art (5 August), p. 510.
               Seléné is a "more poetic if not a more dramatic produc-
          tion" than Schoonmaker's The Saxons. Seléné, moreover, is
          effectively narrated, despite its occasional poor diction.

   2   ANON. "Seléné." The Reader Magazine, 6 (September), 474-75.
               The narrative of Seléné is presented with "the real
          poet's rapture in rhythm and in delicately tinted phrase."
          Seléné is truly a "dainty volume."

1906 A   BOOKS - NONE

1906 B   SHORTER WRITINGS

   1   ANON. Review of Augustine the Man. Times Literary Supplement
          (13 July), p. 248c.
               Augustine the Man is a set of "four separate scenes,"
          not a play. Concerned with the human aspect of Augustine,
          the scenes constitute a "moving story, very gracefully told
          in sensitive, sympathetic verse." The argument with An-
          tonius is an "excrescence on the theme."

   2   RIVES, AMÉLIE. "Preface," in The Quick or the Dead?: A Study.
          Philadelphia: J. B. Lippincott Company, pp. iii-vii.
               Miss Rives denies that Barbara Pomfret, the heroine of
          her controversial novel, is shaped in her image. Miss
          Rives finds Pomfret "morbid, hysterical, sensitive, intro-
          spective." She defends the novel against charges of in-
          delicacy and indecency.

1907 A   BOOKS - NONE

1907 B   SHORTER WRITINGS

   1   PAINTER, F. V. N. Poets of Virginia. Richmond: B. F.
          Johnson Publishing Company, pp. 238-40.
               Miss Rives is a poet of "extraordinary versatility and
          power." Most of her work is quite "subjective" and belongs
          to the "school of George Eliot." Tanis, the Sang-Digger is
          a "strong and steady piece." Much of her poetry attains a
          "high degree of poetic insight and artistic power."

2   RUTHERFORD, MILDRED LEWIS. The South in History and Litera-
    ture: A Handbook of Southern Authors. Atlanta, Georgia:
    The Franklin-Turner Company, pp. 598-600.
        Miss Rives's first work, "A Brother to Dragons," had
    "daring originality." The Quick or the Dead? caused a sen-
    sation but "reflects no credit upon the author." Herod and
    Mariamne, although in need of good editing, is a "strong
    play." Barbara Dering is free of offensive subject matter.

1908 A   BOOKS - NONE

1908 B   SHORTER WRITINGS

1   ANON. "Current Fiction." The Nation, 86 (28 May), 492-94.
        Although The Golden Rose deals with an "abnormal situa-
    tion," the characters are "sweet at heart." The author's
    style is fortunately not as excessive as it once was.

2   ANON. "The Golden Rose." The Independent, 65 (16 July),
    153-54.
        Miss Rives's treatment of love is "artificial and senti-
    mental." Merand, the protagonist of the new novel, is
    quite "morbid." The unfortunate thing about a novel like
    The Golden Rose is that it feeds "an element of insincerity
    in women readers." The novel, moreover, suffers from the
    author's usual weaknesses, and much of it "should never
    have been written."

3   ANON. "A Review of the Season's Fiction." The American
    Review of Reviews, 37 (June), 760-68.
        Miss Rives's The Golden Rose contains a "charmingly told
    emotional story."

4   MARSH, EDWARD CLARK. "Miss Rives's The Golden Rose." The
    Bookman, 27 (June), 413-14.
        Everything Miss Rives publishes will be judged in terms
    of The Quick or the Dead? Hichens had an analogous problem
    with The Green Carnation. Rives's hallmark as a writer is
    her "extravagance." The Golden Rose demonstrates "occa-
    sional flashes of intelligence" and contains "some delicious
    representations of Negro character and manners."

1909

<u>1909 A BOOKS - NONE</u>

<u>1909 B SHORTER WRITINGS</u>

1   DUKE, R. T. W. "Amélie Rives (Princess Troubetzkoy)," in
     <u>Library of Southern Literature</u>. Edited by Edwin Anderson
     Alderman, et al. 17 volumes. Atlanta: Martin & Hoyt
     Company, vol. 10, pp. 4453-76.
         Miss Rives's ancestry is an illustrious one, including
     Pages, Nelsons, Cabells, Walkers, etc. She spent the win-
     ters from 1873 to 1884 in Mobile, Alabama, the summers at
     "Castle Hill." After 1884 "Castle Hill" became her per-
     manent home. It was "Castle Hill" that shaped the disposi-
     tion of the woman and most influenced her work. The his-
     tory of Miss Rives's first publication, "A Brother to
     Dragons," is recounted, and the repercussions from publi-
     cation of <u>The Quick or the Dead</u>? are examined. The mood of
     her best works is "sometimes dangerously tense and again
     dreamily sensuous." Characterization, however, is not one
     of the strengths of her fiction. Her best work is that
     which reverts to an ideal world of the sixteenth and seven-
     teenth centuries as in "A Brother to Dragons," "Nurse Crum-
     pet Tells the Story," and "The Farrier Lass o' Piping Peb-
     worth." Her poetry is of high merit.

2   SIMONDS, WILLIAM EDWARD. <u>A Student's History of American</u>
     <u>Literature</u>. Boston: Houghton Mifflin Company, p. 347.
         Miss Rives's reputation in literature is owed primarily
     to <u>The Quick or the Dead</u>?

<u>1910 A BOOKS - NONE</u>

<u>1910 B   SHORTER WRITINGS</u>

1   ANON. "Current Fiction." <u>The Nation</u>, 90 (3 February), 112-16.
         The protagonist of <u>Trix and Over the Moon</u> is a somewhat
     masculine woman created for women readers. The mammy and
     the Scotch nurse are a good contrast in the novel which, in
     general, has "merits of tone and finish beyond anything"
     that Miss Rives has ever written.

2   ANON. "Current Fiction." <u>The Nation</u>, 91 (8 December), 550-51.
         In Dione, the heroine of <u>Pan's Mountain</u>, "Exalted happi-
     ness and unfathomable bitterness find expression in words
     and actions that are consonant with her direct, elemental
     nature." She is quite original as a character of fiction.
     Miss Rives's only weakness in <u>Pan's Mountain</u> is in style--
     her excessive use of similes and confusion of <u>lie</u> and <u>lay</u>.

3   ANON. "New Novels." The Athenaeum, 4334 (19 November),
     621-22.
          Pan's Mountain is a "clever romantic novel" that ends in
     tragedy. Dione, the heroine, breaks many social conven-
     tions. Italian dialect and superstition are quite good.

4   ANON. "Some Notable Books of the Year." The Independent, 69
     (17 November), 1087-1104.
          Although the reviewer once admired The Quick or the Dead?,
     he finds Pan's Mountain "absurd." The novel could appeal
     only to "childish old ladies" and "serving maids and shop
     girls."

5   ANON. "Trix and Over the Moon." The Independent, 68
     (10 February), 318.
          The heroine of Trix and Over the Moon is unlike all other
     Rives heroines, for she is quite "sporty," "'horsey.'"

6   MOSES, MONTROSE J. The Literature of the South. New York:
     Thomas Y. Crowell & Company, p. 471.
          Although Miss Rives's work is not "vital," it is "enter-
     taining literature, pleasurable in its associations."

1912 A BOOKS - NONE

1912 B SHORTER WRITINGS

1   ANON. "Chronicle and Comment." The Bookman, 35 (June),
     337-57.
          Three "marked developments in English fiction" of the
     1890's were owed to American inspiration. The third de-
     velopment--the "semi-erotic novel"--may be traced in part,
     to Miss Rives's The Quick or the Dead?, which caused quite
     a stir in its day and age.

2   ANON. "Current Fiction: Hidden House." The Nation, 94
     (27 June), 640.
          The reviewer notes that the "theme of double personality"
     has been frequently used but that Miss Rives adds nothing
     new to it in her new novel. (Both Miss Alice Brown and
     W. H. Mallock have used it lately.) Miss Rives, moreover,
     demonstrates little growth in style or feeling in the new
     work.

3   ANON. "Literary Notes." The Independent, 72 (18 April),
     847-48.

1912

> Miss Rives's works are "like hysterical women. They
> vacillate between a gentle, pure-souled passivity and a
> virago attack of impetuosity." Hidden House is marked by
> sound descriptions, highflown sentences, and "superstitious
> mysticism."

4   ANON. "The New Books." The Outlook, 100 (6 April), 792-95.
        Hidden House takes up an old problem--dual personality.
The new novel is marked by a "perfervid" style. Better
stories have dealt with the same theme.

5   ANON. "Recent Fiction." The Literary Digest, 44 (6 April),
        696-98.
        Miss Rives has always been attracted to the "mysterious,
the elfish and ghostlike." Hidden House reveals that at-
traction, and the novel exhibits "novelty, mystery, and
power."

6   BANCROFT, BURTON. "Amélie Rives's Hidden House." The Bookman,
        35 (June), 431.
        The Quick or the Dead? revealed merely "Youth riding its
Pegasus without bridle or halter." The Scottish poem in
Hidden House is excellent. The novel itself undertakes the
subject of dual personality.

7   BURTON, RICHARD. "The Bellman's Bookshelf." The Bellman, 12
        (4 May), 563.
        Hidden House is a truly "weird" novelette. Although it
has moments of power, its conclusion is far from intense.

1914 A   BOOKS - NONE

1914 B   SHORTER WRITINGS

1   ANON. "A Few New Novels." The American Review of Reviews, 49
        (14 June), 761.
        World's End contains a "poignant love story." Miss
Rives has never drawn a better character than that of
Phoebe Nelson, the heroine.

2   ANON. "Amélie Rives Today." Boston Evening Transcript
        (29 April), p. 25.
        World's End is a "vivid, well-written story of distinct
originality." Richard Bryce is "one of the best drawn
characters."

3   ANON. "The New Books." The Independent, 79 (13 July), 72-74.
     World's End is a disappointment if compared with The
     Quick or the Dead? The villain of the new novel is skill-
     fully drawn.

*4   ANON. Review of World's End. Springfield Republican (14 May),
     p. 5.
          Unlocatable. Listed in Book Review Digest for 1914,
     p. 541.

5   ANON. "World's End." The Athenaeum, 4528 (8 August), 178.
          World's End is devoted to a "study of the contrast be-
     tween selfish and unselfish love." As a whole the novel is
     too long, the latter half needing far more "compression."

6   ANON. "World's End." New York Times Book Review (14 June),
     part 6, p. 277.
          World's End, like The Quick or the Dead?, is a "romance
     of human emotions rather than of episodes." The work
     demonstrates "how a woman's impulses even though wrong,
     may ultimately be supplanted by her reason if properly ap-
     pealed to." Minor characters are quite convincingly drawn.

7   GREENLEAF, MARGARET. "Castle Hill, Virginia, the Country
     Home of the Prince and Princess Troubetzkoy." Country
     Life in America, 36 (October), 41-43.
          A description and brief history of the Rives estate.

8   METCALF, JOHN CALVIN. American Literature. Richmond: B. F.
     Johnson Publishing Company, p. 344.
          Rives was a successful writer of stories.

1915 A BOOKS - NONE

1915 B SHORTER WRITINGS

1   ANON. "The New Books." The American Review of Reviews, 52
     (October), 502-09.
          Shadows of Flames is a tribute to Miss Rives's superb
     "character analysis and her power of dramatic realism."

2   ANON. "Novels by Amélie Rives and Mrs. Barr: Heroines Whose
     Lives Illustrate Some of the Social Problems of the Day
     Depicted in Shadows of Flame and The Measure of Man--
     Entertaining Fiction from Other Authors." New York Times
     Book Review (5 September), part 5, p. 314.

1915

Sophy Tallaferro, the heroine of Shadows of Flames,
holds the reader's attention throughout her many loves.
The male characters are equally fascinating, and the novel
is generally "interesting, well written, and carefully
thought out."

3   ANON. "Shadows of Flame." The Athenaeum, No. 4585
       (11 September), p. 174.
       Miss Rives's depiction of an addict-alcoholic stands in
       sharp contrast to her pleasant view of rural Virginia life
       in Shadows of Flame. It is odd, however, that the heroine
       of the novel should venture a third marriage after two un-
       happy ones.

4   EDGETT, EDWIN FRANCIS. "Amélie Rives The Modern." Boston
       Evening Transcript (1 September), p. 20.
       Those who remember Miss Rives for The Quick or the Dead?
       will be surprised at the "virile force" of Shadows of Flame,
       a novel demonstrating "exceptional knowledge of life and a
       distinctive skill in its vital presentation." Miss Rives's
       use of detail is truly excellent.

5   KELLY, FLORENCE FINCH. "Light-Hearted Novels." The Bookman,
       42 (November), 324-28.
       Miss Rives has come a long way since The Quick or the
       Dead? Shadows of Flames articulates a philosophy in "story
       form." The narrative is told with "intimate detail and
       artistic restraint."

1916 A   BOOKS - NONE

1916 B   SHORTER WRITINGS

1   PAINTER, FRANKLIN VERZELIUS NEWTON. Introduction to American
       Literature. Boston: Sibley & Company, p. 320.
       Miss Rives is a "writer of prose and poetry of unusual
       gifts." Notes that The Quick or the Dead? was "a freakish,
       perverse production that had considerable vogue."

2   PATTEE, FRED LEWIS. A History of American Literature Since
       1870. New York: The Century Company, p. 318.
       Although Rives's The Quick or the Dead? created a sensa-
       tion in its day and age, "it had little significance either
       local or otherwise."

1918 A   BOOKS - NONE

1918 B   SHORTER WRITINGS

1   ANON. "<u>The Ghost Garden</u>." <u>New York Times Review of Books</u>
    (1 September), part 6, p. 370.
        <u>The Ghost Garden</u> is Miss Rives's best novel to date.   In
    it she is able to make the supernatural seem quite real.
    By depending upon beauty rather than horror in her work,
    she has achieved a new kind of ghost story.

2   ANON. "The New Books." <u>The Outlook</u>, 120 (2 October), 187-93.
        <u>The Ghost Garden</u> is written with "delicacy of style and
    treatment and with a fineness of diction."   Its narrative
    seems both psychological and supernatural.

3   ANON. "Troubetzkoy, Amélie (Rives) Chanler. <u>The Ghost</u>
    <u>Garden</u>." <u>American Library Association Booklist</u>, 15
    (November), 71.
        <u>The Ghost Garden</u> is written in a "poetic, colorful style
    with charming pictures in words and the supernatural element
    very well managed."

1919 A   BOOKS - NONE

1919 B   SHORTER WRITINGS

1   ANON. "<u>The Ghost Garden</u>." <u>The Independent</u>, 97 (15 February),
    232.
        The age-old "eternal triangle" is given new perspective
    in Miss Rives's new novel since one of the lovers involved
    in the triangle is a ghost.

2   ANON. "In the Name of the Past." <u>The Nation</u>, 108
    (1 February), 173-74.
        <u>The Ghost Garden</u> uses the "'stock'" complication of
    current fiction.

1920 A   BOOKS - NONE

1920 B   SHORTER WRITINGS

1   ANON. "Poetry." New York <u>Evening Post</u> (27 November), part 3,
    p. 12.
        Although she has a "brilliant, many faceted personality,"
    Miss Rives has produced "unsatisfying" poetry in <u>As the Wind</u>

1920

Blew. The poetry in the new volume employs a "derivative method."

1923 A BOOKS -- NONE

1923 B SHORTER WRITINGS

1   GORDON, ARMISTEAD C. Virginian Writers of Fugitive Verse.
     New York: James T. White & Co., pp. 12, 66, 82, 128, 340,
     341.
          Sees Miss Rives as a writer of "many beautiful lyrics."
     Cites "Grief and Faith," "My Laddie," "A Mood," "Surrender,"
     "Love's Seasons," and "A Dream" as "high achievement" in
     poetry.

1924 A BOOKS -- NONE

1924 B SHORTER WRITINGS

1   EDGERTON, GILES. "The Laboratory Theatre: A New Stage Ideal."
     Arts and Decoration, 21 (May), 29-30.
          The Sea-Woman's Cloak is a "thrilling story of the an-
     cient Irish folk." The play is "written simply about po-
     etical, romantic, half-fairy-like folk." The Gaelic poetic
     quality of the work is truly remarkable. Producer Boles-
     lawsky has wisely chosen to initiate his new theater with
     the production of the Rives Play.

1926 A BOOKS -- NONE

1926 B SHORTER WRITINGS

1   ANON. "The Awkward Age." New York Times Book Review (6 June),
     part 3, p. 22.
          The Queerness of Celia is an "excellent romantic novel."
     The novel contains a "lively plot" certain to appeal to the
     romantic reader.

2   KRUTCH, JOSEPH WOOD. "Drama: Weak Women." The Nation, 122
     (28 April), 484.
          "Love in a Mist" is a "highly amusing farce comedy."
     The farce was written by Rives in conjunction with Gilbert
     Emery.

1927 A BOOKS - NONE

1927 B SHORTER WRITINGS

1   ZETLAND, LAWRENCE JOHN LUMLEY DUNDAS, Second Marquis of
     Ronaldshay. The Life of Lord Curzon. 2 volumes. London:
     Ernest Benn, Ltd., vol. 1, p. 127.
          Lord Curzon notes that The Quick or the Dead? was filled
     with "sensuous phrases and morbid turns of thought."

1929 A BOOKS - NONE

1929 B SHORTER WRITINGS

1   CHILDS, JAMES RIVES. Reliques of the Rives. Lynchburg,
     Virginia: J. A. Bell Company, Inc., pp. 273, 578, 585.
          A genealogical account of the Rives family. In his
     entry for Amélie Louise Rives, Childs includes her place
     and date of birth, her marriages, a list of her published
     writings, and a list of her plays produced in New York.

1930 A BOOKS - NONE

1930 B SHORTER WRITINGS

1   ANON. "Firedamp by Amélie Rives." New York Herald Tribune
     (13 April), p. 18.
          Although Firedamp is set in the contemporary world, it
     tends toward the melodrama so popular in the past with its
     "Niagara of tears and tenderness." A fragile novel, there
     is no "mute strength" underlying the situation. Despite
     such weakness, however, the "pomp of the melodrama" sweeps
     the reader onward.

2   ANON. "The Leisure Arts." The Outlook, 154 (12 February),
     266-68.
          Firedamp attains a beauty of characterization, conversa-
     tion, and description that makes narrative seem unimportant.

3   ANON. "Lord of the Manor." New York Times Book Review
     (16 February), part 6, p. 25 ff.
          Rives has "moments of rare insight" in Firedamp, despite
     the "effects of staginess" and the broken unity of the
     novel.

1930

4   PATTEE, FRED LEWIS. The New American Literature: 1890-1930.
     New York: The Century Company, p. 245.
        The Quick or the Dead? was one of four American novels
     by female writers to shock American readers prior to the
     publication of Stephen Crane's Maggie.

1931 A   BOOKS - NONE

1931 B   SHORTER WRITINGS

1   CLARK, EMILY. "Amélie Rives (Princess Troubetzkoy)," in
     Innocence Abroad. New York: Alfred A. Knopf, pp. 73-84.
        Recounts Miss Rives's relationship to the newly founded
     Richmond magazine The Reviewer (1921). On her first visit
     to "Castle Hill" in July 1921, Clark was greatly impressed
     by the estate, which she contends was the setting for every
     novel Rives ever wrote. Clark sees her as unmistakably
     "modern" and in this sense compares her with Helen of Troy.
     References to Rives's London stay, her friendships with
     Lord Curzon and Oscar Wilde, and her introduction to
     Troubetzkoy are included. During her London years Thomas
     Hardy, Henry James, and George Meredith were among her ac-
     quaintances. Her preference for European literature is
     briefly discussed.

2   WARREN, ALBERT V. "Romance of Publishing Venture Here
     Described." Richmond Times-Dispatch (15 March), part 2,
     p. 3.
        A satirical review of Emily Clark's recently published
     Innocence Abroad (See 1931.B1). Satirizes the Virginia
     myth of Rives's beauty and nobility.

1932 A   BOOKS - NONE

1932 B   SHORTER WRITINGS

1   KNIGHT, GRANT C. American Literature and Culture. New York:
     Ray Long and Richard R. Smith, Inc., p. 446.
        The popularity of Rives's work was part of a growing
     discontent with urban life of the period.

2   NEWMAN, JOHN W. "'Castle Hill,' the Old Home of Dr. Thomas
     Walker." Kentucky Progress Magazine, 4 (April), 23, 32-33.
        Recounts here a tour of "Castle Hill" and a meeting with
     Prince Troubetzkoy, Miss Landon Rives, and Amélie Rives her-
     self. The majority of the article is devoted to a descrip-
     tion of the estate and its ties to early Kentucky history.

1934 A   BOOKS - NONE

1934 B   SHORTER WRITINGS

1   CHANLER, MRS. WINTHROP [MARGARET TERRY]. Roman Spring.
     Boston: Little, Brown, and Company, pp. 209-11.
          Mrs. Chanler recalls that The Quick or the Dead? had a
     "certain succès de scandale" when it was first published.
     She adds that "There was a good deal of long kissing" in
     the work. Recalls a spring long past when she and her hus-
     band paid a visit to "Castle Hill." Miss Rives's effect,
     at that time, on the young men was "dazzling." Following
     a description of Rives, Mrs. Chanler concludes that she
     was "a siren, a goddess, perhaps a genius." Shortly after
     that visit, Mrs. Chanler's brother-in-law John Armstrong
     Chanler married Miss Rives.

1935 A   BOOKS - NONE

1935 B   SHORTER WRITINGS

1   KNIGHT, GRANT C. James Lane Allen and the Genteel Tradition.
     Chapel Hill: The University of North Carolina Press,
     pp. 85, 94.
          Thomas Nelson Page considered Miss Rives one of the
     "chief Southern writers since the war."

2   MEADE, JULIAN R. I Live in Virginia. New York and Toronto:
     Longmans, Green, and Company, pp. 143-53.
          Recounts the pleasures of his visit to "Castle Hill,"
     his greeting from Prince Troubetzkoy, etc. His impression-
     istic description of the household and the estate is in-
     cluded. Notes Miss Rives's belief in psychic communication
     and her many famous friends (James, Wilde, Curzon, and
     Hardy). Cultural life at "Castle Hill" is quite impressive.

1936 A   BOOKS - NONE

1936 B   SHORTER WRITINGS

1   FULLERTON, B[RADFORD] M[ORTON]. Selective Bibliography of
     American Literature 1775-1900. New York: Dial Press,
     pp. 276-77.
          A brief sketch of Miss Rives's development and signifi-
     cance. Points out the author's rebellion "against Victorian
     conventions." The two works cited in the bibliography are

1936

> A Brother to Dragons and Other Old-Time Tales and The Quick
> or the Dead? The latter is "bibliographically an interest-
> ing book."

2   QUINN, ARTHUR HOBSON. A History of the American Drama From
    the Civil War to the Present Day. 2 volumes. New York:
    Appleton-Century-Crofts, vol. 2, p. 80.
       Rives and Gilbert Emery collaborated on Love in a Mist
    (1926), a "charming comedy."

3   WORDEN, HELEN. Society Circus: From Ring to Ring With A
    Large Cast. New York: Corici Friede Publishers, p. 155.
       Recalls Miss Rives's former ties to the Chanler family:
    "The Princess Troubetzkoy (Amélie Rives), the author, was
    the first Mrs. John Armstrong Chaloner [Chanler]."

1938 A   BOOKS - NONE

1938 B   SHORTER WRITINGS

1   PURCELL, JAMES SLICER, JR. "The Southern Poor White in
    Fiction." Unpublished M.A. thesis, Duke University,
    pp. 109-10.
       The heroine of Virginia of Virginia was the "spirited,
    independent daughter of an overseer," a Virginia poor
    white. The protagonist of the novel "could only fight cir-
    cumstances; never rise above them." Miss Rives, therefore,
    seems to have believed that "the poor white could rise so
    far but no further."

1942 A   BOOKS - NONE

1942 B   SHORTER WRITINGS

1   "Troubetzkoy, Amélie (Rives), Princess," in Twentieth Century
    Authors. Edited by Stanley J. Kunitz and Howard Haycroft.
    New York: The H. W. Wilson Company, p. 1421.
       An account of Rives's early development. Miss Rives's
    own favorite work was her blank verse drama Augustine the
    Man. Her novel The Quick or the Dead? caused quite a stir
    when it first appeared.

1945 A BOOKS - NONE

1945 B SHORTER WRITINGS

 1   ANON. "Amélie Rives, Authoress, Dies, Aged 81." Richmond
        Times-Dispatch (17 June), p. B-14.
            The Quick or the Dead? received much harsh criticism
        owing to its candid treatment of subject matter.

 2   ANON. "Amélie Rives Dies; Popular Novelist." New York Times
        (17 June), part 2, p. 26.
            The Quick or the Dead? brought notoriety to Rives primar-
        ily because of its candid treatment of sex.

 3   ANON. "Amélie Rives, Gifted Virginia Woman Dies." Richmond
        News Leader (16 June), p. 9.
            Miss Rives will be remembered for her authorship of
        widely popular romantic fiction.

 4   ANON. "Troubetzkoy Rites are Conducted at 'Castle Hill.'"
        Richmond Times-Dispatch (19 June), p. 15.
            Miss Rives will be remembered for her work as "author
        and playwright."

 5   ROBERTSON, DOROTHY. "Valentine Museum Displaying Mementoes of
        Amélie Rives." Richmond Times-Dispatch (17 September),
        p. 14.
            Miss Rives's novels were considered "rather shocking"
        and "risqué" even as late as 1914 when World's End was
        published.

1946 A BOOKS - NONE

1946 B SHORTER WRITINGS

 1   HOLMAN, HARRIET R. "A Letter from Henry W. Grady Regarding
        Southern Authors and the Piedmont Chautauqua." Georgia
        Historical Quarterly, 30 (December), 308-11.
            In his letter to Thomas Nelson Page, Henry W. Grady
        notes that he plans to have Amélie Rives as one of the best
        Southern writers at the Piedmont Chautauqua in Atlanta.
        Notes that Miss Rives did not attend.

1947

1947 A   BOOKS - NONE

1947 B   SHORTER WRITINGS

  1   MOTT, FRANK LUTHER. Golden Multitudes: The Story of the
        Best Sellers in the United States. New York: The Mac-
        millan Company, pp. 249, 323.
           The Quick or the Dead? owed much of its popularity to its
        naughtiness and sensationalism. The novelette contained a
        "morbid theme and some scenes of hysterical passion." The
        work was frequently parodied.

1951 A   BOOKS - NONE

1951 B   SHORTER WRITINGS

  1   GOHDES, CLARENCE. "The Later Nineteenth Century," in The
        Literature of the American People. Edited by Arthur Hobson
        Quinn. New York: Appleton-Century-Crofts, Inc., p. 740.
           Although a somewhat frank treatment of sex was impossible
        in late nineteenth century American realism, some fiction
        of a "'semi-erotic'" nature did appear. The "heat" of a
        novel like The Quick or the Dead?, for example, appears
        "unconsciously genuine," the heroine "suddenly touched with
        nymphomania."

1953 A   BOOKS - NONE

1953 B   SHORTER WRITINGS

  1   ANDERSON, SHERWOOD. Letters of Sherwood Anderson. Edited by
        Howard Mumford Jones and Walter B. Rideout. Boston:
        Little, Brown, and Company, p. 252.
           In his letter dated 24 October 1931 to Laura Lou Copen-
        haver, Anderson briefly notes his visit to "Castle Hill."

1955 A   BOOKS - NONE

1955 B   SHORTER WRITINGS

  1   "Troubetzkoy, Amélie Rives," in Twentieth Century Authors.
        Edited by Stanley J. Kunitz. New York: H. W. Wilson
        Company, p. 1009.
           An account of Miss Rives's death. According to the
        Boston Transcript, she had "'an exceptional knowledge of
        life and a distinctive skill in its presentation.'"

1958 A BOOKS - NONE

1958 B SHORTER WRITINGS

1   GLASGOW, ELLEN. Letters of Ellen Glasgow. Edited by Blair
     Rouse. New York: Harcourt, Brace and Company, p. 224.
          In her letter of 23 August 1937 to Rives, Miss Glasgow
     quotes from The Golden Rose.

1961 A BOOKS - NONE

1961 B SHORTER WRITINGS

1   ROBINS, PAT. "'Petticoat' Poetry Began Virginia Writer's
     Career." Richmond News Leader (8 August), p. 10.
          The publication of The Quick or the Dead?, Miss Rives's
     excursion into veiled autobiography, caused a sensation in
     its day.

1962 A BOOKS - NONE

1962 B SHORTER WRITINGS

1   GALLUP, DONALD. "More Letters of American Writers." Yale
     University Library Gazette, 37 (July), 30-35.
          Cites a letter dated 13 April 1888 from Miss Rives to a
     Miss Dickinson. According to Rives, there was no model for
     Barbara Pomfret, heroine of The Quick or the Dead?

2   WILDE, OSCAR. The Letters of Oscar Wilde. Edited by Rupert
     Hart-Davis. New York: Harcourt, Brace, and World, Inc.,
     p. 340.
          Oscar Wilde wrote to Miss Rives in January 1889 to send
     her a copy of "The Decay of Lying."

1963 A BOOKS - NONE

1963 B SHORTER WRITINGS

1   HART, JAMES D. The Popular Book: A History of America's
     Literary Taste. Berkeley and Los Angeles: University of
     California Press, p. 199.
          The Quick or the Dead? was geared to American taste for
     romance, a taste giving rise to "sophisticated treatments
     of moral issues in high society."

1963

2   TAYLOR, WELFORD DUNAWAY. "Amélie Rives: A Virginia Princess."
     Virginia Calvalcade, 12 (Spring), pp. 11-17.
          A largely biographical account. Notes that "A Brother
     to Dragons" "smacked of the Elizabethan idiom, and the plot
     was overly romantic." The Quick or the Dead?, a "contro-
     versial" novel sold "300,000 copies."

1965 A BOOKS - NONE

1965 B SHORTER WRITINGS

1   BRYAN, J., III. "Johnny Jacknapes, The Merry-Andrew of the
     Merry Mills." The Virginia Magazine of History and
     Biography, 73 (January), 3-21.
          Miss Rives and her fiancé John Armstrong Chanler were
     identified by many as the lovers in The Quick or the Dead?

2   HART, JAMES D. The Oxford Companion to American Literature.
     Fourth edition. New York: Oxford University Press,
     p. 715.
          Miss Rives was under the influence of the "attenuated
     impressionism of the fin de siècle authors, as is revealed
     in her novelette, The Quick or the Dead?"

3   LOGAN, ANDY. "That Was New York: Town Topics." The New
     Yorker, 46 (21 August), 41-98.
          Cites Rives's The Fear Market as an example of dramatic
     treatment of a "criminal proceeding." Running for 118 per-
     formances in 1916, the play dealt with "the venal day-to-
     day operations of a scandal magazine owned by a rambunc-
     tious retired military figure," one Colonel William D'Alton
     Mann.

4   PAGE, RICHARD CHANNING MOORE. Genealogy of the Page Family
     in Virginia. Bridgewater, Virginia: C. J. Carrier
     Company, p. 232.
          An account of Miss Rives's ancestry on her father's
     side.

1967 A BOOKS - NONE

1967 B SHORTER WRITINGS

1   MOORE, JOHN HAMMOND. "Amélie Louise Rives and the Charge of
     the Light Brigade." The Virginia Magazine of History and
     Biography, 75 (January), 89-96.
          An account of Rives's namesake.

Amélie Rives Troubetzkoy: A Reference Guide

1968 A BOOKS - NONE

1968 B SHORTER WRITINGS

1   MOORE, JOHN HAMMOND. "The Vagabond and the Lady: Letters
     from Richard Hovey to Amélie Rives." The Mississippi
     Quarterly, 20 (Spring), 131-43.
          The relationship of the American poet Richard Hovey and
     Amélie Rives began in spring 1888. Because of the deep ad-
     miration Hovey had for her, one suspects that she may be
     the mysterious "Miriam" of his life. Included in the ar-
     ticle are a number of letters and poems written by Hovey to
     Rives.

1969 A BOOKS

1   LONGEST, GEORGE CALVIN. "Amélie Rives Troubetzkoy: A
     Biography." Ph.D. dissertation, University of Georgia,
     120 pp.
          Miss Rives is primarily an American local colorist who
     chose as the settings for most of her fiction Albemarle
     County, Virginia, her birthplace and permanent home. As an
     artist, she was a product of the fin de siècle, and a major
     exponent of the school of American local color. Like James
     and Howells, she was primarily a realist in technique,
     though unlike either, she utilized sensuality in a marked
     manner. In many ways, her works anticipate later American
     female writers like Gertrude Atherton. An internationalist,
     Miss Rives formed acquaintances with Oscar Wilde, George
     Meredith, Thomas Hardy, Henry James, and Lord Curzon.
     American acquaintances included Ellen Glasgow, Thomas Nel-
     son Page, Samuel Langhorne Clemens, H. L. Mencken, James
     Branch Cabell, Richard Hovey, Joseph Hergesheimer, Sinclair
     Lewis, and Emily Clark. Miss Rives's unpleasant stay in
     Mobile, Alabama from 1871 to 1883 merely intensified her
     inherent romanticism. Romantic thought and subject matter,
     though in large part the substance of her fiction, were
     conveyed in realistic manner. Her contributions to Ameri-
     can literature appear to have been made in such areas as
     the widening of the latitude of the artist, regionalism,
     social history, local color, the notion of the American
     abroad, and realism of a somewhat advanced nature. In-
     cluded in the critical biography are discussions of A
     Brother to Dragons and Other Old-Time Tales, The Quick or
     the Dead?, According to St. John, Firedamp, The Ghost Gar-
     den, The Golden Rose, Virginia of Virginia, and Tanis, the
     Sang-Digger.

1969

1969 B SHORTER WRITINGS

1 HERZBERG, MAX J., ed. The Reader's Encyclopedia of American
     Literature. New York: Thomas Y. Crowell Company, p. 1154.
        An account of Miss Rives's birth, marriages, and publi-
     cations. Best known for The Quick or the Dead?, she never
     again equalled that popularity. She is best remembered as
     a member of the Erotic School, which rebelled against the
     stricter rules of Mrs. Grundy and which bore the "influence
     of the art-for-art's-sake movement in England."

2 MENKE, PAMELA GLENN. "Amélie Rives (1863-1945)," in A
     Bibliographical Guide to the Study of Southern Literature.
     Edited by Louis D. Rubin, Jr. Baton Rouge: Louisiana
     State University Press, pp. 279-81.
        The Quick or the Dead? and Barbara Dering were the only
     two works to receive "critical attention." Considerable
     attention, on the other hand, has been devoted to Miss
     Rives's glamorous life. Lists twelve items in the
     bibliography.

1971 A BOOKS - NONE

1971 B SHORTER WRITINGS

1 EICHELBERGER, CLAYTON L., ed. A Guide to Critical Reviews of
     United States Fiction, 1870-1910. Metuchen, New Jersey:
     The Scarecrow Press, vol. 1, p. 305.
        Lists 28 reviews of Rives fiction.

2 TAYLOR, WELFORD DUNAWAY. "A 'Soul' Remembers Oscar Wilde."
     English Literature in Transition, vol. 14, pp. 43-48.
        Oscar Wilde is the real subject of Miss Rives's novel
     Shadows of Flames. She came to know Wilde during the sum-
     mers of 1889 and 1894.

1972 A BOOKS - NONE

1972 B SHORTER WRITINGS

1 TAYLOR, W. D. "Rives, Amélie," in Virginia Authors: Past and
     Present. Edited by W. D. Taylor. Richmond: The William
     Byrd Press, Inc., p. 97.
        Best known for The Quick or the Dead?, Amélie Rives was
     most influenced by her life at "Castle Hill" and by her mar-
     riages to John Armstrong Chanler and subsequently to Prince
     Pierre Troubetzkoy.

1973 A   BOOKS

1   TAYLOR, WELFORD DUNAWAY. Amélie Rives (Princess Troubetzkoy).
     New York: Twayne Publishers, 162 pp.
         Miss Rives's home "Castle Hill" became her "objective
     correlative conveying a feeling of permanence and stability
     in the midst of a changing American society, which to the
     author was anything but permanent and stable." Opening
     chapters discuss her childhood and education, her contact
     with Thomas Bailey Aldrich, editor of the Atlantic Monthly,
     her publication of "A Brother to Dragons" in March, 1886,
     and her growth into realism, which culminated in the 1888
     publication of The Quick or the Dead? The book considers
     the circumstances of her tragic marriage to John Armstrong
     Chanler in April, 1888, her idyllic marriage to Prince
     Pierre Troubetzkoy in 1896, and the influence of the two
     marriages on her development as both woman and writer. Dis-
     cusses all her major works including According to St. John,
     As the Wind Blew, Athelwold, Firedamp, The Ghost Garden,
     The Golden Rose, Virginia of Virginia, and Tanis, the Sang-
     Digger. Critical attention is focused on Miss Rives's em-
     phasis on femininity and her marital attitudes, especially
     in Barbara Dering.

1973 B   SHORTER WRITINGS - NONE

1974 A   BOOKS - NONE

1974 B   SHORTER WRITINGS

1   EICHELBERGER, CLAYTON L., ed. A Guide to Critical Reviews of
     United States Fiction, 1870-1910. Metuchen, New Jersey:
     The Scarecrow Press, Inc., vol. 2, p. 269.
         Lists 20 reviews of Rives fiction.

Three Virginia Writers/Index

Index to Mary Johnston

Laird of Glenfernie, The, 1919.B3

Landscape, landscape painting, 1898.B3; 1899.B4; 1900.B3, B10, B12, B16, B17; 1907.B3; 1908.B3, B15; 1914.B6; 1916.B2; 1922.B6; 1924.B4; 1926.B1, B2; 1927.B11; 1931.B1; 1958.B1

Leisy, Ernest E., 1950.B1; 1958.B1

Leonard, Priscilla, 1904.B8

Lewis Rand, 1908.B1-B6, B8-B11, B16; 1909.B1, B3, B5; 1910.B1; 1928.B2; 1936.A1, B7, B9; 1938.B1; 1941.A1; 1958.B1; 1961.B1; 1966.A1; 1972.A2

Lillard, Richard G., 1956.B1

Literature of the American People, The, 1951.B1

Lively, Robert A., 1957.B1

Long Roll, The, 1911.B1-B12, B14-B19, B21, B23-B27; 1912.B1; 1914.B10; 1915.B15; 1922.B6; 1924.B5; 1926.B8; 1928.B2; 1930.B3, B4; 1936.A1, B7; 1941.A1; 1957.B1; 1966.A1; 1972.A2

Loveman, Amy, 1923.B9

Lublin, Curtis, 1913.B17

Lutz, Mark, 1933.B8

Lynd, Robert, 1915.B17

Mann, Dorothea Lawrance, 1924.B7

"Mary Johnston and the Historic Imagination," 1961.B1

"Mary Johnston as a Novelist," 1941.A1

"Mary Johnston--From Virginian to American," 1966.A1

Marley, Harold P., 1928.B1

Melodramatic, 1900.B7, B17; 1902.B6, B7; 1915.B13; 1927.B11; 1954.B1

Michael Forth, 1919.B4, B8; 1920.B1, B2, B4, B8, B11; 1924.B8; 1928.B2; 1936.A1; 1941.A1; 1952.B2; 1966.A1; 1972.A2

Mims, Edwin, 1909.B5; 1926.B8

Miss Delicia Allen, 1933.B1-B9; 1936.A1; 1941.A1; 1966.A1; 1972.A2

Moss, Mary, 1904.B9

Mott, Frank Luther, 1947.B1

Mysticism, 1919.B4; 1920.B1, B4, B6, B8-B11; 1921.B1, B2; 1922.B1, B2, B5, B11; 1924.B4, B6, B8; 1926.B2; 1927.B2, B5, B8, B10; 1930.B4; 1933.B7; 1934.B5; 1941.A1; 1942.B2; 1961.B1; 1966.A1; 1972.A2

Nelson, Lawrence G., 1961.B1

"Novels of Mary Johnston: A Critical Study, The," 1972.A2

O'Connor, Mrs. T. P., 1914.B21

Odum, Howard W., 1930.B2

Old Dominion, The, 1899.B2, B3

Overton, Grant S., 1922.B12; 1924.B8; 1928.B2

Oxford Companion to American Literature, The, 1965.B1

Painter, Franklin Verzelius Newton, 1916.B4

Pangborn, H. L., 1922.B13; 1924.B9

Parsons, Alice B., 1926.B9

Paterson, Isabel, 1926.B10

Pattee, Fred Lewis, 1916.B5; 1930.B3

Patterson, Dorothya Rentfro, 1941.A1

Payne, William Morton, 1898.B7; 1900.B17; 1902.B16; 1904.B10; 1908.B16; 1911.B24

Pearson, Edmund, 1927.B12

"Penwoman of Virginia's Feminists," 1956.B2

Pioneers of the Old South, 1919.B5, B6, B7; 1920.B5

Polk, Noel, 1975.B1

Popular Book, The, 1963.B1

Pratt, Cornelia Atwood, 1900.B18

Prisoners of Hope, 1898.B1-B7; 1899.B1, B4; 1902.B13;

1903.B1; 1907.B3; 1909.B6;
1924.B5; 1927.B11; 1936.A1,
B7, B9; 1941.A1; 1952.B2;
1961.B1; 1966.A1; 1972.A2
Purcell, James Slicer, Jr.,
1938.B1

Quinn, Arthur Hobson, 1936.B7,
B8; 1951.B1

Reader's Encyclopedia of American
Literature, The, 1969.B1
Realism, 1911.B7, B12; 1912.B2;
1914.B12; 1915.B2; 1923.B9;
1926.B8; 1930.B4
Realism, lack of, 1904.B5;
1926.B10; 1927.B1, B8;
1936.B2
"Rediscovery of Mary Johnston,"
1942.B2
Reely, Mary Katharine, 1914.B22
Richardson, Eudora Ramsay,
1930.B4
Roberson, John R., 1956.B5
Rogers, Joseph M., 1911.B25
Romance, 1898.B6, B7; 1900.B2,
B18; 1902.B2, B7, B12, B15;
1904.B1, B3, B8; 1914.B3;
1915.B10, B17; 1932.B4;
1963.B2; 1969.B1; 1972.A2
Romanticism, 1902.B5, B9;
1914.B20; 1918.B4; 1920.B3;
1930.B3, B4; 1931.B6;
1941.A1; 1942.B1
Rouse, Blair, 1969.B2
Rubin, Louis D., Jr., 1976.B1
Rutherford, Mildred Lewis,
1907.B3

Sales, 1900.B6, B10, B11;
1903.B2; 1914.B1; 1916.B5;
1918.B3; 1945.B1; 1947.B1;
1954.B1; 1956.B4; 1963.B1,
B3; 1967.B1
70 Years of Best Sellers,
1967.B1
Sherman, Caroline B., 1942.B2
Silver Cross, 1922.B1-B4, B6-B11,
B16; 1928.B2; 1941.A1;
1942.B1; 1969.B1; 1972.A2

Simkins, Francis Butler,
1963.B2
Simonds, William E., 1900.B19;
1909.B7
Sir Mortimer, 1904.B1-B10;
1909.B6; 1936.B9; 1941.A1;
1961.B1; 1967.B1; 1972.A2
60 Years of Best Sellers,
1956.B4
Slave Ship, The, 1924.B1-B4, B6,
B7, B9; 1925.B1; 1927.B9;
1928.B2; 1936.A1; 1941.A1;
1961.B1; 1963.B2; 1966.A1;
1972.A2
Smertenko, Johan J., 1922.B15
"Southern Poor White in Fiction,
The," 1938.B1
Southern Writers: Appraisals in
Our Time, 1961.B1
Spiller, Robert E., 1955.B1;
1963.B3
Sweet Rocket, 1920.B3, B6, B7,
B9, B10; 1921.B1, B2;
1924.B5, B8; 1928.B2;
1936.B9; 1941.A1; 1966.A1;
1972.A2

Taylor, W. D., 1972.B1
Tinker, Edward Larocque,
1933.B9; 1934.B5
To Have and to Hold, 1900.B2, B4,
B6-B12, B14-B19; 1902.B11,
B13, B14; 1903.B1; 1904.B7;
1907.B3; 1908.B11; 1918.B3;
1924.B5; 1928.B2; 1930.B3;
1932.B2, B4; 1936.A1, B7, B9;
1941.A1; 1945.B1; 1947.B1;
1951.B1; 1952.B2; 1956.B4;
1958.B1; 1961.B1; 1963.B1,
B3; 1966.A1; 1972.A2
Torrence, William Clayton,
1911.B26
Townsend, R. D., 1922.B16
Twentieth Century Authors,
1942.B1
"Two Virginia Novelists on
Woman's Suffrage: An Exchange
of Letters Between Mary Johnston and Thomas Nelson Page,"
1956.B5
Tyler, Alice, 1912.B9

Unity, 1902.B9, B11, B14;
 1904.B8; 1907.B2; 1918.B4;
 1926.B3
VanAuke, Sheldon, 1948.B2
Van Doren, Carl, 1921.B3
Virginia Authors: Past and
 Present, 1972.B1
"Virginia History in the Histori-
 cal Novels of Mary Johnston,
 The," 1936.A1
Virginia Tradition, The,
 1956.B3

Wagenknecht, Edward, 1936.B9;
 1952.B2
Wanderers, The, 1917.B1-B10;
 1918.B5; 1941.A1; 1961.B1;
 1972.A2
White, William Allen, 1930.B5
Willcocks, M. P., 1915.B18
William Elliott Shoots a Bear,
 1976.B1
Witch, The, 1914.B1-B3, B5-B8,
 B11-B18; 1924.B8; 1941.A1;
 1961.B1; 1972.A2
Woolsey, D. B., 1927.B13
"World and Mary Johnston, The,"
 1936.B9

Index to Thomas Nelson Page

1913.B1-B3, B8, B10, B12, B13, B17, B18; 1916.B1, B2; 1917.B1-B6; 1918.B1-B3; 1919.B1; 1922.B3; 1923.A1, B1, B6-B9, B14, B16, B17; 1924.B6, B11; 1925.B3, B4; 1926.B1; 1927.A1; 1928.B1; 1933.A3; 1938.B1; 1940.B1; 1941.B1; 1944.A1; 1945.B1; 1946.B1, B2; 1947.A1; 1950.A1; 1953.B6-B8; 1954.B1; 1956.B3; 1957.B2; 1959.B2; 1961.B1, B3; 1964.A1; 1965.B5; 1967.A1; 1969.B2; 1970.B2-B4; 1976.B1

Bittinger, Mary Shirkey, 1945.A1

Blackford, W. W., 1945.B2

Bred in the Bone, 1904.B1-B3, B6; 1905.B4, B7; 1906.B2; 1927.A1; 1931.A2; 1932.A1; 1933.A1, A2; 1936.B2; 1964.A1; 1967.A1

Bridgers, Frank Ernst, Jr., 1933.A3

Bridges, Robert, 1913.B14

"Brief for the South, A," 1899.B15

Brodin, Pierre, 1937.B1

Brooks, Van Wyck, 1953.B4

Brown, Dorothy Ware, 1950.A1

Brown, Sterling A., 1939.B1

Buck, Paul H., 1937.B2

Burial of the Guns, The, 1894.B1, B2, B9, B11, B17; 1895.B1, B2, B4; 1903.B18; 1907.B8; 1931.A2; 1932.A1; 1933.A1-A3; 1962.B1; 1964.A1; 1967.A1

Burlingame, Roger, 1946.B1

Cable, George Washington, 1900.B4; 1909.B8

Cairns, William B., 1912.B10

Cambridge History of American Literature, The, 1918.B4

Captured Santa Claus, A, 1902.B1; 1903.B3

"Case of the Carpet-Baggers, The," 1899.B14

Cash, W. J., 1941.B2

Cavalcade of the American Novel, 1952.B2

Cavalier and Yankee, 1961.B5

Chamberlayne, Lewis Parke, 1913.B15

Character, emphasis on, 1903.B7, B9, B14; 1904.B1; 1908.B4; 1909.B11; 1923.B13; 1932.B2; 1936.B2; 1959.B2, B3; 1960.B1

Characterization, 1898.B13, B15; 1900.B4, B5; 1903.B7, B9, B14; 1904.B6; 1905.B4; 1907.B5; 1909.B3; 1916.B3; 1923.B4; 1927.A1, B2; 1931.A1, A2; 1932.B2; 1933.A1-A4; 1939.B2; 1945.A1; 1947.A1, B1; 1950.A1; 1952.B1; 1961.B2, B5; 1964.A1; 1965.B3, B4; 1967.A1; 1971.B4; 1973.B2; 1976.B1

"Charming Old Gentleman, A," 1900.B4

Chew, Samuel C., 1922.B5

Children, fiction for, 1888.B2, B3, B5; 1892.B8, B13, B14; 1898.B1, B7, B11; 1931.A1; 1944.A1; 1947.A1

"Children in Thomas Nelson Page's Stories of Children," 1931.A1

Clark, Kate Upson, 1891.B12

Coan, Otis W., 1956.B1

Coast of Bohemia, The, 1907.B1, B3, B7; 1968.A1

Coleman, Charles W., 1887.B9

Comic Imagination in American Literature, The, 1973.B3

Commemorative Tributes to Page, Wilson, and Bacon, 1925.B3

Compared with other authors, Allen, James Lane, 1913.B18
Bierce, Ambrose, 1967.B2
Bunyan, John, 1903.B4
Cable, George Washington, 1936.B2; 1964.A1
Clemens, Samuel Langhorne, 1888.B5
Dickens, Charles, 1910.B1

Dixon, Thomas, Jr., 1905.B6
Faulkner, William, 1962.B1, B2
Garland, Hamlin, 1973.B1
Glasgow, Ellen, 1931.A2;
    1933.A4; 1947.B1; 1965.B1
Harris, Joel Chandler,
    1887.B9; 1893.B7; 1896.B1;
    1936.A1; 1947.B1
Harte, Bret, 1923.B4
Hawthorne, Nathaniel,
    1903.B18; 1913.B4
Hesiod, 1893.B5
Kennedy, John Pendleton,
    1960.B2
Murfree, Mary Noailles,
    1923.B4
Norris, Frank, 1973.B1
Russell, Irwin, 1896.B1;
    1903.B18; 1968.A1
Stowe, Harriet Beecher,
    1889.B1; 1906.B5
Thackeray, William Makepeace,
    1903.B18
"Comparison of the Negro Dialect
    Poetry of Irwin Russell and
    Thomas Nelson Page, A,"
    1968.A1
Complete Works, 1906.B2;
    1907.B4, B6
"Conception of the Southern
    Aristocracy in the Fiction
    of Thomas Nelson Page, The,"
    1933.A2
Confident Years, The, 1953.B4
Cooper, Frederick Taber,
    1910.B2
Cowan, Louise, 1959.B1
Cowie, Alexander, 1948.B1
Craver, Sadie B., 1944.A1
Cycle of American Literature,
    The, 1955.B1

Dabney, Virginius, 1932.B1;
    1971.B1
Daly, Augustin, 1917.B5;
    1970.B1
Daly, Joseph Francis, 1917.B5
Dante and His Influence,
    1922.B1, B2, B5; 1923.B2,
    B3, B14
Davis, Charles Belmont, 1917.B6

Davis, Mary Moore, 1931.A1
Development of the American Short
    Story, The, 1923.B13
Dialect, 1886.B1; 1887.B1-B4, B6,
    B7, B9; 1888.B1; 1891.B3;
    1893.B2, B5-B7; 1894.B4, B7;
    1895.B5, B7; 1908.B5;
    1909.B9, B11; 1918.B4;
    1922.B4; 1923.B4, B11;
    1924.B1; 1936.A1, B2;
    1938.B1; 1941.B1; 1945.A1;
    1947.B1; 1968.A1; 1973.B3
Dickinson, A. T., Jr., 1971.B2
Dictionary of American Biography,
    1943.B1
Dodd, William E., 1908.B4
Dowd, Jerome, 1927.B1
Duke, R. T. W., 1899.B13;
    1907.B5

Earle, Mary Tracy, 1898.B13
Eaton, Isabel, 1905.B5
Eccentricities of Genius,
    1900.B5
Edgett, Edwin Francis, 1913.B16
Eichelberger, Clayton L.,
    1971.B3; 1974.B1
Ellwood, Charles A., 1906.B3
"Elsket," 1892.B6, B12, B14;
    1931.A2; 1932.A1; 1933.A1
Elsket and Other Stories,
    1891.B5, B7, B9, B13;
    1892.B5, B6, B13; 1909.B11;
    1923.B12; 1931.A2; 1932.A1;
    1933.A2; 1962.B1
Essays Mostly on Periodical
    Publishing in America,
    1973.B1

Famous Authors (Men), 1906.B5
Ferment of Realism, The,
    1965.B1
Fiction Fights the Civil War,
    1957.B1
Fishwick, Marshall, 1953.B5;
    1956.B2; 1959.B2, B3;
    1961.B1
Frontier in American Literature,
    The, 1927.B2
Fugitive Group, The, 1959.B1
Fuller, Henry C., 1924.B8

Fullerton, Bradford Morton,
    1936.B1
"Function of Criticism in the
    South, The," 1903.B17

Gaines, Clarence H., 1924.B9
Gaines, Francis Pendleton,
    1924.B10; 1953.B2
Genealogy of the Page Family in
    Virginia, 1965.B5
General Lee: Man and Soldier,
    1909.B2
"Gentleman at Rome, A,"
    1913.B17
Gentlemen of Virginia, 1961.B1
"George Washington Cable and
    Thomas Nelson Page: Two
    Literary Approaches to the
    New South," 1964.A1
"Gerald W. Johnson, Thomas
    Nelson Page, and the South,"
    1961.B4
Gloster, Hugh M., 1948.B2
Gohdes, Clarence, 1951.B1
Gordon, Armistead Churchill,
    1895.B7; 1917.B4; 1927.B7-B9;
    1924.B11
Gordon Keith, 1903.B1, B2,
    B4-B10, B12, B14, B19;
    1904.B5, B7; 1907.B6;
    1909.B11; 1917.B4; 1931.A2;
    1932.A1; 1933.A1-A4;
    1936.B2; 1947.A1; 1953.B5;
    1954.B1; 1960.B1; 1961.B4;
    1964.A1; 1965.B4; 1967.A1;
    1971.B4
Graves, John Temple, 1913.B17
Greever, Garland, 1912.B11
Gross, Theodore, 1961.B2, B3;
    1967.A1, B1; 1971.B4
Guide to Critical Reviews of
    United States Fiction, A,
    1971.B3; 1974.B1
"Guide to Dissertations on
    American Literary Figures,
    1870-1910: Part Two,"
    1975.B1

Halliday, Carl, 1906.B4
Halsey, Francis Whiting,
    1901.B3

Haney, John Louis, 1923.B10
Hanover County: Its History and
    Legends, 1926.B2
Harkins, Edward Francis, 1906.B5
Harrington, F. H., 1937.B3
Harris, Mrs. L. H., 1903.B15
Hart, James D., 1965.B2
Harvests of Change, 1967.B2
Hawkins, Sir Anthony Hope,
    1928.B1
Hazard, Lucy Lockwood, 1927.B2
Henneman, John Bell, 1894.B13;
    1903.B16
"Heritage of American Personal-
    ity, A," 1912.B11
"Heroes and Heroines in Recent
    Fiction," 1903.B15
Heroic Ideal in American Litera-
    ture, The, 1971.B4
Herzberg, Max J., 1969.B1
Hexman, Dave, 1931.B1
Heydrick, Benjamin A., 1911.B2
Higginson, Thomas Wentworth,
    1899.B14
Hinckley, Henry Barrett, 1899.B15
"Historical Validity of Repre-
    sentative Short Stories of
    Thomas Nelson Page, The,"
    1945.A1
History of American Literature,
    A, 1912.B10
History of American Literature
    Since 1870, A, 1916.B5
History of Southern Literature,
    A, 1906.B4
Holman, Harriet R., 1946.B2;
    1947.A1; 1969.B2; 1970.B1-B3;
    1973.B1
Howard, Helen Eugene, 1932.A1
Hubbell, Jay Broadus, 1922.B6;
    1954.B1; 1960.B1
Hyde, Claudia, 1894.B14

Idealism, 1893.B6; 1907.B7;
    1916.B6; 1923.B10; 1933.A2,
    A4; 1936.B1; 1945.A1;
    1947.A1; 1955.B1; 1959.B2;
    1967.A1, B2; 1971.B4
In Ole Virginia, 1887.B1-B9;
    1893.B2, B3; 1894.B13;
    1896.B1; 1897.B2, B7;

1902.B2; 1904.B3; 1906.B2,
B4; 1909.B9; 1916.B5;
1917.B4, B5; 1923.B4, B10,
B12; 1929.B1, B2; 1931.A2;
1932.A1; 1933.A1-A3;
1936.A1; 1937.B2; 1945.A1;
1947.B1; 1951.B1; 1952.B1;
1953.B4; 1959.B2; 1962.B1;
1964.A1; 1967.A1; 1968.B2;
1969.B3; 1970.B1; 1971.B4
"'In Ole Virginia' With Thomas
Nelson Page," 1923.B17
Introduction to American
Literature, 1916.B4
"Introduction" to In Ole Virginia, 1969.B3
Italy and the World War,
1920.B1, B2; 1921.B1-B4;
1922.B4; 1923.B14; 1925.B3

Jacobs, Elizabeth McDowell,
1925.B2
James Lane Allen and the Genteel
Tradition, 1935.B1
"Joel Chandler Harris," 1893.B7
John Fox and Tom Page As They
Were, 1970.B3
John Marvel, Assistant, 1909.B1,
B3-B6, B10, B11; 1910.B2;
1911.B3; 1917.B4; 1931.A2;
1932.A1; 1933.A1, A3, A4;
1944.A1; 1947.A1; 1952.B1;
1953.B5; 1961.B1, B4;
1962.B1; 1964.A1; 1965.B4;
1967.A1; 1971.B4
Johnson, Gerald W., 1960.B2
Johnson, Merle, 1929.B1
Johnson, Robert Underwood,
1923.B11; 1925.B3
Joys and Tribulations of an
Editor, The, 1923.B15

Kent, Charles W., 1907.B6;
1909.B9
"Kentucky Journal of Thomas
Nelson Page, The," 1970.B2
King, James Kimball, 1964.A1;
1965.B3, B4; 1969.B3, B4
Kittrell, T. G., 1893.B7
Knight, Grant C., 1932.B2;
1935.B1

Kunitz, Stanley J., 1938.B1

Land of the Spirit, The,
1913.B4-B7, B11, B16;
1933.A1, A2; 1962.B1;
1973.B1
Lanier, Henry Wysham, 1898.B14
Lee, Susan P., 1893.B8
Leisy, Ernest Erwin, 1929.B2
"Letter from Henry W. Grady Re-
garding Southern Authors and
the Piedmont Chautauqua, A,"
1946.B2
Liberalism in the South,
1932.B1
Life of Augustin Daly, The,
1917.B5
"Literary Aspects of American
Anti-Imperialism," 1937.B3
"Literary Career of Thomas
Nelson Page, 1884-1910, The,"
1947.A1
Literary History of the United
States, 1963.B1
"Literary Life in Washington,
D. C.," 1909.B13
Literature of the American
People, The, 1951.B1
Literature of the South, The,
1910.B3
Literature of the South, The,
1968.B2
"Little Darby," 1938.B2;
1947.A1; 1960.B1; 1967.A1
Littlefield, Walter, 1920.B2
Lively, Robert A., 1957.B1
Local color, 1891.B5; 1900.B4;
1904.B6; 1922.B6; 1923.B17;
1935.B1; 1941.B3; 1945.A1;
1947.A1; 1959.B2; 1965.B2;
1967.A1
Logan, Rayford W., 1954.B2;
1968.B1
Long, Francis Taylor, 1940.B1

Mabie, Hamilton W., 1907.B7
McCarthy, Carlton, 1894.A1, B15
McFadin, Maude, 1927.A1
McFee, William, 1921.B4
McIlwaine, Shields, 1939.B2

Virginia: A New Look at the
  Old Dominion, 1959.B3
Virginian Portraits: Essays in
  Biography, 1924.B11
Virginian Writers of Fugitive
  Verse, 1923.B9
Virginia: The New Dominion,
  1971.B1
Virginia Tradition, The,
  1956.B2

Wagenknecht, Edward, 1952.B1
"Walter Hines Page on Southern
  Literature," 1976.B2
Warfel, Harry R., 1941.B3

Warner Library, The, 1917.B4
War Years With Jeb Stuart,
  1945.B2
Washington and Its Romance,
  1924.B3, B5
Washington, Hugh V., 1889.B1
Whittle, Gilbert S., 1897.B9
Willey, Day Allen, 1909.B13
William Elliott Shoots a Bear,
  1976.B1
"William Faulkner's Two Little
  Confederates," 1962.B2
Wilson, Edmund, 1962.B3
Wilson, James Southall,
  1923.B17

Index to Amélie Rives Troubetzkoy

Index to Thomas Amélie Rives Troubetzkoy

Student's History of American
    Literature, A, 1909.B2

Tanis, The Sang-Digger, 1893.B7,
    B8; 1894.B1; 1907.B1;
    1969.A1; 1973.A1
Tastelessness, 1888.A1, A2, B1,
    B8-B10, B12; 1889.B1, B3,
    B7; 1891.B1, B2, B6;
    1892.B1-B3; 1893.B3, B8, B9;
    1906.B2; 1912.B1; 1945.B1,
    B2, B5; 1947.B1; 1951.B1;
    1969.B1
Taylor, Welford Dunaway,
    1963.B2; 1971.B2; 1972.B1;
    1973.B1
Timson, Robert, 1889.B13
Trix and Over the Moon,
    1910.B1, B5; 1973.A1
Twentieth Century Authors,
    1942.B1; 1955.B1

Virginia Authors: Past and
    Present, 1972.B1
Virginia Writers of Fugitive
    Verse, 1923.B1
Virginia of Virginia, 1888.B3,
    B8, B9, B11, B12; 1889.B1,
    B4, B6, B10; 1938.B1;
    1969.A1; 1973.A1

Wilde, Oscar, 1962.B2; 1969.A1;
    1971.B2; 1973.A1
Witness of the Sun, The,
    1889.B2-B4, B6, B8, B9;
    1969.A1
Women Authors of Our Day in Their
    Homes, 1903.B1
Worden, Helen, 1936.B3
World's End, 1914.B1-B6;
    1973.A1

ENGLISH FAIRY TALES

retold by Flora Annie Steel
illustrated by Arthur Rackham

being a facsimile edition published by

MAYFLOWER BOOKS
NEW YORK

in association with Macmillan

Facsimile Classics Series

ENGLISH FAIRY TALES
by Flora Annie Steel
illustrated by Arthur Rackham

THE WATER-BABIES
by Charles Kingsley
illustrated by Linley Sambourne

THE HEROES OF ASGARD
by A. and E. Keary
illustrated by Charles E. Brock

THE MIKADO
by Sir W. S. Gilbert
illustrated by W. Russell Flint and Charles E. Brock

THE FABLES OF AESOP
edited by Joseph Jacobs
illustrated by Richard Heighway

THE ROMANCE OF KING ARTHUR
by Alfred W. Pollard abridged from Malory
illustrated by Arthur Rackham

Mr. and Mrs. Vinegar at home (page 182).

ENGLISH
FAIRY · TALES
RETOLD · BY · FLORA · ANNIE · STEEL

ILLUSTRATED · BY
ARTHUR · RACKHAM

MACMILLAN · & · Cº · Lᵀᴰ

First published by Macmillan & Co. 1918
First published in this edition 1979 by
MAYFLOWER BOOKS INC.
575 Lexington Avenue New York City 10022

ISBN : 08317-2925-2

Printed in Hong Kong

CONTENTS

ILLUSTRATIONS

IN COLOUR

IN TEXT

ST. GEORGE OF MERRIE ENGLAND

IN the darksome depths of a thick forest lived Kalyb the
fell enchantress. Terrible were her deeds, and few there
were who had the hardihood to sound the brazen trumpet
which hung over the iron gate that barred the way to the
Abode of Witchcraft. Terrible were the deeds of Kalyb ;
but above all things she delighted in carrying off innocent
new-born babes, and putting them to death.

And this, doubtless, she meant to be the fate of the
infant son of the Earl of Coventry, who long long years
ago was Lord High Steward of England. Certain it is that
the babe's father being absent, and his mother dying at his
birth, the wicked Kalyb, with spells and charms, managed
to steal the child from his careless nurses.

But the babe was marked from the first for doughty

I   B

deeds ; for on his breast was pictured the living image of a dragon, on his right hand was a blood-red cross, and on his left leg showed the golden garter.

And these signs so affected Kalyb, the fell enchantress, that she stayed her hand ; and the child growing daily in beauty and stature, he became to her as the apple of her eye. Now, when twice seven years had passed the boy began to thirst for honourable adventures, though the wicked enchantress wished to keep him as her own.

But he, seeking glory, utterly disdained so wicked a creature; thus she sought to bribe him. And one day, taking him by the hand, she led him to a brazen castle and showed him six brave knights, prisoners therein. Then said she :

"Lo ! These be the six champions of Christendom. Thou shalt be the seventh and thy name shall be St. George of Merrie England if thou wilt stay with me."

But he would not.

Then she led him into a magnificent stable where stood seven of the most beautiful steeds ever seen. "Six of these," said she, " belong to the six Champions. The seventh and the best, the swiftest and the most powerful in the world, whose name is Bayard, will I bestow on thee, if thou wilt stay with me."

But he would not.

Then she took him to the armoury, and with her own hand buckled on a corselet of purest steel, and laced on a helmet inlaid with gold. Then, taking a mighty falchion, she gave it into his hand, and said :

" This armour which none can pierce, this sword called Ascalon, which will hew in sunder all it touches, are thine ; surely now thou wilt stop with me ? "

But he would not.

Then she bribed him with her own magic wand, thus giving him power over all things in that enchanted land, saying :

" Surely now wilt thou remain here ? "

But he, taking the wand, struck with it a mighty rock that stood by ; and lo ! it opened, and laid in view a wide cave garnished by the bodies of a vast number of innocent new-born infants whom the wicked enchantress had murdered.

Thus, using her power, he bade the sorceress lead the way into the place of horror, and when she had entered, he raised the magic wand yet again, and smote the rock ; and lo ! it closed for ever, and the sorceress was left to bellow forth her lamentable complaints to senseless stones.

Thus was St. George freed from the enchanted land, and taking with him the six other champions of Christendom on their steeds, he mounted Bayard and rode to the city of Coventry.

Here for nine months they abode, exercising themselves in all feats of arms. So when spring returned they set forth, as knights errant, to seek for foreign adventure.

And for thirty days and thirty nights they rode on, until, at the beginning of a new month, they came to a great wide plain. Now in the centre of this plain, where seven several ways met, there stood a great brazen pillar, and here, with high heart and courage, they bade each other farewell, and each took a separate road.

Hence, St. George, on his charger Bayard, rode till he reached the seashore where lay a good ship bound for the land of Egypt. Taking passage in her, after long journeying he arrived in that land when the silent wings of night were outspread, and darkness brooded on all things. Here, coming to a poor hermitage, he begged a night's lodging, on which the hermit replied :

" Sir Knight of Merrie England—for I see her arms graven on thy breastplate—thou hast come hither in an ill time, when those alive are scarcely able to bury the dead by reason of the cruel destruction waged by a terrible dragon, who ranges up and down the country by day and by night. If he have not an innocent maiden to devour each day, he sends a mortal plague amongst the people. And this has not ceased for twenty and four years, so that there is left throughout the land but one maiden, the beautiful Sâbia, daughter to the King. And to-morrow must she die, unless some brave knight will slay the monster. To such will the King give his daughter in marriage, and the crown of Egypt in due time."

" For crowns I care not," said St. George boldly, " but the beauteous maiden shall not die. I will slay the monster."

So, rising at dawn of day, he buckled on his armour, laced his helmet, and with the falchion Ascalon in his hand, bestrode Bayard, and rode into the Valley of the Dragon. Now on the way he met a procession of old women weeping and wailing, and in their midst the most beauteous damsel he had ever seen.   Moved by compassion he dismounted, and bowing low before the lady entreated her to return to her father's palace, since he was about to kill the dreaded dragon.   Whereupon the beautiful Sâbia, thanking him with smiles and tears, did as he requested, and he, re-mounting, rode on his emprise.

Now, no sooner did the dragon catch sight of the brave Knight than its leathern throat sent out a sound more terrible than thunder, and weltering from its hideous den, it spread its burning wings and prepared to assail its foe.

Its size and appearance might well have made the stoutest heart tremble.   From shoulder to tail ran full forty feet, its body was covered with silver scales, its belly was as gold, and through its flaming wings the blood ran thick and red.

So fierce was its onset, that at the very first encounter the Knight was nigh felled to the ground ; but recovering himself he gave the dragon such a thrust with his spear that the latter shivered to a thousand pieces ; whereupon the furious monster smote him so violently with its tail that both horse and rider were overthrown.

Now, by great good chance, St. George was flung under the shade of a flowering orange tree, whose fragrance hath this virtue in it, that no poisonous beast dare come within the compass of its branches.   So there the valiant knight had time to recover his senses, until with eager courage he rose, and rushing to the combat, smote the burning dragon on his burnished belly with his trusty sword Ascalon ; and

thereinafter spouted out such black venom, as, falling on the
armour of the Knight, burst it in twain. And ill might it
have fared with St. George of Merrie England but for the
orange tree, which once again gave him shelter under its
branches, where, seeing the issue of the fight was in the Hands
of the Most High, he knelt and prayed that such strength
of body should be given him as would enable him to prevail.
Then with a bold and courageous heart, he advanced again,
and smote the fiery dragon under one of his flaming wings,
so that the weapon pierced the heart, and all the grass around
turned crimson with the blood that flowed from the dying
monster. So St. George of England cut off the dreadful
head, and hanging it on a truncheon made of the spear
which at the beginning of the combat had shivered against
the beast's scaly back, he mounted his steed Bayard, and
proceeded to the palace of the King.

Now the King's name was Ptolemy, and when he saw
that the dreaded dragon was indeed slain, he gave orders
for the city to be decorated. And he sent a golden chariot
with wheels of ebony and cushions of silk to bring St. George
to the palace, and commanded a hundred nobles dressed in
crimson velvet, and mounted on milk-white steeds richly
caparisoned, to escort him thither with all honour, while
musicians walked before and after, filling the air with
sweetest sounds.

Now the beautiful Sâbia herself washed and dressed the
weary Knight's wounds, and gave him in sign of betrothal
a diamond ring of purest water. Then, after he had been

invested by the King with the golden spurs of knighthood
and had been magnificently feasted, he retired to rest his
weariness, while the beautiful Sâbia from her balcony lulled
him to sleep with her golden lute.

So all seemed happiness ; but alas ! dark misfortune
was at hand.

Almidor, the black King of Morocco, who had long
wooed the Princess Sâbia in vain, without having the courage
to defend her, seeing that the maiden had given her whole
heart to her champion, resolved to compass his destruction.

So, going to King Ptolemy, he told him—what was
perchance true—namely, that the beauteous Sâbia had
promised St. George to become Christian, and follow him
to England. Now the thought of this so enraged the King
that, forgetting his debt of honour, he determined on an
act of basest treachery.

Telling St. George that his love and loyalty needed
further trial, he entrusted him with a message to the King
of Persia, and forbade him either to take with him his horse
Bayard or his sword Ascalon ; nor would he even allow him
to say farewell to his beloved Sâbia.

St. George then set forth sorrowfully, and surmounting
many dangers, reached the Court of the King of Persia in
safety ; but what was his anger to find that the secret missive
he bore contained nothing but an earnest request to put the
bearer of it to death. But he was helpless, and when sentence
had been passed upon him, he was thrown into a loathly
dungeon, clothed in base and servile weeds, and his arms

strongly fettered up to iron bolts, while the roars of the two hungry lions who were to devour him ere long, deafened his ears. Now his rage and fury at this black treachery was such that it gave him strength, and with mighty effort he drew the staples that held his fetters ; so being part free he tore his long locks of amber-coloured hair from his head and wound them round his arms instead of gauntlets. So prepared he rushed on the lions when they were let loose upon him, and thrusting his arms down their throats choked them, and thereinafter tearing out their very hearts, held them up in triumph to the gaolers who stood by trembling with fear.

After this the King of Persia gave up the hopes of putting St. George to death, and, doubling the bars of the dungeon, left him to languish therein. And there the unhappy Knight remained for seven long years, his thoughts full of his lost Princess ; his only companions rats and mice and creeping worms, his only food and drink bread made of the coarsest bran and dirty water.

At last one day, in a dark corner of his dungeon, he found one of the iron staples he had drawn in his rage and fury. It was half consumed with rust, yet it was sufficient in his hands to open a passage through the walls of his cell into the King's garden. It was the time of night when all things are silent ; but St. George, listening, heard the voices of grooms in the stables ; which, entering, he found two grooms furnishing forth a horse against some business. Whereupon, taking the staple with which he had redeemed himself from prison, he slew the grooms, and mounting the palfrey rode boldly to the city gates, where he told the watchman at the Bronze Tower that St. George having escaped from the dungeon, he was in hot pursuit of him. Whereupon the gates were thrown open, and St. George, clapping spurs to his horse, found himself safe from pursuit before the first red beams of the sun shot up into the sky.

Now, ere long, being most famished with hunger, he saw a tower set on a high cliff, and riding thitherward determined to ask for food. But as he neared the castle he saw a beauteous damsel in a blue and gold robe seated disconsolate at a window. Whereupon, dismounting, he called aloud to her :

" Lady ! If thou hast sorrow of thine own, succour one also in distress, and give me, a Christian Knight, now almost famished, one meal's meat." To which she replied quickly :

" Sir Knight ! Fly quickly an thou canst, for my lord is a mighty giant, a follower of Mahomed, who hath sworn to destroy all Christians."

Hearing this St. George laughed loud and long. " Go tell him then, fair dame," he cried, " that a Christian Knight waits at his door, and will either satisfy his wants within his castle or slay the owner thereof."

Now the giant no sooner heard this valiant challenge than he rushed forth to the combat, armed with a hugeous crowbar of iron. He was a monstrous giant, deformed, with a huge head, bristled like any boar's, with hot, glaring eyes and a mouth equalling a tiger's. At first sight of him

St. George gave himself up for lost, not so much for fear, but for hunger and faintness of body. Still, commending himself to the Most High, he also rushed to the combat with such poor arms as he had, and with many a regret for the loss of his magic sword Ascalon. So they fought till noon, when, just as the champion's strength was nigh finished, the giant stumbled on the root of a tree, and St. George, taking his chance, ran him through the mid-rib, so that he gasped and died.

After which St. George entered the tower ; whereat the beautiful lady, freed from her terrible lord, set before him all manner of delicacies and pure wine with which he sufficed his hunger, rested his weary body, and refreshed his horse.

So, leaving the tower in the hands of the grateful lady, he went on his way, coming ere long to the Enchanted Garden of the necromancer Ormadine, where, embedded in the living rock, he saw a magic sword, the like of which for beauty he had never seen, the belt being beset with jaspers and sapphire stones, while the pommel was a globe of the purest silver chased in gold with these verses :

> My magic will remain most firmly bound
> Till that a knight from the far north be found
> To pull this sword from out its bed of stone.
> Lo ! when he comes wise Ormadine must fall.
> Farewell, my magic power, my spell, my all.

Seeing this St. George put his hand to the hilt, thinking to essay pulling it out by strength ; but lo ! he drew it out with as much ease as though it had hung by a thread of untwisted silk. And immediately every door in the enchanted garden flew open, and the magician Ormadine appeared, his hair standing on end ; and he, after kissing the hand of the champion, led him to a cave where a young man wrapped in a sheet of gold lay sleeping, lulled by the songs of four beautiful maidens.

" The Knight whom thou seest here ! " said the necromancer in a hollow voice, " is none other than thy brother-in-arms, the Christian Champion St. David of Wales. He also attempted to draw my sword but failed. Him hast thou delivered from my enchantments since they come to an end."

Now, as he spoke, came such a rattling of the skies, such a lumbering of the earth as never was, and in the twinkling of an eye the Enchanted Garden and all in it vanished from view, leaving the Champion of Wales, roused from his seven years' sleep, giving thanks to St. George, who greeted his ancient comrade heartily.

After this St. George of Merrie England travelled far and travelled fast, with many adventures by the way, to Egypt where he had left his beloved Princess Sâbia. But, learning to his great grief and horror from the same hermit he had met on first landing, that, despite her denials, her father, King Ptolemy, had consented to Almidor the black King of Morocco carrying her off as one of his many wives, he turned his steps towards Tripoli, the capital of Morocco ; for he was determined at all costs to gain a sight of the dear Princess from whom he had been so cruelly rent.

To this end he borrowed an old cloak of the hermit,

and, disguised as a beggar, gained admittance to the gate
of the Women's Palace, where were gathered together on
their knees many others, poor, frail, infirm.

And when he asked them wherefore they knelt, they
answered :

" Because good Queen Sâbia succours us that we may
pray for the safety of St. George of England, to whom she
gave her heart."

Now when St. George heard this his own heart was like
to break for very joy, and he could scarce keep on his knees
when, lovely as ever, but with her face pale and sad and wan
from long distress, the Princess Sâbia appeared clothed in
deep mourning.

In silence she handed an alms to each beggar in turn ;
but when she came to St. George she started and laid her
hand on her heart.   Then she said softly :

" Rise up, Sir Beggar !   Thou art too like one who
rescued me from death, for it to be meet for thee to kneel
before me ! "

Then St. George rising, and bowing low, said quietly :
" Peerless lady !   Lo !   I am that very knight to whom
thou did'st condescend to give this."

And with this he slipped the diamond ring she had given
him on her finger.   But she looked not at it, but at him,
with love in her eyes.

Then he told her of her father's base treachery and
Almidor's part in it, so that her anger grew hot and she
cried :

"Waste no more time in talk. I remain no longer in this detested place. Ere Almidor returns from hunting we shall have escaped."

So she led St. George to the armoury, where he found his trusty sword Ascalon, and to the stable, where his swift steed Bayard stood ready caparisoned.

Then, when her brave Knight had mounted, and she, putting her foot on his, had leapt like a bird behind him, St. George touched the proud beast lightly with his spurs, and, like an arrow from a bow, Bayard carried them together over city and plain, through woods and forests, across rivers, and mountains, and valleys, until they reached the Land of Greece.

And here they found the whole country in festivity over the marriage of the King. Now amongst other entertainments was a grand tournament, the news of which had spread through the world. And to it had come all the other Six Champions of Christendom ; so St. George arriving made the Seventh. And many of the champions had with them the fair lady they had rescued. St. Denys of France brought beautiful Eglantine, St. James of Spain sweet Celestine, while noble Rosalind accompanied St. Anthony of Italy. St. David of Wales, after his seven years' sleep, came full of eager desire for adventure. St. Patrick of Ireland, ever courteous, brought all the six Swan-princesses who, in gratitude, had been seeking their deliverer St. Andrew of Scotland ; since he, leaving all worldly things, had chosen to fight for the faith.

So all these brave knights and fair ladies joined in the joyful jousting, and each of the Seven Champions was in turn Chief Challenger for a day.

Now in the midst of all the merriment appeared a hundred heralds from a hundred different parts of the Paynim world, declaring war to the death against all Christians.

Whereupon the Seven Champions agreed that each should return to his native land to place his dearest lady in safety, and gather together an army, and that six months later they should meet, and, joining as one legion, go forth to fight for Christendom.

And this was done. So, having chosen St. George as Chief General, they marched on Tripoli with the cry :

"For Christendom we fight,
For Christendom we die."

Here the wicked Almidor fell in single combat with St. George, to the great delight of his subjects, who begged the Champion to be King in his stead. To this he consented, and, after he was crowned, the Christian host went on towards Egypt where King Ptolemy, in despair of vanquishing such stalwart knights, threw himself down from the battlements of the palace and was killed. Whereupon, in recognition of the chivalry and courtesy of the Christian Champions, the nobles offered the Crown to one of their number, and they with acclaim chose St. George of Merrie England.

Thence the Christian host journeyed to Persia, where a fearsome battle raged for seven days, during which two hundred thousand pagans were slain, beside many who were drowned in attempting to escape. Thus they were compelled to yield, the Emperor himself happening into the hands of St. George, and six other viceroys into the hands of the six other Champions.

And these were most mercifully and honourably entreated after they had promised to govern Persia after Christian rules. Now the Emperor, having a heart fraught with despite and tyranny, conspired against them, and engaged a wicked wizard named Osmond to so beguile six of the Champions that they gave up fighting, and lived an easy slothful life. But St. George would not be beguiled; neither would he consent to the enchantment of his brothers; and he so roused them that they never sheathed their swords nor unlocked their armour till the wicked Emperor and his viceroys were thrown into that very dungeon in which St. George had languished for seven long years.

Whereupon St. George took upon himself the government of Persia, and gave the six other Champions the six viceroyalties.

So, attired in a beautiful green robe, richly embroidered, over which was flung a scarlet mantle bordered with white fur and decorated with ornaments of pure gold, he took his seat on the throne which was supported by elephants of translucent alabaster. And the Heralds at arms, amid the shouting of the people, cried :

" Long live St. George of Merrie England, Emperor of Morocco, King of Egypt, and Sultan of Persia ! "

Now, after that he had established good and just laws to such effect that innumerable companies of pagans flocked to become Christians, St. George, leaving the Government in the hands of his trusted counsellors, took truce with the world and returned to England, where, at Coventry, he lived for many years with the Egyptian Princess Sâbia, who bore him three stalwart sons. So here endeth the tale of St. George of Merrie England, first and greatest of the Seven Champions.

THE STORY OF THE THREE BEARS

ONCE upon a time there were three Bears, who lived together in a house of their own, in a wood. One of them was a Little Wee Bear, and one was a Middle-sized Bear, and the other was a Great Big Bear. They had each a bowl for their porridge ; a little bowl for the Little Wee Bear ; and a middle-sized bowl for the Middle-sized Bear ; and a great bowl for the Great Big Bear. And they had each a chair to sit in ; a little chair for the Little Wee Bear ; and a middle-sized chair for the Middle-sized Bear ; and a great chair for the Great Big Bear. And they had each a bed to sleep in ; a little bed for the Little Wee Bear ; and a middle-sized bed for the Middle-sized Bear ; and a great bed for the Great Big Bear.

One day, after they had made the porridge for their breakfast, and poured it into their porridge-bowls, they walked out into the wood while the porridge was cooling, that they might not burn their mouths by beginning too soon, for they were polite, well-brought-up Bears. And while they were away a little girl called Goldilocks, who lived at the other side of the wood and had been sent on an errand by her mother, passed by the house, and looked in at the window. And then she peeped in at the keyhole, for she was not at all a well-brought-up little girl. Then seeing nobody in the house she lifted the latch. The door was not fastened, because the Bears were good Bears, who did nobody any harm, and never suspected that anybody would harm them. So Goldilocks opened the door and went in; and well pleased was she when she saw the porridge on the table. If she had been a well-brought-up little girl she would have waited till the Bears came home, and then, perhaps, they would have asked her to breakfast; for they were good Bears—a little rough or so, as the manner of Bears is, but for all that very good-natured and hospitable. But she was an impudent, rude little girl, and so she set about helping herself.

First she tasted the porridge of the Great Big Bear, and that was too hot for her. Next she tasted the porridge of the Middle-sized Bear, but that was too cold for her. And then she went to the porridge of the Little Wee Bear, and tasted it, and that was neither too hot nor too cold, but just right, and she liked it so well that she ate it all up, every bit!

Then Goldilocks, who was tired, for she had been catching butterflies instead of running on her errand, sate down in the chair of the Great Big Bear, but that was too hard for her. And then she sate down in the chair of the Middle-sized Bear, and that was too soft for her. But when she sat down in the chair of the Little Wee Bear, that was neither too hard nor too soft, but just right.   So she seated herself in it, and there she sate till the bottom of the chair came out, and down she came, plump upon the ground ; and that made her very cross, for she was a bad-tempered little girl.

Now, being determined to rest, Goldilocks went upstairs into the bedchamber in which the Three Bears slept.   And first she lay down upon the bed of the Great Big Bear, but that was too high at the head for her.   And next she lay down upon the bed of the Middle-sized Bear, and that was too high at the foot for her.   And then she lay down upon the bed of the Little Wee Bear, and that was neither too high at the head nor at the foot, but just right.   So she covered herself up comfortably, and lay there till she fell fast asleep.

By this time the Three Bears thought their porridge would be cool enough for them to eat it properly ; so they came home to breakfast.   Now careless Goldilocks had left the spoon of the Great Big Bear standing in his porridge.

'" SOMEBODY HAS BEEN AT MY PORRIDGE ! "

said the Great Big Bear in his great, rough, gruff voice.

Then the Middle-sized Bear looked at his porridge and saw the spoon was standing in it too.

" SOMEBODY HAS BEEN AT MY PORRIDGE ! "

said the Middle-sized Bear in his middle-sized voice.

Then the Little Wee Bear looked at his, and there was

the spoon in the porridge-bowl, but the porridge was all gone !

"SOMEBODY HAS BEEN AT MY PORRIDGE, AND HAS EATEN IT ALL UP ! "

said the Little Wee Bear in his little wee voice.

Upon this the Three Bears, seeing that some one had entered their house, and eaten up the Little Wee Bear's breakfast, began to look about them. Now the careless Goldilocks had not put the hard cushion straight when she rose from the chair of the Great Big Bear.

"SOMEBODY HAS BEEN SITTING IN MY CHAIR ! "

said the Great Big Bear in his great, rough, gruff voice.

And the careless Goldilocks had squatted down the soft cushion of the Middle-sized Bear.

" SOMEBODY HAS BEEN SITTING IN MY CHAIR ! "

said the Middle-sized Bear in his middle-sized voice.

" SOMEBODY HAS BEEN SITTING IN MY CHAIR, AND HAS SATE THE BOTTOM THROUGH ! "

said the Little Wee Bear in his little wee voice.

Then the Three Bears thought they had better make further search in case it was a burglar, so they went upstairs into their bedchamber. Now Goldilocks had pulled the pillow of the Great Big Bear out of its place.

"SOMEBODY HAS BEEN LYING IN MY BED ! "

said the Great Big Bear in his great, rough, gruff voice.

"SOMEBODY HAS BEEN LYING IN MY BED,—AND HERE SHE IS !"

And Goldilocks had pulled the bolster of the Middle-sized Bear out of its place.

"SOMEBODY HAS BEEN LYING IN MY BED !"

said the Middle-sized Bear in his middle-sized voice.

But when the Little Wee Bear came to look at his bed, there was the bolster in its place !

And the pillow was in its place upon the bolster !

And upon the pillow——?

There was Goldilocks' yellow head—which was not in its place, for she had no business there.

"SOMEBODY HAS BEEN LYING IN MY BED,——AND HERE SHE IS STILL ! "

said the Little Wee Bear in his little wee voice.

Now Goldilocks had heard in her sleep the great, rough, gruff voice of the Great Big Bear ; but she was so fast asleep that it was no more to her than the roaring of wind, or the rumbling of thunder.   And she had heard the middle-sized voice of the Middle-sized Bear, but it was only as if she had heard some one speaking in a dream.   But when she heard the little wee voice of the Little Wee Bear, it was so sharp, and so shrill, that it awakened her at once.   Up she started, and when she saw the Three Bears on one side of the bed, she tumbled herself out at the other, and ran to the window. Now the window was open, because the Bears, like good, tidy Bears, as they were, always opened their bedchamber window when they got up in the morning. So naughty, frightened little Goldilocks jumped ; and whether she broke her neck in the fall, or ran into the wood and was lost there, or found her way out of the wood and got whipped for being a bad girl and playing truant, no one can say.   But the Three Bears never saw anything more of her.

"Somebody has been at my porridge, and has eaten it all up!"

TOM-TIT-TOT

ONCE upon a time there was a woman and she baked five pies. But when they came out of the oven they were over-baked, and the crust was far too hard to eat. So she said to her daughter:

"Daughter," says she, "put them pies on to the shelf and leave 'em there awhile. Surely they'll come again in time."

By that, you know, she meant that they would become softer; but her daughter said to herself, "If Mother says the pies will come again, why shouldn't I eat these now?" So, having good, young teeth, she set to work and ate the lot, first and last.

Now when supper-time came the woman said to her daughter, "Go you and get one of the pies. They are sure to have come again by now."

Then the girl went and looked, but of course there was nothing but the empty dishes.

So back she came and said, "No, Mother, they ain't come again."

" Not one o' them ? " asked the mother, taken aback like.

" Not one o' them," says the daughter, quite confident.

" Well," says the mother, " come again, or not come again, I will have one of them pies for my supper."

" But you can't," says the daughter. " How can you if they ain't come ? And they ain't, as sure's sure."

" But I can," says the mother, getting angry. " Go you at once, child, and bring me the best on them. My teeth must just tackle it."

" Best or worst is all one," answered the daughter, quite sulky, " for I've ate the lot, so you can't have one till it comes again—so there ! "

Well, the mother she bounced up to see ; but half an eye told her there was nothing save the empty dishes ; so she was dished up herself and done for.

So, having no supper, she sate her down on the doorstep, and, bringing out her distaff, began to spin. And as she span she sang :

> " My daughter ha' ate five pies to-day,
> My daughter ha' ate five pies to-day,
> My daughter ha' ate five pies to-day,"

for, see you, she was quite flabbergasted and fair astonished.

Now the King of that country happened to be coming down the street, and he heard the song going on and on, but could not quite make out the words. So he stopped his horse, and asked :

" What is that you are singing, my good woman ? "

Now the mother, though horrified at her daughter's appetite, did not want other folk, leastwise the King, to know about it, so she sang instead :

"My daughter ha' spun five skeins to-day,
My daughter ha' spun five skeins to-day,
My daughter ha' spun five skeins to-day."

"Five skeins !" cried the King. "By my garter and my crown, I never heard tell of any one who could do that ! Look you here, I have been searching for a maiden to wife, and your daughter who can spin five skeins a day is the very one for me. Only, mind you, though for eleven months of the year she shall be Queen indeed, and have all she likes to eat, all the gowns she likes to get, all the company she likes to keep, and everything her heart desires, in the twelfth month she must set to work and spin five skeins a day, and if she does not she must die.   Come ! is it a bargain ? "

So the mother agreed.   She thought what a grand marriage it was for her daughter.   And as for the five skeins ? Time enough to bother about them when the year came round.   There was many a slip between cup and lip, and, likely as not, the King would have forgotten all about it by then.

Anyhow, her daughter would be Queen for eleven months. So they were married, and for eleven months the bride was happy as happy could be.   She had everything she liked to eat, and all the gowns she liked to get, all the company she cared to keep, and everything her heart desired.   And her husband the King was kind as kind could be.   But in the tenth month she began to think of those five skeins and wonder if the King remembered.   And in the eleventh month she began to dream about them as well.   But ne'er a word did the King, her husband, say about them ; so she hoped he had forgotten.

But on the very last day of the eleventh month, the King, her husband, led her into a room she had never set eyes on before.   It had one window, and there was nothing in it but a stool and a spinning-wheel.

" Now, my dear," he said quite kind like, " you will be shut in here to-morrow morning with some victuals and some flax, and if by evening you have not spun five skeins, your head will come off."

Well, she was fair frightened, for she had always been such

a gatless thoughtless girl that she had never learnt to spin at all. So what she was to do on the morrow she could not tell; for, see you, she had no one to help her; for, of course, now she was Queen, her mother didn't live nigh her. So she just locked the door of her room, sate down on a stool, and cried and cried and cried until her pretty eyes were all red.

Now as she sate sobbing and crying she heard a queer little noise at the bottom of the door. At first she thought it was a mouse. Then she thought it must be something knocking.

So she upped and opened the door and what did she see? Why! a small, little, black Thing with a long tail that whisked round and round ever so fast.

"What are you crying for?" said that Thing, making a bow, and twirling its tail so fast that she could scarcely see it.

"What's that to you?" said she, shrinking a bit, for that Thing was very queer like.

"Don't look at my tail if you're frightened," says That, smirking. "Look at my toes. Ain't they beautiful?"

And sure enough That had on buckled shoes with high heels and big bows, ever so smart.

So she kind of forgot about the tail, and wasn't so frightened, and when That asked her again why she was crying, she upped and said, " It won't do no good if I do."

" You don't know that," says That, twirling its tail faster and faster, and sticking out its toes. " Come, tell me, there's a good girl."

" Well," says she, " it can't do any harm if it doesn't do good." So she dried her pretty eyes and told That all about the pies, and the skeins, and everything from first to last.

And then that little, black Thing nearly burst with laughing. " If that is all, it's easy mended ! " it says. " I'll come to your window every morning, take the flax, and bring it back spun into five skeins at night. Come ! shall it be a bargain ? "

Now she, for all she was so gatless and thoughtless, said, cautious like :

" But what is your pay ? "

Then That twirled its tail so fast you couldn't see it, and stuck out its beautiful toes, and smirked and looked out of the corners of its eyes. " I will give you three guesses every night to guess my name, and if you haven't guessed it before the month is up, why "—and That twirled its tail faster and stuck out its toes further, and smirked and sniggered more than ever—" you shall be mine, my beauty."

Three guesses every night for a whole month ! She felt sure she would be able for so much ; and there was no other way out of the business, so she just said, " Yes ! I agree ! "

And lor ! how That twirled its tail, and bowed, and smirked, and stuck out its beautiful toes.

Well, the very next day her husband led her to the strange room again, and there was the day's food, and a spinning-wheel and a great bundle of flax.

" There you are, my dear," says he as polite as polite. " And remember ! if there are not five whole skeins to-night, I fear your head will come off ! "

At that she began to tremble, and after he had gone away and locked the door, she was just thinking of a good cry, when she heard a queer knocking at the window. She upped at once and opened it, and sure enough there was the small, little, black Thing sitting on the window-ledge, dangling its beautiful toes and twirling its tail so that you could scarcely see it.

" Good-morning, my beauty," says That. " Come ! hand over the flax, sharp, there's a good girl."

So she gave That the flax and shut the window and, you may be sure, ate her victuals, for, as you know, she had a good appetite, and the King, her husband, had promised to give her everything she liked to eat. So she ate to her heart's content, and when evening came and she heard that queer knocking at the window again, she upped and oped it, and there was the small, little, black Thing with five spun skeins on his arm !

And it twirled its tail faster than ever, and stuck out its beautiful toes, and bowed and smirked and gave her the five skeins.

Then That said, " And now, my beauty, what is That's name ? "

And she answered quite easy like :

" That is Bill."

" No, it ain't," says That, and twirled its tail.

" Then That is Ned," says she.

" No, it ain't," says That, and twirled its tail faster.

" Well," says she a bit more thoughtful, " That is Mark."

" No, it ain't," says That, and laughs and laughs and laughs, and twirls its tail so as you couldn't see it, as away it flew.

Well, when the King, her husband, came in, he was fine and pleased to see the five skeins all ready for him, for he was fond of his pretty wife.

" I shall not have to order your head off, my dear," says he. " And I hope all the other days will pass as happily." Then he said good-night and locked the door and left her.

But next morning they brought her fresh flax and even more delicious foods. And the small, little, black Thing came knocking at the window and stuck out its beautiful toes and twirled its tail faster and faster, and took away the bundle of flax and brought it back all spun into five skeins by evening. Then That made her guess three times what That's name was ; but she could not guess right, and That laughed and laughed and laughed as it flew away.

Now every morning and evening the same thing happened, and every evening she had her three guesses ; but she never guessed right. And every day the small, little, black Thing laughed louder and louder and smirked more and more, and looked at her quite maliceful out of the corners of its eyes until she began to get frightened, and instead of eating all the fine foods left for her, spent the day in trying to think of names to say. But she never hit upon the right one.

So it came to the last day of the month but one, and when the small, little, black Thing arrived in the evening with the five skeins of flax all ready spun, it could hardly say for smirking :

" Ain't you got That's name yet ? "

So says she—for she had been reading her Bible :

" Is That Nicodemus ? "

" No, it ain't," says That, and twirled its tail faster than you could see.

" Is That Samuel ? " says she all of a flutter.

" No, it ain't, my beauty," chuckles That, looking maliceful.

" Well—is That Methuselah ? " says she, inclined to cry.

Then That just fixes her with eyes like a coal a-fire, and says, " No, it ain't that neither, so there is only to-morrow night and then you'll be mine, my beauty."

And away the small, little, black Thing flew, its tail twirling and whisking so fast that you couldn't see it.

Well, she felt so bad she couldn't even cry ; but she heard the King, her husband, coming to the door, so she made bold to be cheerful, and tried to smile when he said, " Well done, wife ! Five skeins again ! I shall not have to order your head off after all, my dear, of that I'm quite sure, so let us enjoy ourselves." Then he bade the servants bring supper, and a stool for him to sit beside his Queen, and down they sate, lover-like, side by side.

But the poor Queen could eat nothing ; she could not forget the small, little, black Thing. And the King hadn't eaten but a mouthful or two when he began to laugh, and he laughed so long and so loud that at last the poor Queen, all lackadaisical as she was, said :

" Why do you laugh so ? "

" At something I saw to-day, my love," says the King. " I was out a-hunting, and by chance I came to a place I'd never been in before. It was in a wood, and there was an old chalk-pit there, and out of the chalk-pit there came a queer kind of a sort of a humming, bumming noise. So I got off my hobby to see what made it, and went quite quiet to the edge of the pit and looked down. And what do you think I saw ? The funniest, queerest, smallest, little, black Thing you ever set eyes upon. And it had a little spinning-wheel and it was spinning away for dear life, but the wheel didn't go so fast as its tail, and that span round and round— *ho-ho-ha-ha!*—you never saw the like. And its little feet had buckled shoes and bows on them, and they went up and down in a desperate hurry. And all the time that small, little, black Thing kept bumming and booming away at these words :

> " Name me, name me not,
> Who'll guess it's Tom-Tit-Tot."

Well, when she heard these words the Queen nearly jumped out of her skin for joy ; but she managed to say nothing, but ate her supper quite comfortably.

And she said no word when next morning the small, little, black Thing came for the flax, though it looked so gleeful and maliceful that she could hardly help laughing, knowing she had got the better of it. And when night came and she heard that knocking against the window-panes, she put on a wry face, and opened the window slowly as if she was afraid. But that Thing was as bold as brass and came right inside, grinning from ear to ear. And oh, my goodness ! how That's tail was twirling and whisking !

" Well, my beauty," says That, giving her the five skeins all ready spun, " what's my name ? "

Then she put down her lip, and says, tearful like, " Is—is—That—Solomon ? "

" No, it ain't," laughs That, smirking out of the corner of That's eye. And the small, little, black Thing came further into the room.

So she tried again—and this time she seemed hardly able to speak for fright.

" Well—is That—Zebedee ? " she says.

" No, it ain't," cried the impet, full of glee. And it came quite close and stretched out its little black hands to her, and O-oh, ITS TAIL . . .!!!

" Take time, my beauty," says That, sort of jeering like, and its small, little, black eyes seemed to eat her up. " Take time ! Remember ! next guess and you're mine ! "

D

Well, she backed just a wee bit from it, for it was just horrible to look at ; but then she laughed out and pointed her finger at it and said, says she :

> " Name me, name me not,
> *Your* name is
>> *Tom*
>> TIT
>> *TOT*."

And you never heard such a shriek as that small, little, black Thing gave out. Its tail dropped down straight, its feet all crumpled up, and away That flew into the dark, and she never saw it no more.

And she lived happy ever after with her husband, the King.

THE GOLDEN SNUFF-BOX

ONCE upon a time, and a very good time too, though it was not in my time, nor your time, nor for the matter of that in any one's time, there lived a man and a woman who had one son called Jack, and he was just terribly fond of reading books. He read, and he read, and then, because his parents lived in a lonely house in a lonely forest and he never saw any other folk but his father and his mother, he became quite crazy to go out into the world and see charming princesses and the like.

So one day he told his mother he must be off, and she called him an air-brained addle-pate, but added that, as he was no use at home, he had better go seek his fortune. Then she asked him if he would rather take a small cake with her blessing to eat on his journey, or a large cake with her curse? Now Jack was a very hungry lad, so he just up and said :

" A big cake, if you please, 'm."

So his mother made a great big cake, and when he started she just off to the top of the house and cast malisons on him, till he got out of sight. You see she had to do it, but after that she sate down and cried.

Well, Jack hadn't gone far till he came to a field where his father was ploughing. Now the goodman was dreadfully put out when he found his son was going away, and still more so when he heard he had chosen his mother's malison. So he cast about what to do to put things straight, and at last he drew out of his pocket a little golden snuff-box, and gave it to the lad, saying :

" If ever you are in danger of sudden death you may open the box ; but not till then. It has been in our family for years and years ; but, as we have lived, father and son, quietly in the forest, none of us have ever been in need of help—perhaps you may."

So Jack pocketed the golden snuff-box and went on his way.

Now, after a time, he grew very tired, and very hungry, for he had eaten his big cake first thing, and night closed in on him so that he could scarce see his way.

But at last he came to a large house and begged board and lodging at the back door. Now Jack was a good-looking young fellow, so the maid-servant at once called him in to the fireside and gave him plenty good meat and bread and beer. And it so happened that while he was eating his supper the master's gay young daughter came into the kitchen and saw him. So she went to her father and said that there was the prettiest young fellow she had ever seen in the back kitchen, and that if her father loved

her he would give the young man some employment. Now
the gentleman of the house was exceedingly fond of his gay
young daughter, and did not want to vex her ; so he went
into the back kitchen and questioned Jack as to what he
could do.

"Anything," said Jack gaily, meaning, of course, that
he could do any foolish bit of work about a house.

But the gentleman saw a way of pleasing his gay young
daughter and getting rid of the trouble of employing Jack ;
so he laughs and says, " If you can do anything, my good
lad," says he, " you had better do this. By eight o'clock
to-morrow morning you must have dug a lake four miles
round in front of my mansion, and on it there must be
floating a whole fleet of vessels. And they must range up in
front of my mansion and fire a salute of guns. And the very
last shot must break the leg of the four-post bed on which
my daughter sleeps, for she is always late of a morning ! "

Well ! Jack was terribly flabbergasted, but he faltered
out :

" And if I don't do it ? "

" Then," said the master of the house quite calmly,
" your life will be the forfeit."

So he bade the servants take Jack to a turret-room and
lock the door on him.

Well ! Jack sate on the side of his bed and tried to
think things out, but he felt as if he didn't know *b* from a
battledore, so he decided to think no more, and after saying
his prayers he lay down and went to sleep. And he did

sleep ! When he woke it was close on eight o'clock, and he
had only time to fly to the window and look out, when the
great clock on the tower began to whirr before it struck the
hour. And there was the lawn in front of the house all
set with beds of roses and stocks and marigolds ! Well !
all of a sudden he remembered the little golden snuff-box.

" I'm near enough to death," quoth he to himself, as
he drew it out and opened it.

And no sooner had he opened it than out hopped three
funny little red men in red night-caps, rubbing their eyes
and yawning ; for, see you, they had been locked up in
the box for years, and years, and years.

"What do you want, Master ? " they said between
their yawns. But Jack heard that clock a-whirring and
knew he hadn't a moment to lose, so he just gabbled off his
orders. Then the clock began to strike, and the little men
flew out of the window, and suddenly

Bang ! bang ! bang ! bang ! bang ! bang !

went the guns, and the last one must have broken the leg
of the four-post bed, for there at the window was the gay
young daughter in her nightcap, gazing with astonishment
at the lake four miles round, with the fleet of vessels floating
on it !

And so did Jack ! He had never seen such a sight in his
life, and he was quite sorry when the three little red men
disturbed him by flying in at the window and scrambling
into the golden snuff-box.

" Give us a little more time when you want us next, Master," they said sulkily. Then they shut down the lid, and Jack could hear them yawning inside as they settled down to sleep.

As you may imagine, the master of the house was fair astonished, while as for the gay young daughter, she declared at once that she would never marry any one else but the young man who could do such wonderful things ; the truth being that she and Jack had fallen in love with each other at first sight.

But her father was cautious. " It is true, my dear," says he, " that the young fellow seems a bully boy ; but for aught we know it may be chance, not skill, and he may have a broken feather in his wing. So we must try him again."

Then he said to Jack, " My daughter must have a fine house to live in. Therefore by to-morrow morning at eight o'clock there must be a magnificent castle standing on twelve golden pillars in the middle of the lake, and there must be a church beside it. And all things must be ready for the bride, and at eight o'clock precisely a peal of bells from the church must ring out for the wedding. If not you will have to forfeit your life."

This time Jack intended to give the three little red men more time for their task ; but what with having enjoyed himself so much all day, and having eaten so much good food, he overslept himself, so that the big clock on the tower was whirring before it struck eight when he woke, leapt out of bed, and rushed to the golden snuff-box. But he had forgotten where he had put it, and so the clock had *really* begun to strike before he found it under his pillow, opened it, and gabbled out his orders. And then you never saw how the three little red men tumbled over each other and yawned and stretched and made haste all at one time, so that Jack thought his life would surely be forfeit. But just as the clock struck its last chime, out rang a peal of merry bells, and there was the Castle standing on twelve golden pillars and a church beside it in the middle of the lake. And the Castle was all decorated for the wedding, and there were crowds and crowds of servants and retainers, all dressed in their Sunday best.

Never had Jack seen such a sight before; neither had the gay young daughter who, of course, was looking out of the next window in her nightcap. And she looked so pretty and so gay that Jack felt quite cross when he had to step back to let the three little red men fly to their golden snuff-box. But they were far crosser than he was, and mumbled and grumbled at the hustle, so that Jack was quite glad when they shut the box down and began to snore.

Well, of course, Jack and the gay young daughter were married, and were as happy as the day is long; and Jack had fine clothes to wear, fine food to eat, fine servants to wait on him, and as many fine friends as he liked.

So he was in luck; but he had yet to learn that a mother's malison is sure to bring misfortune some time or another.

Thus it happened that one day when he was going

a-hunting with all the ladies and gentlemen, Jack forgot to change the golden snuff-box (which he always carried about with him for fear of accidents) from his waistcoat pocket to that of his scarlet hunting-coat ; so he left it behind him. And what should happen but that the servant let it fall on the ground when he was folding up the clothes, and the snuff-box flew open and out popped the three little red men yawning and stretching.

Well ! when they found out that they hadn't really been summoned, and that there was no fear of death, they were in a towering temper and said they had a great mind to fly away with the Castle, golden pillars and all.

On hearing this the servant pricked up his ears.

" Could you do that ? " he asked.

" Could we ? " they said, and they laughed loud. " Why, we can do anything."

Then the servant said ever so sharp, " Then move me this Castle and all it contains right away over the sea where the master can't disturb us."

Now the little red men need not really have obeyed the order, but they were so cross with Jack that hardly had the servant said the words before the task was done ; so when the hunting-party came back, lo and behold ! the Castle, and the church, and the golden pillars had all disappeared !

At first all the rest set upon Jack for being a knave and a cheat ; and, in particular, his wife's father threatened to have at him for deceiving the gay young daughter ; but at last he agreed to let Jack have twelve months and a day to find the Castle and bring it back.

So off Jack starts on a good horse with some money in his pocket.

And he travelled far and he travelled fast, and he travelled east and west, north and south, over hills, and dales, and valleys, and mountains, and woods, and sheepwalks, but never a sign of the missing castle did he see. Now at last he came to the palace of the King of all the Mice in the Wide World. And there was a little mousie in a fine hauberk and a steel cap doing sentry at the front gate, and he was not for letting Jack in until he had told his errand. And when Jack had told it, he passed him on to the next mouse sentry at the inner gate; so by degrees he reached the King's chamber, where he sate surrounded by mice courtiers.

Now the King of the Mice received Jack very graciously, and said that he himself knew nothing of the missing Castle, but, as he was King of all the Mice in the whole world, it was possible that some of his subjects might know more than he. So he ordered his chamberlain to command a Grand Assembly for the next morning, and in the meantime he entertained Jack right royally.

But the next morning, though there were brown mice, and black mice, and grey mice, and white mice, and piebald mice, from all parts of the world, they all answered with one breath:

" If it please your Majesty, we have not seen the missing Castle."

Then the King said, "You must go and ask my elder brother the King of all the Frogs. He may be able to tell you. Leave your horse here and take one of mine. It knows the way and will carry you safe."

So Jack set off on the King's horse, and as he passed the outer gate he saw the little mouse sentry coming away, for its guard was up. Now Jack was a kind-hearted lad, and he had saved some crumbs from his dinner in order to recompense the little sentry for his kindness. So he put his hand in his pocket and pulled out the crumbs.

"Here you are, mousekin," he said. "That's for your trouble!"

Then the mouse thanked him kindly and asked if he would take him along to the King of the Frogs.

"Not I," says Jack. "I should get into trouble with your King."

But the mousekin insisted. "I may be of some use to you," it said. So it ran up the horse's hind leg and up by its tail and hid in Jack's pocket. And the horse set off at a hand gallop, for it didn't half like the mouse running over it.

So at last Jack came to the palace of the King of all the Frogs, and there at the front gate was a frog doing sentry in a fine coat of mail and a brass helmet. And the frog sentry was for not letting Jack in ; but the mouse called out that they came from the King of all the Mice and must be let in without delay. So they were taken to the King's chamber, where he sate surrounded by frog courtiers in fine clothes ; but alas ! he had heard nothing of the Castle on golden pillars, and though he summoned all the frogs of all the world to a Grand Assembly next morning, they all answered his question with :

" Kro kro, Kro kro,"

which every one knows stands for " No " in frog language.

So the King said to Jack, " There remains but one thing. You must go and ask my eldest brother, the King of all the Birds. His subjects are always on the wing, so mayhap they have seen something. Leave the horse you are riding here, and take one of mine. It knows the way, and will carry you safe."

So Jack set off, and being a kind-hearted lad he gave the frog sentry, whom he met coming away from his guard, some crumbs he had saved from his dinner. And the frog asked leave to go with him, and when Jack refused to take him he just gave one hop on to the stirrup, and a second hop on to the crupper, and the next hop he was in Jack's other pocket.

Then the horse galloped away like lightning, for it didn't like the slimy frog coming down " plop " on its back.

Well, after a time, Jack came to the palace of the King of all the Birds, and there at the front gate were a sparrow and a crow marching up and down with matchlocks on their shoulders. Now at this Jack laughed fit to split, and the mouse and the frog from his pockets called out :

" We come from the King ! Sirrahs ! Let us pass."

So that the sentries were right mazed, and let them pass in without more ado.

But when they came to the King's chamber, where he sate surrounded by all manner of birds, tomtits, wrens, cormorants, turtle-doves, and the like, the King said he was sorry, but he had no news of the missing Castle. And though he summoned all the birds of all the world to a Grand Assembly next morning, not one of them had seen or heard tell of it.

So Jack was quite disconsolate till the King said, " But where is the eagle ? I don't see my eagle."

Then the Chamberlain—he was a tomtit—stepped forward with a bow and said :

" May it please your Majesty he is late."

" Late ? " says the King in a fume. " Summon him at once."

So two larks flew up into the sky till they couldn't be seen and sang ever so loud, till at last the eagle appeared all in a perspiration from having flown so fast.

Then the King said, " Sirrah ! Have you seen a missing Castle that stands upon twelve pillars of gold ? "

And the eagle blinked its eyes and said, " May it please your Majesty that is where I've been."

Then everybody rejoiced exceedingly, and when the eagle had eaten a whole calf so as to be strong enough for the journey, he spread his wide wings, on which Jack stood, with the mouse in one pocket and the frog in the other, and started to obey the King's order to take the owner back to his missing Castle as quickly as possible.

And they flew over land and they flew over sea, until at last in the far distance they saw the Castle standing on its twelve golden pillars. But all the doors and windows were fast shut and barred, for, see you, the servant-master who had run away with it had gone out for the day a-hunting, and he always bolted doors and windows while he was absent lest some one else should run away with it.

Then Jack was puzzled to think how he should get hold of the golden snuff-box, until the little mouse said:

"Let me fetch it. There is always a mouse-hole in every castle, so I am sure I shall be able to get in."

So it went off, and Jack waited on the eagle's wings in a fume; till at last mousekin appeared.

"Have you got it?" shouted Jack, and the little mousie cried:

"Yes!"

So every one rejoiced exceedingly, and they set off back to the palace of the King of all the Birds, where Jack had left his horse; for now that he had the golden snuff-box safe he knew he could get the Castle back whenever he chose to send the three little red men to fetch it. But on the way over the sea, while Jack, who was dead tired with standing so long, lay down between the eagle's wings and fell asleep, the mouse and the eagle fell to quarrelling as to which of them had helped Jack the most, and they quarrelled so much that at last they laid the case before the frog. Then the frog, who made a very wise judge, said he must see the whole affair from the very beginning ; so the mouse brought out the golden snuff-box from Jack's pocket, and began to relate where it had been found and all about it. Now, at that very moment Jack awoke, kicked out his leg, and plump went the golden snuff-box down to the very bottom of the sea !

" I thought my turn would come," said the frog, and went plump in after it.

Well, they waited, and waited, and waited for three whole days and three whole nights ; but froggie never came up again, and they had just given him up in despair when his nose showed above the water.

" Have you got it ? " they shouted.

" No ! " says he, with a great gasp.

" Then what do you want ? " they cried in a rage.

" My breath," says froggie, and with that he sinks down again.

Well, they waited two days and two nights more, and at last up comes the little frog with the golden snuff-box in its mouth.

Then they all rejoiced exceedingly, and the eagle flew ever so fast to the palace of the King of the Birds.

But alas and alack-a-day ! Jack's troubles were not ended ; his mother's malison was still bringing him ill-luck, for the King of the Birds flew into a fearsome rage because Jack had not brought the Castle of the golden pillars back with him. And he said that unless he saw it by eight o'clock next morning Jack's head should come off as a cheat and a liar.

Then Jack being close to death opened the golden snuff-box, and out tumbled the three little red men in their three little red caps. They had recovered their tempers and were quite glad to be back with a master who knew that they would only, as a rule, work under fear of death ; for, see you, the servant-master had been for ever disturbing their sleep with opening the box to no purpose.

So before the clock struck eight next morning, there was the Castle on its twelve golden pillars, and the King of the Birds was fine and pleased, and let Jack take his horse and ride to the palace of the King of the Frogs. But there exactly the same thing happened, and poor Jack had to open the snuff-box again and order the Castle to come to the palace of the King of the Frogs. At this the little red men were a wee bit cross ; but they said they supposed it could not be helped ; so, though they yawned, they brought the Castle all right, and Jack was allowed to take his horse and go to the palace of the King of all the Mice in the World. But here the same thing happened, and the little red men tumbled out of the golden snuff-box in a real rage, and said fellows might as well have no sleep at all ! However, they did as they were bidden ; they brought the Castle of the golden pillars from the palace of the King of the Frogs to the palace of the King of the Birds, and Jack was allowed to take his own horse and ride home.

But the year and a day which he had been allowed was

almost gone, and even his gay young wife, after almost weeping her eyes out after her handsome young husband, had given up Jack for lost ; so every one was astounded to see him, and not over-pleased either to see him come without his Castle. Indeed his father-in-law swore with many oaths that if it were not in its proper place by eight o'clock next morning Jack's life should be forfeit.

Now this, of course, was exactly what Jack had wanted and intended from the beginning ; because when death was nigh he could open the golden snuff-box and order about the little red men. But he had opened it so often of late and they had become so cross that he was in a stew what to do ; whether to give them time to show their temper, or to hustle them out of it. At last he decided to

E

do half and half. So just as the hands of the clock were at five minutes to eight he opened the box, and stopped his ears !

Well ! you never heard such a yawning, and scolding, and threatening, and blustering. What did he mean by it ? Why should he take four bites at one cherry ? If he was always in fear of death why didn't he die and have done with it ?

In the midst of all this the tower clock began to whirr——

" Gentlemen ! " says Jack—he was really quaking with fear—" do as you are told."

" For the last time," they shrieked. " We won't stay and serve a master who thinks he is going to die every day."

And with that they flew out of the window.

AND THEY NEVER CAME BACK.

The golden snuff-box remained empty for evermore.

But when Jack looked out of window there was the Castle in the middle of the lake on its twelve golden pillars, and there was his young wife ever so pretty and gay in her nightcap looking out of the window too.

So they lived happily ever after.

TATTERCOATS

IN a great Palace by the sea there once dwelt a very rich old lord, who had neither wife nor children living, only one little granddaughter, whose face he had never seen in all her life. He hated her bitterly, because at her birth his favourite daughter died ; and when the old nurse brought him the baby he swore that it might live or die as it liked, but he would never look on its face as long as it lived.

So he turned his back, and sat by his window looking out over the sea, and weeping great tears for his lost daughter, till his white hair and beard grew down over his shoulders and twined round his chair and crept into the chinks of the floor, and his tears, dropping on to the window-ledge, wore a channel through the stone, and ran away in a little river to the great sea. Meanwhile, his granddaughter grew up with no one to care for her, or clothe her ; only the old nurse, when no one was by, would sometimes give her a dish of scraps from the kitchen, or a torn petticoat from the rag-bag ; while the other servants of the palace would drive her from the house with blows and mocking words, calling

51

her " Tattercoats," and pointing to her bare feet and shoulders, till she ran away, crying, to hide among the bushes.

So she grew up, with little to eat or to wear, spending her days out of doors, her only companion a crippled gooseherd, who fed his flock of geese on the common. And this gooseherd was a queer, merry little chap, and when she was hungry, or cold, or tired, he would play to her so gaily on his little pipe, that she forgot all her troubles, and would fall to dancing with his flock of noisy geese for partners.

Now one day people told each other that the King was travelling through the land, and was to give a great ball to all the lords and ladies of the country in the town near by, and that the Prince, his only son, was to choose a wife from amongst the maidens in the company. In due time one of the royal invitations to the ball was brought to the Palace by the sea, and the servants carried it up to the old lord, who still sat by his window, wrapped in his long white hair and weeping into the little river that was fed by his tears.

But when he heard the King's command, he dried his eyes and bade them bring shears to cut him loose, for his hair had bound him a fast prisoner, and he could not move. And then he sent them for rich clothes, and jewels, which he put on ; and he ordered them to saddle the white horse, with gold and silk, that he might ride to meet the King ; but he quite forgot he had a granddaughter to take to the ball.

Meanwhile Tattercoats sat by the kitchen-door weeping, because she could not go to see the grand doings. And when the old nurse heard her crying she went to the Lord of the

Palace, and begged him to take his granddaughter with him to the King's ball.

But he only frowned and told her to be silent; while the servants laughed and said, " Tattercoats is happy in her rags, playing with the gooseherd! Let her be—it is all she is fit for."

A second, and then a third time, the old nurse begged him to let the girl go with him, but she was answered only by black looks and fierce words, till she was driven from the room by the jeering servants, with blows and mocking words.

Weeping over her ill-success, the old nurse went to look for Tattercoats; but the girl had been turned from the door by the cook, and had run away to tell her friend the gooseherd how unhappy she was because she could not go to the King's ball.

Now when the gooseherd had listened to her story, he bade her cheer up, and proposed that they should go together into the town to see the King, and all the fine things; and when she looked sorrowfully down at her rags and bare feet he played a note or two upon his pipe, so gay and merry, that she forgot all about her tears and her troubles, and before she well knew, the gooseherd had taken her by the hand, and she and he, and the geese before them, were dancing down the road towards the town.

" Even cripples can dance when they choose," said the gooseherd.

Before they had gone very far a handsome young man,

splendidly dressed, riding up, stopped to ask the way to the castle where the King was staying, and when he found that they too were going thither, he got off his horse and walked beside them along the road.

"You seem merry folk," he said, "and will be good company."

"Good company, indeed," said the gooseherd, and played a new tune that was not a dance.

It was a curious tune, and it made the strange young man stare and stare and stare at Tattercoats till he couldn't see her rags—till he couldn't, to tell the truth, see anything but her beautiful face.

Then he said, "You are the most beautiful maiden in the world. Will you marry me?"

Then the gooseherd smiled to himself, and played sweeter than ever.

But Tattercoats laughed. "Not I," said she; "you would be finely put to shame, and so would I be, if you took a goose-girl for your wife! Go and ask one of the great ladies you will see to-night at the King's ball, and do not flout poor Tattercoats."

But the more she refused him the sweeter the pipe played, and the deeper the young man fell in love; till at last he begged her to come that night at twelve to the King's ball, just as she was, with the gooseherd and his geese, in her torn petticoat and bare feet, and see if he wouldn't dance with her before the King and the lords and ladies, and present her to them all, as his dear and honoured bride.

Tattercoats dancing while the gooseherd pipes.

Now at first Tattercoats said she would not ; but the gooseherd said, " Take fortune when it comes, little one."

So when night came, and the hall in the castle was full of light and music, and the lords and ladies were dancing before the King, just as the clock struck twelve, Tattercoats and the gooseherd, followed by his flock of noisy geese, hissing and swaying their heads, entered at the great doors, and walked straight up the ball-room, while on either side the ladies whispered, the lords laughed, and the King seated at the far end stared in amazement.

But as they came in front of the throne Tattercoats' lover rose from beside the King, and came to meet her. Taking her by the hand, he kissed her thrice before them all, and turned to the King.

" Father ! " he said—for it was the Prince himself—" I have made my choice, and here is my bride, the loveliest girl in all the land, and the sweetest as well ! "

Before he had finished speaking, the gooseherd had put his pipe to his lips and played a few notes that sounded like a bird singing far off in the woods ; and as he played Tattercoats' rags were changed to shining robes sewn with glittering jewels, a golden crown lay upon her golden hair, and the flock of geese behind her became a crowd of dainty pages, bearing her long train.

And as the King rose to greet her as his daughter the trumpets sounded loudly in honour of the new Princess, and the people outside in the street said to each other :

" Ah ! now the Prince has chosen for his wife the loveliest girl in all the land ! "

But the gooseherd was never seen again, and no one knew what became of him ; while the old lord went home once more to his Palace by the sea, for he could not stay at Court, when he had sworn never to look on his grand-daughter's face.

So there he still sits by his window,—if you could only see him, as you may some day—weeping more bitterly than ever. And his white hair has bound him to the stones, and the river of his tears runs away to the great sea.

THE THREE FEATHERS

ONCE upon a time there lived a girl who was wooed and married by a man she never saw; for he came a-courting her after nightfall, and when they were married he never came home till it was dark, and always left before dawn.

Still he was good and kind to her, giving her everything her heart could desire, so she was well content for a while. But, after a bit, some of her friends, doubtless full of envy for her good luck, began to whisper that the unseen husband must have something dreadful the matter with him which made him averse to being seen.

Now from the very beginning the girl had wondered why her lover did not come a-courting her as other girls' lovers came, openly and by day, and though, at first, she paid no heed to her neighbours' nods and winks, she began at last to think there might be something in what they said. So she determined to see for herself, and one night when she heard her husband come into her room, she lit her candle suddenly and saw him.

And, lo and behold ! he was handsome as handsome ; beautiful enough to make every woman in the world fall in love with him on the spot. But even as she got her glimpse of him, he changed into a big brown bird which looked at her with eyes full of anger and blame.

" Because you have done this faithless thing," it said, " you will see me no more, unless for seven long years and a day you serve for me faithfully."

And she cried with tears and sobs, " I will serve seven times seven years and a day if you will only come back. Tell me what I am to do."

Then the bird-husband said, " I will place you in service, and there you must remain and do good work for seven years and a day, and you must listen to no man who may seek to beguile you to leave that service. If you do I will never return."

To this the girl agreed, and the bird, spreading its broad brown wings, carried her to a big mansion.

" Here they need a laundry-maid," said the bird-husband. " Go in, ask to see the mistress, and say you will do the work ; but remember you must do it for seven years and a day."

" But I cannot do it for seven days," answered the girl. " I cannot wash or iron."

" That matters nothing," replied the bird. " All you have to do is to pluck three feathers from under my wing close to my heart, and these feathers will do your bidding whatever it may be. You will only have to put them on your hand, and say, ' By virtue of these three feathers from over my true love's heart may this be done,' and it will be done."

So the girl plucked three feathers from under the bird's wing, and after that the bird flew away.

Then the girl did as she was bidden, and the lady of the house engaged her for the place. And never was such a quick laundress; for, see you, she had only to go into the wash-house, bolt the door and close the shutters, so that no one should see what she was at; then she would out with the three feathers and say, "By virtue of these three feathers from over my true love's heart may the copper be lit, the clothes sorted, washed, boiled, dried, folded, mangled, ironed," and lo! there they came tumbling on to the table, clean and white, quite ready to be put away. So her mistress set great store by her and said there never was such a good laundry-maid. Thus four years passed and there was no talk of her leaving. But the other servants grew jealous of her, all the more so, because, being a very pretty girl, all the men-servants fell in love with her and wanted to marry her.

But she would have none of them, because she was always waiting and longing for the day when her bird-husband would come back to her in man's form.

Now one of the men who wanted her was the stout butler, and one day as he was coming back from the cider-house he chanced to stop by the laundry, and he heard a voice say, " By virtue of these three feathers from over my true love's heart may the copper be lit, the clothes sorted, boiled, dried, folded, mangled, and ironed."

He thought this very queer, so he peeped through the keyhole. And there was the girl sitting at her ease in a chair, while all the clothes came flying to the table ready and fit to put away.

Well, that night he went to the girl and said that if she turned up her nose at him and his proposal any longer, he would up and tell the mistress that her fine laundress was nothing but a witch ; and then, even if she were not burnt alive, she would lose her place.

Now the girl was in great distress what to do, since if she were not faithful to her bird-husband, or if she failed to serve her seven years and a day in one service, he would alike fail to return ; so she made an excuse by saying she could think of no one who did not give her enough money to satisfy her.

At this the stout butler laughed. " Money ? " said he. " I have seventy pounds laid by with master. Won't that satisfy thee ? "

" Happen it would," she replied.

So the very next night the butler came to her with the seventy pounds in golden sovereigns, and she held out her apron and took them, saying she was content ; for she had thought of a plan. Now as they were going upstairs together she stopped and said :

" Mr. Butler, excuse me for a minute. I have left the shutters of the wash-house open, and I must shut them, or they will be banging all night and disturb master and missus ! "

Now though the butler was stout and beginning to grow old, he was anxious to seem young and gallant ; so he said at once :

" Excuse me, my beauty, you shall not go. I will go and shut them. I shan't be a moment ! "

So off he set, and no sooner had he gone than she out with her three feathers, and putting them on her hand, said in a hurry :

" By virtue of the three feathers from over my true love's heart may the shutters never cease banging till morning, and may Mr. Butler's hands be busy trying to shut them."

And so it happened.

Mr. Butler shut the shutters, but—bru-u-u ! there they were hanging open again. Then he shut them once more, and this time they hit him on the face as they flew open. Yet he couldn't stop ; he had to go on. So there he was the whole livelong night. Such a cursing, and banging, and swearing, and shutting, never was, until dawn came, and, too tired to be really angry, he crept back to his bed, resolving that come what might he would not tell what had happened to him and thus get the laugh on him. So he kept his own counsel, and the girl kept the seventy pounds, and laughed in her sleeve at her would-be lover.

Now after a time the coachman, a spruce middle-aged man, who had long wanted to marry the clever, pretty laundry-maid, going to the pump to get water for his horses overheard her giving orders to the three feathers, and peeping through the keyhole as the butler had done, saw her sitting at her ease in a chair while the clothes, all washed and ironed and mangled, came flying to the table.

So, just as the butler had done, he went to the girl and said, " I have you now, my pretty. Don't dare to turn up your nose at me, for if you do I'll tell mistress you are a witch."

Then the girl said quite calmly, " I look on none who has no money."

" If that is all," replied the coachman, " I have forty pounds laid by with master. That I'll bring and ask for payment to-morrow night."

So when the night came the girl held out her apron for the money, and as she was going up the stairs she stopped suddenly and said, " Goody me ! I've left my clothes on the line. Stop a bit till I fetch them in."

Now the coachman was really a very polite fellow, so he said at once :

" Let me go. It is a cold, windy night and you'll be catching your death."

So off he went, and the girl out with her feathers and said :

" By virtue of the three feathers from over my true love's heart may the clothes slash and blow about till dawn, and may Mr. Coachman not be able to gather them up or take his hand from the job."

And when she had said this she went quietly to bed, for she knew what would happen. And sure enough it did. Never was such a night as Mr. Coachman spent with the wet clothes flittering and fluttering about his ears, and the sheets wrapping him into a bundle, and tripping him up, while the towels slashed at his legs. But though he smarted all over he had to go on till dawn came, and then a very weary, woebegone coachman couldn't even creep away to his bed, for he had to feed and water his horses! And he, also, kept his own counsel for fear of the laugh going against him; so the clever laundry-maid put the forty pounds with the seventy in her box, and went on with her work gaily. But after a time the footman, who was quite an honest lad and truly in love, going by the laundry peeped through the keyhole to get a glimpse of his dearest dear, and what should he see but her sitting at her ease in a chair, and the clothes coming all ready folded and ironed on to the table.

Now when he saw this he was greatly troubled. So he went to his master and drew out all his savings; and then he went to the girl and told her that he would have to tell the mistress what he had seen, unless she consented to marry him.

"You see," he said, "I have been with master this while back, and have saved up this bit, and you have been here this long while back and must have saved as well. So let us put the two together and make a home, or else stay on at service as pleases you."

Well, she tried to put him off; but he insisted so much that at last she said:

"James! there's a dear, run down to the cellar and fetch me a drop of brandy. You've made me feel so queer!"

And when he had gone she out with her three feathers, and said, " By virtue of the three feathers from over my true love's heart may James not be able to pour the brandy straight, except down his throat."

Well! so it happened. Try as he would, James could not get the brandy into the glass. It splashed a few drops into it, then it trickled over his hand, and fell on the floor. And so it went on and on till he grew so tired that he thought he needed a dram himself. So he tossed off the few drops and began again ; but he fared no better. So he took another little drain, and went on, and on, and on, till he got quite fuddled. And who should come down into the cellar but his master to know what the smell of brandy meant !

Now James the footman was truthful as well as honest, so he told the master how he had come down to get the sick laundry-maid a drop of brandy, but that his hand had shaken so that he could not pour it out, and it had fallen on the ground, and that the smell of it had got to his head.

" A likely tale," said the master, and beat James soundly.

Then the master went to the mistress, his wife, and said : " Send away that laundry-maid of yours. Something has come over my men. They have all drawn out their savings as if they were going to be married, yet they don't leave, and I believe that girl is at the bottom of it."

But his wife would not hear of the laundry-maid being blamed ; she was the best servant in the house, and worth all the rest of them put together ; it was his men who were

at fault. So they quarrelled over it ; but in the end the
master gave in, and after this there was peace, since the
mistress bade the girl keep herself to herself, and none of
the men would say ought of what had happened for fear
of the laughter of the other servants.

So it went on until one day when the master was going
a-driving, the coach was at the door, and the footman was
standing to hold the coach open, and the butler on the steps
all ready, when who should pass through the yard, so saucy
and bright with a great basket of clean clothes, but the
laundry-maid. And the sight of her was too much for
James, the footman, who began to blub.

" She is a wicked girl," he said. " She got all my savings,
and got me a good thrashing besides."

Then the coachman grew bold. " Did she ? " he said.
" That was nothing to what she served me." So he up and
told all about the wet clothes and the awful job he had had
the livelong night. Now the butler on the steps swelled
with rage until he nearly burst, and at last he out with his
night of banging shutters.

" And one," he said, " hit me on the nose."

This settled the three men, and they agreed to tell their
master the moment he came out, and get the girl sent about
her business. Now the laundry-maid had sharp ears and
had paused behind a door to listen ; so when she heard this
she knew she must do something to stop it. So she out
with her three feathers and said, " By virtue of the three
feathers from over my true love's heart may there be striving

F

as to who suffered most between the men so that they get into the pond for a ducking."

Well ! no sooner had she said the words than the three men began disputing as to which of them had been served the worst ; then James up and hit the stout butler, giving him a black eye, and the fat butler fell upon James and pommelled him hard, while the coachman scrambled from his box and belaboured them both, and the laundry-maid stood by laughing.

So out comes the master, but none of them would listen, and each wanted to be heard, and fought, and shoved, and pommelled away until they shoved each other into the pond, and all got a fine ducking.

Then the master asked the girl what it was all about, and she said :

"They all wanted to tell a story against me because I won't marry them, and one said his was the best, and the next said his was the best, so they fell a-quarrelling as to which was the likeliest story to get me into trouble. But they are well punished, so there is no need to do more."

Then the master went to his wife and said, "You are right. That laundry-maid of yours is a very wise girl."

So the butler and the coachman and James had nothing to do but look sheepish and hold their tongues, and the laundry-maid went on with her duties without further trouble.

Then when the seven years and a day were over, who should drive up to the door in a fine gilded coach but the bird-husband restored to his shape as a handsome young man. And he carried the laundry-maid off to be his wife again, and her master and mistress were so pleased at her good fortune that they ordered all the other servants to stand on the steps and give her good luck. So as she passed the butler she put a bag with seventy pounds in it into his hand and said sweetly, "That is to recompense you for shutting the shutters."

And when she passed the coachman she put a bag with forty pounds into his hand and said, "That is your reward for bringing in the clothes." But when she passed the footman she gave him a bag with a hundred pounds in it, and laughed, saying, "That is for the drop of brandy you never brought me!"

So she drove off with her handsome husband, and lived happy ever after.

LAZY JACK

ONCE upon a time there was a boy whose name was Jack, and he lived with his mother on a common. They were very poor, and the old woman got her living by spinning, but Jack was so lazy that he would do nothing but bask in the sun in the hot weather, and sit by the corner of the hearth in the winter-time. So they called him Lazy Jack. His mother could not get him to do anything for her, and at last told him, one Monday, that if he did not begin to work for his porridge she would turn him out to get his living as he could.

This roused Jack, and he went out and hired himself for the next day to a neighbouring farmer for a penny ; but as he was coming home, never having had any money before, he lost it in passing over a brook.

" You stupid boy," said his mother, " you should have put it in your pocket."

" I'll do so another time," replied Jack.

Well, the next day, Jack went out again and hired himself to a cowkeeper, who gave him a jar of milk for his day's

work. Jack took the jar and put it into the large pocket
of his jacket, spilling it all, long before he got home.

" Dear me ! " said the old woman ; " you should have
carried it on your head."

" I'll do so another time," said Jack.

So the following day, Jack hired himself again to a farmer,
who agreed to give him a cream cheese for his services.
In the evening Jack took the cheese, and went home with
it on his head.   By the time he got home the cheese was all
spoilt, part of it being lost, and part matted with his hair.

" You stupid lout," said his mother, " you should have
carried it very carefully in your hands."

" I'll do so another time," replied Jack.

Now the next day, Lazy Jack again went out, and hired
himself to a baker, who would give him nothing for his work
but a large tom-cat.   Jack took the cat, and began carrying
it very carefully in his hands, but in a short time pussy
scratched him so much that he was compelled to let it go.

When he got home, his mother said to him, " You silly
fellow, you should have tied it with a string, and dragged it
along after you."

" I'll do so another time," said Jack.

So on the following day, Jack hired himself to a butcher,
who rewarded him by the handsome present of a shoulder
of mutton.   Jack took the mutton, tied it with a string, and
trailed it along after him in the dirt, so that by the time he
had got home the meat was completely spoilt.   His mother
was this time quite out of patience with him, for the next

day was Sunday, and she was obliged to do with cabbage for her dinner.

" You ninney-hammer," said she to her son, " you should have carried it on your shoulder."

" I'll do so another time," replied Jack.

Well, on the Monday, Lazy Jack went once more and hired himself to a cattle-keeper, who gave him a donkey for his trouble. Now though Jack was strong he found it hard to hoist the donkey on his shoulders, but at last he did it, and began walking home slowly with his prize. Now it so happened that in the course of his journey he passed a house where a rich man lived with his only daughter, a beautiful girl, who was deaf and dumb. And she had never laughed in her life, and the doctors said she would never speak till somebody made her laugh. So the father had given out that any man who made her laugh would receive

The giant Cormoran was the terror of all the country-side.

her hand in marriage. Now this young lady happened to be looking out of the window when Jack was passing by with the donkey on his shoulders ; and the poor beast with its legs sticking up in the air was kicking violently and hee-hawing with all its might. Well, the sight was so comical that she burst out into a great fit of laughter, and immediately recovered her speech and hearing. Her father was over-joyed, and fulfilled his promise by marrying her to Lazy Jack, who was thus made a rich gentleman. They lived in a large house, and Jack's mother lived with them in great happiness until she died.

JACK THE GIANT-KILLER

I

WHEN good King Arthur reigned with Guinevere his Queen, there lived, near the Land's End in Cornwall, a farmer who had one only son called Jack. Now Jack was brisk and ready; of such a lively wit that none nor nothing could worst him.

In those days, the Mount of St. Michael in Cornwall was the fastness of a hugeous giant whose name was Cormoran.

He was full eighteen feet in height, some three yards about his middle, of a grim fierce face, and he was the terror of all the country-side. He lived in a cave amidst the rocky Mount, and when he desired victuals he would wade across the tides to the mainland and furnish himself forth with all that came in his way. The poor folk and the rich folk alike ran out of their houses and hid themselves when they heard the swish-swash of his big feet in the water; for if he saw them, he would think nothing of broiling half-a-dozen or so of them for breakfast. As it was, he seized their cattle by the score, carrying off half-a-dozen fat oxen on his back at a time, and hanging sheep and pigs to his waistbelt like bunches of dip-candles. Now this had gone on for long years, and the poor folk of Cornwall were in despair, for none could put an end to the giant Cormoran.

It so happened that one market day Jack, then quite a young lad, found the town upside down over some new exploit of the giant's. Women were weeping, men were cursing, and the magistrates were sitting in Council over what was to be done. But none could suggest a plan. Then Jack, blithe and gay, went up to the magistrates, and with a fine courtesy—for he was ever polite—asked them what reward would be given to him who killed the giant Cormoran.

" The treasures of the Giant's Cave," quoth they.

" Every whit of it ? " quoth Jack, who was never to be done.

" To the last farthing," quoth they.

" Then will I undertake the task," said Jack, and forthwith set about the business.

It was winter-time, and having got himself a horn, a pickaxe, and a shovel, he went over to the Mount in the dark evening, set to work, and before dawn he had dug a pit, no less than twenty-two feet deep and nigh as big across. This he covered with long thin sticks and straw, sprinkling a little loose mould over all to make it look like solid ground. So, just as dawn was breaking, he planted himself fair and square on the side of the pit that was farthest from the giant's cave, raised the horn to his lips, and with full blast sounded :

"Tantivy ! Tantivy ! Tantivy !"

just as he would have done had he been hunting a fox.

Of course this woke the giant, who rushed in a rage out of his cave, and seeing little Jack, fair and square blowing away at his horn, as calm and cool as may be, he became still more angry, and made for the disturber of his rest, bawling out, "I'll teach you to wake a giant, you little whipper-snapper. You shall pay dearly for your tantivys, I'll take you and broil you whole for break——"

He had only got as far as this when crash—he fell into the pit ! So there was a break indeed ; such an one that it caused the very foundations of the Mount to shake.

But Jack shook with laughter. "Ho, ho !" he cried, "how about breakfast now, Sir Giant ? Will you have me broiled or baked ? And will no diet serve you but poor little Jack ? Faith ! I've got you in Lob's pound now ! You're in the stocks for bad behaviour, and I'll plague you as I like. Would I had rotten eggs ; but this will do as well." And with that he up with his pickaxe and dealt the giant Cormoran such a most weighty knock on the very crown of his head, that he killed him on the spot.

Whereupon Jack calmly filled up the pit with earth again and went to search the cave, where he found much treasure.

Now when the magistrates heard of Jack's great exploit, they proclaimed that henceforth he should be known as—

JACK THE GIANT-KILLER.

And they presented him with a sword and belt, on which these words were embroidered in gold :

> Here's the valiant Cornishman
> Who slew the giant Cormoran.

II

Of course the news of Jack's victory soon spread over all England, so that another giant named Blunderbore who lived to the north, hearing of it, vowed if ever he came across Jack he would be revenged upon him. Now this giant Blunderbore was lord of an enchanted castle that stood in the middle of a lonesome forest.

It so happened that Jack, about four months after he had killed Cormoran, had occasion to journey into Wales, and on the road he passed this forest. Weary with walking, and finding a pleasant fountain by the wayside, he lay down to rest and was soon fast asleep.

Now the giant Blunderbore, coming to the well for water, found Jack sleeping, and knew by the lines embroidered on his belt that here was the far-famed giant-killer. Rejoiced at his luck, the giant, without more ado, lifted Jack to his shoulder and began to carry him through the wood to the enchanted castle.

But the rustling of the boughs awakened Jack, who, finding himself already in the clutches of the giant, was terrified ; nor was his alarm decreased by seeing the court-yard of the castle all strewn with men's bones.

"Yours will be with them ere long," said Blunderbore as he locked poor Jack into an immense chamber above the castle gateway. It had a high-pitched, beamed roof, and one window that looked down the road. Here poor Jack was to stay while Blunderbore went to fetch his brother-giant, who lived in the same wood, that he might share in the feast.

Now, after a time, Jack, watching through the window, saw the two giants tramping hastily down the road, eager for their dinner.

"Now," quoth Jack to himself, "my death or my deliverance is at hand." For he had thought out a plan. In one corner of the room he had seen two strong cords. These he took, and making a cunning noose at the end of each, he hung them out of the window, and, as the giants were unlocking the iron door of the gate, managed to slip them over their heads without their noticing it. Then, quick as thought, he tied the other ends to a beam, so that as the giants moved on the nooses tightened and throttled them until they grew black in the face. Seeing this, Jack slid down the ropes, and drawing his sword, slew them both.

So, taking the keys of the castle, he unlocked all the doors and set free three beauteous ladies who, tied by the hair of their heads, he found almost starved to death.

" Sweet ladies," quoth Jack, kneeling on one knee—
for he was ever polite—" here are the keys of this
enchanted castle. I have destroyed the giant Blunderbore and his brutish brother, and thus have restored to
you your liberty. These keys should bring you all else
you require."

So saying he proceeded on his journey to Wales.

III

He travelled as fast as he could ; perhaps too fast, for,
losing his way, he found himself benighted and far from
any habitation. He wandered on always in hopes, until
on entering a narrow valley he came on a very large, dreary-
looking house standing alone. Being anxious for shelter
he went up to the door and knocked. You may imagine
his surprise and alarm when the summons was answered by
a giant with two heads. But though this monster's look
was exceedingly fierce, his manners were quite polite ; the
truth being that he was a Welsh giant, and as such double-
faced and smooth, given to gaining his malicious ends by
a show of false friendship.

So he welcomed Jack heartily in a strong Welsh accent,
and prepared a bedroom for him, where he was left with
kind wishes for a good rest. Jack, however, was too tired
to sleep well, and as he lay awake, he overheard his host
muttering to himself in the next room. Having very keen

ears he was able to make out these words, or something like them :

"Though here you lodge with me this night,
You shall not see the morning light.
My club shall dash your brains outright."

" Say'st thou so ! " quoth Jack to himself, starting up at once. " So that is your Welsh trick, is it ? But I will be even with you." Then, leaving his bed, he laid a big billet of wood among the blankets, and taking one of these to keep himself warm, made himself snug in a corner of the room, pretending to snore, so as to make Mr. Giant think he was asleep.

And sure enough, after a little time, in came the monster on tiptoe as if treading on eggs, and carrying a big club. Then—

WHACK ! WHACK ! WHACK !

Jack could hear the bed being belaboured until the Giant, thinking every bone of his guest's skin must be broken, stole out of the room again ; whereupon Jack went calmly to bed once more and slept soundly ! Next morning the giant couldn't believe his eyes when he saw Jack coming down the stairs fresh and hearty.

" Odds splutter hur nails ! " he cried, astonished. " Did she sleep well ? Was there not nothing felt in the night ? "

" Oh," replied Jack, laughing in his sleeve, " I think a rat did come and give me two or three flaps of his tail."

On this the giant was dumbfoundered, and led Jack to breakfast, bringing him a bowl which held at least four

Taking the keys of the castle, Jack unlocked all the doors.

gallons of hasty-pudding, and bidding him, as a man of
such mettle, eat the lot. Now Jack when travelling wore
under his cloak a leathern bag to carry his things withal;
so, quick as thought, he hitched this round in front with the
opening just under his chin; thus, as he ate, he could slip
the best part of the pudding into it without the giant's being
any the wiser. So they sate down to breakfast, the giant

gobbling down his own measure of hasty-pudding, while Jack made away with his.

"See," says crafty Jack when he had finished. "I'll show you a trick worth two of yours," and with that he up with a carving-knife and, ripping up the leathern bag, out fell all the hasty-pudding on the floor !

"Odds splutter hur nails ! " cried the giant, not to be outdone. "Hur can do that hurself ! " Whereupon he seized the carving-knife, and ripping open his own belly fell down dead.

Thus was Jack quit of the Welsh giant.

IV

Now it so happened that in those days, when gallant knights were always seeking adventures, King Arthur's only son, a very valiant Prince, begged of his father a large sum of money to enable him to journey to Wales, and there strive to set free a certain beautiful lady who was possessed by seven evil spirits. In vain the King denied him ; so at last he gave way and the Prince set out with two horses, one of which he rode, the other laden with gold pieces. Now after some days' journey the Prince came to a market-town in Wales where there was a great commotion. On asking the reason for it he was told that, according to law, the corpse of a very generous man had been arrested on its way to the grave, because, in life, it had owed large sums to the money-lenders.

"That is a cruel law," said the young Prince. "Go, bury the dead in peace, and let the creditors come to my lodgings; I will pay the debts of the dead."

So the creditors came, but they were so numerous that by evening the Prince had but twopence left for himself, and could not go further on his journey.

Now it so happened that Jack the Giant-Killer on his way to Wales passed through the town, and, hearing of the Prince's plight, was so taken with his kindness and generosity that he determined to be the Prince's servant. So this was agreed upon, and next morning, after Jack had paid the reckoning with his last farthing, the two set out together. But as they were leaving the town, an old woman ran after the Prince and called out, "Justice! Justice! The dead man owed me twopence these seven years. Pay me as well as the others."

And the Prince, kind and generous, put his hand to his pocket and gave the old woman the twopence that was left to him. So now they had not a penny between them, and when the sun grew low the Prince said:

"Jack! Since we have no money, how are we to get a night's lodging?"

Then Jack replied, "We shall do well enough, Master; for within two or three miles of this place there lives a huge and monstrous giant with three heads, who can fight four hundred men in armour and make them fly from him like chaff before the wind."

"And what good will that be to us?" quoth the Prince. "He will for sure chop us up in a mouthful."

G

" Nay," said Jack, laughing. " Let me go and prepare
the way for you. By all accounts this giant is a dolt.
Mayhap I may manage better than that."

So the Prince remained where he was, and Jack pricked
his steed at full speed till he came to the giant's castle, at
the gate of which he knocked so loud that he made the
neighbouring hills resound.

On this the giant roared from within in a voice like
thunder :

" Who's there ? "

Then said Jack as bold as brass, " None but your poor
cousin Jack."

" Cousin Jack ! " quoth the giant, astounded. " And
what news with my poor cousin Jack ? " For, see you, he
was quite taken aback ; so Jack made haste to reassure
him.

" Dear coz, heavy news, God wot ! "

" Heavy news," echoed the giant, half afraid. " God
wot, no heavy news can come to me. Have I not three
heads ? Can I not fight five hundred men in armour ?
Can I not make them fly like chaff before the wind ? "

" True," replied crafty Jack, " but I came to warn you
because the great King Arthur's son with a thousand men
in armour is on his way to kill you."

At this the giant began to shiver and to shake. " Ah !
Cousin Jack ! Kind cousin Jack ! This is heavy news
indeed," quoth he. " Tell me, what am I to do ? "

" Hide yourself in the vault," says crafty Jack, ' and I

will lock and bolt and bar you in; and keep the key till the Prince has gone. So you will be safe."

Then the giant made haste and ran down into the vault, and Jack locked, and bolted, and barred him in. Then being thus secure, he went and fetched his master, and the two made themselves heartily merry over what the giant was to have had for supper, while the miserable monster shivered and shook with fright in the underground vault.

Well, after a good night's rest Jack woke his master in early morn, and having furnished him well with gold and silver from the giant's treasure, bade him ride three miles forward on his journey. So when Jack judged that the

Prince was pretty well out of the smell of the giant, he took the key and let his prisoner out. He was half dead with cold and damp, but very grateful ; and he begged Jack to let him know what he would be given as a reward for saving the giant's life and castle from destruction, and he should have it.

" You're very welcome," said Jack, who always had his eyes about him. " All I want is the old coat and cap, together with the rusty old sword and slippers which are at your bed-head."

When the giant heard this he sighed and shook his head. " You don't know what you are asking," quoth he. " They are the most precious things I possess, but as I have promised, you must have them. The coat will make you invisible, the cap will tell you all you want to know, the sword will cut asunder whatever you strike, and the slippers will take you wherever you want to go in the twinkling of an eye ! "

So Jack, overjoyed, rode away with the coat and cap, the sword and the slippers, and soon overtook his master ; and they rode on together until they reached the castle where the beautiful lady lived whom the Prince sought.

Now she was very beautiful, for all she was possessed of seven devils, and when she heard the Prince sought her as a suitor, she smiled and ordered a splendid banquet to be prepared for his reception. And she sate on his right hand, and plied him with food and drink.

And when the repast was over she took out her own

handkerchief and wiped his lips gently, and said, with a smile :

"I have a task for you, my lord ! You must show me that kerchief to-morrow morning or lose your head."

And with that she put the handkerchief in her bosom and said, " Good-night ! "

The Prince was in despair, but Jack said nothing till his master was in bed. Then he put on the old cap he had got from the giant, and lo ! in a minute he knew all that he wanted to know. So, in the dead of the night, when the beautiful lady called on one of her familiar spirits to carry her to Lucifer himself, Jack was beforehand with her, and putting on his coat of darkness and his slippers of swiftness, was there as soon as she was. And when she gave the handkerchief to the Devil, bidding him keep it safe, and he put it away on a high shelf, Jack just up and nipped it away in a trice !

So the next morning, when the beauteous enchanted lady looked to see the Prince crestfallen, he just made a fine bow and presented her with the handkerchief.

At first she was terribly disappointed, but, as the day drew on, she ordered another and still more splendid repast to be got ready. And this time, when the repast was over, she kissed the Prince full on the lips and said :

"I have a task for you, my lover. Show me to-morrow morning the last lips I kiss to-night or you lose your head."

Then the Prince, who by this time was head over ears in love, said tenderly, "If you will kiss none but mine, I will."

Now the beauteous lady, for all she was possessed by seven devils, could not but see that the Prince was a very handsome young man ; so she blushed a little, and said :

" That is neither here nor there : you must show me them, or death is your portion."

So the Prince went to his bed, sorrowful as before ; but Jack put on the cap of knowledge and knew in a moment all he wanted to know.

Thus when, in the dead of the night, the beauteous lady called on her familiar spirit to take her to Lucifer himself, Jack in his coat of darkness and his shoes of swiftness was there before her.

" Thou hast betrayed me once," said the beauteous lady to Lucifer, frowning, " by letting go my handkerchief. Now will I give thee something none can steal, and so best the Prince, King's son though he be."

With that she kissed the loathly demon full on the lips, and left him. Whereupon Jack with one blow of the rusty sword of strength cut off Lucifer's head, and, hiding it under his coat of darkness, brought it back to his master.

Thus next morning when the beauteous lady, with malice in her beautiful eyes, asked the Prince to show her the lips she had last kissed, he pulled out the demon's head by the horns. On that the seven devils, which possessed the poor lady, gave seven dreadful shrieks and left her. Thus the enchantment being broken, she appeared in all her perfect beauty and goodness.

So she and the Prince were married the very next

morning.   After which they journeyed back to the court of King Arthur, where Jack the Giant-Killer, for his many exploits, was made one of the Knights of the Round Table.

V

This, however, did not satisfy our hero, who was soon on the road again searching for giants.   Now he had not gone far when he came upon one, seated on a huge block of timber near the entrance to a dark cave.   He was a most terrific giant.   His goggle eyes were as coals of fire, his countenance was grim and gruesome ; his cheeks, like huge flitches of bacon, were covered with a stubbly beard, the bristles of which resembled rods of iron wire, while the locks of hair that fell on his brawny shoulders showed like curled snakes or hissing adders.   He held a knotted iron club, and breathed so heavily you could hear him a mile away. Nothing daunted by this fearsome sight, Jack alighted from his horse and, putting on his coat of darkness, went close up to the giant and said softly : " Hullo ! is that you ?   It will not be long before I have you fast by your beard."

So saying he made a cut with the sword of strength at the giant's head, but, somehow, missing his aim, cut off the nose instead, clean as a whistle !   My goodness !   How the giant roared !   It was like claps of thunder, and he began to lay about him with the knotted iron club, like one possessed.   But Jack in his coat of darkness easily dodged

the blows, and running in behind, drove the sword up to the hilt into the giant's back, so that he fell stone dead.

Jack then cut off the head and sent it to King Arthur by a waggoner whom he hired for the purpose. After which he began to search the giant's cave to find his treasure. He passed through many windings and turnings until he came to a huge hall paved and roofed with freestone. At the upper end of this was an immense fireplace where hung an iron cauldron, the like of which, for size, Jack had never seen before. It was boiling and gave out a savoury steam; while beside it, on the right hand, stood a big massive table set out with huge platters and mugs. Here it was that the giants used to dine. Going a little further he came upon a sort of window barred with iron, and looking within beheld a vast number of miserable captives.

"Alas! Alack!" they cried on seeing him. "Art come, young man, to join us in this dreadful prison?"

"That depends," quoth Jack; "but first tell me wherefore you are thus held imprisoned?"

"Through no fault," they cried at once. "We are captives of the cruel giants and are kept here and well nourished until such time as the monsters desire a feast. Then they choose the fattest and sup off them."

On hearing this Jack straightway unlocked the door of the prison and set the poor fellows free. Then, searching the giants' coffers, he divided the gold and silver equally amongst the captives as some redress for their sufferings, and taking them to a neighbouring castle gave them a right good feast.

VI

Now as they were all making merry over their deliverance, and praising Jack's prowess, a messenger arrived to say that one Thunderdell, a huge giant with two heads, having heard of the death of his kinsman, was on his way from the northern dales to be revenged, and was already within a mile or two of the castle, the country folk with their flocks and herds flying before him like chaff before the wind.

Now the castle with its gardens stood on a small island that was surrounded by a moat twenty feet wide and thirty

feet deep, having very steep
sides.   And   this   moat   was
spanned by a drawbridge. This, without a moment's delay, Jack ordered
should be sawn on both sides at the
middle, so as to only leave one plank
uncut over which he in his invisible coat
of darkness passed swiftly to meet his
enemy, bearing in his hand the wonderful sword of strength.

Now though the giant could not, of course, see Jack,
he could smell him, for giants have keen noses. Therefore
Thunderdell cried out in a voice like his name :

> " Fee, fi, fo, fum !
> I smell the blood of an Englishman.
> Be he alive, or be he dead,
> I'll grind his bones to make my bread ! "

" Is that so ? " quoth Jack, cheerful as ever. " Then art thou a monstrous miller for sure ! "

On this the giant, peering round everywhere for a glimpse of his foe, shouted out :

" Art thou, indeed, the villain who hath killed so many of my kinsmen ? Then, indeed, will I tear thee to pieces with my teeth, suck thy blood, and grind thy bones to powder."

" Thou'lt have to catch me first," quoth Jack, laughing, and throwing off his coat of darkness and putting on his slippers of swiftness, he began nimbly to lead the giant a pretty dance, he leaping and doubling light as a feather, the monster following heavily like a walking tower, so

that the very foundations of the earth seemed to shake at
every step. At this game the onlookers nearly split their
sides with laughter, until Jack, judging there had been
enough of it, made for the drawbridge, ran neatly over the
single plank, and reaching the other side waited in teasing
fashion for his adversary.

On came the giant at full speed, foaming at the mouth
with rage, and flourishing his club. But when he came to
the middle of the bridge his great weight, of course, broke
the plank, and there he was fallen headlong into the moat,
rolling and wallowing like a whale, plunging from place to
place, yet unable to get out and be revenged.

The spectators greeted his efforts with roars of laughter,
and Jack himself was at first too overcome with merriment
to do more than scoff. At last, however, he went for a
rope, cast it over the giant's two heads, so, with the help of
a team of horses, drew them shorewards, where two blows
from the sword of strength settled the matter.

VII

After some time spent in mirth and pastimes, Jack began
once more to grow restless, and taking leave of his companions
set out for fresh adventures.

He travelled far and fast, through woods, and vales,
and hills, till at last he came, late at night, on a lonesome
house set at the foot of a high mountain.

Knocking at the door, it was opened by an old man whose head was white as snow.

"Father," said Jack, ever courteous, "can you lodge a benighted traveller?"

"Ay, that will I, and welcome to my poor cottage," replied the old man.

Whereupon Jack came in, and after supper they sate together chatting in friendly fashion. Then it was that the old man, seeing by Jack's belt that he was the famous Giant-Killer, spoke in this wise:

"My son! You are the great conqueror of evil monsters. Now close by there lives one well worthy of your prowess. On the top of yonder high hill is an enchanted castle kept by a giant named Galligantua, who, by the help of a wicked old magician, inveigles many beautiful ladies and valiant knights into the castle, where they are transformed into all sorts of birds and beasts, yea, even into fishes and insects. There they live pitiably in confinement; but most of all do I grieve for a duke's daughter whom they kidnapped in her father's garden, bringing her hither in a burning chariot drawn by fiery dragons. Her form is that of a white hind; and though many valiant knights have tried their utmost to break the spell and work her deliverance, none have succeeded; for, see you, at the entrance to the castle are two dreadful griffins who destroy every one who attempts to pass them by."

Now Jack bethought him of the coat of darkness which had served him so well before, and he put on the cap of knowledge, and in an instant he knew what had to be done. Then the very next morning, at dawn-time, Jack arose and put on his invisible coat and his slippers of swiftness. And in the twinkling of an eye there he was on the top of the mountain ! And there were the two griffins guarding the castle gates—horrible creatures with forked tails and tongues. But they could not see him because of the coat of darkness, so he passed them by unharmed.

And hung to the doors of the gateway he found a golden trumpet on a silver chain, and beneath it was engraved in red lettering :

> Whoever shall this trumpet blow
> Will cause the giant's overthrow.
> The black enchantment he will break,
> And gladness out of sadness make.

No sooner had Jack read these words than he put the horn to his lips and blew a loud

"Tantivy ! Tantivy ! Tantivy !"

Now at the very first note the castle trembled to its vast foundations, and before he had finished the measure, both the giant and the magician were biting their thumbs and tearing their hair, knowing that their wickedness must now come to an end. But the giant showed fight and took up his club to defend himself ; whereupon Jack, with one clean cut of the sword of strength, severed his head from his body, and would doubtless have done the same to the magician, but that the latter was a coward, and, calling up

The giant Galligantua and the wicked old magician transform the
duke's daughter into a white hind.

a whirlwind, was swept away by it into the air, nor has he ever been seen or heard of since. The enchantments being thus broken, all the valiant knights and beautiful ladies, who had been transformed into birds and beasts and fishes and reptiles and insects, returned to their proper shapes, including the duke's daughter, who, from being a white hind, showed as the most beauteous maiden upon whom the sun ever shone. Now, no sooner had this occurred than the whole castle vanished away in a cloud of smoke, and from that moment giants vanished also from the land.

So Jack, when he had presented the head of Galligantua to King Arthur, together with all the lords and ladies he had delivered from enchantment, found he had nothing more to do. As a reward for past services, however, King Arthur bestowed the hand of the duke's daughter upon honest Jack the Giant-Killer. So married they were, and the whole kingdom was filled with joy at their wedding. Furthermore, the King bestowed on Jack a noble castle with a magnificent estate belonging thereto, whereon he, his lady, and their children lived in great joy and content for the rest of their days.

THE THREE SILLIES

ONCE upon a time, when folk were not so wise as they are nowadays, there lived a farmer and his wife who had one daughter. And she, being a pretty lass, was courted by the young squire when he came home from his travels.

Now every evening he would stroll over from the Hall to see her and stop to supper in the farm-house, and every evening the daughter would go down into the cellar to draw the cider for supper.

So one evening when she had gone down to draw the cider and had turned the tap as usual, she happened to look up at the ceiling, and there she saw a big wooden mallet stuck in one of the beams.

It must have been there for ages and ages, for it was all covered with cobwebs; but somehow or another she had never noticed it before, and at once she began thinking how dangerous it was to have the mallet just there.

" For," thought she, " supposing him and me was
96

married, and supposing we was to have a son, and supposing he were to grow up to be a man, and supposing he were to come down to draw cider like as I'm doing, and supposing the mallet were to fall on his head and kill him, how dreadful it would be ! "

And with that she put down the candle she was carrying and, seating herself on a cask, began to cry. And she cried and cried and cried.

Now, upstairs, they began to wonder why she was so long drawing the cider ; so after a time her mother went down to the cellar to see what had come to her, and found her, seated on the cask, crying ever so hard, and the cider running all over the floor.

" Lawks a mercy me ! " cried her mother, " whatever is the matter ? "

" O mother ! " says she between her sobs, " it's that horrid mallet. Supposing him and me was married, and supposing we was to have a son, and supposing he was to grow up to be a man, and supposing he was to come down to draw cider like as I'm doing, and supposing the mallet were to fall on his head and kill him, how dreadful it would be ! "

" Dear heart ! " said the mother, seating herself beside her daughter and beginning to cry : " How dreadful it would be ! "

So they both sat a-crying.

Now after a time, when they did not come back, the farmer began to wonder what had happened, and going

H

down to the cellar found them seated side by side on the cask, crying hard, and the cider running all over the floor.

" Zounds ! " says he, " whatever is the matter ? "

" Just look at that horrid mallet up there, father," moaned the mother. " Supposing our daughter was to marry her sweetheart, and supposing they was to have a son, and supposing he was to grow to man's estate, and supposing he was to come down to draw cider like as we're doing, and supposing that there mallet was to fall on his head and kill him, how dreadful it would be ! "

" Dreadful indeed ! " said the father and, seating himself beside his wife and daughter, started a-crying too.

Now upstairs the young squire wanted his supper ; so at last he lost patience and went down into the cellar to see for himself what they were all after. And there he found them seated side by side on the cask a-crying, with their feet all a-wash in cider, for the floor was fair flooded. So the first thing he did was to run straight and turn off the tap. Then he said :

" What are you three after, sitting there crying like babies, and letting good cider run over the floor ? "

Then they all three began with one voice, " Look at that horrid mallet ! Supposing you and $\frac{me}{she}$ was married, and supposing $\frac{we}{you}$ had a son, and supposing he was to grow to man's estate, and supposing he was to come down here to draw cider like as we be, and supposing that there mallet was to fall down on his head and kill him, how dreadful it would be ! "

Then the young squire burst out a-laughing, and laughed till he was tired. But at last he reached up to the old mallet and pulled it out, and put it safe on the floor. And he shook his head and said, " I've travelled far and I've travelled fast, but never have I met with three such sillies as you three. Now I can't marry one of the three biggest sillies in the world. So I shall start again on my travels, and if I can find three bigger sillies than you three, then I'll come back and be married—not otherwise."

So he wished them good-bye and started again on his travels, leaving them all crying ; this time because the marriage was off !

Well, the young man travelled far and he travelled fast, but never did he find a bigger silly, until one day he came upon an old woman's cottage that had some grass growing on the thatched roof.

And the old woman was trying her best to cudgel her cow into going up a ladder to eat the grass. But the poor thing was afraid and durst not go. Then the old woman tried coaxing, but it wouldn't go. You never saw such a sight ! The cow getting more and more flustered and obstinate, the old woman getting hotter and hotter.

At last the young squire said, " It would be easier if *you* went up the ladder, cut the grass, and threw it down for the cow to eat."

" A likely story that," says the old woman. " A cow

can cut grass for herself. And the foolish thing will be quite safe up there, for I'll tie a rope round her neck, pass the rope down the chimney, and fasten t'other end to my wrist, so as when I'm doing my bit o' washing, she can't fall off the roof without my knowing it. So mind your own business, young sir."

Well, after a while the old woman coaxed and codgered and bullied and badgered the cow up the ladder, and when she got it on to the roof she tied a rope round its neck, passed the rope down the chimney, and fastened t'other end to her wrist. Then she went about her bit of washing, and young squire he went on his way.

But he hadn't gone but a bit when he heard the awfullest hullabaloo. He galloped back, and found that the cow had fallen off the roof and got strangled by the rope round its neck, while the weight of the cow had pulled the old woman by her wrist up the chimney, where she had got stuck half-way and been smothered by the soot!

"That is one bigger silly," quoth the young squire as he journeyed on. "So now for two more!"

He did not find any, however, till late one night he arrived at a little inn. And the inn was so full that he had to share a room with another traveller. Now his room-fellow proved quite a pleasant fellow, and they forgathered, and each slept well in his bed.

But next morning, when they were dressing, what does the stranger do but carefully hang his breeches on the knobs of the tallboy!

" What are you doing ? " asks young squire.

" I'm putting on my breeches," says the stranger ; and with that he goes to the other end of the room, takes a little run, and tried to jump into the breeches.

But he didn't succeed, so he took another run and another try, and another and another and another, until he got quite hot and flustered, as the old woman had got over her cow that wouldn't go up the ladder. And all the time young squire was laughing fit to split, for never in his life did he see anything so comical.

Then the stranger stopped a while and mopped his face with his handkerchief, for he was all in a sweat. " It's very well laughing," says he, " but breeches are the most awkwardest things to get into that ever were. It takes me the best part of an hour every morning before I get them on. How do you manage yours ? "

Then young squire showed him, as well as he could for laughing, how to put on his breeches, and the stranger was ever so grateful and said he never should have thought of that way.

" So that," quoth young squire to himself, " is a second bigger silly." But he travelled far and he travelled fast without finding the third, until one bright night when the moon was shining right overhead he came upon a village. And outside the village was a pond, and round about the pond was a great crowd of villagers. And some had got rakes, and some had got pitchforks, and some had got brooms. And they were as busy as busy, shouting out, and raking, and forking, and sweeping away at the pond.

"What is the matter?" cried young squire, jumping off his horse to help. "Has any one fallen in?"

"Aye! Matter enough," says they. "Can't 'ee see moon's fallen into the pond, an' we can't get her out nohow."

And with that they set to again raking, and forking, and sweeping away. Then the young squire burst out laughing, told them they were fools for their pains, and bade them look up over their heads where the moon was riding broad and full. But they wouldn't, and they wouldn't believe that what they saw in the water was only a reflection. And when he insisted they began to abuse him roundly and threaten to duck him in the pond. So he got on his horse again as quickly as he could, leaving them raking, and forking, and sweeping away; and for all we know they may be at it yet!

But the young squire said to himself, "There are many more sillies in this world than I thought for; so I'll just go back and marry the farmer's daughter. She is no sillier than the rest."

So they were married, and if they didn't live happy ever after, that has nothing to do with the story of the three sillies.

The Bogles in the Courtyard

THE GOLDEN BALL

ONCE upon a time there lived two lasses, who were sisters, and as they came from the fair they saw a right handsome young man standing at a house door before them. They had never seen such a handsome young man before. He had gold on his cap, gold on his finger, gold on his neck, gold at his waist! And he had a golden ball in each hand. He gave a ball to each lass, saying she was to keep it; but if she lost it, she was to be hanged.

Now the youngest of the lasses lost her ball, and this is how. She was by a park paling, and she was tossing her ball, and it went up, and up, and up, till it went fair over the paling; and when she climbed to look for it, the ball ran along the green grass, and it ran right forward to the door of a house that stood there, and the ball went into the house and she saw it no more.

So she was taken away to be hanged by the neck till she was dead, because she had lost her ball.

But the lass had a sweetheart, and he said he would go and get the ball. So he went to the park gate, but 'twas shut; then he climbed the railing, and when he got to the top of it an old woman rose up out of the ditch before him and said that if he wanted to get the ball he must sleep three nights in the house: so he said he would.

Well! when it was evening, he went into the house, and looked everywhere for the ball, but he could not find it, nor any one in the house at all; but when night came on he thought he heard bogles moving about in the courtyard; so he looked out o' window, and, sure enough, the yard was full of them!

Presently he heard steps coming upstairs, so he hid behind the door, and was as still as a mouse. Then in came a big giant five times as tall as the lad, and looked around; but seeing nothing he went to the window and bowed himself to look out; and as he bowed on his elbows to see the bogles in the yard, the lad stepped behind him, and with one blow of his sword he cut him in twain, so that the top part of him fell in the yard, and the bottom part remained standing looking out of the window.

Well! there was a great cry from the bogles when they saw half the giant come tumbling down to them, and they called out, " There comes half our master ; give us the other half."

Then the lad said, " It's no use of thee, thou pair of legs, standing alone at the window, as thou hast no eye to see with, so go join thy brother " ; and he cast the lower part of the giant after the top part. Now when the bogles had gotten all the giant they were quiet.

Next night the lad went to sleep in the house again, and this time a second giant came in at the door, and as he came in the lad cut him in twain ; but the legs walked on to the fire and went straight up the chimney.

" Go, get thee after thy legs," said the lad to the head, and he cast the other half of the giant up the chimney.

Now the third night nothing happened, so the lad got into bed ; but before he went to sleep he heard the bogles striving under the bed, and he wondered what they were at. So he peeped, and saw that they had the ball there, and were playing with it, casting it to and fro.

Now after a time one of them thrust his leg out from under the bed, and quick as anything the lad brings his sword down, and cuts it off. Then another bogle thrust his arm out at t'other side of the bed, and in a twinkling the lad cuts that off too. So it went on, till at last he had maimed them all, and they all went off, crying and wailing, and forgot the ball ! Then the lad got out of bed, found the ball, and went off at once to seek his true love.

Now the lass had been taken to York to be hanged ; she was brought out on the scaffold, and the hangman said,

"Now, lass, thou must hang by the neck till thou be'st dead." But she cried out :

> " Stop, stop, I think I see my mother coming !
> O mother, hast thou brought my golden ball
>   And come to set me free ? "

And the mother answered :

> " I've neither brought thy golden ball
>   Nor come to set thee free,
> But I have come to see thee hung
>   Upon this gallows-tree."

Then the hangman said, " Now, lass, say thy prayers for thou must die."   But she said :

> " Stop, stop, I think I see my father coming !
> O father, hast thou brought my golden ball
> And come to set me free ? "

And the father answered :

> " I've neither brought thy golden ball
>   Nor come to set thee free,
> But I have come to see thee hung
>   Upon this gallows-tree."

Then the hangman said, " Hast thee done thy prayers ? Now, lass, put thy head into the noose."

But she answered, " Stop, stop, I think I see my brother coming ! "   And again she sang her little verse, and the brother sang back the same words.   And so with her sister, her uncle, her aunt, and her cousin.   But they all said the same :

> " I've neither brought thy golden ball
>   Nor come to set thee free,
> But I have come to see thee hung
>   Upon this gallows-tree."

Then the hangman said, " I will stop no longer, thou'rt making game of me.   Thou must be hung at once."

But now, at long last, she saw her sweetheart coming through the crowd, so she cried to him :

> " Stop, stop, I see my sweetheart coming !
> Sweetheart, hast thou brought my golden ball
> And come to set me free ? "

Then her sweetheart held up her golden ball and cried :

> " Aye, I have brought to thee thy golden ball
> And come to set thee free ;
> I have not come to see thee hung
> Upon this gallows-tree."

So he took her home, then and there, and they lived happy ever after.

THE TWO SISTERS

ONCE upon a time there were two sisters who were as like each other as two peas in a pod ; but one was good, and the other was bad-tempered. Now their father had no work, so the girls began to think of going to service.

" I will go first and see what I can make of it," said the younger sister, ever so cheerfully, " then you, sis, can follow if I have good luck."

So she packed up a bundle, said good-bye, and started to find a place ; but no one in the town wanted a girl, and she went farther afield into the country. And as she journeyed she came upon an oven in which a lot of loaves were baking. Now as she passed, the loaves cried out with one voice :

" Little girl ! Little girl ! Take us out ! Please take us out ! We have been baking for seven years, and no one has come to take us out. Do take us out or we shall soon be burnt ! "

Then, being a kind, obliging little girl, she stopped, put down her bundle, took out the bread, and went on her way saying :

" You will be more comfortable now."

After a time she came to a cow lowing beside an empty pail, and the cow said to her :

" Little girl ! Little girl ! Milk me ! Please milk me ! Seven years have I been waiting, but no one has come to milk me !"

So the kind girl stopped, put down her bundle, milked the cow into the pail, and went on her way saying :

" Now you will be more comfortable."

By and by she came to an apple tree so laden with fruit that its branches were nigh to break, and the apple tree called to her :

" Little girl ! Little girl ! Please shake my branches. The fruit is so heavy I can't stand straight !"

Then the kind girl stopped, put down her bundle, and shook the branches so that the apples fell off, and the tree could stand straight. Then she went on her way saying :

" You will be more comfortable now."

So she journeyed on till she came to a house where an old witch-woman lived. Now this witch-woman wanted a servant-maid, and promised good wages. Therefore the girl agreed to stop with her and try how she liked service. She had to sweep the floor, keep the house clean and tidy, the fire bright and cheery. But there was one thing the witch-woman said she must never do ; and that was look up the chimney !

" If you do," said the witch-woman, " something will fall down on you, and you will come to a bad end."

"Tree of mine! O Tree of mine! Have you seen my naughty
little maid?"

Well! the girl swept, and dusted, and made up the fire ; but ne'er a penny of wages did she see. Now the girl wanted to go home as she did not like witch-service ; for the witch used to have boiled babies for supper, and bury the bones under some stones in the garden. But she did not like to go home penniless ; so she stayed on, sweeping, and dusting, and doing her work, just as if she was pleased. Then one day, as she was sweeping up the hearth, down tumbled some soot, and, without remembering she was forbidden to look up the chimney, she looked up to see where the soot came from. And, lo and behold! a big bag of gold fell plump into her lap.

Now the witch happened to be out on one of her witch errands ; so the girl thought it a fine opportunity to be off home.

So she kilted up her petticoats and started to run home ; but she had only gone a little way when she heard the witch-woman coming after her on her broomstick. Now the apple tree she had helped to stand straight happened to be quite close ; so she ran to it and cried :

> " Apple tree ! Apple tree, hide me
> So the old witch can't find me,
> For if she does she'll pick my bones,
> And bury me under the garden stones."

Then the apple tree said, " Of course I will. You helped me to stand straight, and one good turn deserves another."

So the apple tree hid her finely in its green branches ; and when the witch flew past saying :

> " Tree of mine !   O Tree of mine !
> Have you seen my naughty little maid
> With a willy willy wag and a great big bag,
> She's stolen my money—all I had ? "

the apple tree answered :

> " No, mother dear,
> Not for seven year ! "

So the witch flew on the wrong way, and the girl got down, thanked the tree politely, and started again. But just as she got to where the cow was standing beside the pail, she heard the witch coming again, so she ran to the cow and cried :

> " Cow !   Cow, please hide me
> So the witch can't find me ;
> If she does she'll pick my bones,
> And bury me under the garden stones ! "

" Certainly I will," answered the cow. " Didn't you milk me and make me comfortable ?   Hide yourself behind me and you'll be quite safe."

And when the witch flew by and called to the cow :

> " O Cow of mine !   Cow of mine !
> Have you seen my naughty little maid
> With a willy willy wag and a great big bag,
> Who stole my money—all that I had ? "

she just said politely :

> " No, mother dear,
> Not for seven year ! "

Then the old witch went on in the wrong direction, and the

girl started afresh on her way home ; but just as she got to where the oven stood, she heard that horrid old witch coming behind her again ; so she ran as fast as she could to the oven and cried :

> "O Oven ! Oven ! hide me
> So as the witch can't find me,
> For if she does she'll pick my bones,
> And bury them under the garden stones."

Then the oven said, " I am afraid there is no room for you, as another batch of bread is baking ; but there is the baker —ask him."

So she asked the baker, and he said, " Of course I will. You saved my last batch from being burnt ; so run into the bakehouse, you will be quite safe there, and I will settle the witch for you."

So she hid in the bakehouse, only just in time, for there was the old witch calling angrily :

> "O Man of mine ! Man of mine !
> Have you seen my naughty little maid
> With a willy willy wag and a great big bag,
> Who's stole my money—all I had ? "

Then the baker replied, " Look in the oven. She may be there."

And the witch alighted from her broomstick and peered into the oven : but she could see no one.

" Creep in and look in the farthest corner," said the baker slyly, and the witch crept in, when——

Bang !——

I

he shut the door in her face, and there she was roasting. And when she came out with the bread she was all crisp and brown, and had to go home as best she could and put cold cream all over her !

But the kind, obliging little girl got safe home with her bag of money.

Now the ill-tempered elder sister was very jealous of this good luck, and determined to get a bag of gold for herself. So she in her turn packed up a bundle and started to seek service by the same road.   But when she came to the oven, and the loaves begged her to take them out because they had been baking seven years and were nigh to burning, she tossed her head and said :

" A likely story indeed, that I should burn my fingers to save your crusts.   No, thank you ! "

And with that she went on till she came across the cow standing waiting to be milked beside the pail.   But when the cow said :

" Little girl !   Little girl !   Milk me !   Please milk me, I've waited seven years to be milked——"

She only laughed and replied, " You may wait another seven years for all I care.   I'm not your dairymaid ! "

And with that she went on till she came to the apple tree, all overburdened by its fruit.   But when it begged her to shake its branches, she only giggled, and plucking one ripe apple, said :

" One is enough for me : you can keep the rest your-self."

And with that she went on munching the apple, till she came to the witch-woman's house.

Now the witch-woman, though she had got over being crisp and brown from the oven, was dreadfully angry with all little maid-servants, and made up her mind this one should not trick her. So for a long time she never went out of the house ; thus the ill-tempered sister never had a chance of looking up the chimney, as she had meant to do at once. And she had to dust, and clean, and brush, and sweep ever so hard, until she was quite tired out.

But one day, when the witch-woman went into the garden to bury her bones, she seized the moment, looked up the chimney, and, sure enough, a bag of gold fell plump into her lap !

Well ! she was off with it in a moment, and ran and ran till she came to the apple tree, when she heard the witch-woman behind her. So she cried as her sister had done :

> " Apple tree ! Apple tree, hide me
> So the old witch can't find me,
> For if she does she'll break my bones,
> Or bury me under the garden stones."

But the apple tree said :

" No room here ! I've too many apples."

So she had to run on ; and when the witch-woman on her broomstick came flying by and called :

> " O Tree of mine ! Tree of mine !
> Have you seen a naughty little maid
> With a willy willy wag and a great big bag,
> Who's stolen my money—all I had ? "

the apple tree replied :

> " Yes, mother dear,
> She's gone down there."

Then the witch-woman went after her, caught her, gave her a thorough good beating, took the bag of money away from her, and sent her home without a penny payment for all her dusting, and sweeping, and brushing, and cleaning.

THE LAIDLY WORM

IN Bamborough Castle there once lived a King who had two children, a son named Childe Wynde, and a daughter who was called May Margret. Their mother, a fair woman, was dead, and the King mourned her long and faithfully. But, after his son Childe Wynde went to seek his fortune, the King, hunting in the forest, came across a lady of such great beauty that he fell in love with her at once and determined to marry her.

Now Princess May Margret was not over-pleased to think that her mother's place should be taken by a strange woman, nor was she pleased to think that she would have to give up keeping house for her father the King. For she had always taken a pride in her work. But she said nothing, though she stood long on the castle walls looking out across the sea wishing for her dear brother's return ; for, see you, they had mothered each other.

Still no news came of Childe Wynde ; so on the day when the old King was to bring the new Queen home, May Margret counted over the keys of the castle chambers, knotted them on a string, and after casting them over her left shoulder for luck—more for her father's sake than for the new Queen's regard—she stood at the castle gate ready to hand over the keys to her stepmother.

Now as the bridal procession approached with all the lords of the north countrie, and some of the Scots lords in attendance, she looked so fair and so sweet, that the lords whispered to one another of her beauty. And when, after saying in a voice like a mavis—

> " Oh welcome, welcome, father,
> Unto your halls and towers !
> And welcome too, my stepmother,
> For all that's here is yours ! "

she turned upon the step and tripped into the yard, the Scots lords said aloud :

> " Forsooth ! May Margret's grace
> Surpasses all that we have met, she has so fair a face ! "

Now the new Queen overheard this, and she stamped

her foot and her face flushed with anger as she turned her
about and called :

> " You might have excepted me,
> But I will bring May Margret to a Laidly Worm's degree ;
> I'll bring her low as a Laidly Worm
> That warps about a stone,
> And not till the Childe of Wynde come back
> Will the witching be undone."

Well ! hearing this May Margret laughed, not knowing
that her new stepmother, for all her beauty, was a witch ;
and the laugh made the wicked woman still more angry.
So that same night she left her royal bed, and, returning to
the lonely cave where she had ever done her magic, she cast
Princess May Margret under a spell with charms three times
three, and passes nine times nine.   And this was her spell :

> " I weird ye to a Laidly Worm,
>   And such sall ye ever be
> Until Childe Wynde the King's dear son
>   Comes home across the sea.
> Until the world comes to an end
>   Unspelled ye'll never be,
> Unless Childe Wynde of his own free will
>   Sall give you kisses three ! "

So it came to pass that Princess May Margret went to
her bed a beauteous maiden, full of grace, and rose next
morning a Laidly Worm ; for when her tire-women came
to dress her they found coiled up in her bed an awesome
dragon, which uncoiled itself and came towards them.   And

when they ran away terrified, the Laidly Worm crawled and crept, and crept and crawled down to the sea till it reached the rock of the Spindlestone which is called the Heugh. And there it curled itself round the stone, and lay basking in the sun.

Then for seven miles east and seven miles west and seven miles north and south the whole country-side knew the hunger of the Laidly Worm of Spindlestone Heugh, for it drove the awesome beast to leave its resting-place at night and devour everything it came across.

At last a wise warlock told the people that if they wished to be quit of these horrors, they must take every drop of the milk of seven white milch kine every morn and every eve to the trough of stone at the foot of the Heugh, for the Laidly Worm to drink. And this they did, and after that the Laidly Worm troubled the country-side no longer; but lay warped about the Heugh, looking out to sea with its terrible snout in the air.

But the word of its doings had gone east and had gone west; it had even gone over the sea and had come to Childe Wynde's ears; and the news of it angered him; for he thought perchance it had something to do with his beloved sister May Margret's disappearance. So he called his men-at-arms together and said:

" We must sail to Bamborough and land by Spindlestone, so as to quell and kill this Laidly Worm."

Then they built a ship without delay, laying the keel with wood from the rowan tree. And they made masts of rowan wood also, and oars likewise ; and, so furnished, set forth.

Now the wicked Queen knew by her arts they were coming, so she sent out her imps to still the winds so that the fluttering sails of silk hung idle on the masts.   But Childe Wynde was not to be bested ; so he called out the oarsmen. Thus it came to pass that one morn the wicked Queen, looking from the Keep, saw the gallant ship in Bamborough Bay, and she sent out all her witch-wives and her impets to raise a storm and sink the ship ; but they came back unable to hurt it, for, see you, it was built of rowan wood, over which witches have no power.

Then, as a last device, the Witch Queen laid spells upon the Laidly Worm saying :

> " Oh !   Laidly Worm !   Go make their topmast heel,
> Go !   Worm the sand, and creep beneath the keel."

Now the Laidly Worm had no choice but to obey.   So :

> " The Worm leapt up, the Worm leapt down
>   And plaited round each plank,
>   And aye as the ship came close to shore
>   She heeled as if she sank."

Three times three did Childe Wynde attempt to land, and three times three the Laidly Worm kept the good ship from the shore.   At last Childe Wynde gave the word to put the ship about, and the Witch Queen, who was watching from the Keep, thought he had given up : but he was not to be bested : for he only rounded the next point to Budley sands.   And there, jumping into the shoal water, he got safely to land, and drawing his sword of proof, rushed up to fight the awesome Worm.   But as he raised his sword to strike he heard a voice, soft as the western wind :

> " Oh quit thy sword, unbend thy bow,
>   And give me kisses three,
> For though I seem a Laidly Worm
>   No harm I'll do to thee ! "

And the voice seemed to him like the voice of his dear sister May Margret.   So he stayed his hand.   Then once again the Laidly Worm said :

> " Oh quit thy sword, unbend thy bow,
>   My laidly form forget.
> Forgive the wrong and kiss me thrice
>   For love of May Margret."

Then Childe Wynde, remembering how he had loved his sister, put his arms round the Laidly Worm and kissed it once.   And he kissed the loathly thing twice.   And he kissed it yet a third time as he stood with the wet sand at his feet.

Then with a hiss and a roar the Laidly Worm sank to the sand, and in his arms was May Margret !

He wrapped her in his mantle, for she trembled in the cold sea air, and carried her to Bamborough Castle, where the wicked Queen, knowing her hour was come, stood, all deserted by her imps and witch-wives, on the stairs, twisting her hands.

Then Childe Wynde looking at her cried :

> "Woe ! Woe to thee, thou wicked Witch !
> An ill fate shalt thine be !
> The doom thou dreed on May Margret
> The same doom shalt thou dree.

> Henceforth thou'lt be a Laidly Toad
> That in the clay doth wend,
> And unspelled thou wilt never be
> Till this world hath an end."

And as he spoke the wicked Queen began to shrivel, and she shrivelled and shrivelled to a horrid wrinkled toad that hopped down the castle steps and disappeared in a crevice.

But to this day a loathsome toad is sometimes seen haunting Bamborough Keep ; and that Laidly Toad is the wicked Witch Queen !

But Childe Wynde and Princess May Margret loved each other as much as ever, and lived happily ever after.

TITTY MOUSE AND TATTY MOUSE

TITTY MOUSE and Tatty Mouse both lived in a house.

Titty Mouse went a-gleaning, and Tatty Mouse went a-gleaning.

So they both went a-gleaning.

Titty Mouse gleaned an ear of corn, and Tatty Mouse gleaned an ear of corn.

So they both gleaned an ear of corn.

Titty Mouse made a pudding, and Tatty Mouse made a pudding.

So they both made a pudding.

And Tatty Mouse put her pudding into the pot to boil.

But when Titty went to put hers in, the pot tumbled over, and scalded her to death, and Tatty sat down and wept.

Then the three-legged stool said, " Tatty, why do you weep ? "

" Titty's dead," said Tatty, " and so I weep."

" Then," said the stool, " I'll hop," so the stool hopped.

Then a broom in the corner of the room said, " Stool, why do you hop ? "

" Oh ! " said the stool, " Titty's dead, and Tatty weeps, and so I hop."

" Then," said the broom, " I'll sweep," so the broom began to sweep.

Then said the door, " Broom, why do you sweep ? "

" Oh ! " said the broom, " Titty's dead, and Tatty weeps, and the stool hops, and so I sweep."

" Then," said the door, " I'll jar," so the door jarred.

Then the window said, " Door, why do you jar ? "

" Oh ! " said the door, " Titty's dead, and Tatty weeps, and the stool hops, and the broom sweeps, and so I jar."

" Then," said the window, " I'll creak," so the window creaked.

Now there was an old form outside the house, and when the window creaked, the form said, " Window, why do you creak ? "

" Oh ! " said the window, " Titty's dead, and Tatty weeps, and the stool hops, and the broom sweeps, the door jars, and so I creak ! "

" Then," said the old form, " I'll gallop round the house." So the old form galloped round the house.

Now there was a fine large walnut tree growing by the cottage, and the tree said to the form, " Form, why do you gallop round the house ? "

" Oh ! " says the form, " Titty's dead, and Tatty weeps, and the stool hops, and the broom sweeps, the door jars, and the window creaks, and so I gallop round the house."

" Then," said the walnut tree, " I'll shed my leaves." So the walnut tree shed all its beautiful green leaves.

Now there was a little bird perched on one of the boughs of the tree, and when all the leaves fell, it said, " Walnut tree, why do you shed your leaves ? "

" Oh ! " said the tree, " Titty's dead, and Tatty weeps, the stool hops, and the broom sweeps, the door jars, and the window creaks, the old form gallops round the house, and so I shed my leaves."

" Then," said the little bird, " I'll moult all my feathers," so he moulted all his gay feathers.

Now there was a little girl walking below, carrying a jug of milk for her brothers' and sisters' supper, and when she saw the poor little bird moult all its feathers, she said, " Little bird, why do you moult all your feathers ? "

" Oh ! " said the little bird, " Titty's dead, and Tatty weeps, the stool hops, and the broom sweeps, the door jars, and the window creaks, the old form gallops round the house, the walnut tree sheds its leaves, and so I moult all my feathers."

" Then," said the little girl, " I'll spill the milk." So she dropt the pitcher and spilt the milk.

Now there was an old man just by on the top of a ladder thatching a rick, and when he saw the little girl spill the milk, he said, " Little girl, what do you mean by spilling the milk? your little brothers and sisters must go without their suppers."

Then said the little girl, " Titty's dead, and Tatty weeps, the stool hops, and the broom sweeps, the door jars, and the window creaks, the old form gallops round the house, the walnut tree sheds all its leaves, the little bird moults all its feathers, and so I spill the milk."

" Oh ! " said the old man, " then I'll tumble off the ladder and break my neck."

So he tumbled off the ladder and broke his neck ; and when the old man broke his neck, the great walnut tree fell down with a crash and upset the old form and house, and the house falling knocked the window out, and the window knocked the door down, and the door upset the broom, and the broom upset the stool, and poor little Tatty Mouse was buried beneath the ruins.

JACK AND THE BEANSTALK

ALONG long time ago, when most of the world was young and folk did what they liked because all things were good, there lived a boy called Jack.

His father was bed-ridden, and his mother, a good soul, was busy early morns and late eves planning and placing how to support her sick husband and her young son by selling the milk and butter which Milky-White, the beautiful cow, gave them without stint. For it was summer-time. But winter came on ; the herbs of the fields took refuge from the frosts in the warm earth, and though his mother sent Jack to gather what fodder he could get in the hedgerows, he came back as often as not with a very empty sack ; for Jack's eyes were so often full of wonder at all the things he saw that sometimes he forgot to work !

So it came to pass that one morning Milky-White gave no milk at all—not one drain ! Then the good hard-working mother threw her apron over her head and sobbed :

" What shall we do ? What shall we do ? "

Now Jack loved his mother ; besides, he felt just a bit

sneaky at being such a big boy and doing so little to help, so he said, " Cheer up ! Cheer up ! I'll go and get work somewhere." And he felt as he spoke as if he would work his fingers to the bone ; but the good woman shook her head mournfully.

" You've tried that before, Jack," she said, " and nobody would keep you. You are quite a good lad but your wits go a-wool-gathering. No, we must sell Milky-White and live on the money. It is no use crying over milk that is not here to spill ! "

You see, she was a wise as well as a hard-working woman, and Jack's spirits rose.

" Just so," he cried. " We will sell Milky-White and be richer than ever. It's an ill wind that blows no one good. So, as it is market-day, I'll just take her there and we shall see what we shall see."

" But——" began his mother.

" But doesn't butter parsnips," laughed Jack. " Trust me to make a good bargain."

So, as it was washing-day, and her sick husband was more ailing than usual, his mother let Jack set off to sell the cow.

" Not less than ten pounds," she bawled after him as he turned the corner.

Ten pounds, indeed ! Jack had made up his mind to twenty ! Twenty solid golden sovereigns !

He was just settling what he should buy his mother as a fairing out of the money, when he saw a queer little old man on the road who called out, " Good-morning, Jack ! "

K

"Good-morning," replied Jack, with a polite bow, wondering how the queer little old man happened to know his name; though, to be sure, Jacks were as plentiful as blackberries.

"And where may you be going?" asked the queer little old man. Jack wondered again — he was always wondering, you know—what the queer little old man had to do with it; but, being always polite, he replied:

"I am going to market to sell Milky-White—and I mean to make a good bargain."

"So you will! So you will!" chuckled the queer little old' man. "You look the sort of chap for it. I bet you know how many beans make five?"

"Two in each hand and one in my mouth," answered Jack readily. He really was sharp as a needle.

"Just so, just so!" chuckled the queer little old man; and as he spoke he drew out of his pocket five beans. "Well, here they are, so give us Milky-White."

Jack was so flabbergasted that he stood with his mouth open as if he expected the fifth bean to fly into it.

"What!" he said at last. "My Milky-White for five common beans! Not if I know it!"

"But they aren't common beans," put in the queer little old man, and there was a queer little smile on his queer little face. "If you plant these beans over-night, by morning they will have grown up right into the very sky."

Jack was too flabbergasted this time even to open his mouth; his eyes opened instead.

"Did you say right into the very sky?" he asked at last; for, see you, Jack had wondered more about the sky than about anything else.

"RIGHT UP INTO THE VERY SKY," repeated the queer old man, with a nod between each word. "It's a good bargain, Jack; and, as fair play's a jewel, if they don't—why! meet me here to-morrow morning and you shall have Milky-White back again. Will that please you?"

"Right as a trivet," cried Jack, without stopping to think, and the next moment he found himself standing on an empty road.

"Two in each hand and one in my mouth," repeated

Jack. " That is what I said, and what I'll do. Everything
in order, and if what the queer little old man said isn't
true, I shall get Milky-White back to-morrow morning."

So whistling and munching the bean he trudged home
cheerfully, wondering what the sky would be like if he ever
got there.

" What a long time you've been ! " exclaimed his
mother, who was watching anxiously for him at the gate.
" It is past sun-setting ; but I see you have sold Milky-
White.   Tell me quick how much you got for her."

" You'll never guess," began Jack.

" Laws-a-mercy ! You don't say so," interrupted the
good woman.   " And I worriting all day lest they should
take you in. What was it ? Ten pounds—fifteen—sure it
can't be twenty ! "

Jack held out the beans triumphantly.

" There," he said.   " That's what I got for her, and a
jolly good bargain too ! "

It was his mother's turn to be flabbergasted ; but all she
said was :

" What !   Them beans ! "

" Yes," replied Jack, beginning to doubt his own wisdom ;
" but they're *magic* beans. If you plant them over-night,
by morning they—grow—right up—into—the—sky—Oh !
Please don't hit so hard ! "

For Jack's mother for once had lost her temper, and
was belabouring the boy for all she was worth.   And
when she had finished scolding and beating, she flung the

miserable beans out of window and sent him, supperless, to bed.

If this was the magical effect of the beans, thought Jack ruefully, he didn't want any more magic, if you please.

However, being healthy and, as a rule, happy, he soon fell asleep and slept like a top.

When he woke he thought at first it was moonlight, for everything in the room showed greenish.   Then he stared at the little window.   It was covered as if with a curtain by leaves.   He was out of bed in a trice, and the next moment, without waiting to dress, was climbing up the biggest bean-stalk you ever saw.   For what the queer little old man had said was true !   One of the beans which his mother had chucked into the garden had found soil, taken root, and grown in the night. . . .

Where ? . . .

Up to the very sky ?   Jack meant to see at any rate.

So he climbed, and he climbed, and he climbed.   It was easy work, for the big beanstalk with the leaves growing out of each side was like a ladder ;   for all that he soon was out of breath.   Then he got his second wind, and was just beginning to wonder if he had a third when he saw in front of him a wide, shining white road stretching away, and away, and away.

So he took to walking, and he walked, and walked, and walked, till he came to a tall, shining white house with a wide white doorstep.

And on the doorstep stood a great big woman with a

black porridge-pot in her hand. Now Jack, having had
no supper, was hungry as a hunter, and when he saw the
porridge-pot he said quite politely :

" Good-morning, 'm. I wonder if you *could* give me
some breakfast ? "

" Breakfast ! " echoed the woman, who, in truth, was
an ogre's wife. " If it is breakfast you're wanting, it's
breakfast you'll likely be ; for I expect my man home every
instant, and there is nothing he likes better for breakfast
than a boy—a fat boy grilled on toast."

Now Jack was not a bit of a coward, and when he wanted
a thing he generally got it, so he said cheerful-like :

" I'd be fatter if I'd had my breakfast ! " Whereat the
ogre's wife laughed and bade Jack come in ; for she was
not, really, half as bad as she looked. But he had hardly
finished the great bowl of porridge and milk she gave him
when the whole house began to tremble and quake. It
was the ogre coming home !

Thump ! Thump !! THUMP !!!

" Into the oven with you, sharp ! " cried the ogre's
wife ; and the iron oven door was just closed when the ogre
strode in. Jack could see him through the little peep-hole
slide at the top where the steam came out.

He was a big one for sure. He had three sheep strung
to his belt, and these he threw down on the table. " Here,
wife," he cried, " roast me these snippets for breakfast ;
they are all I've been able to get this morning, worse luck !

I hope the oven's hot ? " And he went to touch the handle, while Jack burst out all of a sweat, wondering what would happen next.

" Roast ! " echoed the ogre's wife. " Pooh ! the little things would dry to cinders. Better boil them."

So she set to work to boil them ; but the ogre began sniffing about the room. " They don't smell—mutton meat," he growled. Then he frowned horribly and began the real ogre's rhyme :

> " *Fee-fi-fo-fum,*
> *I smell the blood of an Englishman.*
> *Be he alive, or be he dead,*
> *I'll grind his bones to make my bread.*"

" Don't be silly ! " said his wife. " It's the bones of the little boy you had for supper that I'm boiling down for soup ! Come, eat your breakfast, there's a good ogre ! "

So the ogre ate his three sheep, and when he had done he went to a big oaken chest and took out three big bags of golden pieces. These he put on the table, and began to count their contents while his wife cleared away the breakfast things. And by and by his head began to nod, and at last he began to snore, and snored so loud that the whole house shook.

Then Jack nipped out of the oven and, seizing one of the bags of gold, crept away, and ran along the straight, wide, shining white road as fast as his legs would carry him till he came to the beanstalk. He couldn't climb down it with the bag of gold, it was so heavy, so he just flung his burden down first, and, helter-skelter, climbed after it.

And when he came to the bottom, there was his mother picking up gold pieces out of the garden as fast as she could ; for, of course, the bag had burst.

" Laws-a-mercy me ! " she says. " Wherever have you been ? See ! It's been rainin' gold ! "

" No, it hasn't," began Jack. " I climbed up——" Then he turned to look for the beanstalk ; but, lo and behold ! it wasn't there at all ! So he knew, then, it was all real magic.

After that they lived happily on the gold pieces for a long time, and the bedridden father got all sorts of nice things to eat ; but, at last, a day came when Jack's mother showed a doleful face as she put a big yellow sovereign into Jack's hand and bade him be careful marketing, because there was not one more in the coffer. After that they must starve.

That night Jack went supperless to bed of his own accord. If he couldn't make money, he thought, at any rate he could eat less money. It was a shame for a big boy to stuff himself and bring no grist to the mill.

He slept like a top, as boys do when they don't overeat themselves, and when he woke . . .

Hey, presto ! the whole room showed greenish, and there was a curtain of leaves over the window ! Another bean had grown in the night, and Jack was up it like a lamplighter before you could say knife.

This time he didn't take nearly so long climbing until he reached the straight, wide, white road, and in a trice he found himself before the tall white house, where on the wide white steps the ogre's wife was standing with the black porridge-pot in her hand.

And this time Jack was as bold as brass. " Good-morning, 'm," he said. " I've come to ask you for breakfast, for I had no supper, and I'm as hungry as a hunter."

" Go away, bad boy ! " replied the ogre's wife. " Last time I gave a boy breakfast my man missed a whole bag of gold. I believe you are the same boy."

" Maybe I am, maybe I'm not," said Jack, with a laugh. " I'll tell you true when I've had my breakfast ; but not till then."

So the ogre's wife, who was dreadfully curious, gave him a big bowl full of porridge ; but before he had half finished it he heard the ogre coming—

Thump ! THUMP ! THUMP !

" In with you to the oven," shrieked the ogre's wife. " You shall tell me when he has gone to sleep."

This time Jack saw through the steam peep-hole that the ogre had three fat calves strung to his belt.

" Better luck to-day, wife ! " he cried, and his voice shook the house. " Quick ! Roast these trifles for my breakfast ! I hope the oven's hot ? "

And he went to feel the handle of the door, but his wife cried out sharply :

" Roast ! Why, you'd have to wait hours before they were done ! I'll broil them—see how bright the fire is ! "

"Umph!" growled the ogre. And then he began sniffing and calling out:

> "*Fee-fi-fo-fum,*
> *I smell the blood of an Englishman.*
> *Be he alive, or be he dead,*
> *I'll grind his bones to make my bread.*"

"Twaddle!" said the ogre's wife. "It's only the bones of the boy you had last week that I've put into the pig-bucket!"

"Umph!" said the ogre harshly; but he ate the broiled calves, and then he said to his wife, "Bring me my hen that lays the magic eggs. I want to see gold."

So the ogre's wife brought him a great big black hen with a shiny red comb. She plumped it down on the table and took away the breakfast things.

Then the ogre said to the hen, "Lay!" and it promptly laid—what do you think?—a beautiful, shiny, yellow, golden egg!

"None so dusty, henny-penny," laughed the ogre. "I shan't have to beg as long as I've got you." Then he said, "Lay!" once more; and, lo and behold! there was another beautiful, shiny, yellow, golden egg!

Jack could hardly believe his eyes, and made up his mind that he would have that hen, come what might. So, when the ogre began to doze, he just out like a flash from the oven, seized the hen, and ran for his life! But, you see, he reckoned without his prize; for hens, you know, always cackle when they leave their nests after laying an egg, and this one set up such a scrawing that it woke the ogre.

"Where's my hen?" he shouted, and his wife came rushing in, and they both rushed to the door; but Jack had got
the better of them by a good start, and all they could see was
a little figure right away down the wide white road, holding
a big, scrawing, cackling, fluttering black hen by the legs!

How Jack got down the beanstalk he never knew.   It
was all wings, and leaves, and feathers, and cacklings; but
get down he did, and there was his mother wondering if
the sky was going to fall!

But the very moment Jack touched ground he called
out, "Lay!" and the black hen ceased cackling and laid
a great, big, shiny, yellow, golden egg.

So every one was satisfied; and from that moment
everybody had everything that money could buy.   For,
whenever they wanted anything, they just said, "Lay!"
and the black hen provided them with gold.

But Jack began to wonder if he couldn't find something
else besides money in the sky.   So one fine moonlight
midsummer night he refused his supper, and before he went
to bed stole out to the garden with a big watering-can and
watered the ground under his window; for, thought he,
"there must be two more beans somewhere, and perhaps
it is too dry for them to grow."   Then he slept like a top.

And, lo and behold! when he woke, there was the green
light shimmering through his room, and there he was in an
instant on the beanstalk, climbing, climbing, climbing for
all he was worth.

But this time he knew better than to ask for his breakfast ; for the ogre's wife would be sure to recognise him. So he just hid in some bushes beside the great white house, till he saw her in the scullery, and then he slipped out and hid himself in the copper ; for he knew she would be sure to look in the oven first thing.

And by and by he heard—

Thump ! Thump ! THUMP !

And peeping through a crack in the copper-lid, he could see the ogre stalk in with three huge oxen strung at his belt. But this time, no sooner had the ogre got into the house than he began shouting :

> " *Fee-fi-fo-fum,*
> *I smell the blood of an Englishman.*
> *Be he alive, or be he dead,*
> *I'll grind his bones to make my bread.*"

For, see you, the copper-lid didn't fit tight like the oven door, and ogres have noses like a dog's for scent.

" Well, I declare, so do I ! " exclaimed the ogre's wife. " It will be that horrid boy who stole the bag of gold and the hen. If so, he's hid in the oven ! "

But when she opened the door, lo and behold ! Jack wasn't there ! Only some joints of meat roasting and sizzling away. Then she laughed and said, " You and me be fools for sure. Why, it's the boy you caught last night as I was getting ready for your breakfast. Yes, we be fools to take dead meat for live flesh ! So eat your breakfast, there's a good ogre ! "

But the ogre, though he enjoyed roast boy very much, wasn't satisfied, and every now and then he would burst out with "*Fee-fi-fo-fum*," and get up and search the cupboards, keeping Jack in a fever of fear lest he should think of the copper.

But he didn't. And when he had finished his breakfast he called out to his wife, "Bring me my magic harp! I want to be amused."

So she brought out a little harp and put it on the table. And the ogre leant back in his chair and said lazily :

"Sing!"

And, lo and behold! the harp began to sing. If you want to know what it sang about? Why! It sang about everything! And it sang so beautifully that Jack forgot to be frightened, and the ogre forgot to think of "*Fee-fi-fo-fum*," and fell asleep and

did

NOT

SNORE.

Then Jack stole out of the copper like a mouse and crept hands and knees to the table, raised himself up ever so softly and laid hold of the magic harp; for he was determined to have it.

But, no sooner had he touched it, than it cried out quite loud, "Master! Master!" So the ogre woke, saw Jack making off, and rushed after him.

My goodness, it was a race! Jack was nimble, but the ogre's stride was twice as long. So, though Jack turned, and twisted, and doubled like a hare, yet at last, when he got to the beanstalk, the ogre was not a dozen yards behind him. There wasn't time to think, so Jack just flung himself on to the stalk and began to go down as fast as he could, while the harp kept calling, "Master! Master!" at the very top of its voice. He had only got down about a quarter of the way when there was the most awful lurch you can think of, and Jack nearly fell off the beanstalk. It was the ogre beginning to climb down, and his weight made the stalk sway like a tree in a storm. Then Jack knew it was life or death, and he climbed down faster and faster, and as he climbed he shouted, "Mother! Mother! Bring an axe! Bring an axe!"

Now his mother, as luck would have it, was in the back-yard chopping wood, and she ran out thinking that this time the sky must have fallen. Just at that moment Jack touched ground, and he flung down the harp—which immediately began to sing of all sorts of beautiful things—and he seized the axe and gave a great chop at the beanstalk, which shook and swayed and bent like barley before a breeze.

"Have a care!" shouted the ogre, clinging on as hard as he could. But Jack *did* have a care, and he dealt that beanstalk such a shrewd blow that the whole of it, ogre and all, came toppling down, and, of course, the ogre broke his crown, so that he died on the spot.

"Fee-fi-fo-fum, I smell the blood of an Englishman."

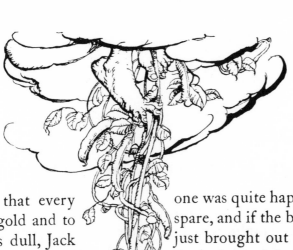

After that every one was quite happy. For
they had gold and to spare, and if the bedridden
father was dull, Jack just brought out the harp
and said, "Sing!" And, lo and behold! it
sang about everything under the sun.
So Jack ceased won-dering so much and became
quite a useful person.

And the last bean hasn't grown yet. It is
still in the garden.

I wonder if it will ever grow?
And what little child will climb its beanstalk into
the sky?

And what will that child find?
Goody me!

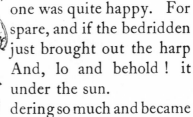

THE BLACK BULL OF NORROWAY

LONG ago in Norroway there lived a lady who had three daughters. Now they were all pretty, and one night they fell a-talking of whom they meant to marry.

And the eldest said, " I will have no one lower than an Earl."

And the second said, " I will have none lower than a Lord."

But the third, the prettiest and the merriest, tossed her head and said, with a twinkle in her eye, " Why so proud ? As for me I would be content with the Black Bull of Norroway."

At that the other sisters bade her be silent and not talk lightly of such a monster. For, see you, is it not written :

> To wilder measures now they turn,
> The black black Bull of Norroway ;
> Sudden the tapers cease to burn,
> The minstrels cease to play.

So, no doubt, the Black Bull of Norroway was held to be a horrid monster.

But the youngest daughter would have her laugh, so she said three times that she would be content with the Black Bull of Norroway.

Well! It so happened that the very next morning a coach-and-six came swinging along the road, and in it sate an Earl who had come to ask the hand of the eldest daughter in marriage. So there were great rejoicings over the wedding, and the bride and bridegroom drove away in the coach-and-six.

Then the next thing that happened was that a coach-and-four with a Lord in it came swinging along the road ; and he wanted to marry the second daughter. So they were wed, and there were great rejoicings, and the bride and bridegroom drove away in the coach-and-four.

Now after this there was only the youngest, the prettiest and the merriest, of the sisters left, and she became the apple of her mother's eye. So you may imagine how the mother felt when one morning a terrible bellowing was heard at the door, and there was a great big Black Bull waiting for his bride.

She wept and she wailed, and at first the girl ran away and hid herself in the cellar for fear, but there the Bull stood waiting, and at last the girl came up and said :

" I promised I would be content with the Black Bull of Norroway, and I must keep my word. Farewell, mother, you will not see me again."

Then she mounted on the Black Bull's back, and it walked away with her quite quietly. And ever it chose the

L

smoothest paths and the easiest roads, so that at last the girl grew less afraid. But she became very hungry and was nigh to faint when the Black Bull said to her, in quite a soft voice that wasn't a bellow at all:

> " Eat out of my left ear,
> Drink out of my right,
> And set by what you leave
> To serve the morrow's night."

So she did as she was bid, and, lo and behold! the left ear was full of delicious things to eat, and the right was full of the most delicious drinks, and there was plenty left over for several days.

Thus they journeyed on, and they journeyed on, through many dreadful forests and many lonely wastes, and the Black Bull never paused for bite or sup, but ever the girl he carried ate out of his left ear and drank out of his right, and set by what she left to serve the morrow's night. And she slept soft and warm on his broad back.

Now at last they reached a noble castle where a large company of lords and ladies were assembled, and greatly the company wondered at the sight of these strange companions. And they invited the girl to supper, but the Black Bull they turned into the field, and left to spend the night after his kind.

But when the next morning came, there he was ready for his burden again. Now, though the girl was loth to leave her pleasant companions, she remembered her promise, and mounted on his back, so they journeyed on, and journeyed

on, and journeyed on, through many tangled woods and over
many high mountains. And ever the Black Bull chose the
smoothest paths for her and set aside the briars and brambles,
while she ate out of his left ear and drank out of his right.

So at last they came to a magnificent mansion where
Dukes and Duchesses and Earls and Countesses were enjoying
themselves. Now the company, though much surprised at
the strange companions, asked the girl in to supper ; and
the Black Bull they would have turned into the park for the
night, but that the girl, remembering how well he had cared
for her, asked them to put him into the stable and give him
a good feed.

So this was done, and the next morning he was waiting
before the hall-door for his burden ; and she, though somewhat loth at leaving the fine company, mounted him cheerfully enough, and they rode away, and they rode away,
and they rode away, through thick briar brakes and up
fearsome cliffs. But ever the Black Bull trod the brambles
underfoot and chose the easiest paths, while she ate out of
his left ear and drank out of his right, and wanted for nothing,
though he had neither bite nor sup. So it came to pass that
he grew tired and was limping with one foot when, just as
the sun was setting, they came to a beautiful palace where
Princes and Princesses were disporting themselves with ball
on the green grass. Now, though the company greatly
wondered at the strange companions, they asked the girl
to join them, and ordered the grooms to lead away the Black
Bull to a field.

But she, remembering all he had done for her, said, "Not so! He will stay with me!" Then seeing a large thorn in the foot with which he had been limping, she stooped down and pulled it out.

And, lo and behold! in an instant, to every one's surprise, there appeared, not a frightful monstrous bull, but one of the most beautiful Princes ever beheld, who fell at his deliverer's feet, thanking her for having broken his cruel enchantment.

A wicked witch-woman who wanted to marry him had, he said, spelled him until a beautiful maiden of her own free will should do him a favour.

"But," he said, "the danger is not all over. You have broken the enchantment by night; that by day has yet to be overcome."

So the next morning the Prince had to resume the form of a bull, and they set out together; and they rode, and they rode, and they rode, till they came to a dark and ugsome glen. And here he bade her dismount and sit on a great rock.

"Here you must stay," he said, "while I go yonder and fight the Old One. And mind! move neither hand nor foot whilst I am away, else I shall never find you again. If everything around you turns blue, I shall have beaten the Old One; but if everything turns red, he will have conquered me."

And with that, and a tremendous roaring bellow, he set off to find his foe.

Well, she sate as still as a mouse, moving neither hand nor foot, nor even her eyes, and waited, and waited, and waited. Then at last everything turned blue. But she was so overcome with joy to think that her lover was victorious that she forgot to keep still, and lifting one of her feet, crossed it over the other !

So she waited, and waited, and waited. Long she sate, and aye she wearied ; and all the time he was seeking for her, but he never found her.

At last she rose and went she knew not whither, determined to seek for her lover through the whole wide world. So she journeyed on, and she journeyed on, and she journeyed on, until one day in a dark wood she came to a little hut where lived an old, old woman who gave her food and shelter, and bid her God-speed on her errand, giving her three nuts, a walnut, a filbert, and a hazel nut, with these words :

> " When your heart is like to break,
> And once again is like to break,
> Crack a nut and in its shell
> That will be that suits you well."

After this she felt heartened up, and wandered on till her road was blocked by a great hill of glass ; and though she tried all she could to climb it, she could not ; for aye she slipped back, and slipped back, and slipped back ; for it was like ice.

Then she sought a passage elsewhere, and round and about the foot of the hill she went sobbing and wailing, but

ne'er a foothold could she find.   At last she came to a smithy ;
and the smith promised if she would serve him faithfully for
seven years and seven days, that he would make her iron
shoon wherewith to climb the hill of glass.   So for seven long
years and seven short days she toiled, and span, and swept,
and washed in the smith's house.   And for wage he gave
her a pair of iron shoon, and with them she clomb the glassy
hill and went on her way.

Now she had not gone far before a company of fine lords
and ladies rode past her talking of all the grand doings that
were to be done at the young Duke of Norroway's wedding.
Then she passed a number of people carrying all sorts of
good things which they told her were for the Duke's wedding.
And at last she came to a palace castle where the courtyards
were full of cooks and bakers, some running this way, some
running that, and all so busy that they did not know what
to do first.

Then she heard the horns of hunters and cries of " Room !
Room for the Duke of Norroway and his bride ! "

And who should ride past but the beautiful Prince she
had but half unspelled, and by his side was the witch-woman
who was determined to marry him that very day.

Well ! at the sight she felt that her heart was indeed like
to break, and over again was like to break, so that the time
had come for her to crack one of the nuts.   So she broke
the walnut, as it was the biggest, and out of it came a wonderful wee woman carding wool as fast as ever she could card.

Now when the witch-woman saw this wonderful thing

she offered the girl her choice of anything in the castle
for it.

"If you will put off your wedding with the Duke for
a day, and let me watch in his room to-night," said the girl,
"you shall have it."

Now, like all witch-women, the bride wanted everything
her own way, and she was so sure she had her groom safe,
that she consented ; but before the Duke went to rest she
gave him, with her own hands, a posset so made that any
one who drank it would sleep till morning.

Thus, though the girl was allowed alone into the Duke's
chamber, and though she spent the livelong night sighing
and singing :

> "Far have I sought for thee,
> Long have I wrought for thee,
> Near am I brought to thee,
> Dear Duke o' Norroway ;
> Wilt thou say naught to me ?"

the Duke never wakened, but slept on.   So when day came
the girl had to leave him without his ever knowing she had
been there.

Then once again her heart was like to break, and over and
over again like to break, and she cracked the filbert nut,
because it was the next biggest.   And out of it came a
wonderful wee, wee woman spinning away as fast as ever
she could spin.   Now when the witch-bride saw this wonderful thing she once again put off her wedding so that she
might possess it.   And once again the girl spent the livelong
night in the Duke's chamber sighing and singing :

" Far have I sought for thee,
Long have I wrought for thee,
Near am I brought to thee,
Dear Duke o' Norroway ;
Wilt thou say naught to me ? "

But the Duke, who had drunk the sleeping-draught from the hands of his witch-bride, never stirred, and when dawn came the girl had to leave him without his ever knowing she had been there.

Then, indeed, the girl's heart was like to break, and over and over and over again like to break, so she cracked the last nut—the hazel nut—and out of it came the most wonderful wee, wee, wee-est woman reeling away at yarn as fast as she could reel.

And this marvel so delighted the witch-bride that once again she consented to put off her wedding for a day, and allow the girl to watch in the Duke's chamber the night through, in order to possess it.

Now it so happened that when the Duke was dressing that morning he heard his pages talking amongst themselves of the strange sighing and singing they had heard in the night ; and he said to his faithful old valet, " What do the pages mean ? "

And the old valet, who hated the witch-bride, said :

" If the master will take no sleeping-draught to-night, mayhap he may also hear what for two nights has kept me awake."

At this the Duke marvelled greatly, and when the witch-bride brought him his evening posset, he made excuse it was not sweet enough, and while she went away to get honey to sweeten it withal, he poured away the posset and made believe he had swallowed it.

So that night when dark had come, and the girl stole in to his chamber with a heavy heart thinking it would be the very last time she would ever see him, the Duke was really broad awake. And when she sate down by his bedside and began to sing :

" Far have I sought for thee,"

he knew her voice at once, and clasped her in his arms.

Then he told her how he had been in the power of the witch-woman and had forgotten everything, but that now he remembered all and that the spell was broken for ever and aye.

So the wedding feast served for their marriage, since the witch-bride, seeing her power was gone, quickly fled the country and was never heard of again.

CATSKIN

ONCE upon a time there lived a gentleman who owned fine lands and houses, and he very much wanted to have a son to be heir to them. So when his wife brought him a daughter, though she was bonny as bonny could be, he cared nought for her, and said :

" Let me never see her face."

So she grew up to be a beautiful maiden, though her father never set eyes on her till she was fifteen years old and was ready to be married.

Then her father said roughly, " She shall marry the first that comes for her." Now when this became known, who should come along and be first but a nasty, horrid old man ! So she didn't know what to do, and went to the hen-wife and asked her advice. And the hen-wife said, " Say you will not take him unless they give you a coat of silver cloth." Well, they gave her a coat of silver cloth, but she wouldn't take him for all that, but went again to the hen-wife, who said, " Say you will not take him unless they give you a coat of beaten gold." Well, they gave her a coat of beaten gold, but still she would not take the old man, but went again to the hen-wife, who said, " Say you will not take him unless they give you a coat made of the feathers of all the birds of the air." So they sent out a man with a great heap of peas ; and the man cried to all the birds of the air, " Each bird take a pea and put down a feather." So each bird took a pea and put down one of its feathers : and they took all the feathers and made a coat of them and gave it to her ; but still she would not take the nasty, horrid old man, but asked the hen-wife once again what she was to do, and the hen-wife said, " Say they must first make you a coat of catskin." Then they made her a coat of catskin ; and she put it on, and tied up her other coats into a bundle, and when it was night-time ran away with it into the woods.

Now she went along, and went along, and went along, till at the end of the wood she saw a fine castle. Then she hid her fine dresses by a crystal waterfall and went up to the castle gates and asked for work. The lady of the castle saw her, and told her, " I'm sorry I have no better place, but if you like you may be our scullion." So down she went into the kitchen, and they called her Catskin, because of her dress. But the cook was very cruel to her, and led her a sad life.

Well, soon after that it happened that the young lord of the castle came home, and there was to be a grand ball in honour of the occasion. And when they were speaking about it among the servants, " Dear me, Mrs. Cook," said Catskin, " how much I should like to go ! "

"What! You dirty, impudent slut," said the cook, "you go among all the fine lords and ladies with your filthy catskin? A fine figure you'd cut!" and with that she took a basin of water and dashed it into Catskin's face. But Catskin only shook her ears and said nothing.

Now when the day of the ball arrived, Catskin slipped out of the house and went to the edge of the forest where she had hidden her dresses. Then she bathed herself in a crystal waterfall, and put on her coat of silver cloth, and hastened away to the ball. As soon as she entered all were overcome by her beauty and grace, while the young lord at once lost his heart to her. He asked her to be his partner for the first dance; and he would dance with none other the livelong night.

When it came to parting time, the young lord said, "Pray tell me, fair maid, where you live?"

But Catskin curtsied and said:

> "Kind sir, if the truth I must tell,
> At the sign of the ' Basin of Water ' I dwell."

Then she flew from the castle and donned her catskin robe again, and slipped into the scullery, unbeknown to the cook.

The young lord went the very next day and searched for the sign of the "Basin of Water"; but he could not find it. So he went to his mother, the lady of the castle, and declared he would wed none other but the lady of the silver dress, and would never rest till he had found her.

So another ball was soon arranged in hopes that the beautiful maid would appear again.

So Catskin said to the cook, " Oh, how I should like to go !" Whereupon the cook screamed out in a rage, "What, you, you dirty, impudent slut ! You would cut a fine figure among all the fine lords and ladies." And with that she up with a ladle and broke it across Catskin's back. But Catskin only shook her ears, and ran off to the forest, where, first of all, she bathed, and then she put on her coat of beaten gold, and off she went to the ball-room.

As soon as she entered all eyes were upon her ; and the young lord at once recognised her as the lady of the " Basin of Water," claimed her hand for the first dance, and did not leave her till the last. When that came, he again asked her where she lived. But all that she would say was :

> " Kind sir, if the truth I must tell,
> At the sign of the ' Broken Ladle ' I dwell " ;

and with that she curtsied and flew from the ball, off with her golden robe, on with her catskin, and into the scullery without the cook's knowing.

Next day, when the young lord could not find where the sign of the " Basin of Water " was, he begged his mother to have another grand ball, so that he might meet the beautiful maid once more.

Then Catskin said to the cook, " Oh, how I wish I could go to the ball !" Whereupon the cook called out : " A fine figure you'd cut !" and broke the skimmer across

her head. But Catskin only shook her ears, and went off
to the forest, where she first bathed in the crystal spring,
and then donned her coat of feathers, and so off to the ball-
room.

When she entered every one was surprised at so beautiful
a face and form dressed in so rich and rare a dress ; but the
young lord at once recognised his beautiful sweetheart, and
would dance with none but her the whole evening. When
the ball came to an end he pressed her to tell him where she
lived, but all she would answer was :

> " Kind sir, if the truth I must tell,
> At the sign of the ' Broken Skimmer ' I dwell " ;

and with that she curtsied, and was off to the forest. But
this time the young lord followed her, and watched her
change her fine dress of feathers for her catskin dress, and
then he knew her for his own scullery-maid.

Next day he went to his mother, and told her that he
wished to marry the scullery-maid, Catskin.

" Never," said the lady of the castle—" never so long as
I live."

Well, the young lord was so grieved that he took to his
bed and was very ill indeed. The doctor tried to cure him,
but he would not take any medicine unless from the hands
of Catskin. At last the doctor went to the mother, and said
that her son would die if she did not consent to his marriage
with Catskin ; so she had to give way. Then she summoned Catskin to her, and Catskin put on her coat of beaten

She went along, and went along, and went along.

gold before she went to see the lady ; and she, of course, was overcome at once, and was only too glad to wed her son to so beautiful a maid.

So they were married, and after a time a little son was born to them, and grew up a fine little lad. Now one day, when he was about four years old, a beggar woman came to the door, and Lady Catskin gave some money to the little lord and told him to go and give it to the beggar woman. So he went and gave it, putting it into the hand of the woman's baby child ; and the child leant forward and kissed the little lord.

Now the wicked old cook (who had never been sent away, because Catskin was too kind-hearted) was looking on, and she said, " See how beggars' brats take to one another ! "

This insult hurt Catskin dreadfully : and she went to her husband, the young lord, and told him all about her father, and begged he would go and find out what had become of her parents. So they set out in the lord's grand coach, and travelled through the forest till they came to the house of Catskin's father. Then they put up at an inn near, and Catskin stopped there, while her husband went to see if her father would own she was his daughter.

Now her father had never had any other child, and his wife had died ; so he was all alone in the world, and sate moping and miserable. When the young lord came in he hardly looked up, he was so miserable. Then Catskin's husband drew a chair close up to him, and asked him, " Pray, sir, had you not once a young daughter whom you would never see or own ? "

And the miserable man said with tears, " It is true ; I am a hardened sinner. But I would give all my worldly goods if I could but see her once before I die."

Then the young lord told him what had happened to Catskin, and took him to the inn, and afterwards brought his father-in-law to his own castle, where they lived happy ever afterwards.

THE THREE LITTLE PIGS

ONCE upon a time there was an old sow who had three little pigs, and as she had not enough for them to eat, she said they had better go out into the world and seek their fortunes.

Now the eldest pig went first, and as he trotted along the road he met a man carrying a bundle of straw. So he said very politely :

" If you please, sir, could you give me that straw to build me a house ? "

And the man, seeing what good manners the little pig had, gave him the straw, and the little pig set to work and built a beautiful house with it.

Now, when it was finished, a wolf happened to pass that way ; and he saw the house, and *he smelt the pig inside.*

So he knocked at the door and said :

" *Little pig ! Little pig ! Let me in ! Let me in !* "

But the little pig saw the wolf's big paws through the keyhole, so he answered back :

" *No ! No ! No ! by the hair of my chinny chin chin !* "

Then the wolf showed his teeth and said :

"*Then I'll huff and I'll puff and I'll blow your house in.*"

So he huffed and he puffed and he blew the house in.
Then he ate up little piggy and went on his way.

Now, the next piggy, when he started, met a man
carrying a bundle of furze, and, being very polite, he said
to him :

"If you please, sir, could you give me that furze to build
me a house ? "

And the man, seeing what good manners the little pig
had, gave him the furze, and the little pig set to work and
built himself a beautiful house.

Now it so happened that when the house was finished
the wolf passed that way ; and he saw the house, and *he
smelt the pig inside.*

So he knocked at the door and said :

"*Little pig !   Little pig !   Let me in !   Let me in !*"

But the little pig peeped through the keyhole and saw
the wolf's great ears, so he answered back :

"*No ! No ! No ! by the hair of my chinny chin chin !*"

Then the wolf showed his teeth and said :

"*Then I'll huff and I'll puff and I'll blow your house in!*"

So he huffed and he puffed and he blew the house in. Then he ate up little piggy and went on his way.

Now the third little piggy, when he started, met a man carrying a load of bricks, and, being very polite, he said :

"If you please, sir, could you give me those bricks to build me a house?"

And the man, seeing that he had been well brought up, gave him the bricks, and the little pig set to work and built himself a beautiful house.

And once again it happened that when it was finished the wolf chanced to come that way ; and he saw the house, and *he smelt the pig inside.*

So he knocked at the door and said :

"*Little pig! Little pig! Let me in! Let me in!*"

But the little pig peeped through the keyhole and saw the wolf's great eyes, so he answered :

"*No! No! No! by the hair of my chinny chin chin!*"

Now the third little piggy, met a man carrying a load of bricks, and asked him to get it, too.

The piggy built a beautiful house, but the wolf came and tried to blow the house in.

" Then I'll huff and I'll puff and I'll blow your house in! "
says the wolf, showing his teeth.

Well! he huffed and he puffed.   He puffed and he huffed.   And he huffed, huffed, and he puffed, puffed ; but he could *not* blow the house down.   At last he was so out of breath that he couldn't huff and he couldn't puff any more.   So he thought a bit.   Then he said :

"Little pig !   I know where there is ever such a nice field of turnips."

"Do you," says little piggy, "and where may that be ? "

"I'll show you," says the wolf; "if you will be ready at six o'clock to-morrow morning, I will call round for you, and we can go together to Farmer Smith's field and get turnips for dinner."

"Thank you kindly," says the little piggy.   "I will be ready at six o'clock sharp."

But, you see, the little pig was not one to be taken in with chaff, so he got up at five, trotted off to Farmer Smith's field, rooted up the turnips, and was home eating them for breakfast when the wolf clattered at the door and cried :

(W) " Little pig ! Little pig ! Aren't you ready ? "

(P) " Ready ? " ~~says the little piggy.~~ " Why ! what a sluggard you are ! I've been to the field and come back again, and I'm having a nice potful of turnips for breakfast."

Then the wolf grew red with rage ; but he was determined to eat little piggy, so he said, as if he didn't care :

(W) " I'm glad you like them ; but I know of something better than turnips."

(P) " Indeed," ~~says little piggy,~~ " and what may that be ? "

(W) " A nice apple tree down in Merry gardens with the juiciest, sweetest apples on it ! So if you will be ready at five o'clock to-morrow morning I will come round for you and we can get the apples together."

(P) " Thank you kindly," ~~says little piggy.~~ " I will sure and be ready at five o'clock sharp."

Now the next morning he bustled up ever so early, and it wasn't four o'clock when he started to get the apples ; but, ~~you see,~~ the wolf had been taken in once and wasn't going to be taken in again, so he also started at four o'clock, and the little pig had but just got his basket half full of apples when he saw the wolf coming down the road licking his lips.

(W) " Hullo ! " ~~says the wolf,~~ " here already ! You *are* an early bird ! Are the apples nice ? "

(P) " Very nice," ~~says little piggy ;~~ " I'll throw you down one to try."

And he threw it so far away, that when the wolf had gone

to pick it up, the little pig was able to jump down with his basket and run home.

Well, the wolf was fair angry ; but he went next day to the little piggy's house and called through the door, as mild as milk :

"Little pig ! Little pig ! You are so clever, I should like to give you a fairing; so if you will come with me to the fair this afternoon you shall have one."

"Thank you kindly," ~~says little piggy.~~ "What time shall we start ? "

"At three o'clock sharp," ~~says the wolf,~~ "so be sure to be ready."

"I'll be ready before three," ~~sniggered the little piggy.~~ And he was ! He started early in the morning and went to the fair, and rode in a swing, and enjoyed himself ever so much, and bought himself a butter-churn as a fairing, and trotted away towards home long before three o'clock. But just as he got to the top of the hill, what should he see but the wolf coming up it, all panting and red with rage !

Well, there was no place to hide in but the butter-churn ; so he crept into it, and was just pulling down the cover when the churn started to roll down the hill—

Bumpety, bumpety, bump !

~~Of course~~ piggy, ~~inside,~~ began to squeal, and when the wolf heard the noise, and saw the butter-churn rolling down on top of him—

Bumpety, bumpety, bump !

—he was so frightened that he turned tail and ran away.

But he was still determined to get the little pig for his dinner; so he went next day to the house and told the little pig how sorry he was not to have been able to keep his promise of going to the fair, because of an awful, dreadful, terrible Thing that had rushed at him, making a fearsome noise.

"Dear me!" says the little piggy, "that must have been me! I hid inside the butter-churn when I saw you coming, and it started to roll! I am sorry I frightened you!"

But this was too much. The wolf danced about with rage and swore he would come down the chimney and eat up the little pig for his supper. But while he was climbing on to the roof the little pig made up a blazing fire and put on a big pot full of water to boil. Then, just as the wolf was coming down the chimney, the little piggy off with the lid, and plump! in fell the wolf into the scalding water.

So the little piggy put on the cover again, boiled the wolf up, and ate him for supper.

NIX NAUGHT NOTHING

ONCE upon a time there lived a King and a Queen who didn't differ much from all the other kings and queens who have lived since Time began. But they had no children, and this made them very sad indeed. Now it so happened that the King had to go and fight battles in a far country, and he was away for many long months. And, lo and behold ! while he was away the Queen at long last bore him a little son. As you may imagine, she was fair delighted, and thought how pleased the King would be when he came home and found that his dearest wish had been fulfilled. And all the courtiers were fine and pleased too, and set about at once to arrange a grand festival for the naming of the little Prince. But the Queen said, " No ! The child shall have no name till his father gives it to him. Till then we will call him ' Nix ! Naught ! Nothing ! ' because his father knows nothing about him ! "

So little Prince Nix Naught Nothing grew into a strong, hearty little lad ; for his father did not come back for a long time, and did not even know that he had a son.

But at long last he turned his face homewards. Now, on the way, he came to a big rushing river which neither he nor his army could cross, for it was flood-time and the water was full of dangerous whirlpools, where nixies and water-wraiths lived, always ready to drown men.

So they were stopped, until a huge giant appeared, who could take the river, whirlpool and all, in his stride ; and he said kindly, " I'll carry you all over, if you like." Now, though the giant smiled and was very polite, the King knew enough of the ways of giants to think it wiser to have a hard and fast bargain. So he said, quite curt, "What's your pay ? "

" Pay ? " echoed the giant, with a grin, " what do you take me for ? Give me Nix Naught Nothing, and I'll do the job with a glad heart."

Now the King felt just a trifle ashamed at the giant's generosity ; so he said, " Certainly, certainly. I'll give you nix naught nothing and my thanks into the bargain."

So the giant carried them safely over the stream and past the whirlpools, and the King hastened homewards. If he was glad to see his dear wife, the Queen, you may imagine how he felt when she showed him his young son, tall and strong for his age.

" And what's your name, young sir ? " he asked of the child fast clasped in his arms.

" Nix Naught Nothing," answered the boy ; " that's what they call me till my father gives me a name."

Well ! the King nearly dropped the child, he was so

horrified. " What have I done ? " he cried. " I promised to give nix naught nothing to the giant who carried us over the whirlpools where the nixies and water-wraiths live."

At this the Queen wept and wailed ; but being a clever woman she thought out a plan whereby to save her son. So she said to her husband the King, " If the giant comes to claim his promise, we will give him the hen-wife's youngest boy. She has so many she will not mind if we give her a crown piece, and the giant will never know the difference."

Now sure enough the very next morning the giant appeared to claim Nix Naught Nothing, and they dressed up the hen-wife's boy in the Prince's clothes and wept and wailed when the giant, fine and satisfied, carried his prize off on his back. But after a while he came to a big stone and sat down to ease his shoulders. And he fell a-dozing. Now, when he woke, he started up in a fluster, and called out :

> " Hodge, Hodge, on my shoulders ! Say
> What d'ye make the time o' day ? "

And the hen-wife's little boy replied :

> " Time that my mother the hen-wife takes
> The eggs for the wise Queen's breakfast cakes ! "

Then the giant saw at once the trick that had been played on him, and he threw the hen-wife's boy on the ground, so that his head hit on the stone and he was killed.

Then the giant strode back to the palace in a tower of a temper, and demanded " Nix Naught Nothing." So this time they dressed up the gardener's boy, and wept and wailed when the giant, fine and satisfied, carried his prize off on his back. Then the same thing happened. The giant grew weary of his burden, and sate down on the big stone to rest. So he fell a-dozing, woke with a start, and called out :

> " Hodge, Hodge, on my shoulders ! Say
> What d'ye make the time o' day ? "

And the gardener's boy replied :

> " Time that my father the gardener took
> Greens for the wise Queen's dinner to cook ! "

So the giant saw at once that a second trick had been played on him and became quite mad with rage. He flung the boy from him so that he was killed, and then strode back to the palace, where he cried with fury : " Give me what you promised to give, Nix Naught Nothing, or I will destroy you all, root and branch."

So then they saw they must give up the dear little Prince, and this time they really wept and wailed as the giant carried off the boy on his back. And this time, after the giant had had his rest at the big stone, and had woke up and called :

> " Hodge, Hodge, on my shoulders ! Say
> What d'ye make the time o' day ? "

the little Prince replied :

> " Time for the King my father to call,
> ' Let supper be served in the banqueting hall.' "

Then the giant laughed with glee and rubbed his hands saying, " I've got the right one at last." So he took Nix Naught Nothing to his own house under the whirlpools ; for the giant was really a great Magician who could take any form he chose. And the reason he wanted a little prince so badly was that he had lost his wife, and had only one little daughter who needed a playmate sorely. So Nix Naught Nothing and the Magician's daughter grew up together, and every year made them fonder and fonder of each other, until she promised to marry him.

Now the Magician had no notion that his daughter should marry just an ordinary human prince, the like of whom he had eaten a thousand times, so he sought some way in which he could quietly get rid of Nix Naught Nothing. So he said one day, " I have work for you, Nix Naught Nothing ! There is a stable hard by which is seven miles long, and seven miles broad, and it has not been cleaned for seven years. By to-morrow evening you must have cleaned it, or I will have you for my supper."

Well, before dawn, Nix Naught Nothing set to work at his task ; but, as fast as he cleared the muck, it just fell back again. So by breakfast-time he was in a terrible sweat ; yet not one whit nearer the end of his job was he. Now the Magician's daughter, coming to bring him his breakfast, found him so distraught and distracted that he could scarce speak to her.

" We'll soon set that to rights," she said. So she just clapped her hands and called :

> " Beasts and birds o' each degree,
> Clean me this stable for love o' me."

And, lo and behold ! in a minute the beasts of the fields came trooping, and the sky was just dark with the wings of birds, and they carried away the muck, and the stable was clean as a new pin before the evening.

Now when the Magician saw this, he grew hot and angry, and he guessed it was his daughter's magic that had wrought the miracle. So he said : " Shame on the wit that helped you ; but I have a harder job for you to-morrow. Yonder is a lake seven miles long, seven miles broad, and seven miles deep. Drain it by nightfall, so that not one drop remains, or, of a certainty, I eat you for supper."

So once again Nix Naught Nothing rose before dawn, and began his task ; but though he baled out the water without ceasing, it ever ran back, so that though he sweated and laboured, by breakfast-time he was no nearer the end of his job.

But when the Magician's daughter came with his breakfast she only laughed and said, " I'll soon mend that ! " Then she clapped her hands and called :

> " Oh ! all ye fish of river and sea,
> Drink me this water for love of me ! "

And, lo and behold ! the lake was thick with fishes. And they drank and drank, till not one drop remained.

Now when the Magician returned in the morning and saw this he was as angry as angry. And he knew it was his daughter's magic, so he said : " Double shame on the wit that helped you ! Yet it betters you not, for I will give you a yet harder task than the last. If you do that, you may have my daughter. See you, yonder is a tree, seven miles high, and no branch to it till the top, and there on the fork is a nest with some eggs in it. Bring those eggs down without breaking one or, sure as fate, I'll eat you for my supper."

Then the Magician's daughter was very sad ; for with all her magic she could think of no way of helping her lover to fetch the eggs and bring them down unbroken. So she sate with Nix Naught Nothing underneath the tree, and thought, and thought, and thought ; until an idea came to her, and she clapped her hands and cried :

> " Fingers of mine, for love of me,
> Help my true lover to climb the tree."

Then her fingers dropped off her hands one by one and ranged themselves like the steps of a ladder up the tree ; but they were not quite enough of them to reach the top, so she cried again :

> " Oh ! toes of mine, for love o' me,
> Help my true lover to climb the tree."

Then her toes began to drop off one by one and range themselves like the rungs of a ladder ; but when the toes of one foot had gone to their places the ladder was tall enough. So Nix Naught Nothing climbed up it, reached the nest, and got the seven eggs. Now, as he was coming down with the last, he was so overjoyed at having finished his task, that he turned to see if the Magician's daughter was overjoyed too : and lo ! the seventh egg slipped from his hand and fell

Crash !

" Quick ! Quick ! " cried the Magician's daughter, who, as you will observe, always had her wits about her. " There is nothing for it now but to fly at once. But first I must have my magic flask, or I shall be unable to help. It is in my room and the door is locked. Put your fingers, since I have none, in my pocket, take the key, unlock the door, get the flask, and follow me fast. I shall go slower than you, for I have no toes on one foot ! "

So Nix Naught Nothing did as he was bid, and soon caught up the Magician's daughter. But alas ! they could not run very fast, so ere long the Magician, who had once again taken a giant's form in order to have a long stride, could be seen behind them. Nearer and nearer he came until he was just going to seize Nix Naught Nothing, when the Magician's daughter cried : " Put your fingers, since I have none, into my hair, take my comb and throw it down." So Nix Naught Nothing did as he was bid, and, lo and behold ! out of every one of the comb-prongs there sprang up a prickly briar, which grew so fast that the Magician found himself in the middle of a thorn hedge ! You may guess how angry and scratched he was before he tore his way out. So Nix Naught Nothing and his sweetheart had time for a good start ; but the Magician's daughter could not run fast because she had lost her toes on one foot ! Therefore the Magician in giant form soon caught them up, and he was just about to grip Nix Naught Nothing when the Magician's daughter cried : " Put your fingers, since I have none, to my breast. Take out my veil-dagger and throw it down."

So he did as he was bid, and in a moment the dagger had grown to thousands and thousands of sharp razors, criss-cross on the ground, and the Magician giant was howling with pain as he trod among them. You may guess how he danced and stumbled and how long it took for him to pick his way through as if he were walking on eggs !

So Nix Naught Nothing and his sweetheart were nearly out of sight ere the giant could start again ; yet it wasn't long before he was like to catch them up ; for the Magician's daughter, you see, could not run fast because she had lost her toes on one foot ! She did what she could, but it was no use. So just as the giant was reaching out a hand to lay hold of Nix Naught Nothing she cried breathlessly :

" There's nothing left but the magic flask. Take it out and sprinkle some of what it holds on the ground."

And Nix Naught Nothing did as he was bid ; but in his hurry he nearly emptied the flask altogether ; and so the big, big wave of water which instantly welled up, swept him off his feet, and would have carried him away, had not the Magician's daughter's loosened veil caught him and held him fast. But the wave grew, and grew, and grew behind them, until it reached the giant's waist ; then it grew and

grew until it reached his shoulders ; and it grew and grew
until it swept over his head : a great big sea-wave full of
little fishes and crabs and sea-snails and all sorts of strange
creatures.

So that was the last of the Magician giant. But the poor
little Magician's daughter was so weary that, after a time,
she couldn't move a step further, and she said to her lover,
" Yonder are lights burning. Go and see if you can find a
night's lodging : I will climb this tree by the pool where I
shall be safe, and by the time you return I shall be rested."

Now, by chance, it happened that the lights they saw
were the lights of the castle where Nix Naught Nothing's
father and mother, the King and Queen, lived (though, of
course, he did not know this) ; so, as he walked towards the
castle, he came upon the hen-wife's cottage and asked for a
night's lodging.

" Who are you ? " asked the hen-wife suspiciously.

" I am Nix Naught Nothing," replied the young man.

Now the hen-wife still grieved over her boy who had
been killed, so she instantly resolved to be revenged.

" I cannot give you a night's lodging," she said. " But
you shall have a drink of milk, for you look weary. Then
you can go on to the castle and beg for a bed there."

So she gave him a cup of milk ; but, being a witch-
woman, she put a potion to it so that the very moment he
saw his father and mother he should fall fast asleep, and none
should be able to waken him. So he would be no use to
anybody, and would not recognise his father and mother.

N

Now the King and Queen had never ceased grieving for their lost son, so they were always very kind to wandering young men, and when they heard that one was begging a night's lodging, they went down to the hall to see him. And lo ! the moment Nix Naught Nothing caught sight of his father and mother, there he was on the floor fast asleep, and none could waken him ! And he did not recognise his father and mother and they did not recognise him.

But Prince Nix Naught Nothing had grown into a very handsome young man, so they pitied him very much, and when none, do what they would, could waken him, the King said, " A maiden will likely take more trouble to waken him than others, seeing how handsome he is ; so send forth a proclamation that if any maiden in my realm can waken this young man, she shall have him in marriage, and a handsome dowry to boot."

So the proclamation was sent forth, and all the pretty maidens of the realm came to try their luck ; but they had no success.

Now the gardener whose boy had been killed by the giant had a daughter who was very ugly indeed—so ugly that she thought it no use to try her luck, and went about her work as usual. So she took her pitcher to the pool to fill it. Now the Magician's daughter was still hiding in the tree waiting for her lover to return. Thus it came to pass that the gardener's ugly daughter, bending down to fill her pitcher in the pool, saw a beautiful shadow in the water, and thought it was her own !

" If I am as pretty as that," she cried, " I'll draw water no longer ! "

So she threw down her pitcher, and went straight to the castle to see if she hadn't a chance of the handsome stranger and the handsome dowry. But of course she hadn't ; though at the sight of Nix Naught Nothing she fell so much in love with him, that, knowing the hen-wife to be a witch, she went straight to her, and offered all her savings for a charm by which she could awaken the sleeper.

Now when the hen-wife witch heard her tale, she thought it would be a rare revenge to marry the King and Queen's long-lost son to a gardener's ugly daughter ; so she straight-way took the girl's savings and gave her a charm by which she could unspell the Prince or spell him again at her pleasure.

So away went the gardener's daughter to the castle, and sure enough, no sooner had she sung her charm, than Nix Naught Nothing awoke.

" I am going to marry you, my charmer," she said coaxingly ; but Nix Naught Nothing said he would prefer sleep. So she thought it wiser to put him to sleep again till the marriage feast was ready and she had got her fine clothes. So she spelled him asleep again.

Now the gardener had, of course, to draw the water himself, since his daughter would not work. And he took the pitcher to the pool ; and he also saw the Magician's daughter's shadow in the water ; but he did not think the face was his own, for, see you, he had a beard !

Then he looked up and saw the lady in the tree.

She, poor thing, was half dead with sorrow, and hunger, and fatigue, so, being a kind man, he took her to his house and gave her food. And he told her that that *very day* his daughter was to marry a handsome young stranger at the castle, and to get a handsome dowry to boot from the King and Queen, in memory of their son, Nix Naught Nothing, who had been carried off by a giant when he was a little boy.

Then the Magician's daughter felt sure that something had happened to her lover ; so she went to the castle, and there she found him fast asleep in a chair.

But she could not waken him, for, see you, her magic had gone from her with the magic flask which Nix Naught Nothing had emptied.

So, though she put her fingerless hands on his and wept and sang :

> " I cleaned the stable for love o' thee,
> I laved the lake and I clomb the tree,
> Wilt thou not waken for love o' me ? "

he never stirred nor woke.

Now one of the old servants there, seeing how she wept, took pity on her and said, " She that is to marry the young man will be back ere long, and unspell him for the wedding. Hide yourself and listen to her charm."

So the Magician's daughter hid herself, and, by and by, in comes the gardener's daughter in her fine wedding-dress, and begins to sing her charm. But the Magician's daughter didn't wait for her to finish it ; for the moment Nix Naught

Nothing opened his eyes, she rushed out of her hiding-place, and put her fingerless hands in his.

Then Nix Naught Nothing remembered everything. He remembered the castle, he remembered his father and mother, he remembered the Magician's daughter and all that she had done for him.

Then he drew out the magic flask and said, " Surely, surely there must be enough magic in it to mend your hands." And there was. There were just fourteen drops left, ten for the fingers and four for the toes ; but there was not one for the little toe, so it could not be brought back. Of course, after that there was great rejoicing, and Prince Nix Naught Nothing and the Magician's daughter were married and lived happy ever after, even though she only had four toes on one foot. As for the hen-wife witch, she was burnt, and so the gardener's daughter got back her earnings ; but she was not happy, because her shadow in the water was ugly again.

MR. AND MRS. VINEGAR

MR. AND MRS. VINEGAR, a worthy couple, lived in a glass pickle-jar. The house, though small, was snug, and so light that each speck of dust on the furniture showed like a mole-hill; so while Mr. Vinegar tilled his garden with a pickle-fork and grew vegetables for pickling, Mrs. Vinegar, who was a sharp, bustling, tidy woman, swept, brushed, and dusted, brushed and dusted and swept to keep the house clean as a new pin. Now one day she lost her temper with a cobweb and swept so hard after it that bang! bang! the broom-handle went right through the glass, and crash! crash! clitter! clatter! there was the pickle-jar house about her ears all in splinters and bits.

She picked her way over these as best she might, and rushed into the garden.

"Oh, Vinegar, Vinegar!" she cried. "We are clean ruined and done for! Quit these vegetables! they won't be wanted! What is the use of pickles if you haven't a pickle-jar to put them in, and—I've broken ours—into little bits!" And with that she fell to crying bitterly.

But Mr. Vinegar was of different mettle ; though a small man, he was a cheerful one, always looking at the best side of things, so he said, " Accidents will happen, lovey ! But there are as good pickle-bottles in the shop as ever came out of it. All we need is money to buy another. So let us go out into the world and seek our fortunes."

" But what about the furniture ? " sobbed Mrs. Vinegar.

" I will take the door of the house with me, lovey," quoth Mr. Vinegar stoutly. " Then no one will be able to open it, will they ? "

Mrs. Vinegar did not quite see how this fact would mend matters, but, being a good wife, she held her peace. So off they trudged into the world to seek fortune, Mr. Vinegar bearing the door on his back like a snail carries its house.

Well, they walked all day long, but not a brass farthing did they make, and when night fell they found themselves in a dark, thick forest. Now Mrs. Vinegar, for all she was a smart, strong woman, was tired to death, and filled with fear of wild beasts, so she began once more to cry bitterly ; but Mr. Vinegar was cheerful as ever.

" Don't alarm yourself, lovey," he said. " I will climb into a tree, fix the door firmly in a fork, and you can sleep there as safe and comfortable as in your own bed."

So he climbed the tree, fixed the door, and Mrs. Vinegar lay down on it, and being dead tired was soon fast asleep. But her weight tilted the door sideways, so, after a time, Mr. Vinegar, being afraid she might slip off, sate down on the other side to balance her and keep watch.

Now in the very middle of the night, just as he was beginning to nod, what should happen but that a band of robbers should meet beneath that very tree in order to divide their spoils. Mr. Vinegar could hear every word said quite distinctly, and began to tremble like an aspen as he listened to the terrible deeds the thieves had done to gain their ends.

" Don't shake so ! " murmured Mrs. Vinegar, half asleep. " You'll have me off the bed."

" I'm not shaking, lovey," whispered back Mr. Vinegar in a quaking voice. " It is only the wind in the trees."

But for all his cheerfulness he was not really *very* brave *inside*, so he went on trembling and shaking, and shaking and trembling, till, just as the robbers were beginning to parcel out the money, he actually shook the door right out of the tree-fork, and down it came—with Mrs. Vinegar still asleep upon it—right on top of the robbers' heads !

As you may imagine, they thought the sky had fallen, and made off as fast as their legs would carry them, leaving their booty behind them. But Mr. Vinegar, who had saved himself from the fall by clinging to a branch, was far too frightened to go down in the dark to see what had happened. So up in the tree he sate like a big bird until dawn came.

Then Mrs. Vinegar woke, rubbed her eyes, yawned, and said, " Where am I ? "

" On the ground, lovey," answered Mr. Vinegar, scrambling down.

And when they lifted up the door, what do you think they found ?

One robber squashed flat as a pancake, and forty golden guineas all scattered about !

My goodness ! How Mr. and Mrs. Vinegar jumped for joy !

" Now, Vinegar ! " said his wife when they had gathered up all the gold pieces, " I will tell you what we must do. You must go to the next market-town and buy a cow ; for, see you, money makes the mare to go, truly ; but it also goes itself. Now a cow won't run away, but will give us milk and butter, which we can sell. So we shall live in comfort for the rest of our days."

" What a head you have, lovey ! " said Mr. Vinegar admiringly, and started off on his errand.

" Mind you make a good bargain," bawled his wife after him.

" I always do," bawled back Mr. Vinegar. " I made a good bargain when I married such a clever wife, and I made a better one when I shook her down from the tree. I am the happiest man alive ! "

So he trudged on, laughing and jingling the forty gold pieces in his pocket.

Now the first thing he saw in the market was an old red cow.

" I am in luck to-day," he thought ; " that is the very beast for me. I shall be the happiest of men if I get that cow." So he went up to the owner, jingling the gold in his pocket.

" What will you take for your cow ? " he asked.

And the owner of the cow, seeing he was a simpleton, said, " What you've got in your pocket."

" Done ! " said Mr. Vinegar, handed over the forty guineas, and led off the cow, marching her up and down the market, much against her will, to show off his bargain.

Now, as he drove it about, proud as Punch, he noticed a man who was playing the bagpipes. He was followed about by a crowd of children who danced to the music, and a perfect shower of pennies fell into his cap every time he held it out.

" Ho, ho ! " thought Mr. Vinegar. " That is an easier way of earning a livelihood than by driving about a beast of a cow ! Then the feeding, and the milking, and the churning ! Ah, I should be the happiest man alive if I had those bagpipes ! "

So he went up to the musician and said, " What will you take for your bagpipes ? "

" Well," replied the musician, seeing he was a simpleton, " it is a beautiful instrument, and I make so much money by it, that I cannot take anything less than that red cow."

" Done ! " cried Mr. Vinegar in a hurry, lest the man should repent of his offer.

So the musician walked off with the red cow, and Mr. Vinegar tried to play the bagpipes. But, alas and alack ! though he blew till he almost burst, not a sound could he make at first, and when he did at last, it was such a terrific squeal and screech that all the children ran away frightened, and the people stopped their ears.

But he went on and on, trying to play a tune, and never earning anything, save hootings and peltings, until his fingers were almost frozen with the cold, when of course the noise he made on the bagpipes was worse than ever.

Then he noticed a man who had on a pair of warm gloves, and he said to himself, " Music is impossible when one's fingers are frozen. I believe I should be the happiest man alive if I had those gloves."

So he went up to the owner and said, " You seem, sir, to have a very good pair of gloves." And the man replied, " Truly, sir, my hands are as warm as toast this bitter November day."

That quite decided Mr. Vinegar, and he asked at once what the owner would take for them ; and the owner, seeing he was a simpleton, said, " As your hands seem frozen, sir, I will, as a favour, let you have them for your bagpipes."

" Done ! " cried Mr. Vinegar, delighted, and made the exchange.

Then he set off to find his wife, quite pleased with himself. " Warm hands, warm heart ! " he thought. " I'm the happiest man alive ! "

But as he trudged he grew very, very tired, and at last began to limp. Then he saw a man coming along the road with a stout stick.

" I should be the happiest man alive if I had that stick," he thought. " What is the use of warm hands if your feet ache ! " So he said to the man with the stick, " What will you take for your stick ? " and the man, seeing he was a simpleton, replied :

" Well, I don't want to part with my stick, but as you are so pressing I'll oblige you, as a friend, for those warm gloves you are wearing."

" Done for you ! " cried Mr. Vinegar delightedly ; and trudged off with the stick, chuckling to himself over his good bargain.

But as he went along a magpie fluttered out of the hedge and sate on a branch in front of him, and chuckled and laughed as magpies do. " What are you laughing at ? " asked Mr. Vinegar.

" At you, forsooth ! " chuckled the magpie, fluttering just a little further. " At *you*, Mr. Vinegar, you foolish man—you simpleton—you blockhead ! You bought a cow for forty guineas when she wasn't worth ten, you exchanged her for bagpipes you couldn't play — you changed the bagpipes for a pair of gloves, and the pair of gloves for a miserable stick. Ho, ho ! Ha, ha ! So you've nothing to show for your forty guineas save a stick you might have cut in any hedge. Ah, you fool ! you simpleton ! you blockhead ! "

And the magpie chuckled, and chuckled, and chuckled in such guffaws, fluttering from branch to branch as Mr. Vinegar trudged along, that at last he flew into a violent rage and flung his stick at the bird. And the stick stuck in a tree out of his reach ; so he had to go back to his wife without anything at all.

But he was glad the stick had stuck in a tree, for Mrs. Vinegar's hands were quite hard enough.

When it was all over Mr. Vinegar said cheerfully, " You are too violent, lovey. You broke the pickle-jar, and now you've nearly broken every bone in my body. I think we had better turn over a new leaf and begin afresh. I shall take service as a gardener, and you can go as a housemaid, until we have enough money to buy a new pickle-jar. There are as good ones in the shop as ever came out of it."

And that is the story of Mr. and Mrs. Vinegar.

And that is the story of Mr. and Mrs. Vinegar.

THE TRUE HISTORY OF SIR THOMAS THUMB

AT the court of great King Arthur, who lived, as all know, when knights were bold, and ladies were fair indeed, one of the most renowned of men was the wizard Merlin. Never before or since was there such another. All that was to be known of wizardry he knew, and his advice was ever good and kindly.

Now once when he was travelling in the guise of a beggar, he chanced upon an honest ploughman and his wife who, giving him a hearty welcome, supplied him, cheerfully, with a big wooden bowl of fresh milk and some coarse brown bread on a wooden platter. Still, though both they and the little cottage where they dwelt were neat and tidy, Merlin noticed that neither the husband nor the wife seemed happy ; and when he asked the cause they said it was because they had no children.

" Had I but a son, no matter if he were no bigger than my goodman's thumb," said the poor woman, " we should be quite content."

Now this idea of a boy no bigger than a man's thumb

so tickled Wizard Merlin's fancy that he promised straight
away that such a son should come in due time to bring the
good couple content. This done, he went off at once to pay
a visit to the Queen of the Fairies, since he felt that the
little people would best be able to carry out his promise.
And, sure enough, the droll fancy of a mannikin no bigger
than his father's thumb tickled the Fairy Queen also, and she
set about the task at once.

So behold the ploughman and his wife as happy as King
and Queen over the tiniest of tiny babies; and all the happier
because the Fairy Queen, anxious to see the little fellow,
flew in at the window, bringing with her clothes fit for the
wee mannikin to wear.

> An oak-leaf hat he had for his crown;
> His jacket was woven of thistle-down.
> His shirt was a web by spiders spun;
> His breeches of softest feathers were done.
> His stockings of red-apple rind were tyne
> With an eyelash plucked from his mother's eyne.
> His shoes were made of a mouse's skin,
> Tanned with the soft furry hair within.

Dressed in this guise he looked the prettiest little fellow
ever seen, and the Fairy Queen kissed him over and over
again, and gave him the name of Tom Thumb.

Now as he grew older—though, mind you, he never
grew bigger—he was so full of antics and tricks that he was
for ever getting into trouble. Once his mother was making
a batter pudding, and Tom, wanting to see how it was made,
climbed up to the edge of the bowl. His mother was so busy

beating the batter that she didn't notice him ; and when his foot slipped, and he plumped head and ears into the bowl, she just went on beating until the batter was light enough. Then she put it into the pudding-cloth and set it on the fire to boil.

Now the batter had so filled poor Tom's mouth that he couldn't cry ; but no sooner did he feel the hot water than he began to struggle and kick so much that the pudding bobbed up and down, and jumped about in such strange fashion that the ploughman's wife thought it was bewitched, and in a great fright flung it to the door.

Here a poor tinker passing by picked it up and put it in his wallet. But by this time Tom had got his mouth clear of the batter, and he began holloaing, and making such a to-do, that the tinker, even more frightened than Tom's mother had been, threw the pudding in the road, and ran away as fast as he could run. Luckily for Tom, this second fall broke the pudding string and he was able to creep out, all covered with half-cooked batter, and make his way home, where his mother, distressed to see her little dear in such a woeful state, put him into a teacup of water to clean him, and then tucked him up in bed.

Another time Tom's mother went to milk her red cow in the meadow and took Tom with her, for she was ever afraid lest he should fall into mischief when left alone. Now the wind was high, and fearful lest he should be blown away, she tied him to a thistle-head with one of her own long hairs, and then began to milk. But the red cow, nosing about for

o

something to do while she was being milked, as all cows will, spied Tom's oak-leaf hat, and thinking it looked good, curled its tongue round the thistle-stalk and——

There was Tom dodging the cow's teeth, and roaring as loud as he could :

"Mother! Mother! Help! Help!"

"Lawks-a-mercy-me," cried his mother, "where's the child got to now? Where are you, you bad boy?"

"Here!" roared Tom, "in the red cow's mouth!"

With that his mother began to weep and wail, not knowing what else to do ; and Tom, hearing her, roared louder than ever. Whereat the red cow, alarmed—and no wonder ! —at the dreadful noise in her throat, opened her mouth, and Tom dropped out, luckily into his mother's apron ; otherwise he would have been badly hurt falling so far.

Adventures like these were not Tom's fault. He could not help being so small, but he got into dreadful trouble once for which he was entirely to blame. This is what happened. He loved playing cherry-stones with the big boys, and when he had lost all his own he would creep unbeknownst into the other players' pockets or bags, and make off with cherry-stones enough and galore to carry on the game !

Now one day it so happened that one of the boys saw Master Tom on the point of coming out of a bag with a whole fistful of cherry-stones. So he just drew the string of the bag tight.

"Ha! ha! Mr. Thomas Thumb," says he jeeringly,

" so you were going to pinch my cherry-stones, were you ? Well ! you shall have more of them than you like." And with that he gave the cherry-stone bag such a hearty shake that all Tom's body and legs were sadly bruised black and blue ; nor was he let out till he had promised never to steal cherry-stones again.

So the years passed, and when Tom was a lad, still no bigger than a thumb, his father thought he might begin to make himself useful. So he made him a whip out of a barley straw, and set him to drive the cattle home. But Tom, in trying to climb a furrow's ridge—which to him, of course, was a steep hill—slipped down and lay half stunned, so that a raven, happening to fly over, thought he was a frog, and picked him up intending to eat him. Not relishing the morsel, however, the bird dropped him above the battlements of a big castle that stood close to the sea. Now the castle belonged to one Grumbo, an ill-tempered giant who happened to be taking the air on the roof of his tower. And when Tom dropped on his bald pate the giant put up his great hand to catch what he thought was an impudent fly, and finding something that smelt man's meat, he just swallowed the little fellow as he would have swallowed a pill !

He began, however, to repent very soon, for Tom kicked and struggled in the giant's inside as he had done in the red cow's throat until the giant felt quite squeamish, and finally got rid of Tom by being sick over the battlements into the sea.

And here, doubtless, would have been Tom Thumb's

end by drowning, had not a big fish, thinking that he was a shrimp, rushed at him and gulped him down !

Now by good chance some fishermen were standing by with their nets, and when they drew them in, the fish that had swallowed Tom was one of the haul. Being a very fine fish it was sent to the Court kitchen, where, when the fish was opened, out popped Tom on the dresser, as spry as spry, to the astonishment of the cook and the scullions ! Never had such a mite of a man been seen, while his quips and pranks kept the whole buttery in roars of laughter. What is more, he soon became the favourite of the whole Court, and when the King went out a-riding Tom sat in the Royal waistcoat pocket ready to amuse Royalty and the Knights of the Round Table.

After a while, however, Tom wearied to see his parents again ; so the King gave him leave to go home and take with him as much money as he could carry. Tom therefore chose a threepenny bit, and putting it into a purse made of a water bubble, lifted it with difficulty on to his back, and trudged away to his father's house, which was some half a mile distant.

It took him two days and two nights to cover the ground, and he was fair outwearied by his heavy burden ere he reached home. However, his mother put him to rest in a walnut shell by the fire and gave him a whole hazel nut to eat ; which, sad to say, disagreed with him dreadfully. However, he recovered in some measure, but had grown so thin and light that to save him the trouble of walking back to the Court, his mother tied him to a dandelion-clock, and as there was a high wind, away he went as if on wings. Unfortunately, however, just as he was flying low in order to alight, the Court cook, an ill-natured fellow, was coming across the palace yard with a bowl of hot furmenty for the King's supper. Now Tom was unskilled in the handling of dandelion horses, so what should happen but that he rode straight into the furmenty, spilt the half of it, and splashed the other half, scalding hot, into the cook's face.

He was in a fine rage, and going straight to King Arthur said that Tom, at his old antics, had done it on purpose.

Now the King's favourite dish was hot furmenty; so he also fell into a fine rage and ordered Tom to be tried for high treason. He was therefore imprisoned in a mouse-trap, where he remained for several days tormented by a cat, who, thinking him some new kind of mouse, spent its time in sparring at him through the bars. At the end of a week, however, King Arthur, having recovered the loss of the furmenty, sent for Tom and once more received him into favour. After this Tom's life was happy and successful. He became so renowned for his dexterity and wonderful activity, that he was knighted by the King under the name of Sir Thomas Thumb, and as his clothes, what with the batter and the furmenty, to say nothing of the insides of giants and fishes, had become somewhat shabby, His Majesty ordered him a new suit of clothes fit for a mounted knight to wear. He also gave him a beautiful prancing grey mouse as a charger.

It was certainly very diverting to see Tom dressed up to the nines, and as proud as Punch.

> Of butterflies' wings his shirt was made,
> His boots of chicken hide,
> And by a nimble fairy blade,
> All learned in the tailoring trade,
> His coat was well supplied.
> A needle dangled at his side,
> And thus attired in stately pride
> A dapper mouse he used to ride.

In truth the King and all the Knights of the Round Table were ready to expire with laughter at Tom on his fine curveting steed.

But one day, as the hunt was passing a farm-house, a big cat, lurking about, made one spring and carried both Tom and the mouse up a tree. Nothing daunted, Tom boldly drew his needle sword and attacked the enemy with such fierceness that she let her prey fall. Luckily one of the nobles caught the little fellow in his cap, otherwise he must have been killed by the fall. As it was he became very ill, and the doctor almost despaired of his life. However, his friend and guardian, the Queen of the Fairies, arrived in a chariot drawn by flying mice, and then and there carried Tom back with her to Fairyland, where, amongst folk of his own size, he, after a time, recovered. But time runs swiftly in Fairyland, and when Tom Thumb returned to Court he was surprised to find that his father and mother and nearly all his old friends were dead, and that King

Thunstone reigned in King Arthur's place. So every one was astonished at his size, and carried him as a curiosity to the Audience Hall.

"Who art thou, mannikin?" asked King Thunstone. "Whence dost come? And where dost live?"

To which Tom replied with a bow:

> "My name is well known.
> From the Fairies I come.
> When King Arthur shone,
> This Court was my home.
> By him I was knighted,
> In me he delighted
> —Your servant—Sir Thomas Thumb."

This address so pleased His Majesty that he ordered a little golden chair to be made, so that Tom might sit beside him at table. Also a little palace of gold, but a span high, with doors a bare inch wide, in which the little fellow might take his ease.

Now King Thunstone's Queen was a very jealous woman, and could not bear to see such honours showered on the little fellow; so she up and told the King all sorts of bad tales about his favourite; amongst others, that he had been saucy and rude to her.

Whereupon the King sent for Tom; but forewarned is forearmed, and knowing by bitter experience the danger of royal displeasure, Tom hid himself in an empty snail-shell, where he lay till he was nigh starved. Then seeing a fine large butterfly on a dandelion close by, he climbed up and managed to get astride it. No sooner had he gained his seat than the butterfly was off, hovering from tree to tree, from flower to flower.

At last the royal gardener saw it and gave chase, then the nobles joined in the hunt, even the King himself, and finally the Queen, who forgot her anger in the merriment. Hither and thither they ran, trying in vain to catch the pair, and almost expiring with laughter, until poor Tom, dizzy with so much fluttering, and doubling, and flittering, fell from his seat into a watering-pot, where he was nearly drowned.

So they all agreed he must be forgiven, because he had afforded them so much amusement.

Thus Tom was once more in favour; but he did not live long to enjoy his good luck, for a spider one day attacked him, and though he fought well, the creature's poisonous breath proved too much for him; he fell dead on the

ground where he stood, and the spider soon sucked every drop of his blood.

Thus ended Sir Thomas Thumb ; but the King and the Court were so sorry at the loss of their little favourite that they went into mourning for him. And they put a fine white marble monument over his grave whereon was carven the following epitaph :

Here lyes Tom Thumb, King Arthur's Knight,
Who died by a spider's fell despite.
He was well known in Arthur's Court,
Where he afforded gallant sport.
He rode at tilt and tournament,
And on a mouse a-hunting went.
Alive he filled the Court with mirth,
His death to sadness must give birth.
So wipe your eyes and shake your head,
And say, " Alas, Tom Thumb is dead ! "

HENNY-PENNY

ONE day Henny-penny was picking up corn in the rickyard when—whack!—an acorn hit her upon the head. "Goodness gracious me!" said Henny-penny, "the sky's a-going to fall; I must go and tell the King."

So she went along, and she went along, and she went along, till she met Cocky-locky. "Where are you going, Henny-penny?" says Cocky-locky. "Oh! I'm going to tell the King the sky's a-falling," says Henny-penny. "May I come with you?" says Cocky-locky. "Certainly," says Henny-penny. So Henny-penny and Cocky-locky went to tell the King the sky was falling.

They went along, and they went along, and they went along, till they met Ducky-daddles. "Where are you going to, Henny-penny and Cocky-locky?" says Ducky-daddles. "Oh! we're going to tell the King the sky's a-falling," said Henny-penny and Cocky-locky. "May I come with you?" says Ducky-daddles. "Certainly," said Henny-penny and Cocky-locky. So Henny-penny, Cocky-locky, and Ducky-daddles went to tell the King the sky was a-falling.

So they went along, and they went along, and they went along, till they met Goosey-poosey. "Where are you going to, Henny-penny, Cocky-locky, and Ducky-daddles?" said Goosey-poosey. "Oh! we're going to tell the King the sky's a-falling," said Henny-penny and Cocky-locky and Ducky-daddles. "May I come with you?" said Goosey-poosey. "Certainly," said Henny-penny, Cocky-locky, and Ducky-daddles. So Henny-penny, Cocky-locky, Ducky-daddles, and Goosey-poosey went to tell the King the sky was a-falling.

So they went along, and they went along, and they went along, till they met Turkey-lurkey. "Where are you going, Henny-penny, Cocky-locky, Ducky-daddles, and Goosey-poosey?" says Turkey-lurkey. "Oh! we're going to tell the King the sky's a-falling," said Henny-penny, Cocky-locky, Ducky-daddles, and Goosey-poosey. "May I come with you, Henny-penny, Cocky-locky, Ducky-daddles, and Goosey-poosey?" said Turkey-lurkey. "Oh, certainly, Turkey-lurkey," said Henny-penny, Cocky-locky, Ducky-daddles, and Goosey-poosey. So Henny-penny, Cocky-locky, Ducky-daddles, Goosey-poosey, and Turkey-lurkey all went to tell the King the sky was a-falling.

So they went along, and they went along, and they went along, till they met Foxy-woxy, and Foxy-woxy said to Henny-penny, Cocky-locky, Ducky-daddles, Goosey-poosey, and Turkey-lurkey, "Where are you going, Henny-penny, Cocky-locky, Ducky-daddles, Goosey-poosey, and Turkey-lurkey?" And Henny-penny, Cocky-locky, Ducky-daddles, Goosey-poosey, and Turkey-lurkey said to Foxy-woxy, "We're going to tell the King the sky's a-falling." "Oh! but this is not the way to the King, Henny-penny, Cocky-locky, Ducky-daddles, Goosey-poosey, and Turkey-lurkey," says Foxy-woxy; "I know the proper way; shall I show it you?" "Oh, certainly, Foxy-woxy," said Henny-penny, Cocky-locky, Ducky-daddles, Goosey-poosey, and Turkey-lurkey. So Henny-penny, Cocky-

locky, Ducky - daddles, Goosey - poosey,
Turkey-lurkey, and Foxy-woxy all went
to tell the King the sky was a-falling.
So they went along, and they went along,
and they went along, till they came to
a narrow and dark hole.   Now this
was the door of Foxy-woxy's burrow.
But Foxy - woxy said to Henny-
penny,   Cocky - locky,   Ducky -
daddles, Goosey - poosey, and Tur-

key-lurkey, "This is the short cut to the King's palace : you'll soon get there if you follow me. I will go first and you come after, Henny-penny, Cocky-locky, Ducky-daddles, Goosey-poosey, and Turkey-lurkey." "Why, of course, certainly, without doubt, why not?" said Henny-penny, Cocky-locky, Ducky-daddles, Goosey-poosey, and Turkey-lurkey.

So Foxy-woxy went into his burrow, and he didn't go very far but turned round to wait for Henny-penny, Cocky-locky, Ducky-daddles, Goosey-poosey, and Turkey-lurkey. Now Turkey-lurkey was the first to go through the dark hole into the burrow. He hadn't got far when—

"Hrumph!"

Foxy-woxy snapped off Turkey-lurkey's head and threw his body over his left shoulder. Then Goosey-poosey went in, and—

"Hrumph!"

Off went her head and Goosey-poosey was thrown beside Turkey-lurkey. Then Ducky-daddles waddled down, and—

" Hrumph ! "

Foxy-woxy had snapped off Ducky-daddles' head and Ducky-daddles was thrown alongside Turkey-lurkey and Goosey-poosey.   Then Cocky-locky strutted down into the burrow, and he hadn't gone far when—

" Hrumph ! "

But Cocky-locky *will* always crow whether you want him to do so or not, and so he had just time for one " Cock-a-doo-dle d——" before he went to join Turkey-lurkey, Goosey - poosey, and Ducky - daddles over Foxy - woxy's shoulders.

Now when Henny-penny, who had just got into the dark burrow, heard Cocky-locky crow, she said to herself :

" My goodness ! it must be dawn.   Time for me to lay my egg."

So she turned round and bustled off to her nest ; so she escaped, but she never told the King the sky was falling !

They thanked her and said-good-bye, and she went on her journey.

THE THREE HEADS OF THE WELL

ONCE upon a time there reigned a King in Colchester, valiant, strong, wise, famous as a good ruler.

But in the midst of his glory his dear Queen died, leaving him with a daughter just touching woman's estate ; and this maiden was renowned, far and wide, for beauty, kindness, grace. Now strange things happen, and the King of Colchester, hearing of a lady who had immense riches, had a mind to marry her, though she was old, ugly, hook-nosed, and ill-tempered ; and though she was, furthermore, possessed of a daughter as ugly as herself. None could give the reason why, but only a few weeks after the death of his dear Queen, the King brought this loathly bride to Court, and married her with great pomp and festivities. Now the very first thing she did was to poison the King's mind against his own beautiful, kind, gracious daughter, of whom, naturally, the ugly Queen and her ugly daughter were dreadfully jealous.

Now when the young Princess found that even her father had turned against her, she grew weary of Court life, and longed to get away from it ; so, one day, happening to meet the King alone in the garden, she went down on her knees, and begged and prayed him to give her some help, and let her go out into the world to seek her fortune. To this the King agreed, and told his consort to fit the girl out for her enterprise in proper fashion. But the jealous woman only gave her a canvas bag of brown bread and hard cheese, with a bottle of small-beer.

Though this was but a pitiful dowry for a King's daughter, the Princess was too proud to complain ; so she took it, returned her thanks, and set off on her journey through woods and forests, by rivers and lakes, over mountain and valley.

At last she came to a cave at the mouth of which, on a stone, sate an old, old man with a white beard.

" Good morrow, fair damsel," he said ; " whither away so fast ? "

" Reverend father," replies she, " I go to seek my fortune."

" And what hast thou for dowry, fair damsel," said he, " in thy bag and bottle ? "

" Bread and cheese and small-beer, father," says she, smiling. " Will it please you to partake of either ? "

" With all my heart," says he, and when she pulled out her provisions he ate them nearly all. But once again she made no complaint, but bade him eat what he needed, and welcome.

Now when he had finished he gave her many thanks, and said :

" For your beauty, and your kindness, and your grace, take this wand. There is a thick thorny hedge before you which seems impassable. But strike it thrice with this wand, saying each time, ' Please, hedge, let me through,' and it will open a pathway for you. Then, when you come to a well, sit down on the brink of it ; do not be surprised at anything you may see, but, whatever you are asked to do, that do ! "

So saying the old man went into the cave, and she went on her way. After a while she came to a high, thick thorny hedge ; but when she struck it three times with the wand, saying, " Please, hedge, let me through," it opened a wide pathway for her. So she came to the well, on the brink of which she sate down, and no sooner had she done so, than a golden head without any body came up through the water, singing as it came :

> " Wash me, and comb me, lay me on a bank to dry
> Softly and prettily to watch the passers-by."

" Certainly," she said, pulling out her silver comb. Then, placing the head on her lap, she began to comb the golden hair. When she had combed it, she lifted the golden head softly, and laid it on a primrose bank to dry. No sooner had she done this than another golden head appeared, singing as it came :

> " Wash me, and comb me, lay me on a bank to dry
> Softly and prettily to watch the passers-by."

" Certainly," says she, and after combing the golden

hair, placed the golden head softly on the primrose bank, beside the first one.

Then came a third head out of the well, and it said the same thing:

"Wash me, and comb me, lay me on a bank to dry
Softly and prettily to watch the passers-by."

"With all my heart," says she graciously, and after taking the head on her lap, and combing its golden hair with her silver comb, there were the three golden heads in a row on the primrose bank. And she sate down to rest herself and looked at them, they were so quaint and pretty; and as she rested she cheerfully ate and drank the meagre portion of the brown bread, hard cheese, and small-beer which the old man had left to her; for, though she was a king's daughter, she was too proud to complain.

Then the first head spoke. "Brothers, what shall we weird for this damsel who has been so gracious unto us? I weird her to be so beautiful that she shall charm every one she meets."

"And I," said the second head, "weird her a voice that shall exceed the nightingale's in sweetness."

"And I," said the third head, "weird her to be so fortunate that she shall marry the greatest King that reigns."

"Thank you with all my heart," says she; "but don't you think I had better put you back in the well before I go on? Remember you are golden, and the passers-by might steal you."

To this they agreed ; so she put them back.   And when they had thanked her for her kind thought and said good-bye, she went on her journey.

Now she had not travelled far before she came to a forest where the King of the country was hunting with his nobles, and as the gay cavalcade passed down the glade she stood back to avoid them ; but the King caught sight of her, and drew up his horse, fairly amazed at her beauty.

" Fair maid," he said, " who art thou, and whither goest thou through the forest thus alone ? "

" I am the King of Colchester's daughter, and I go to seek my fortune," says she, and her voice was sweeter than the nightingale's.

Then the King jumped from his horse, being so struck by her that he felt it would be impossible to live without her, and falling on his knee begged and prayed her to marry him without delay.

And he begged and prayed so well that at last she consented.   So, with all courtesy, he mounted her on his horse behind him, and commanding the hunt to follow, he returned to his palace, where the wedding festivities took place with all possible pomp and merriment.   Then, ordering out the royal chariot, the happy pair started to pay the King of Colchester a bridal visit : and you may imagine the surprise and delight with which, after so short an absence, the people of Colchester saw their beloved, beautiful, kind, and gracious princess return in a chariot all gemmed with gold, as the bride of the most powerful King in the world.   The bells rang out, flags flew, drums beat, the people huzzaed, and all was gladness, save for the ugly Queen and her ugly daughter, who were ready to burst with envy and malice; for, see you, the despised maiden was now above them both, and went before them at every Court ceremonial.

So, after the visit was ended, and the young King and his bride had gone back to their own country, there to live happily ever after, the ugly ill-natured princess said to her mother, the ugly Queen:

"I also will go into the world and seek my fortune. If that drab of a girl with her mincing ways got so much, what may I not get?"

So her mother agreed, and furnished her forth with silken dresses and furs, and gave her as provisions sugar, almonds, and sweetmeats of every variety, besides a large flagon of Malaga sack. Altogether a right royal dowry.

Armed with these she set forth, following the same road as her step-sister. Thus she soon came upon the old man with a white beard, who was seated on a stone by the mouth of a cave.

"Good morrow," says he. "Whither away so fast?"

"What's that to you, old man?" she replied rudely.

"And what hast thou for dowry in bag and bottle?" he asked quietly.

"Good things with which you shall not be troubled," she answered pertly.

"Wilt thou not spare an old man something?" he said.

Then she laughed. " Not a bite, not a sup, lest they
should choke you : though that would be small matter to
me," she replied, with a toss of her head.

" Then ill luck go with thee," remarked the old man
as he rose and went into the cave.

So she went on her way, and after a time came to the
thick thorny hedge, and seeing what she thought was a gap
in it, she tried to pass through ; but no sooner had she got
well into the middle of the hedge than the thorns closed in
around her so that she was all scratched and torn before she
won her way. Thus, streaming with blood, she went on
to the well, and seeing water, sate on the brink intending to
cleanse herself. But just as she dipped her hands, up came
a golden head singing as it came :

"Wash me, and comb me, lay me on the bank to dry
Softly and prettily to watch the passers-by."

"A likely story," says she. "I'm going to wash myself." And with that she gave the head such a bang with her bottle that it bobbed below the water. But it came up again, and so did a second head, singing as it came:

"Wash me, and comb me, lay me on the bank to dry
Softly and prettily to watch the passers-by."

"Not I," scoffs she. "I'm going to wash *my* hands and face and have my dinner." So she fetches the second head a cruel bang with the bottle, and both heads ducked down in the water.

But when they came up again all draggled and dripping, the third head came also, singing as it came:

"Wash me, and comb me, lay me on the bank to dry
Softly and prettily to watch the passers-by."

By this time the ugly princess had cleansed herself, and, seated on the primrose bank, had her mouth full of sugar and almonds.

"Not I," says she as well as she could. "I'm not a washerwoman nor a barber. So take that for your washing and combing."

And with that, having finished the Malaga sack, she flung the empty bottle at the three heads.

But this time they didn't duck. They looked at each other and said, "How shall we weird this rude girl for her bad manners?" Then the first head said:

" I weird that to her ugliness shall be added blotches on her face."

And the second head said :

" I weird that she shall ever be hoarse as a crow and speak as if she had her mouth full."

Then the third head said :

" And I weird that she shall be glad to marry a cobbler."

Then the three heads sank into the well and were no more seen, and the ugly princess went on her way. But, lo and behold ! when she came to a town, the children ran from her ugly blotched face screaming with fright, and when she tried to tell them she was the King of Colchester's daughter, her voice squeaked like a corn-crake's, was hoarse as a crow's, and folk could not understand a word she said, because she spoke as if her mouth was full !

Now in the town there happened to be a cobbler who not long before had mended the shoes of a poor old hermit ; and the latter, having no money, had paid for the job by the gift of a wonderful ointment which would cure blotches on the face, and a bottle of medicine that would banish any hoarseness.

So, seeing the miserable, ugly princess in great distress, he went up to her and gave her a few drops out of his bottle ; and then understanding from her rich attire and clearer speech that she was indeed a King's daughter, he craftily said that if she would take him for a husband he would undertake to cure her.

"Anything! Anything!" sobbed the miserable princess.

So they were married, and the cobbler straightway set off with his bride to visit the King of Colchester. But the bells did not ring, the drums did not beat, and the people, instead of huzzaing, burst into loud guffaws at the cobbler in leather, and his wife in silks and satins.

As for the ugly Queen, she was so enraged and disappointed that she went mad, and hanged herself in wrath. Whereupon the King, really pleased at getting rid of her so soon, gave the cobbler a hundred pounds and bade him go about his business with his ugly bride.

Which he did quite contentedly, for a hundred pounds means much to a poor cobbler. So they went to a remote part of the kingdom and lived unhappily for many years, he cobbling shoes, and she spinning the thread for him.

MR. FOX

LADY MARY was young and Lady Mary was fair, and she had more lovers than she could count on the fingers of both hands.

She lived with her two brothers, who were very proud and very fond of their beautiful sister, and very anxious that she should choose well amongst her many suitors.

Now amongst them there was a certain Mr. Fox, handsome and young and rich ; and though nobody quite knew who he was, he was so gallant and so gay that every one liked him. And he wooed Lady Mary so well that at last she promised to marry him. But though he talked much of the beautiful home to which he would take her, and described the castle and all the wonderful things that furnished it, he never offered to show it to her, neither did he invite Lady Mary's brothers to see it.

Now this seemed to her very strange indeed ; and, being a lass of spirit, she made up her mind to see the castle if she could.

So one day, just before the wedding, when she knew Mr.

Fox would be away seeing the lawyers with her brothers, she just kilted up her skirts and set out unbeknownst—for, see you, the whole household was busy preparing for the marriage feastings—to see for herself what Mr. Fox's beautiful castle was like.

After many searchings, and much travelling, she found it at last ; and a fine strong building it was, with high walls and a deep moat to it. A bit frowning and gloomy, but when she came up to the wide gateway she saw these words carven over the arch :

BE BOLD—BE BOLD.

So she plucked up courage, and the gate being open, went through it and found herself in a wide, empty, open courtyard. At the end of this was a smaller door, and over this was carven :

BE BOLD, BE BOLD ; BUT NOT TOO BOLD.

So she went through it to a wide, empty hall, and up the wide, empty staircase. Now at the top of the staircase there was a wide, empty gallery at one end of which were wide windows with the sunlight streaming through them from a beautiful garden, and at the other end a narrow door, over the archway of which was carven :

BE BOLD, BE BOLD ; BUT NOT TOO BOLD,
LEST THAT YOUR HEART'S BLOOD SHOULD RUN COLD.

Now Lady Mary was a lass of spirit, and so, of course, she turned her back on the sunshine, and opened the narrow, dark door. And there she was in a narrow, dark passage.

But at the end there was a chink of light. So she went forward and put her eye to the chink—and what do you think she saw?

Why! a wide saloon lit with many candles, and all round it, some hanging by their necks, some seated on chairs, some lying on the floor, were the skeletons and bodies of numbers of beautiful young maidens in their wedding-dresses that were all stained with blood.

Now Lady Mary, for all she was a lass of spirit, and brave as brave, could not look for long on such a horrid sight, so she turned and fled. Down the dark narrow passage, through the dark narrow door (which she did not forget to close behind her), and along the wide gallery she fled like a hare, and was just going down the wide stairs into the wide hall when, what did she see, through the window, but Mr. Fox dragging a beautiful young lady across the wide courtyard! There was nothing for it, Lady Mary decided, but to hide herself as quickly and as best she might; so she fled faster down the wide stairs, and hid herself behind a big wine-butt that stood in a corner of the wide hall. She was only just in time, for there at the wide door was Mr. Fox dragging the poor young maiden along by the hair; and he dragged her across the wide hall and up the wide stairs. And when she clutched at the bannisters to stop herself, Mr. Fox cursed and swore dreadfully; and at last he drew his sword and brought it down so hard on the poor young lady's wrist that the hand, cut off, jumped up into the air so that the diamond ring on the finger flashed in the sunlight as it fell, of all places in the world, into Lady Mary's very lap as she crouched behind the wine-butt !

Then she was fair frightened, thinking Mr. Fox would be sure to find her ; but after looking about a little while in vain (for, of course, he coveted the diamond ring), he continued his dreadful task of dragging the poor, beautiful young maiden upstairs to the horrid chamber, intending, doubtless, to return when he had finished his loathly work, and seek for the hand.

But by that time Lady Mary had fled ; for no sooner did she hear the awful, dragging noise pass into the gallery, than she upped and ran for dear life—through the wide door with

BE BOLD, BE BOLD; BUT NOT TOO BOLD

engraven over the arch, across the wide courtyard past the wide gate with

BE BOLD—BE BOLD

engraven over it, never stopping, never thinking till she reached her own chamber. And all the while the hand with the diamond ring lay in her kilted lap.

Now the very next day, when Mr. Fox and Lady Mary's brothers returned from the lawyers, the marriage-contract had to be signed. And all the neighbourhood was asked to witness it and partake of a splendid breakfast. And there was Lady Mary in bridal array, and there was Mr. Fox, looking so gay and so gallant. He was seated at the table just opposite Lady Mary, and he looked at her and said :

" How pale you are this morning, dear heart."

Then Lady Mary looked at him quietly and said, " Yes, dear sir ! I had a bad night's rest, for I had horrible dreams."

Then Mr. Fox smiled and said, " Dreams go by contraries, dear heart ; but tell me your dream, and your sweet voice will speed the time till I can call you mine."

" I dreamed," said Lady Mary, with a quiet smile, and her eyes were clear, " that I went yesterday to seek the castle that is to be my home, and I found it in the woods with high walls and a deep dark moat. And over the gateway were carven these words :

BE BOLD—BE BOLD."

Then Mr. Fox spoke in a hurry. " But it is not so— nor it was not so."

" Then I crossed the wide courtyard and went through a wide door over which was carven :

BE BOLD, BE BOLD ; BUT NOT TOO BOLD,"

went on Lady Mary, still smiling, and her voice was cold ; " but, of course, it is not so, and it was not so."

And Mr. Fox said nothing ; he sate like a stone.

" Then I dreamed," continued Lady Mary, still smiling, though her eyes were stern, " that I passed through a wide hall and up a wide stair and along a wide gallery until I came to a dark narrow door, and over it was carven :

BE BOLD, BE BOLD ; BUT NOT TOO BOLD,
LEST THAT YOUR HEART'S BLOOD SHOULD RUN COLD.

But it is not so, of course, and it was not so."

And Mr. Fox said nothing ; he sate frozen.

" Then I dreamed that I opened the door and went down a dark narrow passage," said Lady Mary, still smiling, though her voice was ice. " And at the end of the passage there was a door, and the door had a chink in it. And through the chink I saw a wide saloon lit with many candles, and all round it were the bones and bodies of poor dead maidens, their clothes all stained with blood ; but of course it is not so, and it was not so."

By this time all the neighbours were looking Mr. Fox-ways with all their eyes, while he sate silent.

But Lady Mary went on, and her smiling lips were set :

" Then I dreamed that I ran downstairs and had just time to hide myself when you, Mr. Fox, came in dragging a young lady by the hair. And the sunlight glittered on her diamond ring as she clutched the stair-rail, and you out with your sword and cut off the poor lady's hand."

Then Mr. Fox rose in his seat stonily and glared about him as if to escape, and his eye-teeth showed like a fox beset by the dogs, and he grew pale.

And he said, trying to smile, though his whispering voice could scarcely be heard :

" But it is not so, dear heart, and it was not so, and God forbid it should be so ! "

Then Lady Mary rose in her seat also, and the smile left her face, and her voice rang as she cried :

> " But it is so, and it was so ;
> Here's hand and ring I have to show."

Many's the beating he had from the broomstick or the ladle.

And with that she pulled out the poor dead hand with the glittering ring from her bosom and pointed it straight at Mr. Fox.

At this all the company rose, and drawing their swords cut Mr. Fox to pieces.

And served him very well right.

DICK WHITTINGTON AND HIS CAT

MORE than five hundred years ago there was a little boy named Dick Whittington, and this is true. His father and mother died when he was too young to work, and so poor little Dick was very badly off. He was quite glad to get the parings of the potatoes to eat and a dry crust of bread now and then, and more than that he did not often get, for the village where he lived was a very poor one and the neighbours were not able to spare him much.

Now the country folk in those days thought that the people of London were all fine ladies and gentlemen, and that there was singing and dancing all the day long, and so rich were they there that even the streets, they said, were paved with gold. Dick used to sit by and listen while all these strange tales of the wealth of London were told, and it made him long to go and live there and have plenty to eat and fine clothes to wear, instead of the rags and hard fare that fell to his lot in the country.

So one day when a great waggon with eight horses stopped on its way through the village, Dick made friends

with the waggoner and begged to be taken with him to
London.   The man felt sorry for poor little Dick when he
heard that he had no father or mother to take care of him,
and saw how ragged and how badly in need of help he was.
So he agreed to take him, and off they set.

How far it was and how many days they took over the
journey I do not know, but in due time Dick found himself
in the wonderful city which he had heard so much of and
pictured to himself so grandly.   But oh ! how disappointed
he was when he got there.   How
dirty it was !   And the people,
how unlike the gay company,
with music and singing, that he
had dreamt of !   He wandered
up and down the streets, one
after another, until he was tired
out, but not one did he find
that was paved with gold.   Dirt
in plenty he could see, but none
of the gold that he thought to
have put in his pockets as fast
as he chose to pick it up.

Little Dick ran about till he
was tired and it was growing
dark.   And at last he sat himself down in a corner and fell
asleep.   When morning came
he was very cold and hungry,

and though he asked every one he met to help him, only one or two gave him a halfpenny to buy some bread. For two or three days he lived in the streets in this way, only just able to keep himself alive, when he managed to get some work to do in a hayfield, and that kept him for a short time longer, till the haymaking was over.

After this he was as badly off as ever, and did not know where to turn. One day in his wanderings he lay down to rest in the doorway of the house of a rich merchant whose name was Fitzwarren. But here he was soon seen by the cook-maid, who was an unkind, bad-tempered woman, and she cried out to him to be off. "Lazy rogue," she called him ; and she said she'd precious quick throw some dirty dish-water over him, boiling hot, if he didn't go. However, just then Mr. Fitzwarren himself came home to dinner, and when he saw what was happening, he asked Dick why he was lying there. "You're old enough to be at work, my boy," he said. "I'm afraid you have a mind to be lazy."

"Indeed, sir," said Dick to him, "indeed that is not so " ; and he told him how hard he had tried to get work to do, and how ill he was for want of food. Dick, poor fellow, was now so weak that though he tried to stand he had to lie down again, for it was more than three days since he had had anything to eat at all. The kind merchant gave orders for him to be taken into the house and gave him a good dinner, and then he said that he was to be kept, to do what work he could to help the cook.

And now Dick would have been happy enough in this

good family if it had not been for the ill-natured cook, who did her best to make life a burden to him. Night and morning she was for ever scolding him. Nothing he did was good enough. It was " Look sharp here " and " Hurry up there," and there was no pleasing her. And many's the beating he had from the broomstick or the ladle, or whatever else she had in her hand.

At last it came to the ears of Miss Alice, Mr. Fitzwarren's daughter, how badly the cook was treating poor Dick. And she told the cook that she would quickly lose her place if she didn't treat him more kindly, for Dick had become quite a favourite with the family.

After that the cook's behaviour was a little better, but Dick still had another hardship that he bore with difficulty. For he slept in a garret where were so many holes in the walls and the floor that every night as he lay in bed the room was overrun with rats and mice, and sometimes he could hardly sleep a wink. One day when he had earned a penny for cleaning a gentleman's shoes, he met a little girl with a cat in her arms, and asked whether she would not sell it to him. " Yes, she would," she said, though the cat was such a good mouser that she was sorry to part with her. This just suited Dick, who kept pussy up in his garret, feeding her on scraps of his own dinner that he saved for her every day. In a little while he had no more bother with the rats and mice. Puss soon saw to that, and he slept sound every night.

Soon after this Mr. Fitzwarren had a ship ready to sail ; and as it was his custom that all his servants should be given a chance of good fortune as well as himself, he called them all into the counting-house and asked them what they would send out.

They all had something that they were willing to venture except poor Dick, who had neither money nor goods, and so could send nothing. For this reason he did not come into the room with the rest. But Miss Alice guessed what was the matter, and ordered him to be called in. She then said, " I will lay down some money for him out of my own purse " ; but her father told her that would not do, for it must be something of his own.

When Dick heard this he said, " I have nothing whatever but a cat, which I bought for a penny some time ago."

" Go, my boy, fetch your cat then," said his master, " and let her go."

Dick went upstairs and fetched poor puss, but there were tears in his eyes when he gave her to the captain. " For," he said, " I shall now be kept awake all night by the rats and mice." All the company laughed at Dick's odd venture, and Miss Alice, who felt sorry for him, gave him some money to buy another cat.

Now this, and other marks of kindness shown him by Miss Alice, made the ill-tempered cook jealous of poor Dick, and she began to use him more cruelly than ever, and was always making game of him for sending his cat to sea. " What do you think your cat will sell for ? " she'd ask. " As much money as would buy a stick to beat you with ? "

At last poor Dick could not bear this usage any longer,

and he thought he would run away. So he made a bundle
of his things—he hadn't many—and started very early in the
morning, on All-hallows Day, the first of November. He
walked as far as Holloway, and there he sat down to rest
on a stone, which to this day, they say, is called " Whittington's Stone," and began to wonder to himself which road
he should take.

While he was thinking what he should do the Bells of
Bow Church in Cheapside began to chime, and as they rang
he fancied that they were singing over and over again :

> " Turn again, Whittington,
> Lord Mayor of London."

" Lord Mayor of London ! " said he to himself. " Why,
to be sure, wouldn't I put up with almost anything now to

be Lord Mayor of London, and ride in a fine coach, when
I grow to be a man ! Well, I'll go back, and think nothing
of the cuffing and scolding of the cross old cook if I am to
be Lord Mayor of London at last."

So back he went, and he was lucky enough to get into
the house and set about his work before the cook came
down.

But now you must hear what befell Mrs. Puss all this
while. The ship *Unicorn* that she was on was a long time
at sea, and the cat made herself useful, as she would, among
the unwelcome rats that lived on board too. At last the ship
put into harbour on the coast of Barbary, where the only
people are the Moors. They had never before seen a ship
from England, and flocked in numbers to see the sailors,
whose different colour and foreign dress were a great wonder
to them. They were soon eager to buy the goods with
which the ship was laden, and patterns were sent ashore for
the King to see. He was so much pleased with them that
he sent for the captain to come to the palace, and honoured
him with an invitation to dinner. But no sooner were they
seated, as is the custom there, on the fine rugs and carpets
that covered the floor, than great numbers of rats and mice
came scampering in, swarming over all the dishes, and helping
themselves from all the good things there were to eat. The
captain was amazed, and wondered whether they didn't find
such a pest most unpleasant.

" Oh yes," said they, " it was so, and the King would
give half his treasure to be freed of them, for they not only

When Puss saw the rats and mice she didn't wait to be told.

spoil his dinner, but they even attack him in his bed at night, so that a watch has to be kept while he is sleeping, for fear of them."

The captain was overjoyed ; he thought at once of poor Dick Whittington and his cat, and said he had a creature on board ship that would soon do for all these vermin if she were there.   Of course, when the King heard this he was eager to possess this wonderful animal.

"Bring it to me at once," he said ; "for the vermin are dreadful, and if only it will do what you say, I will load your ship with gold and jewels in exchange for it."

The captain, who knew his business, took care not to underrate the value of Dick's cat.   He told His Majesty how inconvenient it would be to part with her, as when she was gone the rats might destroy the goods in the ship ; however, to oblige the King, he would fetch her.

"Oh, make haste, do !" cried the Queen ; "I, too, am all impatience to see this dear creature."

Off went the captain, while another dinner was got ready.   He took Puss under his arm and got back to the palace just in time to see the carpet covered with rats and mice once again.   When Puss saw them, she didn't wait to be told, but jumped out of the captain's arms, and in no time almost all the rats and mice were dead at her feet, while the rest of them had scuttled off to their holes in fright.

The King was delighted to get rid so easily of such an intolerable plague, and the Queen desired that the animal who had done them such a service might be brought to her.

Upon which the captain called out, " Puss, puss, puss," and she came running to him.   Then he presented her to the Queen, who was rather afraid at first to touch a creature who had made such a havoc with her claws.   However, when the captain called her, " Pussy, pussy," and began to stroke her, the Queen also ventured to touch her and cried, " Putty, putty," in imitation of the captain, for she hadn't learned to speak English.   He then put her on to the Queen's lap, where she purred and played with Her Majesty's hand and was soon asleep.

The King having seen what Mrs. Puss could do, and learning that her kittens would soon stock the whole country, and keep it free from rats, after bargaining with the captain for the whole ship's cargo, then gave him ten times as much for the cat as all the rest amounted to.

The captain then said farewell to the court of Barbary, and after a fair voyage reached London again with his precious load of gold and jewels safe and sound.

One morning early Mr. Fitzwarren had just come to his counting-house and settled himself at the desk to count the cash, when there came a knock at the door.   " Who's there ? " said he.   " A friend," replied a voice.   " I come with good news of your ship the *Unicorn*."   The merchant in haste opened the door, and who were there but the ship's captain and the mate, bearing a chest of jewels and a bill of lading.   When he had looked this over he lifted his eyes and thanked heaven for sending him such a prosperous voyage.

The honest captain next told him all about the cat, and

showed him the rich present the King had sent for her to poor Dick.   Rejoicing on behalf of Dick as much as he had done over his own good fortune, he called out to his servants to come and to bring up Dick :

> " Go fetch him, and we'll tell him of his fame ;
> Pray call him Mr. Whittington by name."

The servants, some of them, hesitated at this, and said so great a treasure was too much for a lad like Dick ; but Mr. Fitzwarren now showed himself the good man that he was and refused to deprive him of the value of a single penny. " God forbid ! " he cried.   " It's all his own, and he shall have it, to a farthing."

He then sent for Dick, who at the moment was scouring pots for the cook and was black with dirt.   He tried to excuse himself from coming into the room in such a plight, but the merchant made him come, and had a chair set for him.   And he then began to think they must be making game of him, so he begged them not to play tricks on a poor simple boy, but to let him go downstairs again back to his work in the scullery.

" Indeed, Mr. Whittington," said the merchant, " we are all quite in earnest with you, and I most heartily rejoice at the news that these gentlemen have brought.   For the captain has sold your cat to the King of Barbary, and brings you in return for her more riches than I possess in the whole world ; and may you long enjoy them ! "

Mr. Fitzwarren then told the men to open the great

treasure they had brought with them, saying, "There is nothing more now for Mr. Whittington to do but to put it in some place of safety."

Poor Dick hardly knew how to behave himself for joy. He begged his master to take what part of it he pleased, since he owed it all to his kindness. "No, no," answered Mr. Fitzwarren, "this all belongs to you; and I have no doubt that you will use it well."

Dick next begged his mistress, and then Miss Alice, to accept a part of his good fortune, but they would not, and at the same time told him what great joy they felt at his great success. But he was far too kind-hearted to keep it all to himself; so he made a present to the captain, the mate, and the rest of Mr. Fitzwarren's servants; and even to his old enemy, the cross cook.

After this Mr. Fitzwarren advised him to send for a tailor and get himself dressed like a gentleman, and told him he was welcome to live in his house till he could provide himself with a better.

When Whittington's face was washed, his hair curled, and he was dressed in a smart suit of clothes, he was just as handsome and fine a young man as any who visited at Mr. Fitzwarren's, and so thought fair Alice Fitzwarren, who had once been so kind to him and looked upon him with pity. And now she felt he was quite fit to be her sweetheart, and none the less, no doubt, because Whittington was always thinking what he could do to please her, and making her the prettiest presents that could be.

Mr. Fitzwarren soon saw which way the wind blew, and ere long proposed to join them in marriage, and to this they both readily agreed.   A day for the wedding was soon fixed ; and they were attended to church by the Lord Mayor, the court of aldermen, the sheriffs, and a great number of the richest merchants in London, whom they afterwards treated with a magnificent feast.

History tells us that Mr. Whittington and his lady lived in great splendour, and were very happy.   They had several children.   He was Sheriff, and thrice Lord Mayor of London, and received the honour of knighthood from Henry V.

After the King's conquest of France, Sir Richard Whittington entertained him and the Queen at dinner at the Mansion House in so sumptuous a manner that the King said, " Never had Prince such a subject ! "   To which Sir Richard replied, " Never had subject such a Prince."

THE OLD WOMAN AND HER PIG

AN old woman was sweeping her house, and she found a little crooked sixpence. "What," said she, "shall I do with this little sixpence? I will go to market, and buy a little pig."

So she bought a little pig; but as she was coming home, she came to a stile, and the piggy would not go over the stile.

She went a little further, and she met a dog. So she said to him, "Dog! dog! bite pig; piggy won't go over the stile; and I shan't get home till midnight." But the dog wouldn't.

She went a little further, and she met a stick. So she said, " Stick ! stick ! beat dog ; dog won't bite pig ; piggy won't get over the stile ; and I shan't get home till midnight." But the stick wouldn't.

She went a little further, and she met a fire. So she said, " Fire ! fire ! burn stick ; stick won't beat dog ; dog won't bite pig ; pig won't get over the stile ; and I shan't get home till midnight." But the fire wouldn't.

She went a little further, and she met some water. So she said, " Water ! water ! quench fire ; fire won't burn stick ; stick won't beat dog ; dog won't bite pig ; pig won't get over the stile ; and I shan't get home till midnight." But the water wouldn't.

She went a little further, and she met an ox. So she said, " Ox ! ox ! drink water ; water won't quench fire ; fire won't burn stick ; stick won't beat dog ; dog won't bite pig ; pig won't get over the stile ; and I shan't get home till midnight." But the ox wouldn't.

She went a little further, and she met a butcher. So she said, " Butcher ! butcher ! kill ox ; ox won't drink water ; water won't quench fire ; fire won't burn stick ; stick won't beat dog ; dog won't bite pig ; pig won't get over the stile ; and I shan't get home till midnight." But the butcher wouldn't.

She went a little further, and she met a rope. So she said, " Rope ! rope ! hang butcher ; butcher won't kill ox ; ox won't drink water ; water won't quench fire ; fire won't burn stick ; stick won't beat dog ; dog won't bite pig ;

pig won't get over the stile; and I shan't get home till midnight." But the rope wouldn't.

She went a little further, and she met a rat. So she said, " Rat! rat! gnaw rope; rope won't hang butcher; butcher won't kill ox; ox won't drink water; water won't quench fire; fire won't burn stick; stick won't beat dog; dog won't bite pig; pig won't get over the stile; and I shan't get home till midnight." But the rat wouldn't.

She went a little further, and she met a cat. So she said, " Cat! cat! kill rat; rat won't gnaw rope; rope won't hang butcher; butcher won't kill ox; ox won't drink water; water won't quench fire; fire won't burn stick; stick won't beat dog; dog won't bite pig; pig won't get over the stile; and I shan't get home till midnight." But the cat said to her, " If you will go to yonder cow, and fetch me a saucer of milk, I will kill the rat." So away went the old woman to the cow.

But the cow said to her, " If you will go to yonder haystack, and fetch me a handful of hay, I'll give you the milk." So away went the old woman to the haystack; and she brought the hay to the cow.

As soon as the cow had eaten the hay, she gave the old woman the milk; and away she went with it in a saucer to the cat.

As soon as the cat had lapped up the milk, the cat began to kill the rat; the rat began to gnaw the rope; the rope began to hang the butcher; the butcher began to kill the ox ; the ox began to drink the water ; the water began to quench the fire ; the fire began to burn the stick ; the stick began to beat the dog ; the dog began to bite the pig ; the little pig squealed and jumped over the stile ; and so the old woman got home before midnight.

THE WEE BANNOCK

ONCE upon a time there was an old man and his old wife who lived in a wee cottage beside a wee burnie. They had two cows, five hens, and a cock, a cat and two kittens. Now the old man looked after the cows, the cock looked after the hens, the cat looked after a mouse in the cupboard, and the two kittens looked after the old wife's spindle as it twirled and tussled about on the hearthstone. But though the old wife should have looked after the kittens, the more she said, "Sho! Sho! Go away, kitty!" the more they looked after the spindle!

So, one day, when she was quite tired out with saying, "Sho! Sho!" the old wife felt hungry and thought she could take a wee bite of something. So she up and baked two wee oatmeal bannocks and set them to toast before the fire. Now just as they were toasting away, smelling so fresh and tasty, in came the old man, and seeing them look so crisp and nice, takes up one of them and snaps a piece out of it. On this the other bannock thought it high time to be off, so up it jumps and away it trundles as fast as ever it could. And away ran the old wife after it as fast as she could run, with her spindle in one hand and her distaff in the other. But the wee bannock trundled faster than she could run, so it was soon out of sight, and the old wife was obliged to go back and tussle with the kittens again.

The wee bannock meanwhile trundled gaily down the hill till it came to a big thatched house, and it ran boldly in at the door and sate itself down by the fireside quite comfortably. Now there were three tailors in the room working away on a big bench, and being tailors they were, of course, dreadfully afraid, and jumped up to hide behind the goodwife who was carding wool by the fire.

"Hout-tout!" she cried. "What are ye a-feared of? 'Tis naught but a wee bit bannock. Just grip hold o' it, and I'll give ye a sup o' milk to drink with it."

So up she gets with the carders in her hands, and the tailor had his iron goose, and the apprentices, one with the big scissors and the other with the ironing-board, and they all made for the wee bannock; but it was too clever for them, and dodged about the fireside until the apprentice, thinking to snap it with the big scissors, fell into the hot ashes and got badly burnt. Then the tailor cast the goose at it, and the other apprentice the ironing-board; but it wouldn't do. The wee bannock got out at the doorway, where the goodwife flung the carders at it; but it dodged them and trundled away gaily till it came to a small house by the road-side. So in it ran bold as bold and sate itself down by the hearth where the wife was winding a clue of

R

yarn for her husband, the weaver, who was click-clacking away at his loom.

"Tibby!" quoth the weaver. "Whatever's that?"

"Naught but a wee bannock," quoth she.

"Well, come and welcome," says he, "for the porridge was thin the morn; so grip it, woman! grip it!"

"Aye," says she, and reaches out her hand to it. But the wee bannock just dodged.

"Man!" says she, "yon's a clever wee bannockie! Catch it, man! Catch it if you can."

But the wee bannock just dodged. "Cast the clue at it, woman!" shouted the weaver.

But the wee bannock was out at the door, trundling away over the hill like a new tarred sheep or a mad cow!

And it trundled away till it came to a cowherd's house where the goodwife was churning her butter.

"Come in by," cried the goodwife when she saw the wee bannock all crisp and fresh and tasty; "I've plenty cream to eat with you."

But at this the wee bannock began dodging about, and it dodged so craftily that the goodwife overset the churn in trying to grip it, and before she set it straight again the wee bannock was off, trundling away down the hill till it came to a mill-house where the miller was sifting meal. So in it ran and sate down by the trough.

"Ho, ho!" says the miller. "It's a sign o' plenty when the likes of you run about the country-side with none to look after you. But come in by. I like bannock and cheese for supper, so I'll give ye a night's quarters." And with that he tapped his fat stomach.

At this the wee bannock turned and ran; it wasn't going to trust itself with the miller and his cheese; and the miller, having nothing but the meal to fling after it, just stood and stared; so the wee bannock trundled quietly along the level till it came to the smithy where the smith was welding horse-nails.

"Hullo!" says he, "you're a well-toasted bannock. You'll do fine with a glass of ale! So come in by and I'll give you a lodging inside." And with that he laughed, and tapped his fat stomach.

But the wee bannock thought the ale was as bad as the cheese, so it up and away, with the smith after it. And when he couldn't come up with it, he just cast his hammer at it. But the hammer missed and the wee bannock was out of sight in a crack, and trundled and trundled till it came to a farm-house where the goodman and his wife were beating out flax and combing it. So it ran in to the fireside and began to toast itself again.

"Janet," says the goodman, "yon is a well-toasted wee bannock. I'll have the half of it."

"And I'll take t'other half," says the goodwife, and reached out a hand to grip it. But the wee bannock played dodgings again.

"My certy," says the wife, "but you're spirity!" And with that she cast the flax comb at it. But it was too clever for her, so out it trundled through the door and away was it down the road, till it came to another house where the goodwife was stirring the scalding soup and the goodman was plaiting a thorn collar for the calf. So it trundled in, and sate down by the fire.

" Ho, Jock !" quoth the goodwife, " you're always crying on a well-toasted bannock. Here's one ! Come and eat it !"

Then the wee bannock tried dodgings again, and the goodwife cried on the goodman to help her grip it.

" Aye, mother !" says he, " but where's it gone ? "

" Over there !" cries she. " Quick ! run to t'other side o' yon chair." And the chair upset, and down came the goodman among the thorns. And the goodwife she flung the soup spoon at it, and the scalding soup fell on the goodman and scalded him, so the wee bannock ran out in a crack and was away to the next house, where the folk were just sitting down to their supper and the goodwife was scraping the pot.

" Look !" cries she, " here's a wee well-toasted bannock for him as catches it !"

" Let's shut the door first," says the cautious goodman, " afore we try to get a grip on it."

Now when the wee bannock heard this it judged it was time to be off ; so away it trundled and they after it helter-skelter. But though they threw their spoons at it, and the goodman cast his best hat, the wee bannock was too clever for them, and was out of sight in a crack.

Then away it trundled till it came to a house where the folk were just away to their beds. The goodwife she was raking out the fire, and the goodman had taken off his breeches.

"What's yon?" says he, for it was nigh dark.

"It will just be a wee bannock," says she.

"I could eat the half of it," says he.

"And I could eat t'other," quoth she.

Then they tried to grip it; but the wee bannock tried dodging. And the goodman and the goodwife tumbled against each other in the dark and grew angry.

"Cast your breeches at it, man!" cries the goodwife at last. "What's the use of standing staring like a stuck pig?"

So the goodman cast his breeches at it and thought he had smothered it sure enough; but somehow it wriggled out, and away it was, the goodman after it without his breeches. You never saw such a race—a real clean chase over the park, and through the whins, and round by the bramble patch. But there the goodman lost sight of it and had to go back all scratched and tired and shivering.

The wee bannock, however, trundled on till it was too dark even for a wee bannock to see.

Then it came to a fox's hole in the side of a big whin-bush and trundled in to spend the night there; but the fox had had no meat for three whole days, so he just said, "You're welcome, friend! I wish there were two of you!"

And there were two! For he snapped the wee bannock into halves with one bite. So that was an end of *it*!

JIGGELTY-JOLT

HOW JACK WENT OUT TO SEEK HIS FORTUNE

ONCE on a time there was a boy named Jack, and one morning he started to go and seek his fortune.

He hadn't gone very far before he met a cat.

" Where are you going, Jack ? " said the cat.

" I am going to seek my fortune."

" May I go with you ? "

" Yes," said Jack, " the more the merrier."

So on they went, Jack and the cat. Jiggelty-jolt, jiggelty-jolt, jiggelty-jolt !

They went a little farther and they met a dog.

" Where are you going, Jack ? " said the dog.

" I am going to seek my fortune."

" May I go with you ? "

" Yes," said Jack, " the more the merrier."

So on they went, Jack, the cat, and the dog! Jiggelty-jolt, jiggelty-jolt, jiggelty-jolt!

They went a little farther and they met a goat.

"Where are you going, Jack?" said the goat.

"I am going to seek my fortune."

"May I go with you?"

"Yes," said Jack, "the more the merrier."

So on they went, Jack, the cat, the dog, and the goat. Jiggelty-jolt, jiggelty-jolt, jiggelty-jolt!

They went a little farther and they met a bull.

"Where are you going, Jack?" said the bull.

"I am going to seek my fortune."

"May I go with you?"

"Yes," said Jack, "the more the merrier."

So on they went, Jack, the cat, the dog, the goat, and the bull. Jiggelty-jolt, jiggelty-jolt, jiggelty-jolt!

They went a little farther and they met a rooster.

"Where are you going, Jack?" said the rooster.

"I am going to seek my fortune."

"May I go with you?"

"Yes," said Jack, "the more the merrier."

So on they went, Jack, the cat, the dog, the goat, the bull, and the rooster. Jiggelty-jolt, jiggelty-jolt, jiggelty-jolt!

And they went on jiggelty-jolting till it was about dark, and it was time to think of some place where they could spend the night. Now, after a bit, they came in sight of a house, and Jack told his companions to keep still while he went up and looked in through the window to see if all was safe. And what did he see through the window but a band of robbers seated at a table counting over great bags of gold !

" That gold shall be mine," quoth Jack to himself. " I have found my fortune already."

Then he went back and told his companions to wait till he gave the word, and then to make all the noise they possibly could in their own fashion. So when they were all ready Jack gave the word, and the cat mewed, and the dog barked, and the goat bleated, and the bull bellowed, and the rooster crowed, and all together they made such a terrific hubbub that the robbers jumped up in a fright and ran away, leaving their gold on the table. So, after a good laugh, Jack and his companions went in and took possession of the house and the gold.

Now Jack was a wise boy, and he knew that the robbers would come back in the dead of the night to get their gold, and so when it came time to go to bed he put the cat in the rocking-chair, and he put the dog under the table, and he put the goat upstairs, and he put the bull in the cellar, and bade the rooster fly up on to the roof.

Then he went to bed.

Now sure enough, in the dead of the night, the robbers sent one man back to the house to look after their money. But before long he came back in a great fright and told them a fearsome tale !

" I went back to the house," said he, " and went in and

tried to sit down in the rocking-chair, and there was an old woman knitting there, and she—oh my !—stuck her knitting-needles into me."

(*That was the cat, you know.*)

" Then I went to the table to look after the money, but there was a shoemaker under the table, and my ! how he stuck his awl into me."

(*That was the dog, you know.*)

" So I started to go upstairs, but there was a man up there threshing, and goody ! how he knocked me down with his flail ! "

(*That was the goat, you know.*)

" Then I started to go down to the cellar, but—oh dear me !—there was a man down there chopping wood, and he knocked me up and he knocked me down just terrible with his axe."

(*That was the bull, you know.*)

" But I shouldn't have minded all that if it hadn't been for an awful little fellow on the top of the house by the kitchen chimney, who kept a-hollering and hollering, ' Cook him in a stew ! Cook him in a stew ! Cook him in a stew ! ' "

(*And that, of course, was the cock-a-doodle-doo.*)

Then the robbers agreed that they would rather lose their gold than meet with such a fate ; so they made off, and Jack next morning went gaily home with his booty. And each of the animals carried a portion of it. The cat hung a bag on its tail (a cat when it walks always carries its tail stiff), the dog on his collar, the goat and the bull on their horns, but Jack made the rooster carry a golden guinea in its beak to prevent it from calling all the time :

" Cock-a-doodle-doo,
Cook him in a stew ! "

THE BOGEY-BEAST

THERE was once a woman who was very, very cheerful, though she had little to make her so; for she was old, and poor, and lonely. She lived in a little bit of a cottage and earned a scant living by running errands for her neighbours, getting a bite here, a sup there, as reward for her services. So she made shift to get on, and always looked as spry and cheery as if she had not a want in the world.

Now one summer evening, as she was trotting, full of smiles as ever, along the high road to her hovel, what should she see but a big black pot lying in the ditch!

"Goodness me!" she cried, "that would be just the very thing for me if I only had something to put in it! But I haven't! Now who could have left it in the ditch?"

And she looked about her expecting the owner would not be far off; but she could see nobody.

"Maybe there is a hole in it," she went on, "and that's why it has been cast away. But it would do fine to put a flower in for my window; so I'll just take it home with me."

And with that she lifted the lid and looked inside.
" Mercy me ! " she cried, fair amazed.   " If it isn't full of
gold pieces.   Here's luck ! "

And so it was, brimful of great gold coins.   Well, at first
she simply stood stock-still, wondering if she was standing
on her head or her heels.   Then she began saying :

" Lawks !   But I *do* feel rich.   I feel awful rich ! "

After she had said this many times, she began to wonder
how she was to get her treasure home.   It was too heavy
for her to carry, and she could see no better way than to tie
the end of her shawl to it and drag it behind her like a
go-cart.

" It will soon be dark," she said to herself as she trotted
along.   " So much the better !   The neighbours will not see
what I'm bringing home, and I shall have all the night to
myself, and be able to think what I'll do !   Mayhap I'll
buy a grand house and just sit by the fire with a cup o' tea
and do no work at all like a queen.   Or maybe I'll bury
it at the garden foot and just keep a bit in the old china
teapot on the chimney - piece.   Or maybe —— Goody !
Goody !   I feel that grand I don't know myself."

By this time she was a bit tired of dragging such a heavy
weight, and, stopping to rest a while, turned to look at her
treasure.

And lo ! it wasn't a pot of gold at all !   It was nothing
but a lump of silver.

She stared at it, and rubbed her eyes, and stared at it
again.

"Well! I never!" she said at last. "And me thinking it was a pot of gold! I must have been dreaming. But this is luck! Silver is far less trouble—easier to mind, and not so easy stolen. Them gold pieces would have been the death o' me, and with this great lump of silver——"

So she went off again planning what she would do, and feeling as rich as rich, until becoming a bit tired again she stopped to rest and gave a look round to see if her treasure was safe ; and she saw nothing but a great lump of iron !

"Well! I never!" says she again. "And I mistaking it for silver! I must have been dreaming. But this is luck! It's real convenient. I can get penny pieces for old iron, and penny pieces are a deal handier for me than your gold and silver. Why! I should never have slept a wink for fear of being robbed. But a penny piece comes in useful, and I shall sell that iron for a lot and be real rich—rolling rich."

So on she trotted full of plans as to how she would spend her penny pieces, till once more she stopped to rest and looked round to see her treasure was safe. And this time she saw nothing but a big stone.

"Well! I never!" she cried, full of smiles. "And to think I mistook it for iron. I must have been dreaming. But here's luck indeed, and me wanting a stone terrible bad to stick open the gate. Eh my! but it's a change for the better! It's a fine thing to have good luck."

So, all in a hurry to see how the stone would keep the gate open, she trotted off down the hill till she came to her own cottage. She unlatched the gate and then turned to unfasten her shawl from the stone which lay on the path behind her. Aye! it was a stone sure enough. There was plenty light to see it lying there, douce and peaceable as a stone should.

So she bent over it to unfasten the shawl end, when——
" Oh my ! "

All of a sudden it gave a jump, a squeal, and in one moment was as big as a haystack. Then it let down four great lanky legs and threw out two long ears, flourished a great long tail and romped off, kicking and squealing and whinnying and laughing like a naughty, mischievous boy !

The old woman stared after it till it was fairly out of sight, then she burst out laughing too.

" Well ! " she chuckled, " I am in luck ! Quite the luckiest body hereabouts. Fancy my seeing the Bogey-Beast all to myself ; and making myself so free with it too ! My goodness ! I do feel that uplifted — that *GRAND !* "——

So she went into her cottage and spent the evening chuckling over her good luck.

"Well!" she chuckled, "I am in luck!"

LITTLE RED RIDING-HOOD

ONCE upon a time there was a little girl who was called little Red Riding-Hood, because she was quite small and because she always wore a red cloak with a big red hood to it, which her grandmother had made for her.

Now one day her mother, who had been churning and baking cakes, said to her :

" My dear, put on your red cloak with the hood to it, and take this cake and this pot of butter to your Grannie, and ask how she is, for I hear she is ailing."

Now little Red Riding-Hood was very fond of her grandmother, who made her so many nice things, so she put on her cloak joyfully and started on her errand. But her grandmother lived some way off, and to reach the cottage little Red Riding-Hood had to pass through a vast lonely forest. However, some wood-cutters were at work in it, so little Red Riding-Hood was not so very much alarmed when she saw a great big wolf coming towards her, because she knew that wolves were cowardly things.

And sure enough the wolf, though but for the wood-cutters he would surely have eaten little Red Riding-Hood, only stopped and asked her politely where she was going.

"I am going to see Grannie, take her this cake and this pot of butter, and ask how she is," says little Red Riding-Hood.

"Does she live a very long way off?" asks the wolf craftily.

"Not so very far if you go by the straight road," replied little Red Riding-Hood. "You only have to pass the mill and the first cottage on the right is Grannie's; but I am going by the wood path because there are such a lot of nuts and flowers and butterflies."

"I wish you good luck," says the wolf politely. "Give my respects to your grandmother and tell her I hope she is quite well."

And with that he trotted off. But instead of going his ways he turned back, took the straight road to the old woman's cottage, and knocked at the door.

Rap! Rap! Rap!

"Who's there?" asked the old woman, who was in bed.

"Little Red Riding-Hood," sings out the wolf, making his voice as shrill as he could. "I've come to bring dear Grannie a pot of butter and a cake from mother, and to ask how you are."

"Pull the bobbin, and the latch will go up," says the old woman, well satisfied.

So the wolf pulled the bobbin, the latch went up, and—

oh my !—it wasn't a minute before he had gobbled up old Grannie, for he had had nothing to eat for a week.

Then he shut the door, put on Grannie's night-cap, and, getting into bed, rolled himself well up in the clothes.

By and by along comes little Red Riding-Hood, who had been amusing herself by gathering nuts, running after butterflies, and picking flowers.

So she knocked at the door.

Rap ! Rap ! Rap !

" Who's there ? " says the wolf, making his voice as soft as he could.

Now little Red Riding-Hood heard the voice was very gruff, but she thought her grandmother had a cold ; so she said :

" Little Red Riding-Hood, with a pot of butter and a cake from mother, to ask how you are."

" Pull the bobbin, and the latch will go up."

So little Red Riding-Hood pulled the bobbin, the latch went up, and there, she thought, was her grandmother in the bed ; for the cottage was so dark one could not see well. Besides, the crafty wolf turned his face to the wall at first. And he made his voice as soft, as soft as he could, when he said :

" Come and kiss me, my dear."

Then little Red Riding-Hood took off her cloak and went to the bed.

" Oh, Grandmamma, Grandmamma," says she, " what big arms you've got ! "

s

" All the better to hug you with," says he.

" But, Grandmamma, Grandmamma, what big legs you have ! "

" All the better to run with, my dear."

" Oh, Grandmamma, Grandmamma, what big ears you've got ! "

" All the better to hear with, my dear."

" But, Grandmamma, Grandmamma, what big eyes you've got ! "

" All the better to see you with, my dear ! "

" Oh, Grandmamma, Grandmamma, what big teeth you've got ! "

" All the better to eat you with, my dear ! " says that wicked, wicked wolf, and with that he gobbled up little Red Riding-Hood.

CHILDE ROWLAND

CHILDE ROWLAND and his brothers twain
Were playing at the ball.
Their sister, Burd Helen, she played
In the midst among them all.

For Burd Helen loved her brothers, and they loved her
exceedingly. At play she was ever their companion and
they cared for her as brothers should. And one day when
they were at ball close to the churchyard—

Childe Rowland kicked it with his foot
And caught it on his knee.
At last as he plunged among them all,
O'er the church he made it flee.

Now Childe Rowland was Burd Helen's youngest,
dearest brother, and there was ever a loving rivalry between
them as to which should win. So with a laugh—

Burd Helen round about the aisle
To seek the ball is gone.

Now the ball had trundled to the right of the church;
so, as Burd Helen ran the nearest way to get it, she ran

contrary to the sun's course, and the light, shining full on her face, sent her shadow behind her. Thus that happened which will happen at times when folk forget and run widershins, that is against the light, so that their shadows are out of sight and cannot be taken care of properly.

Now what happened you will learn by and by ; meanwhile, Burd Helen's three brothers waited for her return.

> But long they waited, and longer still,
> And she came not back again.

Then they grew alarmed, and—

> They sought her east, they sought her west,
> They sought her up and down.
> And woe were the hearts of her brethren,
> Since she was not to be found.

Not to be found anywhere—she had disappeared like dew on a May morning.

So at last her eldest brother went to Great Merlin the Magician, who could tell and foretell, see and foresee all things under the sun and beyond it, and asked him where Burd Helen could have gone.

"Fair Burd Helen," said the Magician, "must have been carried off with her shadow by the fairies when she was running round the church widershins ; for fairies have power when folk go against the light. She will now be in the Dark Tower of the King of Elfland, and none but the boldest knight in Christendom will be able to bring her back."

"If it be possible to bring her back," said the eldest brother, "I will do it, or perish in the attempt."

"Possible it is," quoth Merlin the Magician gravely. "But woe be to the man or mother's son who attempts the task if he be not well taught beforehand what he is to do."

Now the eldest brother of fair Burd Helen was brave indeed, danger did not dismay him, so he begged the Magician to tell him exactly what he should do, and what he should not do, as he was determined to go and seek his sister. And the Great Magician told him, and schooled him, and after he had learnt his lesson right well he girt on his sword, said good-bye to his brothers and his mother, and set out for the Dark Tower of Elfland to bring Burd Helen back.

> But long they waited, and longer still,
> With doubt and muckle pain.
> But woe were the hearts of his brethren,
> For he came not back again.

So after a time Burd Helen's second brother went to Merlin the Magician and said :

"School me also, for I go to find my brother and sister in the Dark Tower of the King of Elfland and bring them back." For he also was brave indeed, danger did not dismay him.

Then when he had been well schooled and had learnt his lesson, he said good-bye to Childe Rowland, his brother, and to his mother the good Queen, girt on his sword, and

set out for the Dark Tower of Elfland to bring back Burd
Helen and her brother.

> But long they waited, and longer still,
> With muckle doubt and pain.
> And woe were his mother's and brother's hearts,
> For he came not back again.

Now when they had waited and waited a long, long
time, and none had come back from the Dark Tower of
Elfland, Childe Rowland, the youngest, the best beloved
of Burd Helen's brothers, besought his mother to let him
also go on the quest ; for he was the bravest of them all,
and neither death nor danger could dismay him.   But at
first his mother the Queen said :

"Not so ! You are the last of my children ; if you
are lost, all is lost indeed !"

But he begged so hard that at length the good Queen
his mother bade him God-speed, and girt about his waist
his father's sword, the brand that never struck in vain, and
as she girt it on she chanted the spell that gives victory.

So Childe Rowland bade her good-bye and went to the
cave of the Great Magician Merlin.

"Yet once more, Master," said the youth, "and but
once more, tell how man or mother's son may find fair
Burd Helen and her brothers twain in the Dark Tower of
Elfland."

"My son," replied the wizard Merlin, "there be things
twain ; simple they seem to say, but hard are they to per-
form.   One thing is to do, and one thing is not to do.

Now the first thing you have to do is this: after you have once entered the Land of Faery, *whoever speaks to you*, you must out with your father's brand and cut off their head. In this you must not fail. And the second thing you have not to do is this: after you have entered the Land of Faery, bite no bit, sup no drop; for if in Elfland you sup one drop or bite one bit, never again will you see Middle Earth."

Then Childe Rowland said these two lessons over and over until he knew them by heart; so, well schooled, he thanked the Great Master and went on his way to seek the Dark Tower of Elfland.

And he journeyed far, and he journeyed fast, until at last on a wide moorland he came upon a horse-herd feeding his horses; and the horses were wild, and their eyes were like coals of fire.

Then he knew they must be the horses of the King of Elfland, and that at last he must be in the Land of Faery.

So Childe Rowland said to the horse-herd, "Canst tell me where lies the Dark Tower of the Elfland King?"

And the horse-herd answered, "Nay, that is beyond my ken; but go a little farther and thou wilt come to a cow-herd who mayhap can tell thee."

Then at once Childe Rowland drew his father's sword that never struck in vain, and smote off the horse-herd's head, so that it rolled on the wide moorland and frightened the King of Elfland's horses. And he journeyed further till he came to a wide pasture where a cow-herd was herding cows. And the cows looked at him with fiery eyes, so he knew that they must be the King of Elfland's cows, and that he was still in the Land of Faery. Then he said to the cow-herd :

" Canst tell me where lies the Dark Tower of the Elfland King ? "

And the cow-herd answered, " Nay, that is beyond my ken ; but go a little farther and thou wilt come to a hen-wife who, mayhap, can tell thee."

So at once Childe Rowland, remembering his lesson, out with his father's good sword that never struck in vain, and off went the cow-herd's head spinning amongst the grasses and frightening the King of Elfland's cows.

Then he journeyed further till he came to an orchard where an old woman in a grey cloak was feeding fowls. And the fowls' little eyes were like little coals of fire, so he knew that they were the King of Elfland's fowls, and that he was still in the Land of Faery.

And he said to the hen - wife, " Canst tell me where lies the Dark Tower of the King of Elfland ? "

Now the hen-wife looked at him and smiled. " Surely I can tell you," said she. " Go on a little farther. There you will find a low green hill ; green and low against the sky. And the hill will have three terrace-rings upon it from bottom to top. Go round the first terrace saying :

' Open from within ;
Let me in ! Let me in ! '

Then go round the second terrace and say :

> ' Open wide, open wide ;
> Let me inside.'

Then go round the third terrace and say :

> ' Open fast, open fast ;
> Let me in at last.'

Then a door will open and let you in to the Dark Tower of the King of Elfland. Only remember to go round widershins. If you go round with the sun the door will not open. So good luck to you ! "

Now the hen-wife spoke so fair, and smiled so frank, that Childe Rowland forgot for a moment what he had to do. Therefore he thanked the old woman for her courtesy and was just going on, when, all of a sudden, he remembered his lesson. And he out with his father's sword that never yet struck in vain, and smote off the hen-wife's head, so that it rolled among the corn and frightened the fiery-eyed fowls of the King of Elfland.

After that he went on and on, till, against the blue sky, he saw a round green hill set with three terraces from top to bottom.

Then he did as the hen-wife had told him, not forgetting to go round widershins, so that the sun was always on his face.

Now when he had gone round the third terrace saying :

> " Open fast, open fast ;
> Let me in at last,"

what should happen but that he should see a door in the hill-side. And it opened and let him in. Then it closed behind him with a click, and Childe Rowland was left in the dark ; for he had gotten at last to the Dark Tower of the King of Elfland.

It was very dark at first, perhaps because the sun had part blinded his eyes ; for after a while it became twilight, though where the light came from none could tell, unless through the walls and the roof ; for there were neither windows nor candles. But in the gloaming light he could see a long passage of rough arches made of rock that was transparent and all encrusted with sheep-silver, rock-spar, and many bright stones. And the air was warm as it ever is in Elfland. So he went on and on in the twilight that came from nowhere, till he found himself before two wide doors all barred with iron. But they flew open at his touch, and he saw a wonderful, large, and spacious hall that seemed to him to be as long and as broad as the green hill itself. The roof was supported by pillars wide and lofty beyond the pillars of a cathedral ; and they were of gold and silver, fretted into foliage, and between and around them were woven wreaths of flowers. And the flowers were of diamonds, and rubies, and topaz, and the leaves of emerald. And the arches met in the middle of the roof where hung, by a golden chain, an immense lamp made of a hollowed pearl, white and translucent. And in the middle of this lamp was a mighty carbuncle, blood-red, that kept spinning round and round, shedding its light to the very ends of the huge hall, which thus seemed to be filled with the shining of the setting sun.

Now at one end of the hall was a marvellous, wondrous, glorious couch of velvet, and silk, and gold ; and on it sate fair Burd Helen combing her beautiful golden hair with a golden comb. But her face was all set and wan, as if it were made of stone. And when she saw Childe Rowland she never moved, and her voice came like the voice of the dead as she said :

> " God pity you, poor luckless fool !
> What have you here to do ? "

Now at first Childe Rowland felt he must clasp this semblance of his dear sister in his arms ; but he remembered the lesson which the Great Magician Merlin had taught him, and drawing his father's brand which had never yet been drawn in vain, and turning his eyes from the horrid sight, he struck with all his force at the enchanted form of fair Burd Helen.

And lo ! when he turned to look in fear and trembling, there she was her own self, her joy fighting with her fears. And she clasped him in her arms and cried :

> " Oh, hear you this, my youngest brother,
> Why didn't you bide at home ?
> Had you a hundred thousand lives,
> Ye couldn't spare ne'er a one !

> " But sit you down, my dearest dear,
> Oh ! woe that ye were born,
> For, come the King of Elfland in,
> Your fortune is forlorn."

So with tears and smiles she seated him beside her on the wondrous couch, and they told each other what they each had suffered and done. He told her how he had come to Elfland, and she told him how she had been carried off, shadow and all, because she ran round a church widershins, and how her brothers had been enchanted, and lay intombed as if dead, as she had been, because they had not had the courage to obey the Great Magician's lesson to the letter, and cut off her head.

Now after a time Childe Rowland, who had travelled far and travelled fast, became very hungry, and forgetting all about the second lesson of the Magician Merlin, asked his sister for some food. And she, being still under the spell of Elfland, could not warn him of his danger; she could only look at him sadly as she rose up and brought him a golden basin full of bread and milk.

Now in those days it was manners before taking food from any one to say thank you with your eyes, and so just as Childe Rowland was about to put the golden bowl to his lips, he raised his eyes to his sister's.

And in an instant he remembered what the Great Magician had said : " Bite no bit, sup no drop, for if in Elfland you sup one drop or bite one bit, never again will you see Middle Earth."

So he dashed the bowl to the ground, and standing square and fair, lithe and young and strong, he cried like a challenge :

" Not a sup will I swallow, not a bit will I bite, till fair Burd Helen is set free."

Then immediately there was a loud noise like thunder, and a voice was heard saying :

" Fee, fi, fo, fum,
I smell the blood of a Christian Man.
Be he alive or dead, my brand
Shall dash his brains from his brain-pan."

Then the folding-doors of the vast hall burst open and the King of Elfland entered like a storm of wind. What he was really like Childe Rowland had not time to see, for with a bold cry :

" Strike, Bogle ! thy hardest if thou darest ! " he rushed to meet the foe, his good sword, that never yet did fail, in his hand.

And Childe Rowland and the King of Elfland fought, and fought, and fought, while Burd Helen, with her hands clasped, watched them in fear and hope.

So they fought, and fought, and fought, until at last Childe Rowland beat the King of Elfland to his knees. Whereupon he cried, " I yield me. Thou hast beaten me in fair fight."

Then Childe Rowland said, " I grant thee mercy if thou wilt release my sister and my brothers from all spells and enchantments, and let us go back to Middle Earth."

So that was agreed ; and the Elfin King went to a golden chest whence he took a phial that was filled with a blood-red liquor. And with this liquor he anointed the ears and the eyelids, the nostrils, the lips, and the finger-tips of the bodies of Burd Helen's two brothers that lay as dead in two golden coffers.

And immediately they sprang to life and declared that their souls only had been away, but had now returned.

After this the Elfin King said a charm which took away the very last bit of enchantment, and adown the huge hall that showed as if it were lit by the setting sun, and through the long passage of rough arches made of rock that was transparent and all encrusted with sheep-silver, rock-spar, and many bright stones, where twilight reigned, the three brothers and their sister passed. Then the door opened in the green hill, it clicked behind them, and they left the Dark Tower of the King of Elfland never to return.

For, no sooner were they in the light of day, than they found themselves at home.

But fair Burd Helen took care never to go widershins round a church again.

THE WISE MEN OF GOTHAM

OF BUYING OF SHEEP

THERE were two men of Gotham, and one of them was going to market to Nottingham to buy sheep, and the other came from the market, and they both met together upon Nottingham bridge.

" Where are you going ? " said the one who came from Nottingham.

" Marry," said he that was going to Nottingham, " I am going to buy sheep."

" Buy sheep ? " said the other ; " and which way will you bring them home ? "

" Marry," said the other, " I will bring them over this bridge."

" By Robin Hood," said he that came from Nottingham, " but thou shalt not."

" By Maid Marion," said he that was going thither, " but I will."

" You will not," said the one.

" I will."

Then they beat their staves against the ground, one against the other, as if there had been a hundred sheep between them.

" Hold in," said one ; " beware lest my sheep leap over the bridge."

" I care not," said the other ; " they shall not come this way."

" But they shall," said the other.

Then the other said, " If that thou make much to do, I will put my fingers in thy mouth."

" Will you ? " said the other.

Now, as they were at their contention, another man of Gotham came from the market with a sack of meal upon a horse, and seeing and hearing his neighbours at strife about sheep, though there were none between them, said :

" Ah, fools ! will you ever learn wisdom ? Help me, and lay my sack upon my shoulders."

They did so, and he went to the side of the bridge, unloosened the mouth of the sack, and shook all his meal out into the river.

" Now, neighbours," he said, " how much meal is there in my sack ? "

" Marry," said they, " there is none at all."

" Now, by my faith," said he, " even as much wit as is in your two heads to stir up strife about a thing you have not."

Which was the wisest of these three persons, judge yourself.

Of Hedging a Cuckoo

Once upon a time the men of Gotham would have kept the Cuckoo so that she might sing all the year, and in the midst of their town they made a hedge round in compass and they got a Cuckoo, and put her into it, and said, " Sing there all through the year, or thou shalt have neither meat nor water." The Cuckoo, as soon as she perceived herself within the hedge, flew away. " A vengeance on her ! " said they. " We did not make our hedge high enough."

T

Of Sending Cheeses

There was a man of Gotham who
went to the market at Nottingham
to sell cheese, and as he was going
down the hill to Nottingham bridge, one of his cheeses
fell out of his wallet and rolled down the hill. " Ah,
gaffer," said the fellow, " can you run to market alone ? I
will send one after another after you." Then he laid down
his wallet and took out the cheeses and rolled them down the
hill. Some went into one bush, and some went into another.

" I charge you all to meet me near the market-place,"
cried he ; and when the fellow came to the market to meet
his cheeses, he stayed there till the market was nearly done.
Then he went about to inquire of his friends and neighbours,
and other men, if they did see his cheeses come to the market.

" Who should bring them ? " said one of the market men.

" Marry, themselves," said the fellow ; " they know the way well enough."

He said, " A vengeance on them all.   I did fear, to see them run so fast, that they would run beyond the market. I am now fully persuaded that they must be now almost at York."   Whereupon he forthwith hired a horse to ride to York, to seek his cheeses where they were not ; but to this day no man can tell him of his cheeses.

OF DROWNING EELS

When Good Friday came, the men of Gotham cast their heads together what to do with their white herrings, their red herrings, their sprats, and other salt fish.   One consulted with the other, and agreed that such fish should be cast into their pond (which was in the middle of the town), that they might breed against the next year, and every man that had salt fish left cast them into the pool.

" I have many white herrings," said one.

" I have many sprats," said another.

" I have many red herrings," said the other.

" I have much salt fish.   Let all go into the pond or pool, and we shall fare like lords next year."

At the beginning of next year following the men drew near the pond to have their fish, and there was nothing but a great eel.   " Ah," said they all, " a mischief on this eel, for he has eaten up all our fish."

" What shall we do to him ? " said one to the other.

" Kill him," said one.

" Chop him into pieces," said another.

" Not so," said another ; " let us drown him."

" Be it so," said all.   And they went to another pond, and cast the eel into the pond.   " Lie there and shift for yourself, for no help thou shalt have from us " ; and they left the eel to drown.

Of Sending Rent

Once on a time the men of Gotham had forgotten to pay their landlord. One said to the other, " To-morrow is our pay-day, and what shall we find to send our money to our landlord ? "

The one said, " This day I have caught a hare, and he shall carry it, for he is light of foot."

" Be it so," said all ; " he shall have a letter and a purse to put our money in, and we shall direct him the right way." So when the letters were written and the money put in a purse, they tied it round the hare's neck, saying, " First you go to Lancaster, then thou must go to Loughborough, and Newarke is our landlord, and commend us to him, and there is his dues."

The hare, as soon as he was out of their hands, ran on along the country way. Some cried, " Thou must go to Lancaster first."

" Let the hare alone," said another ; " he can tell a nearer way than the best of us all. Let him go."

Another said, " It is a subtle hare; let her alone ; she will not keep the highway for fear of dogs."

Of Counting

On a certain time there were twelve men of Gotham who went fishing, and some went into the water and some on dry ground ; and, as they were coming back, one of them said, "We have ventured much this day wading ; I pray God that none of us that did come from home be drowned."

"Marry," said one, "let us see about that. Twelve of us came out." And every man did count eleven, and the twelfth man did never count himself.

"Alas !" said one to another, "one of us is drowned." They went back to the brook where they had been fishing, and looked up and down for him that was drowned, and made great lamentation. A courtier came riding by, and he did ask what they were seeking, and why they were so sorrowful. "Oh," said they, "this day we came to fish in this brook, and there were twelve of us, and one is drowned."

"Why," said the courtier, "count me how many of you there be" ; and one counted eleven and did not count himself.

" Well," said the courtier, " what will you give me if I find the twelfth man ? "

" Sir," said they, " all the money we have."

" Give me the money," said the courtier ; and he began with the first, and gave him a whack over the shoulders that he groaned, and said, " There is one," and he served all of them that they groaned ; but when he came to the last he gave him a good blow, saying, " Here is the twelfth man."

" God bless you on your heart," said all the company ; " you have found our neighbour."

CAPORUSHES

ONCE upon a time, a long, long while ago, when all the world was young and all sorts of strange things happened, there lived a very rich gentleman whose wife had died leaving him three lovely daughters. They were as the apple of his eye, and he loved them exceedingly.

Now one day he wanted to find out if they loved him in return, so he said to the eldest, " How much do you love me, my dear ? "

And she answered as pat as may be, " As I love my life."

" Very good, my dear," said he, and gave her a kiss. Then he said to the second girl, " How much do you love me, my dear ? "

And she answered as swift as thought, " Better than all the world beside."

" Good ! " he replied, and patted her on the cheek. Then he turned to the youngest, who was also the prettiest.

" And how much do *you* love me, my dearest ? "

Now the youngest daughter was not only pretty, she was clever. So she thought a moment, then she said slowly :

" I love you as fresh meat loves salt ! "

Now when her father heard this he was very angry, because he really loved her more than the others.

" What ! " he said. " If that is all you give me in return for all I've given you, out of my house you go." So there and then he turned her out of the home where she had been born and bred, and shut the door in her face.

Not knowing where to go, she wandered on, and she wandered on, till she came to a big fen where the reeds grew ever so tall and the rushes swayed in the wind like a field of corn. There she sate down and plaited herself an overall of rushes and a cap to match, so as to hide her fine clothes, and her beautiful golden hair that was all set with milk-white pearls. For she was a wise girl, and thought that in such lonely country, mayhap, some robber might fall in with her and kill her to get her fine clothes and jewels.

It took a long time to plait the dress and cap, and while she plaited she sang a little song :

> " Hide my hair, O cap o' rushes,
> Hide my heart, O robe o' rushes.
> Sure ! my answer had no fault,
> I love him more than he loves salt."

And the fen birds sate and listened and sang back to her :

> " Cap o' rushes, shed no tear,
> Robe o' rushes, have no fear ;
> With these words if fault he'd find,
> Sure your father must be blind."

When her task was finished she put on her robe of rushes and it hid all her fine clothes, and she put on the cap and it hid all her beautiful hair, so that she looked quite a common country girl. But the fen birds flew away, singing as they flew :

> " Cap-o-rushes ! we can see,
> Robe o' rushes ! what you be,
> Fair and clean, and fine and tidy,
> So you'll be whate'er betide ye."

By this time she was very, very hungry, so she wandered on, and she wandered on ; but ne'er a cottage or a hamlet did she see, till just at sun-setting she came on a great house on the edge of the fen. It had a fine front door to it ; but mindful of her dress of rushes she went round to the back. And there she saw a strapping fat scullion washing pots and pans with a very sulky face. So, being a clever girl, she guessed what the maid was wanting, and said :

" If I may have a night's lodging, I will scrub the pots and pans for you."

" Why ! Here's luck," replied the scullery-maid, ever so pleased. " I was just wanting badly to go a-walking with my sweetheart. So if you will do my work you shall share my bed and have a bite of my supper. Only mind you scrub the pots clean or cook will be at me."

Now next morning the pots were scraped so clean that they looked like new, and the saucepans were polished like silver, and the cook said to the scullion, " Who cleaned these pots ? Not you, I'll swear." So the maid had to up and out with the truth. Then the cook would have turned away the old maid and put on the new, but the latter would not hear of it.

"The maid was kind to me and gave me a night's lodging," she said. "So now I will stay without wage and do the dirty work for her."

So Caporushes—for so they called her since she would give no other name—stayed on and cleaned the pots and scraped the saucepans.

Now it so happened that her master's son came of age, and to celebrate the occasion a ball was given to the neighbourhood, for the young man was a grand dancer, and loved nothing so well as a country measure. It was a very fine party, and after supper was served, the servants were allowed to go and watch the quality from the gallery of the ball-room.

But Caporushes refused to go, for she also was a grand dancer, and she was afraid that when she heard the fiddles starting a merry jig, she might start dancing. So she excused herself by saying she was too tired with scraping pots and washing saucepans ; and when the others went off, she crept up to her bed.

But alas ! and alack-a-day ! The door had been left open, and as she lay in her bed she could hear the fiddlers fiddling away and the tramp of dancing feet.

Then she upped and off with her cap and robe of rushes, and there she was ever so fine and tidy. She was in the ball-room in a trice joining in the jig, and none was more beautiful or better dressed than she. While as for her dancing . . . !

Her master's son singled her out at once, and with the finest of bows engaged her as his partner for the rest of the night. So she danced away to her heart's content, while the whole room was agog, trying to find out who the beautiful young stranger could be. But she kept her own counsel and, making some excuse, slipped away before the ball finished ; so when her fellow-servants came to bed, there she was in hers in her cap and robe of rushes, pretending to be fast asleep.

Next morning, however, the maids could talk of nothing but the beautiful stranger.

"You should ha' seen her," they said. "She was the loveliest young lady as ever you see, not a bit like the likes o' we. Her golden hair was all silvered wi' pearls, and her dress—law ! You wouldn't believe how she was dressed. Young master never took his eyes off her."

And Caporushes only smiled and said, with a twinkle in her eye, "I should like to see her, but I don't think I ever shall."

"Oh yes, you will," they replied, "for young master has ordered another ball to-night in hopes she will come to dance again."

But that evening Caporushes refused once more to go to the gallery, saying she was too tired with cleaning pots and scraping saucepans. And once more when she heard the fiddlers fiddling she said to herself, "I must have one dance

—just one with the young master : he dances so beautifully."
For she felt certain he would dance with her.

And sure enough, when she had upped and offed with her
cap and robe of rushes, there he was at the door waiting for her
to come ; for he had determined to dance with no one else.

So he took her by the hand, and they danced down the
ball-room. It was a sight of all sights ! Never were such
dancers ! So young, so handsome, so fine, so gay !

But once again Caporushes kept her own counsel and just
slipped away on some excuse in time, so that when her fellow-
servants came to their beds they found her in hers, pretending
to be fast asleep ; but her cheeks were all flushed and her
breath came fast. So they said, " She is dreaming. We
hope her dreams are happy."

But next morning they were full of what she had missed.
Never was such a beautiful young gentleman as young
master ! Never was such a beautiful young lady ! Never
was such beautiful dancing ! Every one else had stopped
theirs to look on.

And Caporushes, with a twinkle in her eyes, said, " I
should like to see her ; but I'm *sure* I never shall ! "

" Oh yes ! " they replied. " If you come to-night
you're sure to see her ; for young master has ordered another
ball in hopes the beautiful stranger will come again ; for
it's easy to see he is madly in love with her."

Then Caporushes told herself she would not dance again,
since it was not fit for a gay young master to be in love with
his scullery-maid ; but, alas ! the moment she heard the

fiddlers fiddling, she just upped and offed with her rushes, and there she was fine and tidy as ever ! She didn't even have to brush her beautiful golden hair ! And once again she was in the ball-room in a trice, dancing away with young master, who never took his eyes off her, and implored her to tell him who she was. But she kept her own counsel and only told him that she never, never, never would come to dance any more, and that he must say good-bye. And he held her hand so fast that she had a job to get away, and lo and behold ! his ring came off his finger, and as she ran up to her bed there it was in her hand ! She had just time to put on her cap and robe of rushes, when her fellow-servants came trooping in and found her awake.

"It was the noise you made coming upstairs," she made excuse ; but they said, "Not we ! It is the whole place that is in an uproar searching for the beautiful stranger. Young master he tried to detain her ; but she slipped from him like an eel. But he declares he will find her ; for if he doesn't he will die of love for her."

Then Caporushes laughed. "Young men don't die of love," says she. "He will find some one else."

But he didn't. He spent his whole time looking for his beautiful dancer, but go where he might, and ask whom he would, he never heard anything about her. And day by day he grew thinner and thinner, and paler and paler, until at last he took to his bed.

And the housekeeper came to the cook and said, "Cook the nicest dinner you can cook, for young master eats nothing."

Then the cook prepared soups, and jellies, and creams, and roast chicken, and bread sauce ; but the young man would none of them.

And Caporushes cleaned the pots and scraped the saucepans and said nothing.

Then the housekeeper came crying and said to the cook, " Prepare some gruel for young master. Mayhap he'd take that. If not he will die for love of the beautiful dancer. If she could see him now she would have pity on him."

So the cook began to make the gruel, and Caporushes left scraping saucepans and watched her.

" Let me stir it," she said, " while you fetch a cup from the pantry-room."

So Caporushes stirred the gruel, and what did she do but slips young master's ring into it before the cook came back !

Then the butler took the cup upstairs on a silver salver. But when the young master saw it he waved it away, till the butler with tears begged him just to taste it.

So the young master took a silver spoon and stirred the gruel ; and he felt something hard at the bottom of the cup. And when he fished it up, lo ! it was his own ring ! Then he sate up in bed and said quite loud, " Send for the cook ! "

And when she came he asked her who made the gruel.

" I did," she said, for she was half-pleased and half-frightened.

Then he looked at her all over and said, " No, you didn't ! You're too stout ! Tell me who made it and you shan't be harmed ! "

Then the cook began to cry. " If you please, sir, I *did* make it ; but Caporushes stirred it."

" And who is Caporushes ? " asked the young man.

" If you please, sir, Caporushes is the scullion," whimpered the cook.

Then the young man sighed and fell back on his pillow. " Send Caporushes here," he said in a faint voice ; for he really was very near dying.

And when Caporushes came he just looked at her cap and her robe of rushes and turned his face to the wall ; but he asked her in a weak little voice, " From whom did you get that ring ? "

Now when Caporushes saw the poor young man so weak and worn with love for her, her heart melted, and she replied softly :

" From him that gave it me," quoth she, and offed with her cap and robe of rushes, and there she was as fine and tidy as ever with her beautiful golden hair all silvered over with pearls.

And the young man caught sight of her with the tail of his eye, and sate up in bed as strong as may be, and drew her to him and gave her a great big kiss.

So, of course, they were to be married in spite of her being only a scullery-maid, for she told no one who she was. Now every one far and near was asked to the wedding. Amongst the invited guests was Caporushes' father, who, from grief at losing his favourite daughter, had lost his sight, and was very dull and miserable. However, as a friend of the family, he had to come to the young master's wedding.

Now the marriage feast was to be the finest ever seen ; but Caporushes went to her friend the cook and said :

" Dress every dish without one mite of salt."

" That'll be rare and nasty," replied the cook ; but because she prided herself on having let Caporushes stir the gruel and so saved the young master's life, she did as she was asked, and dressed every dish for the wedding breakfast without one mite of salt.

Now when the company sate down to table their faces were full of smiles and content, for all the dishes looked so nice and tasty ; but no sooner had the guests begun to eat than their faces fell ; for nothing can be tasty without salt.

Then Caporushes' blind father, whom his daughter had seated next to her, burst out crying.

" What is the matter ? " she asked.

Then the old man sobbed, " I had a daughter whom I loved dearly, dearly. And I asked her how much she loved me, and she replied, ' As fresh meat loves salt.' And I was angry with her and turned her out of house and home, for I thought she didn't love me at all. But now I see she loved me best of all."

And as he said the words his eyes were opened, and there beside him was his daughter lovelier than ever.

And she gave him one hand, and her husband, the young master, the other, and laughed saying, " I love you both as fresh meat loves salt." And after that they were all happy for evermore.

U

THE BABES IN THE WOOD

NOW ponder well, you parents dear,
  These words which I shall write ;
A doleful story you shall hear,
  In time brought forth to light.
A gentleman of good account
  In Norfolk dwelt of late,
Who did in honour far surmount
  Most men of his estate.

Sore sick he was and like to die,
  No help his life could save ;
His wife by him as sick did lie,
  And both possest one grave.
No love between these two was lost,
  Each was to other kind ;
In love they lived, in love they died,
  And left two babes behind :

The one a fine and pretty boy
　　Not passing three years old,
The other a girl more young than he,
　　And framed in beauty's mould.
The father left his little son,
　　As plainly did appear,
When he to perfect age should come,
　　Three hundred pounds a year ;

And to his little daughter Jane
　　Five hundred pounds in gold,
To be paid down on marriage-day,
　　Which might not be controlled.
But if the children chanced to die
　　Ere they to age should come,
Their uncle should possess their wealth ;
　　For so the will did run.

" Now, brother," said the dying man,
　　" Look to my children dear ;
Be good unto my boy and girl,
　　No friends else have they here ;
To God and you I recommend
　　My children dear this day ;
But little while be sure we have
　　Within this world to stay.

" You must be father and mother both,
　And uncle, all in one ;
God knows what will become of them
　When I am dead and gone."
With that bespake their mother dear :
　" O brother kind," quoth she,
" You are the man must bring our babes
　To wealth or misery.

" And if you keep them carefully,
　Then God will you reward ;
But if you otherwise should deal,
　God will your deeds regard."
With lips as cold as any stone,
　They kissed their children small :
" God bless you both, my children dear ! "
　With that the tears did fall.

These speeches then their brother spake
　To this sick couple there :
" The keeping of your little ones,
　Sweet sister, do not fear ;
God never prosper me nor mine,
　Nor aught else that I have,
If I do wrong your children dear
　When you are laid in grave ! "

The parents being dead and gone,
  The children home he takes,
And brings them straight unto his house,
  Where much of them he makes.
He had not kept these pretty babes
  A twelvemonth and a day,
But, for their wealth, he did devise
  To make them both away.

He bargained with two ruffians strong,
  Which were of furious mood,
That they should take these children young,
  And slay them in a wood.
He told his wife an artful tale
  He would the children send
To be brought up in London town
  With one that was his friend.

Away then went those pretty babes,
  Rejoicing at that tide,
Rejoicing with a merry mind
  They should on cock-horse ride.
They prate and prattle pleasantly,
  As they ride on the way,
To those that should their butchers be
  And work their lives' decay :

So that the pretty speech they had
    Made Murder's heart relent ;
And they that undertook the deed
    Full sore now did repent.
Yet one of them, more hard of heart,
    Did vow to do his charge,
Because the wretch that hirèd him
    Had paid him very large.

The other won't agree thereto,
    So there they fall to strife ;
With one another they did fight
    About the children's life ;
And he that was of mildest mood
    Did slay the other there,
Within an unfrequented wood ;
    The babes did quake for fear !

He took the children by the hand,
    Tears standing in their eye,
And bade them straightway follow him,
    And look they did not cry ;
And two long miles he led them on,
    While they for food complain :
" Stay here," quoth he, " I'll bring you bread,
    When I come back again."

She sate down and plaited herself an overall of rushes and a cap to match.

These pretty babes, with hand in hand,
  Went wandering up and down ;
But never more could see the man
  Approaching from the town.
Their pretty lips with blackberries
  Were all besmeared and dyed ;
And when they saw the darksome night,
  They sat them down and cried.

Thus wandered these poor innocents,
  Till death did end their grief ;
In one another's arms they died,
  As wanting due relief :
No burial this pretty pair
  From any man receives,
Till Robin Redbreast piously
  Did cover them with leaves.

And now the heavy wrath of God
  Upon their uncle fell ;
Yea, fearful fiends did haunt his house,
  His conscience felt an hell :
His barns were fired, his goods consumed,
  His lands were barren made,
His cattle died within the field,
  And nothing with him stayed.

And in a voyage to Portugal
  Two of his sons did die ;
And to conclude, himself was brought
  To want and misery :
He pawned and mortgaged all his land
  Ere seven years came about.
And now at last this wicked act
  Did by this means come out,

The fellow that did take in hand
  These children for to kill,
Was for a robbery judged to die,
  Such was God's blessèd will :
Who did confess the very truth,
  As here hath been displayed :
The uncle having died in jail,
  Where he for debt was laid.

You that executors be made,
  And overseers eke,
Of children that be fatherless,
  And infants mild and meek,
Take you example by this thing,
  And yield to each his right,
Lest God with suchlike misery
  Your wicked minds requite.

THE RED ETTIN

THERE was once a widow that lived on a small bit of
ground, which she rented from a farmer. And she had
two sons ; and by and by it was time for the wife to send
them away to seek their fortune. So she told her eldest son
one day to take a can and bring her water from the well,
that she might bake a cake for him ; and however much or
however little water he might bring, the cake would be
great or small accordingly, and that cake was to be all that
she could give him when he went on his travels.

The lad went away with the can to the well, and filled
it with water, and then came away home again ; but the
can being broken, the most part of the water had run out
before he got back. So his cake was very small ; yet small
as it was, his mother asked him if he was willing to take the
half of it with her blessing, telling him that, if he chose rather
to take the whole, he would only get it with her curse. The
young man, thinking he might have to travel a far way, and
not knowing when or how he might get other provisions,
said he would like to have the whole cake, come of his mother's

malison what might ; so she gave him the whole cake, and her malison along with it. Then he took his brother aside, and gave him a knife to keep till he should come back, desiring him to look at it every morning, and as long as it continued to be clear, then he might be sure that the owner of it was well ; but if it grew dim and rusty, then for certain some ill had befallen him.

So the young man went to seek his fortune. And he went all that day, and all the next day ; and on the third day, in the afternoon, he came up to where a shepherd was sitting with a flock of sheep. And he went up to the shepherd and asked him to whom the sheep belonged ; and he answered :

> " To the Red Ettin of Ireland
>   Who lives in Ballygan,
> He stole King Malcolm's daughter,
>   The king of fair Scotland.
> He beats her, he binds her,
>   He lays her on a band ;
> And every day he strikes her
>   With a bright silver wand.
> 'Tis said there's one predestinate
>   To be his mortal foe ;
> But sure that man is yet unborn,
>   And long may it be so ! "

After this the shepherd told him to beware of the beasts he should next meet, for they were of a very different kind from any he had yet seen.

So the young man went on, and by and by he saw a multitude of very dreadful, terrible, horrible beasts, with two

heads, and on every head four horns! And he was sore
frightened, and ran away from them as fast as he could;
and glad was he when he came to a castle that stood on a
hillock, with the door standing wide open to the wall. And
he went in to the castle for shelter, and there he saw an old
wife sitting beside the kitchen fire. He asked the wife if he
might stay for the night, as he was tired with a long journey;
and the wife said he might, but it was not a good place for
him to be in, as it belonged to the Red Ettin, who was a very
terrible monster with three heads, who spared no living man
it could get hold of. The young man would have gone
away, but he was afraid of the two-headed four-horned beasts
outside; so he beseeched the old woman to hide him as best
she could, and not tell the Ettin he was there. He thought,
if he could put over the night, he might get away in the
morning, without meeting with the dreadful, terrible, horrible
beasts, and so escape.

But he had not been long in his hiding-hole, before the
awful Ettin came in; and no sooner was he in, than he was
heard crying:

"Snouk but! and snouk ben!
I find the smell of an earthly man;
Be he living, or be he dead,
His heart this night shall kitchen my bread."

Well, the monster began to search about, and he soon found
the poor young man, and pulled him from his hiding-place.
And when he had got him out, he told him that if he could
answer him three questions his life should be spared.

So the first head asked : " A thing without an end ;
what's that ? "

But the young man knew not.

Then the second head said : " The smaller the more
dangerous ; what's that ? "

But the young man knew not.

And then the third head asked : " The dead carrying the
living ? riddle me that."

But the young man knew not.

So the lad not being able to answer one of these questions,
the Red Ettin took a mallet from behind the door, knocked
him on the head, and turned him into a pillar of stone.

Now on the morning after this happened the younger
brother took out the knife to look at it, and he was grieved
to find it all brown with rust. So he told his mother that
the time was now come for him to go away upon his travels
also. At first she refused to let him go ; but at last she
requested him to take the can to the well for water, that she
might make a cake for him. So he went, but as he was
bringing home the water, a raven over his head cried to him
to look, and he would see that the water was running out.
Now being a young man of sense, and seeing the water
running out, he took some clay and patched up the holes,
so that he brought home enough water to bake a large cake.
And when his mother put it to him to take the half cake
with her blessing, he took it instead of having the whole with
her malison.

So he went away on his journey with his mother's blessing.

Now after he had travelled a far way, he met with an old woman who asked him if he would give her a bit of his cake. And he said, " I will gladly do that " ; so he gave her a piece of the cake. Then the old woman, who was a fairy, gave him a magic wand, that might yet be of service to him, if he took care to use it rightly ; and she told him a great deal that would happen to him, and what he ought to do in all circumstances ; and after that, she vanished in an instant, out of his sight. Then he went on his way until he came up to the old man who was herding the sheep ; and when he asked him to whom the sheep belonged, the answer was :

" To the Red Ettin of Ireland
  Who lives in Ballygan,
He stole King Malcolm's daughter,
  The king of fair Scotland.
He beats her, he binds her,
  He lays her on a band ;
And every day he strikes her
  With a bright silver wand.
But now I fear his end is near,
  And death is close at hand ;
For you're to be, I plainly see,
  The heir of all his land."

So the younger brother went on his way ; but when he came to the place where the dreadful, terrible, horrible beasts were standing, he did not stop nor run away, but went boldly through amongst them. One came up roaring with open mouth to devour him, when he struck it with his wand, and laid it in an instant dead at his feet. He soon came to the

Ettin's castle, where he found the door shut, but he knocked boldly, and was admitted. Then the old woman who sat by the fire warned him of the terrible Ettin, and what had been the fate of his brother ; but he was not to be daunted, and would not even hide.

Then by and by the monster came in, crying as before :

"Snouk but ! and snouk ben !
I find the smell of an earthly man ;
Be he living, or be he dead,
His heart this night shall kitchen my bread."

Well, he quickly espied the young man, and bade him stand forth on the floor, and told him that if he could answer three questions his life would be spared.

So the first head asked : " What's the thing without an end ? "

Now the younger brother had been told by the fairy to whom he had given a piece of his cake what he ought to say ; so he answered :

" A bowl."

Then the first head frowned, but the second head asked : " The smaller the more dangerous ; what's that ? "

" A bridge," says the younger brother, quite fast.

Then the first and the second heads frowned, but the third head asked :

" When does the dead carry the living ? riddle me that."

At this the young man answered up at once and said :

" When a ship sails on the sea with men inside her."

When the Red Ettin found all his riddles answered, he

knew that his power was gone, so he tried to escape, but the young man took up an axe and hewed off the monster's three heads. Then he asked the old woman to show him where the king's daughter lay ; and the old woman took him upstairs, and opened a great many doors, and out of every door came a beautiful lady who had been imprisoned there by the Red Ettin ; and last of all the ladies was the king's daughter. Then the old woman took him down into a low room, and there stood a stone pillar ; but he had only to touch it with his wand, and his brother started into life.

So the whole of the prisoners were overjoyed at their deliverance, for which they thanked the younger brother again and again. Next day they all set out for the king's court, and a gallant company they made. Then the king married his daughter to the young man who had delivered her, and gave a noble's daughter to his brother.

So they all lived happily all the rest of their days.

THE FISH AND THE RING

ONCE upon a time there lived a Baron who was a great magician, and could tell by his arts and charms everything that was going to happen at any time.

Now this great lord had a little son born to him as heir to all his castles and lands. So, when the little lad was about four years old, wishing to know what his fortune would be, the Baron looked in his Book of Fate to see what it foretold

And, lo and behold ! it was written that this much-loved, much-prized heir to all the great lands and castles was to marry a low-born maiden. So the Baron was dismayed, and set to work by more arts and charms to discover if this maiden were already born, and if so, where she lived.

And he found out that she had just been born in a very poor house, where the poor parents were already burdened with five children.

So he called for his horse and rode away, and away, until he came to the poor man's house, and there he found the poor man sitting at his doorstep very sad and doleful.

" What is the matter, my friend ? " asked he ; and the poor man replied :

" May it please your honour, a little lass has just been born to our house ; and we have five children already, and where the bread is to come from to fill the sixth mouth, we know not."

" If that be all your trouble," quoth the Baron readily, " mayhap I can help you : so don't be down-hearted. I am just looking for such a little lass to companion my son, so, if you will, I will give you ten crowns for her."

Well ! the man he nigh jumped for joy, since he was to get good money, and his daughter, so he thought, a good home. Therefore he brought out the child then and there, and the Baron, wrapping the babe in his cloak, rode away. But when he got to the river he flung the little thing into the swollen stream, and said to himself as he galloped back to his castle :

" There goes Fate ! "

But, you see, he was just sore mistaken. For the little lass didn't sink. The stream was very swift, and her long clothes kept her up till she caught in a snag just opposite a fisherman, who was mending his nets.

Now the fisherman and his wife had no children, and they were just longing for a baby ; so when the goodman saw the little lass he was overcome with joy, and took her home to his wife, who received her with open arms.

And there she grew up, the apple of their eyes, into the most beautiful maiden that ever was seen.

Now, when she was about fifteen years of age, it so happened that the Baron and his friends went a-hunting

x

along the banks of the river and stopped to get a drink of water at the fisherman's hut. And who should bring the water out but, as they thought, the fisherman's daughter.

Now the young men of the party noticed her beauty, and one of them said to the Baron, " She should marry well ; read us her fate, since you are so learned in the art."

Then the Baron, scarce looking at her, said carelessly : " I could guess her fate ! Some wretched yokel or other. But, to please you, I will cast her horoscope by the stars ; so tell me, girl, what day you were born ? "

" That I cannot tell, sir," replied the girl, " for I was picked up in the river about fifteen years ago."

Then the Baron grew pale, for he guessed at once that she was the little lass he had flung into the stream, and that Fate had been stronger than he was. But he kept his own counsel and said nothing at the time. Afterwards, however, he thought out a plan, so he rode back and gave the girl a letter.

" See you ! " he said. " I will make your fortune. Take this letter to my brother, who needs a good girl, and you will be settled for life."

Now the fisherman and his wife were growing old and needed help ; so the girl said she would go, and took the letter.

And the Baron rode back to his castle saying to himself once more :

" There goes Fate ! "

For what he had written in the letter was this :

" DEAR BROTHER,

       Take the bearer and put her to death imme-diately."

But once again he was sore mistaken ; since on the way to the town where his brother lived, the girl had to stop the night in a little inn. And it so happened that that very night a gang of thieves broke into the inn, and not content with carrying off all that the innkeeper possessed, they searched the pockets of the guests, and found the letter which the girl carried. And when they read it, they agreed that it was a mean trick and a shame. So their captain sat down and, taking pen and paper, wrote instead :

" DEAR BROTHER,

       Take the bearer and marry her to my son without delay."

Then, after putting the note into an envelope and sealing it up, they gave it to the girl and bade her go on her way. So when she arrived at the brother's castle, though rather surprised, he gave orders for a wedding feast to be prepared. And the Baron's son, who was staying with his uncle, seeing the girl's great beauty, was nothing loth, so they were fast wedded.

Well ! when the news was brought to the Baron, he was nigh beside himself ; but he was determined not to be done by Fate. So he rode post-haste to his brother's and pre-tended to be quite pleased. And then one day, when no one was nigh, he asked the young bride to come for a walk with

him, and when they were close to some cliffs, seized hold
of her, and was for throwing her over into the sea. But
she begged hard for her life.

"It is not my fault," she said. "I have done nothing.
It is Fate. But if you will spare my life I promise that I
will fight against Fate also. I will never see you or your
son again until you desire it. That will be safer for you ;
since, see you, the sea may preserve me, as the river did."

Well! the Baron agreed to this. So he took off his
gold ring from his finger and flung it over the cliffs into the
sea and said :

"Never dare to show me your face again till you can
show me that ring likewise."

And with that he let her go.

Well! the girl wandered on, and she wandered on, until
she came to a nobleman's castle ; and there, as they needed
a kitchen girl, she engaged as a scullion, since she had been
used to such work in the fisherman's hut.

Now one day, as she was cleaning a big fish, she looked
out of the kitchen window, and who should she see driving
up to dinner but the Baron and his young son, her husband.
At first she thought that, to keep her promise, she must
run away ; but afterwards she remembered they would not
see her in the kitchen, so she went on with her cleaning of
the big fish.

And, lo and behold! she saw something shine in its
inside, and there, sure enough, was the Baron's ring! She
was glad enough to see it, I can tell you ; so she slipped it

on to her thumb. But she went on with her work, and dressed the fish as nicely as ever she could, and served it up as pretty as may be, with parsley sauce and butter.

Well! when it came to table the guests liked it so well that they asked the host who cooked it. And he called to his servants, " Send up the cook who cooked that fine fish, that she may get her reward."

Well! when the girl heard she was wanted she made herself ready, and with the gold ring on her thumb, went boldly into the dining-hall. And all the guests when they saw her were struck dumb by her wonderful beauty. And the young husband started up gladly; but the Baron, recognising her, jumped up angrily and looked as if he would kill her. So, without one word, the girl held up her hand before his face, and the gold ring shone and glittered on it; and she went straight up to the Baron, and laid her hand with the ring on it before him on the table.

Then the Baron understood that Fate had been too strong for him; so he took her by the hand, and, placing her beside him, turned to the guests and said:

" This is my son's wife. Let us drink a toast in her honour."

And after dinner he took her and his son home to his castle, where they all lived as happy as could be for ever afterwards.

LAWKAMERCYME

THERE was an old woman, as I've heard tell,
    She went to the market her eggs for to sell ;
She went to the market, all on a market-day,
And she fell asleep on the king's highway.

There came by a pedlar, whose name it was Stout,
He cut all her petticoats all round about ;
He cut her petticoats up to the knees,
Which made the old woman to shiver and freeze.

When this old woman first did awake,
She 'gan to shiver, she 'gan to shake ;
She 'gan to wonder, she 'gan to cry—
" Lawkamercyme ! this is none of I !

" But if it be I, as I do hope it be,
I've a little dog at home, and sure he'll know me ;
If it be I, he'll wag his little tail,
And if it be not I, then he'll bark and wail."

Home went the old woman, all in the dark ;
Up got the little dog, and he began to bark,
He began to bark, and she began to cry—
" Lawkamercyme ! this is none of I ! "

MASTER OF ALL MASTERS

A GIRL once went to the fair to hire herself for servant.
At last a funny-looking old gentleman engaged her
and took her home to his house. When she got there, he
told her that he had something to teach her, for that in his
house he had his own names for things.

He said to her, " What will you call me ? "

" Master or mister, or whatever you please, sir," says she.

He said, " You must call me ' master of all masters.'
And what would you call this ? " pointing to his bed.

" Bed or couch, or whatever you please, sir."

" No, that's my ' barnacle.' And what do you call
these ? " said he, pointing to his pantaloons.

" Breeches or trousers, or whatever you please, sir."

" You must call them ' squibs and crackers.' And what
would you call her ? " pointing to the cat.

" Cat or kit, or whatever you please, sir."

" You must call her ' white-faced simminy.' And this now," showing the fire, " what would you call this ? "

" Fire or flame, or whatever you please, sir."

" You must call it ' hot cockalorum ' ; and what this ? " he went on, pointing to the water.

" Water or wet, or whatever you please, sir."

" No, ' pondalorum ' is its name. And what do you call all this ? " asked he, as he pointed to the house.

" House or cottage, or whatever you please, sir."

" You must call it ' high topper mountain.' "

That very night the servant woke her master up in a fright and said, " Master of all masters, get out of your barnacle and put on your squibs and crackers. For white-faced simminy has got a spark of hot cockalorum on its tail, and unless you get some pondalorum high topper mountain will be all on hot cockalorum. . . ."

That's all ! !

MOLLY WHUPPIE AND THE DOUBLE-FACED GIANT

ONCE upon a time there was a man and his wife who were not over rich. And they had so many children that they couldn't find meat for them ; so, as the three youngest were girls, they just took them out to the forest one day, and left them there to fend for themselves as best they might.

Now the two eldest were just ordinary girls, so they cried a bit and felt afraid ; but the youngest, whose name was Molly Whuppie, was bold, so she counselled her sisters not to despair, but to try and find some house where they might get a night's lodging. So they set off through the forest, and journeyed, and journeyed, and journeyed, but never a house did they see. It began to grow dark, her sisters were faint with hunger, and even Molly Whuppie began to think of supper. At last in the distance they saw a great big light, and made for it. Now when they drew near they saw that it came from a huge window in a huge house.

" It will be a giant's house," said the two elder girls, trembling with fright.

" If there were two giants in it I mean to have my supper," quoth Molly Whuppie, and knocked at a huge door, as bold as brass. It was opened by the giant's wife, who shook her head when Molly Whuppie asked for victuals and a night's lodging.

" You wouldn't thank me for it," she said, " for my man is a giant, and when he comes home he will kill you of a certainty."

" But if you give us supper at once," says Molly craftily, " we shall have finished it before the giant comes home ; for we are very sharp-set."

Now the giant's wife was not unkindly ; besides, her three daughters, who were just of an age with Molly and her sisters, tugged at her skirts well pleased ; so she took the girls in, set them by the fire, and gave them each a bowl of bread and milk. But they had hardly begun to gobble it up before the door burst open, and a fearful giant strode in saying :

" *Fee-fi-fo-fum,*
I smell the smell of some earthly one."

" Don't put yourself about, my dear," said the giant's wife, trying to make the best of it. " See for yourself. They are only three poor little girlies like our girlies. They were cold and hungry so I gave them some supper ; but they have promised to go away as soon as they have finished.

Now be a good giant and don't touch them. They've eaten
of our salt, so don't *you* be at fault ! "

Now this giant was not at all a straightforward giant.
He was a double-faced giant. So he only said,

"Umph !"

and remarked that as they had come, they had better stay
all night, since they could easily sleep with his three daughters.
And after he had had his supper he made himself quite
pleasant, and plaited chains of straw for the little strangers
to wear round their necks, to match the gold chains his
daughters wore. Then he wished them all pleasant dreams
and sent them to bed.

Dear me ! He *was* a double-faced giant !

But Molly Whuppie, the youngest of the three girls,
was not only bold, she was clever. So when she was in bed,
instead of going to sleep like the others, she lay awake and
thought, and thought, and thought ; until at last she up
ever so softly, took off her own and her sisters' straw chains,
put them round the neck of the ogre's daughters, and placed
their gold chains round her own and her sisters' necks.

And even then she did not go to sleep, but lay still and
waited to see if she was wise ; and she was ! For in the very
middle of the night, when everybody else was dead asleep
and it was pitch dark, in comes the giant, all stealthy, feels
for the straw chains, twists them tight round the wearers'
necks, half strangles his daughters, drags them on to the
floor, and beats them till they were quite dead ; so, all

stealthy and satisfied, goes back to his own bed, thinking
he had been very clever.

But he was no match, you see, for Molly Whuppie; for
she at once roused her sisters, bade them be quiet, and
follow her. Then she slipped out of the giant's house and
ran, and ran, and ran until the dawn broke and they found
themselves before another great house. It was surrounded
by a wide deep moat, which was spanned by a drawbridge.
But the drawbridge was up. However, beside it hung a
Single-Hair rope over which any one very light-footed could
cross.

Now Molly's sisters were feared to try it; besides, they
said that for aught they knew the house might be another
giant's house, and they had best keep away.

"Taste and try," says Molly Whuppie, laughing, and
was over the Bridge of a Single Hair before you could say
knife. And, after all, it was not a giant's house but a King's
castle. Now it so happened that the very giant whom
Molly had tricked was the terror of the whole country-side,
and it was to gain safety from him that the drawbridge
was kept up, and the Bridge of a Single Hair had been made.
So when the sentry heard Molly Whuppie's tale, he took
her to the King and said:

"My lord! Here is a girlie who has tricked the
giant!"

Then the King when he had heard the story said, "You
are a clever girl, Molly Whuppie, and you managed very
well; but if you could manage still better and steal the

giant's sword, in which part of his strength lies, I will give your eldest sister in marriage to my eldest son."

Well! Molly Whuppie thought this would be a very good downsitting for her sister, so she said she would try.

So that evening, all alone, she ran across the Bridge of One Hair, and ran and ran till she came to the giant's house. The sun was just setting, and shone on it so beautifully that Molly Whuppie thought it looked like a castle in Spain, and could hardly believe that such a dreadful, double-faced giant lived within. However, she knew he did; so she slipped into the house unbeknownst, stole up to the giant's room, and crept in behind the bed. By and by the giant came home, ate a huge supper, and came crashing up the stairs to his bed. But Molly kept very still and held her breath. So after a time he fell asleep, and soon he began to snore. Then Molly crept out from under the bed, ever so softly, and crept up the bed-clothes, and crept past his great snoring face, and laid hold of the sword that hung above it. But alas! as she jumped from the bed in a hurry, the sword rattled in the scabbard. The noise woke the giant, and up he jumped and ran after Molly, who ran as she had never run before, carrying the sword over her shoulder. And he ran, and she ran, and they both ran, until they came to the Bridge of One Hair. Then she fled over it light-footed, balancing the sword, but he couldn't. So he stopped, foaming at the mouth with rage, and called after her:

"Woe worth you, Molly Whuppie! Never you dare to come again!"

And she, turning her head about as she sped over the One Hair Bridge, laughed lightly :

" Twice yet, gaffer, will I come to the Castle in Spain ! "

So Molly gave the sword to the King, and, as he had promised, his eldest son wedded her eldest sister.

But after the marriage festivities were over the King says again to Molly Whuppie :

" You're a main clever girl, Molly, and you have managed very well, but if you could manage still better and steal the giant's purse, in which part of his strength lies, I will marry my second son to your second sister.   But you need to be careful, for the giant sleeps with the purse under his pillow ! "

Well !   Molly Whuppie thought this would be a very good downsitting, indeed, for her second sister, so she said she would try her luck.

So that evening, just at sunsetting, she ran over the One Hair Bridge, and ran, and ran, and ran until she came to the giant's house looking for all the world like a castle in the air, all ruddy and golden and glinting.   She could scarce believe such a dreadful double-faced giant lived within.   However, she *knew* he did ; so she slipped into the house unbeknownst, stole up to the giant's room, and crept in below the giant's bed.   By and by the giant came home, ate a hearty supper, and then came crashing upstairs, and soon fell a-snoring.   Then Molly Whuppie slipped from under the bed, and slipped up the bed-clothes, and reaching out her hand slipped it under the pillow, and got hold of the purse. But the giant's head was so heavy on it she had to tug and tug away. At last out it came, she fell backward over the bedside, the purse opened, and some of the money fell out with a crash. The noise wakened the giant, and she had only time to grab the money off the floor, when he was after her. How they ran, and ran, and ran, and ran! At last she reached the One Hair Bridge and, with the purse in one hand, the money in the other, she sped across it while the giant shook his fist at her and cried:

"Woe worth you, Molly Whuppie! Never you dare to come again!"

And she, turning her head, laughed lightly:

"Yet once more, gaffer, will I come to the Castle in Spain."

So she took the purse to the King, and he ordered a splendid marriage feast for his second son and her second sister.

But after the wedding was over the King says to her, says he:

"Molly! You are the most main clever girl in the world; but if you would do better yet, and steal me from his finger the giant's ring, in which all his strength lies, I will give you my dearest, youngest, handsomest son for yourself."

Now Molly thought the King's son was the nicest young prince she had ever seen, so she said she would try, and that evening, all alone, she sped across the One Hair Bridge as light as a feather, and ran, and ran, and ran until she came to the giant's house all lit up with the red setting sun like any castle in the air. And she slipped inside, stole upstairs, and crept under the bed in no time. And the giant came in, and supped, and crashed up to bed, and snored. Oh! he snored louder than ever!

But you know he was a double-faced giant; so perhaps he snored louder on purpose. For no sooner had Molly Whuppie began to tug at his ring than . . . My! . . .

He had her fast between his finger and thumb. And he sate up in bed, and shook his head at her and said, "Molly Whuppie, you are a main clever girl! Now, if I had done as much ill to you as you have done to me, what would you do to me?"

Then Molly thought for a moment and she said, "I'd put you in a sack, and I'd put the cat inside with you, and I'd put the dog inside with you, and I'd put a needle and thread and a pair of shears inside with you, and I'd hang you up on a nail, and I'd go to the wood and cut the thickest stick I could get, and come home and take you down and bang you, and bang, and bang, and bang you till you were dead!"

"Right you are!" cried the giant gleefully, "and that's just what I'll do to you!"

So he got a sack and put Molly into it with the dog and the cat, and the needle and thread and the shears, and hung her on a nail in the wall, and went out to the wood to choose a stick.

Then Molly Whuppie began to laugh like anything, and the dog joined in with barks, and the cat with mews.

Y

Now the giant's wife was sitting in the next room, and when she heard the commotion she went in to see what was up.

" Whatever is the matter ? " quoth she.

" Nothing, 'm," quoth Molly Whuppie from inside the sack, laughing like anything. " Ho, ho ! Ha, ha ! If you saw what we see you'd laugh too. Ho, ho ! Ha, ha ! "

And no matter how the giant's wife begged to know what she saw, there never was any answer but, " Ho, ho ! Ha, ha ! Could ye but see what I see !!! "

At last the giant's wife begged Molly to let her see, so Molly took the shears, cut a hole in the sack, jumped out, helped the giant's wife in, and sewed up the hole ! For of course she hadn't forgotten to take out the needle and thread with her.

Now, just at that very moment, the giant burst in, and Molly had barely time to hide behind the door before he rushed at the sack, tore it down, and began to batter it with a huge tree he had cut in the wood.

" Stop ! stop ! " cried his wife. " It's me ! It's me ! "

But he couldn't hear, for, see you, the dog and the cat had tumbled one on the top of the other, and such a growling and spitting, and yelling and caterwauling you never heard ! It was fair deafening, and the giant would have gone on battering till his wife was dead had he not caught sight of Molly Whuppie escaping with the ring which he had left on the table.

Well, he threw down the tree and ran after her. Never

was such a race. They ran, and they ran, and they ran, and they ran, until they came to the One Hair Bridge. And then, balancing herself with the ring like a hoop, Molly Whuppie sped over the bridge light as a feather, but the giant had to stand on the other side, and shake his fist at her, and cry louder than ever :

"Woe worth you, Molly Whuppie ! Never you dare to come again ! "

And she, turning her head back as she sped, laughed gaily :

" Never more, gaffer, will I come to the castle in the air ! "

So she took the ring to the King, and she and the handsome young prince were married, and no one ever saw the double-faced giant again.

THE ASS, THE TABLE, AND THE STICK

A LAD named Jack was once so unhappy at home through his father's ill-treatment, that he made up his mind to run away and seek his fortune in the wide world.

He ran, and he ran, till he could run no longer, and then he ran right up against a little old woman who was gathering sticks. He was too much out of breath to beg pardon, but the woman was good-natured, and she said he seemed to be a likely lad, so she would take him to be her servant, and would pay him well. He agreed, for he was very hungry, and she brought him to her house in the wood, where he served her for a twelvemonths and a day. When the year had passed, she called him to her, and said she had good wages for him. So she presented him with an ass out of the stable, and he had but to pull Neddy's ears to make him begin at once to hee-haw! And when he brayed there dropped from his mouth silver sixpences, and half-crowns, and golden guineas.

The lad was well pleased with the wage he had received, and away he rode till he reached an inn. There he ordered

the best of everything, and when the innkeeper refused to
serve him without being paid beforehand, the boy went off
to the stable, pulled the ass's ears, and obtained his pocket
full of money. The host had watched all this through a
crack in the door, and when night came on he put an ass of
his own for the precious Neddy belonging to the youth.
So Jack, without knowing that any change had been made,
rode away next morning to his father's house.

Now I must tell you that near his home dwelt a poor
widow with an only daughter. The lad and the maiden
were fast friends and true-loves. So when Jack returned he
asked his father's leave to marry the girl.

"Never till you have the money to keep her," was the reply.

"I have that, father," said the lad, and going to the
ass he pulled its long ears ; well, he pulled, and he pulled,
till one of them came off in his hands ; but Neddy, though
he hee-hawed and he hee-hawed, let fall no half-crowns or
guineas. Then the father picked up a hayfork and beat his
son out of the house.

I promise you he ran ; he ran and ran till he came bang
against a door, and burst it open, and there he was in a
joiner's shop. "You're a likely lad," said the joiner ;
" serve me for a twelvemonths and a day and I will pay you
well." So he agreed, and served the carpenter for a year
and a day. "Now," said the master, "I will give you
your wage " ; and he presented him with a table, telling
him he had but to say, " Table, be covered," and at once
it would be spread with lots to eat and drink.

Jack hitched the table on his back, and away he went with it till he came to the inn. " Well, host," shouted he, putting down the table, " my dinner to-day, and that of the best."

" Very sorry, sir," says the host, " but there is nothing in the house but ham and eggs."

" No ham and eggs for me ! " exclaimed Jack. " I can do better than that.—Come, my table, be covered ! "

So at once the table was spread with turkey and sausages, roast mutton, potatoes, and greens. The innkeeper opened his eyes, but he said nothing, not he ! But that night he fetched down from his attic a table very like the magic one, and exchanged the two, and Jack, none the wiser, next morning hitched the worthless table on to his back and carried it home.

" Now, father, may I marry my lass ? " he asked.

" Not unless you can keep her," replied the father.

" Look here ! " exclaimed Jack. " Father, I have a table which does all my bidding."

" Let me see it," said the old man.

The lad set it in the middle of the room, and bade it be covered ; but all in vain, the table remained bare. Then, in a rage, the father caught the warming-pan down from the wall and warmed his son's back with it so that the boy fled howling from the house, and ran and ran till he came to a river and tumbled in. A man picked him out and bade him help in making a bridge over the river by casting a tree across. Then Jack climbed up to the top of the tree and threw his weight on it, so that when the man had rooted

The fisherman and his wife had no children, and they were just longing
for a baby.

the tree up, Jack and the tree-head dropped on the farther bank.

"Thank you," said the man; "and now for what you have done I will pay you"; so saying, he tore a branch from the tree, and fettled it up into a club with his knife. "There," exclaimed he; "take this stick, and when you say to it, 'Up, stick, and bang him,' it will knock any one down who angers you."

The lad was overjoyed to get this stick, for he had begun to see he had been tricked by the innkeeper, so away he went with it to the inn, and as soon as the man appeared he cried:

"Up, stick, and bang him!"

At the word the cudgel flew from his hand and battered the old fellow on the back, rapped his head, bruised his arms, tickled his ribs, till he fell groaning on the floor; and still the stick belaboured the prostrate man, nor would Jack call it off till he had got back the stolen ass and table. Then he galloped home on the ass, with the table on his shoulders, and the stick in his hand. When he arrived there he found his father was dead, so he brought his ass into the stable, and pulled its ears till he had filled the manger with money.

It was soon known through the town that Jack had returned rolling in wealth, and accordingly all the girls in the place set their caps at him.

"Now," said Jack, "I shall marry the richest lass in the place; so to-morrow do you all come in front of my house with your money in your aprons."

Next morning the street was full of girls with aprons held out, and gold and silver in them; but Jack's own sweetheart was among them, and she had neither gold nor silver; nought but two copper pennies, that was all she had.

"Stand aside, lass," said Jack to her, speaking roughly. "Thou hast no silver nor gold—stand off from the rest." She obeyed, and the tears ran down her cheeks, and filled her apron with diamonds.

"Up, stick, and bang them!" exclaimed Jack; whereupon the cudgel leaped up, and running along the line of girls, knocked them all on the heads and left them senseless on the pavement. Jack took all their money and poured it into his true-love's lap. "Now, lass," he exclaimed, "thou art the richest, and I shall marry thee."

THE WELL OF THE WORLD'S END

ONCE upon a time, and a very good time it was, though it wasn't in my time, nor in your time, nor any one else's time, there was a girl whose mother had died, and her father had married again. And her stepmother hated her because she was more beautiful than she was. And she was very cruel to her ; she used to make her do all the servant's work, and never let her have any peace. At last, one day, the stepmother thought to get rid of her altogether ; so she handed her a sieve and said to her :

" Go, fill it at the Well of the World's End and bring it home to me full, or woe betide you." For she thought she would never be able to find the Well of the World's End, and, if she did, how could she bring home a sieve full of water ?

Well, the girl started off, and asked every one she met to tell her where was the Well of the World's End. But nobody knew, and she didn't know what to do, when a queer little old woman, all bent double, told her where it was, and how she could get to it. So she did what the old

329

woman told her, and at last arrived at the Well of the World's End. But when she dipped the sieve in the cold cold water, it all ran out again. She tried and she tried again, but every time it was the same ; and at last she sate down and cried as if her heart would break.

Suddenly she heard a croaking voice, and she looked up and saw a great frog with goggle eyes looking at her and speaking to her.

" What's the matter, dearie ? " it said.

" Oh dear ! oh dear ! " she said, " my stepmother has sent me all this long way to fill this sieve with water from the Well of the World's End, and I can't fill it no how at all."

" Well," said the frog, " if you promise me to do whatever I bid you for a whole night long, I'll tell you how to fill it."

So the girl agreed, and then the frog said :

> " Stop it with moss and daub it with clay,
> And then it will carry the water away " ;

and then it gave a hop, skip, and jump, and went flop into the Well of the World's End.

So the girl looked about for some moss, and lined the bottom of the sieve with it, and over that she put some clay, and then she dipped it once again into the Well of the World's End ; and this time the water didn't run out, and she turned to go away.

Just then the frog popped up its head out of the Well of the World's End, and said, " Remember your promise."

" All right," said the girl ; for, thought she, " what harm can a frog do me ? "

So she went back to her stepmother, and brought the sieve full of water from the Well of the World's End.   The stepmother was angry as angry, but she said nothing at all.

That very evening they heard something tap-tapping at the door low down, and a voice cried out :

> " Open the door, my hinny, my heart,
>   Open the door, my own darling ;
> Remember the words that you and I spoke,
>   At the World's End Well but this morning."

" Whatever can that be ? " cried out the stepmother.

Then the girl had to tell her all about it, and what she had promised the frog.

" Girls must keep their promises," said the stepmother. who was glad the girl would have to obey a nasty frog. " Go and open the door this instant."

So the girl went and opened the door, and there was the frog from the Well of the World's End.   And it hopped, and it hopped, and it jumped, till it reached the girl, and then it said :

> " Lift me up, my hinny, my heart,
>   Lift to your knee, my own darling ;
> Remember the words that you and I spoke,
>   At the World's End Well but this morning."

But the girl would not do the frog's bidding, till her stepmother said, " Lift it up this instant, you hussy !   Girls *must* keep their promises ! "

So she lifted the frog up on to her lap, and it lay there comfortably for a time ; till at last it said :

> " Give me some supper, my hinny, my heart,
>   Give me some supper, my darling ;
> Remember the words you and I spoke,
>   At the World's End Well but this morning."

Well, that she did not mind doing, so she got it a bowl of milk and bread, and fed it well.   But when the frog had finished, it said :

> " Take me to bed, my hinny, my heart,
>   Take me to bed, my own darling ;
> Remember the promise you promised to me,
>   At the World's End Well but this morning."

But that the girl refused to do, till her stepmother said harshly :

" Do what you promised, girl ; girls *must* keep their promises. Do what you're bid, or out you go, you and your froggie."

So the girl took the frog with her to bed, and kept it as far away from her as she could. Well, just as the day was beginning to break, what should the frog say but :

> " Chop off my head, my hinny, my heart,
>   Chop off my head, my own darling ;
> Remember the promise you promised to me,
>   At the World's End Well but this morning."

At first the girl wouldn't, for she thought of what the frog had done for her at the Well of the World's End. But when the frog said the words over and over again in a

pleading voice, she went and took an axe and chopped off
its head, and, lo and behold! there stood before her a
handsome young prince, who told her that he had been
enchanted by a wicked magician, and he could never be
unspelled till some girl would do his bidding for a whole
night, and chop off his head at the end of it.

The stepmother was surprised indeed when she found
the young prince instead of the nasty frog, and she was not
best pleased, you may be sure, when the prince told her
that he was going to marry her stepdaughter because she
had unspelled him.   But married they were, and went away
to live in the castle of the king, his father ; and all the stepmother had to console her was, that it was all through *her*
that her stepdaughter was married to a prince.

THE ROSE TREE

ONCE upon a time, long long years ago, in the days when one had to be careful about witches, there lived a good man, whose young wife died, leaving him a baby girl.

Now this good man felt he could not look after the baby properly, so he married a young woman whose husband had died leaving her with a baby boy.

Thus the two children grew up together, and loved each other dearly, dearly.

But the boy's mother was really a wicked witch-woman, and so jealous that she wanted all the boy's love for herself, and when the girl-baby grew white as milk, with cheeks like roses and lips like cherries, and when her hair, shining like golden silk, hung down to her feet so that her father and all the neighbours began to praise her looks, the step-mother fairly hated her, and did all in her power to spoil her looks. She would set the child hard tasks, and send her out in all weathers to do difficult messages, and if they were not well performed would beat her and scold her cruelly.

Now one cold winter evening when the snow was drifting fast, and the wild rose tree in the garden under which the children used to play in summer was all brown and barren save for snowflake flowers, the stepmother said to the little girl :

" Child ! go and buy me a bunch of candles at the grocer's. Here is some money ; go quickly, and don't loiter by the way."

So the little girl took the money and set off quickly through the snow, for already it was growing dark. Now there was such a wind blowing that it nearly blew her off her feet, and as she ran her beautiful hair got all tangled and almost tripped her up. However, she got the candles, paid for them, and started home again. But this time the wind was behind her and blew all her beautiful golden hair in front of her like a cloud, so that she could not see her steps, and, coming to a stile, had to stop and put down the bundle of candles in order to see how to get over it. And when she was climbing it a big black dog came by and ran off with the bunch of candles ! Now she was so afraid of her stepmother that she durst not go home, but turned back and bought another bunch of candles at the grocer's, and when she arrived at the stile once more, the same thing happened. A big black dog came down the road and ran away with the bunch of candles. So yet once again she journeyed back to the grocer's through wind and snow, and, with her last penny, bought yet another bunch of candles. To no purpose, for alas, and alack-a-day ! when she laid them down in order to part her beautiful golden hair and to see how to get over the stile, a big black dog ran away with them.

So nothing was left save to go back to her stepmother in fear and trembling. But, for a wonder, her stepmother did not seem very angry. She only scolded her for being so late, for, see you, her father and her little playmate had gone to their beds and were in the Land of Nod.

Then she said to the child, " I must take the tangles out of your hair before you go to sleep. Come, put your head on my lap."

So the little girl put her head on her stepmother's lap, and, lo and behold ! her beautiful yellow-silk hair rolled right over the woman's knees and lay upon the ground.

Then the beauty of it made the stepmother more jealous than before, so she said, " I cannot part your hair properly on my knee, fetch me a billet of wood."

So the little girl fetched one. Then said the step-mother, " Your hair is so thick I cannot part it with a comb ; fetch me an axe ! "

So the child fetched an axe.

" Now," said that wicked, wicked woman, " lay your head down on the billet while I part your hair."

And the child did as she was bid without fear ; and lo ! the beautiful little golden head was off in a second, by one blow of the axe.

Now the wicked stepmother had thought it all out before, so she took the poor little dead girl out to the garden, dug a hollow in the snow under the rose tree, and said to herself, "When spring comes and the snow melts, if people find her bones, they will say she lost her way and fell asleep in the snow."

But first, because she was a wicked witch-woman, knowing spells and charms, she took out the heart of the little girl and made it into two savoury pasties, one for her husband's breakfast and one for the little boy's, for thus would the love they bore to the little girl become hers. Nevertheless, she was mistaken, for when morning came and the little child could not be found, the father sent away his breakfast barely tasted, and the little boy wept so that he could eat nothing.

So they grieved and grieved. And when the snow melted and they found the bones of the poor child, they said, " She must have lost her way that dark night going to the grocer's to buy candles." So they buried the bones under the children's rose tree, and every day the little boy sate there and wept and wept for his lost playmate.

Now when summer came the wild rose tree flowered. It was covered with white roses, and amongst the flowers there sate a beautiful white bird. And it sang and sang and sang like an angel out of heaven ; but what it sang the little boy could never make out, for he could hardly see for weeping, hardly hear for sobbing.

So at last the beautiful white bird unfolded its broad white wings and flew to a cobbler's shop, where a myrtle bush hung over the man and his last, on which he was

making a dainty little pair of rose-red shoes. Then it
perched on a bough and sang ever so sweetly :

> " Stepmother slew me,
> Father nigh ate me,
> He whom I dearly love
> Sits below, I sing above,
> Stick ! Stock ! Stone dead ! "

" Sing that beautiful song again," said the cobbler.
" It is better than a nightingale's."

" That will I gladly," sang the bird, " if you will give
me the little rose-red shoes you are making."

And the cobbler gave them willingly, so the white bird
sang its song once more. Then with the rose-red shoes in
one foot it flew to an ash tree that grew close beside a goldsmith's bench, and sang :

> " Stepmother slew me,
> Father nigh ate me,
> He whom I dearly love
> Sits below, I sing above,
> Stick ! Stock ! Stone dead ! "

" Oh, what a beautiful song ! " cried the goldsmith.
" Sing again, dear bird, it is sweeter than a nightingale's."

" That will I gladly," sang the bird, " if you will give
the gold chain you're making."

d the goldsmith gave the bauble willingly, and the
its song once more. Then with the rose-red
foot and the golden chain in the other, the
oak tree which overhung the mill stream,

beside which three millers were busy picking out a millstone, and, perching on a bough, sang its song ever so
sweetly :

> " My stepmother slew me,
> My father nigh ate me,
> He whom I dearly love
> Sits below, I sing above,
> Stick !—

Just then one of the millers put down his tool and listened.

" Stock ! " sang the bird.

And the second miller put aside his tool and listened.

" Stone," sang the bird.

Then the third miller put aside his tool and listened.

" Dead ! " sang the bird so sweetly that
with one accord the millers looked up and cried with one
voice :

" Oh, what a beautiful song ! Sing it again, dear bird,
it is sweeter than a nightingale's."

" That will I gladly," answered the bird, " if you will
hang the millstone you are picking round my neck."

So the millers hung it as they were asked ; and when
the song was finished, the bird spread its wide white wings
and, with the millstone round its neck and the little rose-red
shoes in one foot, the golden chain in the other, it flew
back to the rose tree. But the little playmate was not
there ; he was inside the house eating his dinner.

Then the bird flew to the house, and rattled the millstone about the eaves until the stepmother cried, " Hearken !
How it thunders ! "

So the little boy ran out to see, and down dropped the dainty rose-red shoes at his feet.

" See what fine things the thunder has brought ! " he cried with glee as he ran back.

Then the white bird rattled the millstone about the eaves once more, and once again the stepmother said, " Hearken ! How it thunders ! "

So this time the father went out to see, and down dropped the golden chain about his neck.

" It is true," he said when he came back. " The thunder does bring fine things ! "

Then once more the white bird rattled the millstone about the eaves, and this time the stepmother said hurriedly, " Hark ! there it is again ! Perhaps it has got something for me ! "

Then she ran out ; but the moment she stepped outside the door, down fell the millstone right on her head and killed her.

So that was an end of her. And after that the little boy was ever so much happier, and all the summer time he sate with his little rose-coloured shoes under the wild rose tree and listened to the white bird's song. But when winter came and the wild rose tree was all barren and bare save for snowflake flowers, the white bird came no longer and the little boy grew tired of waiting for it. So one day he gave up altogether, and they buried him under the rose tree beside his little playmate.

Now when the spring came and the rose tree blossomed,

the flowers were no longer white. They were edged with rose colour like the little boy's shoes, and in the centre of each blossom there was a beautiful tuft of golden silk like the little girl's hair.

And if you look in a wild rose you will find these things there still.

THE END